WABASH ON MY MIND

BYRON K. TRIPPET

BYRON K. TRIPPET

Wabash On My Mind

Edited by
Paul Donald Herring

Assisted by
Byron P. Hollett, Richard O. Ristine,
and Lewis S. Salter

A Sesquicentennial Publication

WABASH COLLEGE
Crawfordsville, Indiana
1982

To the memory of two loyal sons of Wabash, Allan Dale Eby and Ben Hur Watt, without whose influence on my youth these thoughts would never have been recorded.

BKT

CONTENTS

ILLUSTRATIONS

THE TRIPPET YEARS

Between pages 222–223

FOREWORD

The memoirs that follow would nearly stand alone, without explanatory notes or foreword. A brief account of the context of their writing, however, may serve to illuminate why Wabash College considers their publication one of the central events in the celebration of its sesquicentennial.

Wabash on My Mind is not an official history continuing the work of Gronert and Osborne into the college's second century. Nevertheless, it is prime material for later historians of the college, who will find here important and even essential insights for the writing of "The Second Hundred Years." Nor is it a systematic and definitive description of his years in office by one of the most important presidents of the college, useful though that would be. It is, rather, a series of vignettes of individual presidents, trustees, and faculty members of Wabash College. They have been set down by a man who knew each one, and who, as he reflected upon his long experience with the college, was haunted by a recurring question: "What explains the fierce loyalty and devotion to Wabash College on the part of such a diverse group of men and women?" The question of devotion is also addressed in a chapter on his own presidency and in an epilogue on the future of the college.

Brief biographical details of Byron K. Trippet's life may be useful to the reader. He was born in Princeton, Indiana, on September 21, 1908. After graduating from Princeton High School he matriculated at Wabash College in the fall of 1926 and graduated with high honors with the Class of 1930. After a year's study in Geneva, Switzerland, he was elected to a Rhodes Scholarship. He returned to Wabash as assistant professor of history in 1935. In 1936 he married Dorothy Clark O'Neall (who died in 1972). Appointed as assistant to Dean Kendall in 1936, he assumed the full responsibilities of dean of the college in 1939. After service in the U.S. Navy from 1942 to 1946, he resumed his duties as dean. When President Sparks retired in December, 1955, Dean Trippet was immediately named by the Board of Trustees as ninth president of the college. He served for nearly ten years, a period many of us consider to have been the "Golden Age" of Wabash. His resignation in 1965 came during a period of acute personal difficulty. In late 1965 he began an association with La Universidad de Las Americas in Mexico City; he served initially as vice president and consultant to the president, and after an interim returned as acting president for the years 1973–75. (The interim period, 1968–73, he spent in New York as president of the Independent College Funds of America.) It was in Mexico that he met and subsequently married Lorenza Galdeano Tuillas, a native of Spain. He died on August 4, 1982.

When President Trippet announced his resignation to a stunned faculty at one of its regular meetings in the early spring of 1965, representatives were asked to draft a resolution in his honor. The faculty resolution read:

> Outstanding student, Rhodes Scholar, distinguished teacher-turned-administrator, widely-admired president, idol of generations of students, the faculty of this college likes best to think of you as a friend who — considering the task no burden for the dignity of the end in view — brought his alma mater to a level of excellence which once might only have been dreamed. In many men, ourselves not least, you brought to birth a love of the liberal arts which, in the providence of God, may prove to be a living memorial to your efforts.
>
> Although your leaving us is a sadness which only time can assuage, no other man so nearly personifies what is best in the honorable traditions of the college, and thus is ever present in her continued achievements.
>
> Byron Kightly Trippet, no longer can we, with fitting pride, speak of you as our president. Yet it is not alone friendship which leads us to say of the years of your presidency that they are the mark to which future generations will aspire.

It is as a friend and lover of Wabash College that Byron Trippet explores and shapes fifty years of memories, years that have become an "indelible part" of his existence. Recalling his own earlier disappointments with the dryness of materials in the college archives, he tries to find a "different and richer vein to be mined out of the past." His work gives us riches in its glimpses of "the personalities and the characters" whose lives have made "Wabash what is was and what it is."

Lewis S. Salter

Editors' Note: Most of the manuscript was dictated over a period of some months in 1974 and 1975, when its author was living in Mexico. The epilogue and appendix were composed in early 1976 and a section on women at Wabash in late 1979. Because his Mexican secretary took down, literally, his recollections while he had "Wabash on his mind," we have, with the author's approval, deleted some inevitable repetitions. To avoid possible misinterpretations, we have also deleted certain passages in the original manuscript (again, with the author's permission).

The author's footnotes are identified by his initials. We have included a minimum number of informative remarks, noting, on occasion, pertinent passages in *The First Hundred Years* and *These Fleeting Years*. Entries in the index specify, when appropriate, an individual's class year, position or department, and tenure at the college. We have been helped in our annotation of the manuscript by many friends of Wabash, especially Danial Clark, William Degitz, and Robert S. Harvey. Our special thanks go to John F. Charles, chairman of the Sesquicentennial Committee, for his encouragement, suggestions, and proofreading.

PAUL DONALD HERRING,
BYRON P. HOLLETT,
RICHARD O. RISTINE,
LEWIS S. SALTER,
editors.

August, 1982

PREFACE

I have written these Wabash reflections entirely out of my memory. I am a long way from Crawfordsville, Indiana, and I do not have with me diaries or personal notes which might verify the accuracy of my recollections. Nor do I have access to anyone with a shared Wabash experience with whom I might check my remembered impressions. For this reason I have no doubt there are errors in what I have written, especially in matters such as dates. Nevertheless, I believe a certain solidness comes through in these fragments of the history of Wabash in the past fifty years.

My memories of Wabash are vivid. I am amazed to discover, when I put my mind to it, how sharp and clear are the images of people and incidents recalled in memory. In saying this I have in mind not only things intellectually remembered but also matters felt and sensed. I can still see the beauty of the Wabash campus in the spring and the autumn of the year and the drabness of the place in late February and early March. I can still hear specific voices and specific laughter and such sounds as the tolling bell and creaking stairways in Center Hall. Even smells long forgotten come back to me now, like the whiffs of formaldehyde that never completely left old South Hall. Such total recall, I suppose, bears witness to the extent to which Wabash was for many years an indelible part of my existence.

Perhaps it is the persistence of that indelible influence on my life that prompts me to put on paper these random thoughts about Wabash. In any case, what I have written is a matter of personal diversion, that and also perhaps a desire to see if my long association with Wabash makes more sense to me now than it did in the middle 1960s.

Beginning in the late 1920s when I was a student assistant to Professor Gronert during the writing of *The First Hundred Years*[1] and continuing off and

---

1. James Insley Osborne and Theodore Gregory Gronert, *Wabash College: The First Hundred Years, 1832–1932* (Crawfordsville: R. E. Banta, 1932). Bryon Trippet's work on the volume is acknowledged in the preface.

on after that, I spent hours and hours in the Wabash library reconstructing piecemeal the early history of the college. It was a fascinating pastime and often I was enthralled with what I read. And yet I remember being frustrated at finding so little about what kind of people those early Wabash heroes really were. Their speeches, their sermons, their mementos, and some of their letters are there. They tell us much about their lives and times, they reflect their convictions and their prejudices. But there is precious little recorded about their private lives, their innermost thoughts, or their opinions of each other. I used to be disappointed about this as I tried to identify with them in my imagination.

When I was president of Wabash I kept in my desk drawer the diary of Elihu Baldwin.[2] From time to time, especially in moments of discouragement, I used to consult it. The story of his presidency is there — where he had been, whom he saw, how much gift money he had received or had been promised. Those crisp, business-like entries in his diary, to be sure, tell us something about what kind of man this first president of Wabash was, but how much more interesting it would have been had he recorded something of his personal feelings.

The same sort of thing is true of Caleb Mills. Elihu Baldwin was at Wabash only a few years but Caleb Mills was there for the better part of his life. The Wabash archives are full of his speeches and tracts. They tell us much about the public interests and goals of this remarkable educational pioneer. But they give us little insight into his private life. Reading his speeches and his essays always reminded me somehow of that familiar austere portrait of Caleb Mills done late in his life.[3] I found it impossible to hail him across the intervening decades as a fellow Wabash man. It was not until his granddaughter, Helen Condit, gave me typewritten copies of his letters to his son, Marshall, then a Union soldier in the deep South during the Civil War, that I discovered a more human Caleb Mills. I found those chatty letters full of warmth, with touches of sly humor. His admonitions to his son about the wiles of dark-eyed southern belles, for me, made him more real and less formidable than did his numerous speeches about education. So did his letter to Marshall explaining that he was sending his son a bottle of gin. It was to be used as a guard against the "ague" — sparingly! Seen through his letters to his son, Caleb Mills is more likeable than seen through his speeches.

But inevitably college archives must be disappointing as far as the kind of insights into the past of which I am speaking are concerned. They are filled

2. First president of the college, 1834–40.

3. The college has three portraits of Caleb Mills, all unsigned. Two smaller ones hang in the Caleb Mills House and a larger portrait in the Chapel. Trippet's chapel talk on "Caleb Mills and the Love of God" is included in Robert S. Harvey's *These Fleeting Years* (Crawfordsville: Wabash College, 1982), pp. 28–31.

with speeches, sermons, faded diplomas and programs, musty minutes of faculty meetings, stilted resolutions paying tribute to departed colleagues, old photographs and the like. Such things, no doubt, are useful when it comes to writing official college histories but there is a different and richer vein to be mined out of the past, if one can only find it. It provides glimpses of the personalities and characters of people who have made Wabash what it was and what it is. It includes the drama of their lives.

Insofar as what I have just said is true, perhaps these recollections of mine will enrich the Wabash archives for the period from the middle 1920s to the middle 1960s. I see that I have written more about people than I have about events. It was an easy, natural thing for me to do. Looking back on my experience at Wabash I realize that above everything else individual people I admired and liked attracted me to the college in the first place and kept me there for years. The spell which a college like Wabash has repeatedly cast on a long succession of young men who came there as students and who (out of love for the place) stayed there or returned after interludes elsewhere is a multi-sided thing. But the intertwining of human lives is at the heart of the spell.

Even so, I confess that I have omitted much more than I have included in the thoughts I have recorded about Wabash men and women who meant much to me. This is especially true in what I have written about my later years at Wabash. It is a deficit in these recollections which perhaps I can later balance with another set of notes for the college archives in which I will acknowledge my great sense of indebtedness to those who befriended me and pay tribute to sacrificial love squandered in my behalf.

Ten years have now gone by since I left the Wabash campus. It is just as well that I have waited this long to record my recollections, which makes it possible to distinguish between what was important and what was unimportant. What I have written is thus like a pilgrimage to rekindle a torch of love which for a time flickered and smoldered but never died.

BYRON K. TRIPPET
Mexico, 1975

I

WABASH PRESIDENTS

Bemused as I am by history, I have often thought of the story of Wabash as if it were an endless tapestry. It is not a unique tapestry, but it has a character of its own, a fascinating thing to admire and to wonder about. From panel to panel the color tones change and re-emerge, sometimes bright and bold, sometimes pale and indistinct, then bright and bold again. The color changes reflect the drama of a larger world of which Wabash is but a tiny part. But they also represent a drama which is exclusively local, exclusively Wabash.

The tapestry of my imagination is crowded with figures of people, young and old. Most are now anonymous. Some are recognizable by name and a few of these loom larger than others. Especially prominent are the presidents of the college. With notable exceptions, their prominence exaggerates their importance in the Wabash story. And yet there is no denying that through their personalities and by virtue of their strengths or their shortcomings, Wabash presidents have shaped, sometimes decisively, the destiny of the college. It is not surprising that epochs in the history of the college are associated with their individual names.

It is this kind of musing that prompts me to begin these Wabash reflections by writing about Wabash presidents. Of the eight presidents who preceded me I knew three, and of these I knew only two very well. The five presidents who preceded these three I knew only by what reading I could do. I learned less about them than I sought and, apart from a common interest in Wabash, I found it impossible to identify with them. That is not surprising, I suppose. If the nineteenth-century presidents could revisit Wabash in our times I am sure they would find it impossible to identify with the likes of me. No doubt they would be astonished, perhaps troubled, by what they would see and hear. I suspect the second president, Dr. White,[1] and the third, Dr. Tuttle,[2] would be

1. Charles White (brother-in-law of Edmund Hovey), president (1841–61).

2. Joseph Ferrand Tuttle, president (1862–91). For his inaugural address, see "What Do We Mean by 'A College'?" in *These Fleeting Years,* pp. 43–46.

1

appalled to the point of regretting their earlier labors. By their assumptions and definitions, the godless character of current liberal education and the philosophical presuppositions of current faculty members would seem alien if not evil. The reactions of the first president, Elihu Baldwin, and the fourth, George Burroughs,[3] would be more positive, I believe. Once they had recovered from their initial shock, they would understand and approve the modern aims which Wabash tries to pursue.

Elihu Baldwin eminently deserves the prominent place accorded to him in my imaginary tapestry. His presidency was the shortest of the first nine but it was the most important. Without him an infant college might have disappeared completely, as other similar institutions west of the Allegheny Mountains occasionally disappeared. His courage, resolution, and cheerfulness in spite of adversity — for example, after the destruction by fire of the first permanent building (South Hall) — were probably decisive in keeping Wabash alive. Had he despaired, others such as Edmund Hovey and Caleb Mills would also have despaired.

Elihu Baldwin put his concept of the college's purpose indelibly on the character of Wabash. Deeply religious man though he was, his recorded thoughts about liberal education have a secular, timeless ring about them. When we read his statement about "the development of all of [man's] powers... chiefly the improvement of the mind," we may find his words quaint but his ideas are as fresh and appropriate for our times as they were for his. And his statement of what the college must try to become has inspired all of his successors. "Our purpose is never to rest while Wabash College shall lack any advantages . . . ," he said, and this has been something of a commandment to his successors.[4] Certainly it was for me. Elihu Baldwin wore himself out and died in that kind of commitment to Wabash.

I have sometimes wondered if Charles White, Baldwin's successor, was not miscast as a Wabash president. He was above all a preaching minister of a stern Christian gospel. The life of the mind apart from Christian piety would have held minimal interest for him. His tenure as president was four times as long as Baldwin's. It was a period of growth and improvement for Wabash during which Dr. White's influence among church people "back East" was helpful. But there is reason to believe that in Indiana it was the influence of his brother-in-law, Edmund Hovey, and of Caleb Mills that advanced the Wabash cause.

My judgment of President White probably was influenced by conversations I had with Professor Gronert when he was writing the early chapters of

3. George Stockton Burroughs, president (1892–99).

4. For this and the remainder of his inaugural address, see "Liberal Education" in *These Fleeting Years*, pp. 15–26.

The First Hundred Years. Ted Gronert was not an admirer of Dr. White. He spoke of White's sermons being "a trifle spacious." I am not sure what he meant by that, but I was thereafter never able to study Dr. White's enormous full length portrait in Yandes Hall without smiling at the memory of the word "spacious."[5]

Dr. Tuttle, the third Wabash president, deserves his prominent place in my tapestry if for no other reason than for his remarkably long tenure and his immense popularity and prestige. His impact on the academic development of Wabash has always eluded me. But for three decades and more, his imposing presence, his strength of character, and his warm personality won great good will and substantial material support for Wabash. Someone — perhaps it was Insley Osborne — told me that when he was a very small boy in Crawfordsville, the occasional majestic sight of Dr. Tuttle helped him to imagine what God looked like. It was this attribute, among others, that caused generations of students, alumni, and townspeople to identify Dr. Tuttle with all that was good and admirable in the college. That in itself is an important part of the Wabash heritage. Dr. Tuttle stayed in office too long, however, and after his retirement his continuing presence, as he regularly occupied a special chair on the platform during chapel services, must have been a trial for his successor.

I wonder if George Burroughs did not become the most unhappy of all Wabash presidents. When he arrived in Crawfordsville to become the fourth president of Wabash he was young, handsome and brilliant. His coming was greeted with great enthusiasm and high expectations. Students, faculty members, and a majority of the alumni and townspeople had never known any president other than Dr. Tuttle. The prospect of a new personality in that office was bound to have been exciting. And Dr. Burroughs surely must have accepted the position with equal enthusiasm and with high hopes of what he might do for the place. What a happy beginning!

George Burroughs was the only one of the first seven presidents of Wabash who held the Ph.D. degree. Except possibly for Hopkins, he was also the only one with credentials as a professional educator. He wanted to make changes in the academic character of Wabash. Some he managed to bring about, and his presence at Wabash, no doubt, was a positive consideration in winning for the college a chapter of Phi Beta Kappa.[6] But in the main, his proposals were resisted and rather soon he lost his early popularity. The conservatism of the faculty made him feel increasingly like an outsider. When he

5. This portrait (unsigned) now hangs in the south stairwell of Center Hall. Another portrait by Lucille S. Dalrymple hangs in the Chapel. For portions of President White's inaugural address, see "The Duties of Educated Young Men of the West" in *These Fleeting Years,* pp. 39–42.

6. Beta of Indiana, established in 1898.

3

lost his fight to make Wabash coeducational, he resigned.[7] He remained courteous and urbane to the last but he must have been embittered. Misfortune continued to plague him. Soon after he left Wabash, it became apparent that he was suffering from bone cancer. Both arms were amputated. When he died, he was only in his late forties.

Dr. Burroughs' figure in my tapestry is small and ambiguous, reflecting the appraisals of those who opposed him. On ceremonial occasions at Wabash, when it is customary to make fulsome allusions to earlier Wabash heroes, Burroughs is never mentioned. The only one of his successors who may have brooded sympathetically about his memory was the seventh president, Hopkins. Dr. Hopkins was far more successful in achieving what he set out to accomplish for Wabash than was Dr. Burroughs. But the obstacles both men encountered were similar. It was the faculty, joined by the trustees, who frustrated Burroughs. Hopkins had the faculty with him, but alumni and finally trustees turned against him. In both cases the personal heartaches were much the same.

With the coming of the fifth president, William Kane, the color tones of my tapestry become bright and bold again.[8] Dr. Kane was the first of the twentieth century presidents of Wabash. He was a product of the nineteenth century, but it occurs to me that in his thinking about the needs of the college he was closer in spirit to President Sparks than to his predecessors. If he could have revisited the campus in 1950, I believe he would have understood immediately what Frank Sparks was trying to do and he would have been enthusiastic in his approval.

Like his predecessors he was a Presbyterian minister. But he was a pragmatic, "take charge" kind of man, a doer rather than a thinker. He did not have the philosophical turn of mind that characterized his successor, Dr. Mackintosh. Insley Osborne and others who remembered him spoke of his being a "powerful" preacher. I have no doubt he was. But my guess is he was the kind of minister who was especially good at enlarging the size of his church membership, mobilizing his parishioners for church programs, launching and completing a fund drive for a new church building, and so on. A shrewd judge of men and their motives, he was attuned to the prejudices and aspirations of midwesterners, especially Hoosiers.

Such were the personal attributes which Dr. Kane brought to bear on the presidency of Wabash at a dark moment in its history. He was well known and highly respected by faculty members by virtue of his having been a strong president of the Board of Trustees, a post he continued to hold for some time

7. For an account of the fight over coeducation, see *The First Hundred Years,* pp. 207–19. President Burrough's letter of resignation is included in *These Fleeting Years,* pp. 66–68.

8. William Kane, president (1899–1906).

after becoming president of the college. Despite some faculty resistance to his pressure to relax entrance requirements for students, my guess is that the faculty was somewhat cowed by Dr. Kane. The schism within the faculty between scientists and humanists widened during his administration, but until Mackintosh became president voices were subdued.[9] Dr. Kane did not regard himself as an "educator." He would have considered the point irrelevant. His task was to lift Wabash out of the morass into which it had slipped, and he set about that task with a confidence that quickly became contagious.

The presidency of Dr. Kane was one of the shorter Wabash presidencies (seven years) but it was remarkably successful. When he assumed the presidency, student enrollment had shrunk to fewer than 200 students, alumni were estranged, the Crawfordsville establishment was hostile, faculty members were worried and pessimistic, and, as usual, the college was hard pressed financially. When he died a few years later, Wabash was well into that colorful and confident era which has often been called by alumni like Lee McCanliss "the Golden Age of Wabash."

The two burning questions which were on the minds of Wabash men at the turn of the century were these: (1) Does the new popularity and rapid growth of state universities mean that private colleges are doomed to extinction, just as private academies were when public high schools became thoroughly established? and (2) Can Wabash continue to be a viable institution in view of the popularity of coeducation? As far as I could discover, Dr. Kane simply ignored both questions. If he regarded the new popularity of state universities as ominous, he never said so. Instead, he quietly put his influence — and that of the Board of Trustees — to work at making Wabash more attractive and more accessible to graduates of public high schools. Judging by the role he played in trustee meetings during the heated debates about making Wabash coeducational, I suspect he believed that the idea of admitting women to Wabash was something to be dismissed without argument. At any rate, as president of Wabash, Dr. Kane was never publicly on the defensive about these questions. Instead, he talked forcefully and with great conviction about the values of the old-fashioned American college, about education and character, about manhood and rugged competition, about the bright promise for Wabash in the new century.[10] It was the Wabash gospel of upward and onward, pure and simple, and people believed him.

It is an interesting coincidence that that rousing college song, "Old Wabash," was first sung at President Kane's inaugural ceremony. The song is, perhaps, of minor importance for the current generation of Wabash students,

9. See Gronert and Osborne's account in *The First Hundred Years*, pp. 232–36.

10. For Kane's remarks on this subject, see "The Historic Old-fashioned College" (his inaugural address) in *These Fleeting Years*, pp. 69–73.

but for more than a half century, it symbolized and contributed to that cocky, chauvinistic student spirit which the general public in Indiana associated with Wabash. It is something less than a coincidence that in the Kane years the fame of Wabash athletic teams and the proud name "Little Giants" were born. When students and alumni later in the century boasted of the spirit and traditions of "Old Wabash," they were paying sentimental tribute not to the really old Wabash of the nineteenth century but to a new Wabash which emerged shortly after 1900. I dare say few, if any, of them thought about it, but they were, in fact, paying tribute to the impact made on the college by its fifth president.

My sketchy appraisals of the first five Wabash presidents may be quite wide of the mark. Probably what I have written reveals more about my attitudes and biases than theirs. It is the familiar problem in historiography — how can one be sure of an historical judgment? Even for past events it is a difficult task, but when it comes to reconstructing what people believed or felt, one is reduced to relying on inference and imagination. Nor does the length of elapsed time make much difference in such tasks. Today is always becoming yesterday and yesterday (so quickly) recedes into the remote past. Two or three hand shakes separate us now from the founding of Wabash. As a young man I shook hands with James H. Osborne[11] when he was old, and I am quite sure that when he was a young man he shook hands with Caleb Mills when he was old. And there we are back to the beginning of Wabash College! But when we bear in mind the revolutionary changes in the human condition in the twentieth century, including, especially, the profound changes in styles of life and systems of values, 1832 is light-years away from us.

The differences in philosophical assumptions and attitudes of mind between the nineteenth-century presidents of Wabash and their later twentieth-century counterparts are sharp and significant. But for all that, the presidents are more alike than different. And as far as the continuing history of Wabash is concerned, they share a common conviction and a sense of pupose. All have been deeply committed to Wabash as a cause worth advancing for its own sake and for the sake of a higher and larger cause to which the college is dedicated. The nineteenth-century presidents undoubtedly would have defined the higher, larger cause in somewhat different terms than would their twentieth-century successors, but their common sense of purpose remains essentially the same.

Wabash presidents have not been unique in their commitment to the advancement of the college they served. The same thing could be said of college and university presidents generally. However, the history of American higher education reveals numerous examples of college presidents who used their positions to further their own personal interests — advancing in a political

11. James H. (Pat) Osborne was one-time principal of the preparatory department of the college, long-time faculty member, and for many years secretary of the faculty. He was the father of J. Insley Osborne and grandfather of Richard O. Ristine. BKT.

career, for example, or rising in rank in a church hierarchy, or moving to bigger, more prominent positions in education. Wabash presidents have been remarkably free of such self-serving interests. Of the first eight Wabash presidents, four died in office, three retired after lengthy service, and one resigned when he saw his usefulness to the college was finished. While they were in office their dedication to the cause of Wabash was total. They were not equally successful. There were defeats as well as victories. All of them paid some kind of a personal price for their labors, two or three of them a heavy price. But Wabash as we know it today is the consequence of their cumulative, unrelenting effort.

GEORGE LEWIS MACKINTOSH
1906–1926

In May, 1926, I visited the Wabash campus for the first time. Oscar M. Anderson, Dale Eby, and Ben H. Watt, Wabash alumni in Princeton, took Clayton Weist and me to Crawfordsville for a long weekend. I did not know it at the time, but it was to be one of the most important weekends in my life.

Until that weekend I had been headed for DePauw University. I had been accepted for admission there, had visited the campus, and had even pledged to a fraternity. I liked DePauw and had good friends there but I later realized I never felt the emotional appeal about DePauw that I was to feel about Wabash. In part I suppose this was because the plan to study at DePauw was not my decision. It was something I acquiesced in without much reflection. My father had suggested that I go to one of his alma maters, Indiana University or the University of Michigan, but he did not press me. It was the staunch Methodism of my mother and the influence of family friends in the church that made going to DePauw seem like a natural thing to do. My late spring visit to Wabash changed all that abruptly. I was seventeen and had no experience in judging colleges, but it seemed to me that Wabash was what I imagined a college should be. It was a case of love at first sight.

Actually it was not all that sudden. Without realizing it, I had been well conditioned for Wabash before that weekend. I liked and admired "Doc" Anderson, Dale Eby, and Ben Watt. I was especially drawn to Ben Watt who, in 1925, returned to Princeton and who, in my senior year in high school, served as my basketball coach. The contrast between Ben and his predecessor I found exciting. He seemed far better educated, and he had a kind of verve that made youngsters look up to him. I was flattered by the way he talked to me as if I were an adult. His conversations were heavily laden with anecdotes about Wabash. Years later Dale Eby laughed when I recounted this experience. "It was all a part of our conspiracy to get you and Weistie to go to Wa-

7

bash," he said. Ben once took our basketball team to watch Wabash play Indiana State at Terre Haute. Along with my teammates I was thrilled by Benny Devol's fantastic dribbling antics and by Red Robinson's uncanny eye for the basket. And I remember being inpressed by the incredible amount of noise that came from a small Wabash cheering section.

There were other influences at work. My father was a great admirer of Thomas R. Paxton, prominent Princeton banker and trustee of Wabash from 1882 to 1921. One day in the summer of 1925 my father sent me with some legal papers which required Mr. Paxton's signature. I found the old gentleman on the veranda of the large Paxton home. He was reading Herodotus in the original Greek. I remember being astounded. "Reading Herodotus in Greek? For the fun of it? Incredible!" I thought. He drew me into conversation and finally asked me where I planned to go to college. "DePauw, I guess," I answered. Mr. Paxton said nothing but later, my father told me, Mr. Paxton remarked: "Sanford, you ought to send that boy of yours to Wabash." I remember being pleased.

The weekend on the Wabash campus, however, was decisive. I could not have then said why. It was a matter of feeling. The wooded campus charmed me and the friendliness of the students at the old Beta House was appealing. And also, especially, there was Dr. Mackintosh.

On the Friday night of that weekend, while Ben Watt took Weistie to Pete Vaughan's home for a get-acquainted visit,[12] Dale Eby and "Doc" Anderson took me to the Baldwin Oratorical Contest in the Old Chapel in Center Hall. After the final oration, while the judges were making their decisions, Dale took me across the room to meet President Mackintosh. I was greatly impressed. Tall and gaunt, he seemed to tower above us. I had been timid about the introduction, and I was surprised at how quickly he put me at ease. I liked his smile and the warm, friendly look in his eyes. He asked me a few questions and gently led me to talk about myself. He asked me how old I was. I told him. "What do you want to be doing when you are thirty-seven?" he asked. It was a strange question, I thought. "Thirty-seven? — an eternity away!" I mumbled my uncertainty. He smiled again. "Well," he said, "it's perhaps better not to be sure of a career at your age. You have plenty of time. And the important thing, anyway, is to become a good human being." It was a thought that stayed with me. Walking away from the brief visit, Dale said, more to himself than to me, "There is a great man." And that he was.

"Doc Mack" was the last of the Presbyterian minister presidents of Wabash. In temperament and in quality of mind he was also perhaps the last of the nineteenth-century presidents of the college. His higher causes for the

---

12. Clayton Weist, whose devotion to Pete Vaughan began that night, became in the next four years one of the all-time great halfbacks in Wabash football history. BKT.

8

college were love of God and love of country. His celebrated chapel speech in April, 1917, when he exhorted the student body to answer the nation's call to military service and offered to nail shut the doors of Wabash if it would help, contrasts sharply with the mood of the college leadership at the outbreak of World War II.

It is impossible to think of Doc Mack's going through the countless public relations routines later Wabash presidents were to endure as a matter of course — throwing a cocktail party for alumni, calling on corporation executives for financial support, speaking to a variety of publics, and so on. Already, in the middle 1920s, the sight of Dr. Mackintosh striding purposefully down Wabash Avenue toward town, his black, wide preacher's hat squarely on his head, was a little quaint. Later it would have seemed ridiculous. His was an old-fashioned stance — dignified, benevolent, and wise. There was a respectful distance between him and the rest of the college and, yet, I wonder if he was not the most beloved of all Wabash presidents.

Dr. Mackintosh ran the college with a gentle hand. But he ran it. Far more than his successors, he was the administration. The dean of the college was essentially a dean of students, not a key officer in policy determination. The treasurer's office — Jim Wedding and a part time bookkeeper-secretary — was located in downtown Crawfordsville and doubled as a business office for the college. There was no development office, no public relations office, no alumni affairs office, no fully established office of admissions.[13] The registrar was a college functionary. Harry Lebo, who with a pipe wrench and baling wire kept the power plant working — more or less, was virtually a one-man maintenance department. He took his orders from Doc Mack and from no one else. By about 1920 every active faculty member was a Mackintosh appointee. If there was restlessness among the faculty, as there was in the middle 1920s, respect and affection for Doc Mack kept voices subdued and polite.

President Mackintosh was rarely away from Crawfordsville and never for long. When he was in Crawfordsville, he was usually on campus. His office was plain and spartan. He answered his own telephone and he replied to much of his correspondence by letters written in long hand. (For years until shortly before the Hopkins administration, there was only one secretary in Center Hall.) For most of his presidential years, he continued to teach philosophy. His class in ethics was a famous experience for a long succession of students. He spoke in chapel almost every day, almost never repeating himself. Often he led the daily hymn singing. He followed student activities closely and he regu-

---

13. Insley Osborne told me a favorite topic of faculty conversation shortly after Labor Day each year involved speculation about how many students would "turn up" for registration. It is not surprising that when college opened in September more than 500 students would register, but by Thanksgiving there would be fewer than 400 attending classes. BKT.

larly attended home athletic contests. His enthusiasm for Wabash victories was genuine, but restrained. He never cheered.

The "Hell-Roaring 500"-Caveman ambience which swept over Wabash after World War I must have been distasteful to him, but he never said so. He continued to address students in groups as "gentlemen." George Kendall, to whom I am indebted for such insights as I have for the Mackintosh years, told me Doc Mack was incensed about student drinking, partly on moral grounds, but even more so because during Prohibition "gentlemen" should not break the law. Occasionally he would take cases of student discipline into his own hands. He was inconsistent in the punishments he assigned — sometimes terribly severe, sometimes lenient. Apparently it made a difference if Doc Mack had witnessed the offending behavior.

President Mackintosh, despite the superficiality of my acquaintance with him, profoundly influenced my way of thinking about Wabash. Why? It was above all his speeches, I believe — those and his standard of simplicity in everything he did as president. As a student I was enormously moved every time I heard him speak — both by what he had to say and how he said it. I heard him speak in chapel now and then, occasionally at college ceremonial occasions, and also as a candidate for Congress in 1928. Often after hearing him I would return to my room and outline what he had said, so much was I impressed.[14]

By Brigancian standards, Dr. Mackintosh would have drawn low grades as a public speaker. He resorted to no artifices, no gestures, no crescendos of emphasis. He spoke simply, quietly, with restraint, and always briefly. He never used a manuscript or even notes, so far as I could tell. And yet his words flowed with unbelievable grace, carrying with them a kind of conviction that I found irresistible. Always there would be touches of humor and wit, dry and low keyed. He made others who spoke on the same occasion appear awkward, thin, and childish by contrast. I vaguely remember being pained listening to Dr. Hopkins speak at length, following a five-minute talk by Dr. Mackintosh on some occasion at the Wabash Avenue Presbyterian Church.

In 1928 when Doc Mack was the Democratic candidate for Congress against the Republican incumbent from Attica I was one of his volunteer student workers.[15] I, therefore, had a chance to hear him speak on the campaign

14. President Mackintosh's first baccalaureate address, "You Are Our Exhibits," is included in *These Fleeting Years,* pp. 80–81.

15. Once or twice I was included in "campaign strategy meetings" held at the pleasant Mackintosh home on Crawford Street. The tone of the gatherings was anything but political. Foster Fudge, Doc Mack's campaign chairman, and a few party workers from the county or district talked briefly about speaking schedules, plans for rallies, campaign contributions, and the like, but it was all quite relaxed. Doc Mack had little to say. Perhaps he knew it was a hopeless undertaking. At any rate, he remained quiet and serene

trail. Always it seemed to me I was listening to the most practical kind of political wisdom which made his opponent's oratory sound like pure cant. In reacting that way, I undoubtedly was in a small minority of those who heard the two men speak. The Hoover landslide in Indiana in 1928 meant that Dr. Mackintosh never had a chance for election; but even had there been no landslide, I suspect he would have lost. By then he was too old. His hands shook with palsy. Above all his speeches, while gems for me, were entirely too unpolitical and too learned for vote getting.

I remember wondering how Doc Mack prepared his speeches. Did he write them out? Or think them out in advance? Was it simply a gift that enabled him on a moment's notice to call upon his extensive knowledge and transmit part of it to an audience? I was fascinated by the accomplishment, even if I never learned the answers to my questions. Later I took the trouble to search in the college archives for copies of his speeches. I found precious few. One I remember was his tribute at Dr. Kane's funeral. It was a classic — brief, restrained, rich in meaning and beauty.

Dr. Mackintosh's effect on me as a young man illustrates a conviction I was later to hold. I do not believe that one can "teach" a youngster to be courageous, or resolute, or persevering, or even honest. But such attributes of character can be strengthened and nurtured in the young by the example of those who, greatly respected, thus appeal to the human propensity to emulate that which is loved and admired. Certainly Dr. Mackintosh, though he never knew it, was one of my greatest teachers in this respect. Consciously I studied what I could find about his presidency years after his death, when I was beginning my own presidency and was groping for guidance. One example will suffice to clarify what I mean. When I was elected president, public relations-minded trustees immediately began to plan an impressive inauguration. I rejected this proposal and opted for a short chapel service with no outside guests and no publicity. Perhaps I would have insisted on this anyway, but the decisive example in my thinking was the simple inauguration of Dr. Mackintosh — a perfunctory detail in the 1907 commencement exercises.

During 1906–26, Dr. Mackintosh came to be the personification of the character and quality of Wabash as the college was in those years for generations of students, alumni, and (perhaps to a lesser extent) the general public. I must confess that when I became president of Wabash one of my secret personal goals was to earn in the 1950s and 1960s a similar kind of personal identification. The fact that he and I, for all of our marked differences, were

above the political talk. Mrs. Mackintosh served tea and cake and with her compressed smile chatted amiably and primly with each guest in turn. Once or twice she called her husband into another room, ostensibly to answer the telephone, but when he rejoined us his hair would be freshly brushed or his vest would be neatly buttoned again or his coat collar would be rearranged. BKT.

11

the only graduates of Wabash to become presidents of their alma mater up to that time, gave me a sense of identity with him and with the history of the college. My failure to realize this personal aspiration added to my sense of frustration when I resigned in 1965.

There are two portraits of Mackintosh at Wabash. One — head and shoulders — shows him in his younger years. My guess is that this was painted by Dalrymple from a photograph. It never seemed to me to catch the man's strength of character and presence. The other, a full figure seated in a chair, was done after his death by a New York artist commissioned by Norman Treves and John Farber. For me it is a superb likeness, catching as it does the strength of the man toward the end of a long and fruitful life. Even his hands, somewhat awkwardly poised on his knees, are right. And behind those familiar spectacles, one can see in his eyes his wisdom and his kindness.[16]

LOUIS BERTRAM HOPKINS
1926–1940

My acquaintanceship with President Hopkins was extensive and close — especially in the years 1929–31 and 1934–40. Despite the difference in our ages, we became good friends. It finally became easy and natural for me to address him in private as "Hoppy," a term used by those who were closest to him.

Dr. Hopkins came to Wabash in 1926 as its seventh president, just a few weeks before I entered Wabash as a freshman. I had no personal contact with him during that first year, although I heard him speak and saw him frequently going to or from his house across the campus. At the Beta House I was aware of much speculation among upper classmen about the new president, including an occasional invidious comparison with Doc Mack. My reaction to the new president was uncritical. He was president of the college and, therefore, he must be an exceptionally able person. To think otherwise would have been impossible for a green youngster from a small Indiana town brought up to respect those in authority.

It was not until the second semester of my sophomore year that I came to know Dr. Hopkins personally. During that year I participated in the Hays Oratorical Contest.[17] I was fortunate enough to win first prize. The subject of

16. The Dalrymple portrait now hangs in the Arnold Admissions Center. The portrait Trippet prefers was painted by A. Laevens and hangs in the Chapel.

17. Hinkle C. Hays (Wabash 1912) established this contest to encourage public speaking and limited the entrants to freshmen and sophomores. The prizes were no longer offered after his death in 1957.

my speech was "Higher Education — Higher Than What?" I remember little about the content of that speech except that I spoke with enthusiasm about the plan Dr. Hopkins had forged with the faculty for a new Wabash curriculum.[18] Dr. Hopkins was not in the audience that night, but Mrs. Hopkins and one of her daughters were. As the meeting was breaking up, after the judges' decision had been anounced, she warmly congratulated me and seemed genuinely pleased with what I had said about Wabash.

Whether it was because of this I do not know, but thereafter I gradually found myself being included in occasional student conferences with President Hopkins and now and then having a private conversation with him. By my senior year I probably knew Dr. Hopkins as well as any undergraduate. That year I also began driving his car for him occasionally, a practice which became more common after my graduation.

Dr. Hopkins interviewed and advised all members of the senior class. (Later he extended this practice to all freshmen as well.) Perhaps because I had developed a friendship with him, I did not have a formal interview to discuss my plans. We had already talked several times about what they might be. For some years I had intended to study law and then to join my father in practice. Participation in politics was also vaguely in my mind. I had never really thought of any other career. Dr. Hopkins asked me if I had ever thought of becoming a college professor. Without in any way trying to dissuade me from law as a career, he caused me to think of other alternatives for the first time. He had a gift for discussing career options with students, and he brought to bear his considerable knowledge of personnel psychology and his personal interest in helping to fit "round pegs into round holes." When I was invited to stay on at Wabash after graduation as an instructor during John Tomlinson's leave of absence, I accepted without a moment's hesitation. That year's experience (1930–31) was to change my whole life. Perhaps Hoppy knew it would do so.

From the beginning, the Hopkins administration was doomed to falling action as far as the total college community was concerned. I say this looking back over the receding years. I do not mean by "falling action" failure. Nor by "from the beginning" do I mean there were any ominous signals in the year 1926–27. I mean only that in retrospect the odds were against his achieving the kind of college leadership which appeals to the college's constituency and thus helps to lift it to a new plateau of greatness. And the influences working against him so increased as time went on that, in the closing years of his presidency, he was really in an embattled position, harassed and frustrated by those who opposed him.

18. For a description of the new curriculum, see *The First Hundred Years*, pp. 379–81, and *These Fleeting Years*, pp. 89–93.

His administration began on a quite positive, cordial note. To some extent, no doubt, this was merely the result of natural curiosity manifested whenever an unknown newcomer replaces a retiring president. But there was more to it than that. The fact that John Coss, professor of philosophy and director of the summer school at Columbia University, had been chairman of the trustee presidential selection committee, made his choice of Louis Hopkins instantly popular with the faculty. Coss' prestige on the board and the high regard in which he was held undoubtedly gave Hopkins an initial advantage. Businessmen on the board and alumni (to some extent) liked the idea of picking a businessman-educator for president. It was "just what the college needed." The inauguration in December 1926 was a star-studded exercise which gave a thrill to the whole Wabash family.[19]

Despite this happy beginning, the honeymoon with the Hopkins administration was short-lived. His early firm decisions on student discipline, on intercollegiate athletics, and above all, on curriculum revision touched off the first signals of opposition. The financial consequences of the "Great Depression" and the declining enrollment, developments over which he had no control, complicated his life. The deterioration of alumni interest in the college that became so serious in the 1930s actually began in the late 1920s.

Although I was a staunch Hopkins partisan in the controversies that developed in the 1930s, in retrospect I recognize that many of his difficulties with alumni stemmed from his own personality and his way of exercising the responsibilities of his office. Dr. Hopkins lacked the personal attributes of leadership, now fashionably described as "charismatic." He had the head and torso of a big man, but his curiously short and slightly bowed legs decreased his stature. His face was full of character, marked especially by a strong, determined jaw. (The one portrait of Hopkins at Wabash, done I believe without his having sat for it, does not capture the strength of his features.)[20] But, especially for strangers, there was an aloofness and a coldness of demeanor which estranged people from him. His speech and mannerisms were "not Hoosier" and this tended to keep people at arm's length. Except from the few people who knew him well, he did not evoke affection or admiration.

Dr. Hopkins' taste and style in dress contrasted sharply with what Crawfordsville had come to expect as standard garb for the president of Wabash. He was a "tweedy man," who wore sports jackets and slacks of contrasting color, light gray flannel shirts, two-toned brown saddle back shoes and cashmere sweaters. I believe students liked his sporty appearance; certainly I did. But it served to call attention to the sharp difference between the new presi-

19. "The Separate College," President Hopkins' inaugural address, is included in *These Fleeting Years*, pp. 87–89.

20. By Dalrymple, the portrait hangs in the Chapel.

dent and the old. More shocking to some people, Dr. Hopkins smoked cigarettes. Perhaps because of this, one of the college rules he changed in his first
year was that which forbade smoking by students on campus. Eyebrows in
Crawfordsville undoubtedly were raised when it became known that the new
president smoked in public.

More important in contributing to the "falling action," Hopkins was a
poor public speaker. His speeches, when written in advance, read much better
than when he delivered them. His delivery was monotonous and stiff. His was
a New England, not midwestern accent. On occasions when he had to speak
extemporaneously without the security of a manuscript before him, he was
halting in his delivery. I remember my own feeling of acute embarrassment
and sympathy for him at an alumni banquet in the mid-1930s when he forgot
his train of thought altogether and had to pause, asking his listeners "to bear
with me for a moment." The content of his prepared speeches in my judgment
was always quite good. He addressed himself to practical problems. His purpose was to instruct and convince rather than to inspire and persuade. But his
purpose was often blunted by his unfortunate delivery. In private conversations Hopkins could be amusing and disarming, but relatively few people saw
this side of him. He was judged rather by his public speeches and regrettably
this judgment was usually adverse.

I believe Dr. Hopkins found distasteful what he had to do publicly. He
did not like to mix with strangers and avoided this kind of exercise whenever
possible. He was contemptuous of Hoosier folkways, and although he was
careful not to say so, he obviously preferred the New England landscape and
its people. For that reason, each summer, as soon as he could do so, he took
his family back to Perkinsville, Vermont, for a long vacation, a practice which,
as time went by and the college's finances worsened, led to grumbling among
trustees. He had no relish for fund raising and did precious little of it. One time
in the late 1930s, when opposition to him had become quite serious, he told
me he had had an understanding with the Board of Trustees from the beginning that he would not have to raise money. But in such moments he was always soft-spoken in what he said in his behalf, never plaintive and never angry.

Dr. Hopkins' family, by its very nature, reinforced his disposition to avoid
the demands of public relations, money raising, and winning friends for the
college. Nora Hopkins was an unprepossessing, retiring sort of woman. Well-
educated and intelligent, with a quick and delightful sense of humor, she shrank
from the public eye as much as possible. She and her husband almost never
entertained others in their home and at public functions — for example, the
picnic luncheon on campus following commencement, or the "covered dish"
faculty supper just before the opening of college. Nora Hopkins' participation
was one of duty, not pleasure. What she had to do she did, but she kept it to
a minimum. I recall now and then Hoppy's remarking to me and others about

15

some prospective friend of the college who should be cultivated. "I must ask Jim and Marian [Paterson] to have him to dinner so I can get acquainted."[21] And, in fact, the Patersons and the Kendalls did most of the official entertaining normally done by the president.

The Hopkins daughters were more out-going than their mother, especially Margaret, but their personalities and interests did not "open" the Hopkins home or attract to it anyone outside of the small devoted circle of Hopkinses' friends within the college. They were intensely loyal to their father and were quick to take offense at any criticism of him. I have no doubt they were hurt by their Wabash experience, feeling as they did that their father was never fully appreciated.

Florence, the older daughter, was more lonely than Margaret. She went to Western College for Women in Ohio. Her father would arrange for her to have dates for college dances. Once or twice he asked John Tomlinson to go as her escort and once he asked me to do the same. When I returned to Wabash in the mid-1930s I found that my brother, C. Kightly Trippet, who occasionally drove the Hopkinses' car, was serving as her escort. Although it did not occur to me at the time, I can now see in Florence in those years the traces of unhappiness which I understand became more pronounced as she grew older. Margaret was more "simpatica" than her sister, more vivacious, engaging, and cheerful. She had a beautiful soprano voice which pleased people and undoubtedly gave her confidence and self esteem. She was liked and admired but she always seemed more at ease with and appealing to older people. She never married.

This sketch of Dr. Hopkins and his family makes it easier to understand why the opposition that developed against his administration was not blunted or softened by feelings of affection and good will. The major decisions which Dr. Hopkins made or which the faculty made under his leadership were more often than not unpopular with the rank and file of Wabash alumni. The expression of that opposition might have been more temperate and more constructive had there been a reservoir of affection and respect toward Louis Hopkins personally. But, unfortunately, as things were, the criticisms and opposition were often as cruel as they were irrational.

I am guessing, but I believe Dr. Hopkins regarded his mission as president of Wabash to be that of directing the day-to-day operations of the college. His duty was on, not off campus. His obligations were to the faculty and to the students first and to the trustees second. If he had any sense of obligation

21. Jim and Marian (Crane) Paterson often served as unofficial host and hostess for President Hopkins. Jim came in 1926 from Northwestern University as director of physical education and freshman coach of all three major sports. He later became assistant dean, ran the Senior Study Camps, and, after the war, served as director of auxiliary enterprises and even managed all housing. All this in addition to teaching economics.

to alumni, he never betrayed it. Still guessing, I believe he was determined to do what he could to modernize the curriculum of the college, to make it a more rigorous place of learning, to up-grade the quality of the student body and the faculty, to "clean up" the Caveman ambience of the place, and to give the college a new reputation for integrity. If outsiders — including alumni — didn't like what he did, well, that was unfortunate, but really quite irrelevant.

He began with the student Caveman problem, only because he encountered it first. In the late fall of 1926, a sordid incident took place in Center Hall which Hopkins met head-on and quickly. Some student or students brought to the campus one night a wandering young woman, perhaps a stranded prostitute, perhaps a mentally retarded delinquent, and in the old history classroom (now the dean's office) proceeded to organize an impromptu sex orgy. Numerous students were involved, some quite prominent. President Hopkins personally took charge of the appraisal of facts and the punishment that followed. The offending students were identified and summarily dismissed from college. The action was regarded as arbitrary and, because of the social prominence of the families of two or three of the students, intercessions were made by trustess and others, including the formidable Federal Judge A. B. Anderson. Hopkins would not be pressured and the matter was closed, but not without angry feelings.

A little later that year Dr. Hopkins witnessed the brutality of "Rhynie Up" in which all freshmen passed meekly through the gauntlet of the senior class to have their bottoms beaten black and blue with hickory paddles. It was too much for Dr. Hopkins; by presidential decree that was the last year for "Rhynie Up" (which meant, by the way, that my class, 1930, was the last Wabash class to submit to this bloody ordeal). The faculty applauded this courageous stand, but there were mutterings of protest from the heartier element of the student body and from some alumni who loved the "Hell-Roaring 500" image the college had gained in the 1920s. In the months that followed, campus walks were improved and a campus system of electric street lamps was installed, as was a burly night watchman. These were regarded by critics as the beginning of the end of all that was virile and tough in "Old Wabash."

The "assault" on Wabash athletic prowess and the complete reorganization of the academic curriculum came next. The two were not linked together in Dr. Hopkins' mind, but in the public's mind they were. As I understood it, the tightening of admissions requirements was faculty-inspired and had begun the year before Hopkins became president. But Hoppy put his full force behind these faculty efforts and took a direct personal interest in the process that led to the formation of the new curriculum in 1928. Some of the details of that curriculum and the new admissions forms and procedures were essentially his.

It was to be expected, therefore, that all of these changes were associ-

17

ated with Hopkins personally, especially by those who bitterly opposed them. The consequent fall-off in enrollment and the rapid deterioration of Wabash athletic prowess provided a target for the Hopkins critics to attack. Athletic fans concentrated initially on the new foreign language requirement for admission and on the requirement that to be admitted to Wabash (without entrance examination) a high school graduate must rank in the upper two-thirds of his high school class. These requirements, they argued (and with good reason), would deprive Wabash of the kind of athlete who had brought glory to Wabash in the past. I remember a clever but vicious example of this kind of attack which appeared in a prominent sports column in the *Indianapolis Star* in 1928. The column was headed "Hic, haec, hoc." It heaped ridicule on the Wabash foreign language admissions requirement.

In 1929 came Hopkins' public endorsement of the Carnegie Foundation's Bulletin 23 on intercollegiate athletics. With the backing of the trustees, he terminated the separate financial status of the athletic department and brought both the finances and administration of intercollegiate athletics under the direct control of the college administration. It was only a question of time after that until a clash between Hopkins and Harry Scholler, director of athletics, developed. I believe the official college record says that Scholler as well as Pete Vaughan agreed with the Hopkins position. It also shows that in 1931 Scholler resigned. These accounts gloss over the more unpleasant facts. The truth is that Harry Scholler constantly undermined the president's policy and that he was given the choice of resigning or being fired. In a brief conversation on the baseball field, Dr. Hopkins made the choice clear to Harry, and Harry grudgingly agreed to resign.

As student manager of the Wabash baseball team, I came to know "Skipper" Scholler well and I liked him even though I argued with him on matters relating to the Hopkins policy. As far as I could tell, Pete Vaughan, although he may have been equally opposed to the changes Hopkins was making in the college, accepted them and conducted himself correctly and loyally in conversations with his athletes. But not Harry. His resentment and bitterness ran deep, and he could not help betraying his strong feelings to others — to me, to his players, to cronies at the Elk's Club, to alumni. He included in his criticisms Jim Paterson, whom Hoppy had brought from Northwestern to institute a modern program of intramural sports and a student health program. Dissident athletes, especially hold-overs from the Mackintosh years, took comfort in their lamentations to Harry. And Harry infected new athletes with his scorn of the "Easterner" and his "high falutin'" ideas. After the new Chapel was completed in 1928, it became something of a game for batters to try to foul ball the Chapel windows during baseball practice sessions. I remember one near miss accompanied by the taunt, "There's one for your god damned church!" Hoppy was dead right in forcing the "Skipper's" resignation although I remember being depressed about it because of my fondness for Harry.

By my senior year, like other students, I knew of the opposition developing among alumni and townspeople to the Hopkins administration. But it was not until the year 1930–31 when, after a summer's study in Switzerland, I joined the Wabash faculty as an instructor, that I became aware of the gravity of the opposition. I had not known the extent to which dissident alumni were organizing to bring pressure to bear on the Board of Trustees by electing like-minded alumni as trustees. The first target was John Coss, who was identified as the trustee primarily responsible for bringing Hopkins to Wabash and as serving in some ways as his mentor. In the alumni trustee election of 1930, Coss was defeated by the opposition's candidate, Clare McTurnan. The following year Russell Byers was the target, with Herman Wolff as the contender. The campaign for votes in that election was furious, with circulating petitions and campaign letters from both sides and open electioneering.

In 1930–31 I shared an apartment (the upstairs of Mrs. Chapman's house on South Grant Avenue) with Jim Paterson and Ted Henshaw. Neil Hutsinpillar took his meals with us. Because Henshaw was alumni secretary, our apartment became a center of activity for the on-campus pro-Hopkins forces. There were frequent huddles there concerning strategy and tactics. Hoppy himself was not an active participant. But Kendall, Osborne, Myron Phillips and others were. We wrote innumerable letters to alumni in Hoppy's behalf (thus in Russell Byers' behalf). I concentrated on my classmates now eligible to vote and on Beta alumni whom I knew well. My partisanship for Hoppy ran very high and led to opportunities to take part in more important huddles. I remember especially a long session in the law offices of Baker and Daniels in Indianapolis in which Joe Daniels, then a trustee, masterminded a letter blitz to alumni. George Kendall played an important part in that conference, as did Ted Henshaw. Dr. Hopkins may have been there, too, but I do not recall his participation in the discussions.

I did not attach importance to it at the time, but I am now impressed that in countering the opposition to his administration, Hopkins relied on others. What he did in private conversations I do not know, but publicly he never took the counter-offensive — never tried to appeal to alumni with speeches. Perhaps he knew this was simply not his forte. Perhaps he believed the obligation for fighting back belonged to others. At any rate his role was detached and mild. Others did the rallying of support. At the annual alumni banquet in 1930, for example, it was Finley Mount, a trustee, who in an impromptu speech from the floor threw down the gauntlet to the opposition. His was an impassioned defense with all of the stops pulled out. I remember his citing the disappearance of the Haynes Motor Company in Kokomo because "it refused to make changes required by changing times." He thus underscored the wisdom of changes at Wabash. He concluded with an emotional declaration of confidence in President Hopkins and announced that in that day's Board of Trustees meeting, they had unanimously passed a "ringing" resolution of support for Dr. Hopkins and his policies. He sat down amid thunderous applause. I was enormously impressed. Looking back on those controversial years, I again wonder how different matters might have been had Hoppy been able to bring to bear personally the kind of reasoned and emotional appeal that wins support. He simply could not do this.

Russell Byers was re-elected to the board, and in a way this was to be the turning point in the organized effort to force Hopkins out of office. Nevertheless, the curse of the "athletic problem" was to continue to plague Hopkins for the balance of his administration. Much of this I missed because, from the summer of 1931 until the fall of 1934, I was living and studying in England. But occasionally I would hear of the continuing troubles, and, after my return to the faculty, it became obvious to me that the disaffection of alumni was, if anything, greater.

Not all of the continuing opposition came from athletic-minded alumni. The worsening of the college's finances because of the Depression and the consequent doubts about the future of the college's fiscal health were part of the unhappiness. So also were some of the consequences of the new curriculum. In 1932 the first comprehensive examinations for seniors were given. Two seniors, who had met all other requirements for graduation, failed these examinations and thus could not graduate. One of these was from Evansville and his alumni friends there were outraged. Louis Roberts, an Evansville lawyer and an alumnus with no great interest in athletics, later told me emphatically how much he deplored the "elitist educational philosophy" that could perpetrate such "injustices."

But the carping theme in the continuous opposition was athletics. After Wabash stopped playing Big Ten games and dropped down to small college competition exclusively, it had indifferent success in both basketball and football. It was a bitter pill for alumni to swallow, especially in Indianapolis and in Chicago. I do not recall the year in the thirties when I went with Hoppy to attend an annual meeting in Chicago which illustrates what I have in mind. The meeting was well attended. When the program got under way after dinner, Fred Naber, a four-letter athlete at Wabash and also a Phi Beta Kappa, delivered a stinging speech which he had carefully written out. It was polite, but it amounted to a bitter repudiation of the athletic change which had been made under Hopkins at Wabash. The alleged deterioration in the character of Wabash was attributed primarily to the de-emphasis of athletics and the over-emphasis of academic requirements. I remember feeling shaken and humiliated. Dr. Hopkins' response, as was so often the case under such circumstances, was halting and aloof. It was Les Remley, an alumnus with some claim to having been an athlete at Wabash and a good student (Ph.D. in zoology),

20

who "answered" Fred Naber more effectively. Les was then director of athletics at Proviso High School, which gave him credibility for speaking about the effect of athletics on education. He spoke with more feeling than reason, perhaps, but his words softened the harshness of the evening and provided a measure of comfort to those of us present from the campus.

One of Hoppy's last official and controversial acts as president concerned the running sore of athletics. Following a series of meetings in the late 1930s of a faculty-alumni-trustee committee appointed to study ways in which the college's athletic program could be improved, Hoppy fired Lon Goldsberry, head baseball coach and assistant football coach. Goldy was an authentic Wabash athletic hero. His appointment to succeed Harry Scholler in 1931 had been considered a stroke of genius. His dismissal caught people by surprise. Goldy was hurt and angry and his vocal wife, Opal, was enraged — and said so. Again there were hurt feelings and resentment.

I was a member of that special committee, as was John Collett, representing the trustees. Both John and I were aghast at Hoppy's interpretation of the committee's recommendations. Apparently the recommendation that, because of financial reasons, baseball be discontinued temporarily, meant to Hoppy that Goldy had to go, and he acted at once without further consultation. This was not my understanding of what the committee had intended.

It was another unhappy episode in the long controversy about Wabash athletics. But by the year 1939–40, the opposition which had been so intense and so active in the late 1920s and early 1930s had spent itself. Instead, a vast indifference had overtaken the older generations of Wabash alumni.

It seems right to me at this point to digress in some detail about another figure who for a few years played a prominent and somewhat ambiguous role in the Wabash administration. In 1929, Dr. John G. Coulter became vice-president of Wabash. I do not know what led to his appointment or who selected him. I assume it must have been trustees who believed that someone like Coulter was desperately needed to improve the college's public relations, especially with alumni and potential financial donors. "Doc" Coulter appeared on campus in the fall of 1929. He made an immediate and immensely favorable impression on the students and also on the townspeople. His robust good looks, his breezy outgoing manner, his booming laughter, his love of the outdoors, his reputation as an experienced bon-vivant — all of his personal qualities — made him almost overnight a favorite on the Wabash scene. I was among those students who at once liked and enjoyed him. He was a Beta and thus spent a good deal of his time at the Beta House. I was president of the chapter that year and thus had a good opportunity to get acquainted with him.

21

He regaled us with stories of his youth in Crawfordsville when his father had been professor of botany at the college and of his youth at Bloomington when his father left Wabash to become president of Indiana University.[22] He talked much about France where he had lived since World War I and where he continued to keep a "little farm." It was fascinating talk. And he entered into student recreation with gusto. If someone wanted a partner for pitching horseshoes in the back yard, he was ready. Or if a fourth for bridge was needed, he always obliged. It was the same way with gin rummy or poker. He played expertly and with confidence. He did not limit to the Beta House this kind of fraternization. He visited other houses too. He often strolled out to watch football practice in the late afternoons. He visited classes and joined in botany field trips (his Ph.D. was in botany).

It was not all banter and play. Dr. Coulter was good at drawing students into conversations about themselves and about the college. He thus obtained good insight into student interests, their appraisal of their professors, their courses, and their likes and dislikes. He was a good listener. Much of what he learned in this way was later to appear in his book *In Freshman Year,* about which I will write more in a moment.

"Doc" Coulter went over equally well with townspeople and alumni. (When I say "Doc" I am reflecting the title which students affectionately and habitually used. I never called him "Doc." For me it was at first "Doctor Coulter" and gradually this became "John.") Although he had lived in Paris for more than a decade (he must have been in his early fifties when he became vice-president of Wabash) and was something of an expatriate as far as America was concerned, he slipped back into the Hoosier landscape and Hoosier idioms as easily as one's return to old shoes. He used to laugh about this and say "Once a Hoosier always a Hoosier." At any rate he fitted well into the life of Crawfordsville, whether it was hamburgers at Blake's Cafe or dinner at the De Vores. He had great charm for ladies and was lionized for a while in Crawfordsville, in Indianapolis, and, I suppose, wherever he went as an ambassador of the college.

I used the word "ambiguous" when I began writing this digression about Coulter. By that I mean that to those outside of the college administration, it was never clear precisely what Dr. Coulter's responsibilities were. Apparently he was to win friends and raise money for Wabash. No doubt he won friends and rekindled waning interest here and there, but if he raised money it was not conspicuously evident.[23] Also his coming to Wabash when he did and the

22. See *The First Hundred Years,* pp. 150, 154, and 160, for remarks about Professor John M. Coulter.

23. The Crash of 1929 and the Depression, of course, frustrated and postponed Coulter's efforts to raise money for the Centennial.

contrast between him and Hoppy as far as personality was concerned touched off speculation as to whether Coulter was really to become president.

I doubt that John Coulter himself had any such thoughts, and nothing he ever said to me would lend credence to that idea. But I also doubt that he asserted himself to squash that kind of speculation. And at times he even seemed to give encouragement to the Hopkins opponents. For example, in a chapel speech in the winter of 1930–31, after returning to the campus from France, he made a wise crack about the efforts to "disenfranchise" a large number of the alumni in the annual election of alumni trustees. This was a reference to the successful efforts of the Board of Trustees, following the defeat of John Coss, to limit voting privileges to alumni who had completed at least two years of study at Wabash. What Dr. Coulter said could be taken two ways. I took it the light-hearted way. But I later discovered that Hoppy had taken it as a serious criticism of the board's (and therefore of Hoppy's) strategy. It may have been true also that in his occasional visits with Ike Elston in Chicago, Coulter expressed confidential criticism of President Hopkins.

Notwithstanding such tension as this ambiguity may have caused between Dr. Hopkins and Dr. Coulter, Dr. Hopkins obviously wanted to keep Dr. Coulter identified with his administration and to have him serve as a buffer with the alumni. Some years after his death, when I was searching for something else among Dr. Hopkins' papers, I came upon a file of correspondence between the two men. I was fascinated by an exchange of letters written, I believe, in the fall of 1934, possibly somewhat later. Each summer, just as Hoppy returned to Vermont, Dr. Coulter made it a point to return to France. His returns to Wabash from France became progressively later each year. The letters to which I refer — "Dear John," "Dear Hoppy" exchanges — stressed Hoppy's desire to have Dr. Coulter on campus soon. I remember one sentence in Hoppy's letter which ran something like this: "People are wondering why you are not here, and again there is talk about your lack of confidence in this administration." John's reply was reassuring, but it included a sentence like this: "If you must know, I am now going through a divorce here and can not easily return." Neither before then nor afterward, although I was quite close to him, did John Coulter ever mention a wife or a divorce to me. Nor was it ever a matter of discussion with others, so far as I know.

Although it seemed to me at the time (and seems even more so in retrospect) that as a money raiser and public relations man for Wabash John Coulter was not successful, he left his mark on the college in several ways. The most important of these was the institution of the Senior Study Camps at Turkey Run.[24] For the better part of the next thirty years (after 1930) these camps operated as a valuable and happy part of the senior year experience at

24. For an account of the Senior Study Camps, see *These Fleeting Years*, pp. 93–95.

Wabash. And certainly in the beginning and so long as John (and later Jim Paterson) led them, they were an important educational asset in the college's total program. The camps were John's idea, as was the grouping of seniors regardless of fraternity affiliation or major subjects. I was a member of the first group of seniors to go to Turkey Run in late February, 1930. For me and for others in the group, it was a high point in our total undergraduate experience. The program of study in the mornings, nature hikes in the afternoon, and above all the organized bull sessions with a different set of professors each night were both relaxing and exciting at the same time. Becoming as it did a regular part of the total Wabash undergraduate program for many years, the Senior Study Camp added another distinctive idea that was in one form or another adopted by other institutions.

Another contribution which John Coulter made was his writing of *In Freshman Year*.[25] I presume the purpose of this book was to attract high school students to Wabash. As such it was a failure, but as an interesting record of student life in the late 1920s and early 1930s and as a commentary on some of the prominent professors of those years (Osborne, Gronert, Kendall, Bechtel, among others), it is a book of more than casual value for the college archives. While he was writing the book, he asked me and others to read and to criticize certain chapters; or, in my case, he would often read chapters aloud and would digress to discuss his opinions and conclusions. But I did not read the book completely until more than twenty years after its publication. It struck me as a breezy, somewhat "boy-scoutish" story, but for all that I found myself made sentimental and nostalgic by its reminders of my undergraduate Wabash days.

John Coulter enjoyed writing and he wrote well. His books on "Old France" and his book about his uncle, Stanley Coulter, long-time dean at Purdue University, were sprightly and interesting.[26] So far as I know, however, none of his books achieved any prominence. Nor did he care. He wrote for the fun he had in writing. He was that kind of man — at least when I knew him. He did whatever he enjoyed and declined to do what he didn't enjoy.

These are not attributes best suited for the humdrum aspects of college administration, and no doubt this had something to do with his gradually fading from the Wabash scene. His absences from the campus during the summer months became longer as the years went by, and his work for Wabash became more dilatory. During my years in England, we kept in touch with each other. In fact, we became closer personal friends. Two or three times he

25. *In Freshman Year, the Story of a Real Boy and His Dad* (New York: W. H. Wise and Co., 1934).

26. *Old France; a Sort of History* (Paris: John G. Coulter, 1929); *The Dean, an Account of His Career and of His Convictions* (Lafayette: Purdue University Alumni Association, 1940).

visited me for a week or so in England. We toured Wales together during one of these visits and the Midlands during another. Occasionally I would spend a few days with him in Paris, usually when I was en route to Austria where I did much of my Oxford studies. He introduced me to obscure and delightful corners in Paris, which I would never have known otherwise. He never seemed to lack money, but he had no visible routine of work. He made no references to sources of income and, except for speaking occasionally of his "farm," never revealed anything to me about his life in France. Not once did he mention his wife. It was a lazy, aimless kind of life, I decided. He read, wrote a little, enjoyed sitting for hours at a sidewalk cafe table sipping Pernod and water, watching life go by. He was obviously well known and liked in his favorite haunts in Paris, where he was greeted as "Capitan." It was mysterious but, after trying a few times without success to get him to talk about his earlier years in France, I dismissed the mystery and accepted his happy indolence without question.

After my marriage in 1936, I gradually saw less of John, even though he continued to spend some time at Wabash each year until about 1938. He did not like my wife, nor she him. Now and then we would, nevertheless, have the same kind of long conversation which formerly had been so common. He became increasingly gloomy about the gathering war clouds in Europe and, perhaps because of this, pessimistic about Wabash. Dick Banta, who joined the Wabash staff in the late 1930s, added to John's unhappiness. Dick regarded John as a "fake" and John regarded Dick as "overbearing" and "uncouth." These circumstances probably had something to do with his leaving his ambiguous position at Wabash toward the end of the 1930s. They also probably caused him to speak more openly of his private reservations about Dr. Hopkins. He made it clear to me in one of our last conversations before World War II that he thought Hoppy should resign. "Wabash has gone East twice for its presidents," he said, "and each time it was a serious mistake." I presume he was referring to President Burroughs as well as to President Hopkins. But even at the time of his remark, the observation struck me as emotional rather than logical. All four Wabash presidents from 1832 to 1901 were "Easterners."

With the outbreak of the war in Europe in 1939, Dr. Coulter stopped his annual pilgrimages to France. He lived in Indianapolis with old friends and identified himself more and more closely with that city. In the early 1940s he was an unsuccessful candidate for the Republican nomination for Congress. After that I had no personal contact with him while I was in the Navy for the next four years.

The next time I saw John Coulter was shortly after my return to civilian life in the late spring of 1946. It was at a Wabash banquet at the Columbia Club in Indianapolis, where I had been invited to speak. I was shocked at the toll the four years had taken on him. He was thin, stooped, rheumy-eyed. The

25

hearty laughter remained and so did the ruddy complexion, but gone was his robust vitality. Two more years went by without further contact, and then I learned that he was living at the Indiana Soldiers and Sailors Home north of Lafayette. Ted Gronert and I went to see him one day with a few simple gifts. It was a depressing experience. We found him withdrawn in a bare room that smelled of stale tobacco smoke. His color was ashen and he had an uncharacteristic stubble of beard. He had almost nothing to say to us and gave no sign that he was glad we had come to see him. Was his sullenness resentment? Self-pity? Senility? Perhaps it was all three.

I came away from that visit engulfed in sadness, and I rebuked myself for having neglected John. He died shortly after that, penniless and alone. No one at the college was notified at the time. I do not even know where his body is buried.

The observations and judgments which I have made about Dr. Hopkins and his administration probably leave the impression that the Hopkins' years were unhappy as well as controversial years for Wabash. Looked at from the outside, such a conclusion might seem justified. But viewed from within the college — certainly through the eyes of a very young member of the faculty — they were really quite happy years.

I am speaking now of the mid-1930s. In the spring of 1934, Dr. Hopkins wrote to me in England and invited — yes, urged — me to return to Wabash. It was a personal plea. As so often has been the case in my life, it was a proposal involving a one-year commitment. It was a plea I could not reject. Once again I postponed my timetable for law school and with no real hesitation at all I said "yes." I returned to Indiana from Europe in September, 1934. The truth is, I suspect, I had lost interest in studying law and was uncertain what kind of a career I wanted. The thought of returning to Wabash and using the year's interlude to make some decisions about my future I found enormously appealing. As matters turned out, the return was in itself to become an irrevocable decision about the future.

My remark that the Hopkins' years were "really quite happy years" reflects my own experience at Wabash from 1934–35 to Dr. Hopkins' death in 1940. The morale of the faculty in those years was remarkably high. In part this was because the "Great Depression" experience brought about at Wabash, as it did elsewhere in America, a new sense of closeness among people — something like a common bond of privation and concern. Following the "Roaring Twenties" the 1930s brought a simplification of life through a rediscovery of early American values all but forgotten following World War I.

There was also the excitement of the sweeping changes introduced by

26

Franklin Roosevelt in Washington. The "New Deal" produced something like a national war psychology — a central theme of national concern and debate. The majority of the Wabash faculty was pro-New Deal in spite of the pervasive anti-New Deal sentiment in Crawfordsville and much of Indiana. This contributed to a new kind of community sense at Wabash that transcended the bleak institutional problems of the college.

Finally, there was a feeling within the faculty that the academic changes taking place at Wabash were important innovations. They were proud of the new trails the college was blazing, proud of the curiosity these trails aroused at other institutions. The frequency of visitors coming from other campuses to take a look at the new Wabash curriculum — especially the divisional system, the senior reading course, and comprehensive examinations — contributed to the faculty's sense of working at something new and different. No doubt it was an exaggerated sense of importance, but it was exciting.

Moreover, despite the financial problems of Wabash at the operating level, there were new symbols of progress. In 1929 the new Chapel was in use. The simple New England beauty and authenticity which Frederick Larson (then architect for Dartmouth) gave it had a stunning effect on the Wabash campus. In 1938 the second building designed by Larson, Goodrich Hall for physical sciences, was completed and Larson's master plan for the future development of the campus, complete with artists' sketches, began to be publicized far beyond any legitimate hopes for its achievement. It was the beginning of a vague dream of future greatness once "better times" returned.

Yes, faculty morale was high despite low salaries and frequent reminders of financial calamaties (I believe the highest salary in these years, next to the president's, was $3,600 per year. My salary was $1,200 a year in 1934–35). Even when Dr. Hopkins had to announce a fifteen percent cut in salaries, as he did in 1935, the faculty, with few exceptions, took the news calmly and with good grace.

With no money to spend on non-essentials, faculty recreation was simple. But it was very pleasant. Often we would gather in someone's home to read books aloud. I remember numerous such reading sessions at the Gronerts, who were then living at Hovey Cottage, which at that time was located about where Wolcott Hall now stands. It was light reading; Mark Twain and Tarkington were favorites. A variation of such evenings would be simple parties with old fashioned games like charades, or slightly more formal parties with discussion sessions following a light supper. Many of these were at the Kendall home, whose charm reflected the good taste and graciousness of Yvonne Kendall.

The Crawfordsville Dramatic Club provided periodic social highlights, especially during the winter months. The Little Theatre in the Masonic Temple was always packed for amateur productions, and, following the play, the dances in the ballroom downstairs, while somewhat stiff by comparison with student dances, were happy diversions. The majority of the club members were towns-people, but the influence of the college in the Dramatic Club was dispropor-tionately large. Always some one or several from the college had prominent roles in the plays presented, and more often than not it was a faculty member who directed the play. I had never before taken part in amateur dramatic pro-ductions but I quickly found myself drawn into the activity. I had the lead, for example, in *Ten Minute Alibi* and in *Room Service* and minor parts in other plays. The weeks of rehearsals and the "refreshments" in the house of one of the play committee members following rehearsals often encouraged romantic attachments. It was in this way that I met Dorothy Clark O'Neall, whom I later married.

Especially there were the faculty picnics which enlivened the weekends during these lean years. Sometimes these would be held at Turkey Run or the Shades but more commonly they took place in Pine Hills. The rugged beauty and mysterious solitude of Pine Hills worked like a tonic for me on these oc-casions, and for others too, I am sure. Doubling up to save gasoline, we would make our way by caravan in the late afternoons to Pine Hills and then walk the balance of the way to a favorite high cliff overlooking Indian Creek. The men would build a roaring fire, while the women unpacked boxes and baskets of the potluck supper. While the fire died down to hot coals, there would be an hour of hiking. Following supper there were lazy hours sitting around the fire telling stories, arguing about current events, or singing (usually started by Fergus Ormes with his guitar). Finally, we would extinguish the last of the glowing embers and, Indian file, make our way back through the darkness to the cars. They were delightful hours, perhaps the happiest I ever knew at Wabash.

For these outings there was something of an "in" group among the faculty. It changed as time went by, but the central core remained the same. The Ken-dalls (George and Yvonne), the Osbornes (Insley and Frances), the Gronert (Ted and Hazel), the Patersons (Jim and Marian), the Leavenworths (Clar and Annie), the Montgomerys (Henry and Peg), the Polleys (Crawford and Mildred), the Ormeses (Fergus and Emily), and the "bachelors," John Coulter John Tomlinson, Neil Hutsinpillar and I. Occasionally there would be others from the faculty and now and then townspeople like the Collars (George and Helen). As long as this core continued to be important the picnics were much the same. The practice continued after the Hopkins era, but it was less fun. The groups became bigger and less closely knit.

President Hopkins took no part in these simple recreations, perhaps be-cause Nora Hopkins stayed withdrawn from faculty social life. But those who may have regarded Hoppy's life as unrelieved by relaxation were mistaken. Louis Hopkins seems to me to have been a lonely man. At Wabash he had no intimate friends. Perhaps he had close friends in the East, but my superficial observation made me conclude that he was not close to his illustrious brother, Ernest, who was then president of Dartmouth, and still less close to his younger brother, Robert. But he was not an unhappy man. Nor was he moody.

He enjoyed his own private hobbies. One of these was tropical fish. His collection of brilliant guppies in the Caleb Mills House was spectacular. He worked for hours on end at fish tanks, lighting effects, and water flow, becoming something of an expert in such matters. He was equally studious and industrious in photography. Somewhere there must be a large collection of his photographs of campus scenes and of his country home in Vermont. He loved his bull terrier, "Bepo," a love "Bepo" returned. Especially, he loved his old country home on the outskirts of Perkinsville, Vermont. It was a small red brick farmhouse pleasantly located in mountain country. I visited there once or twice and was impressed with the loving care Hoppy had expended improving the place little by little. I presume it was to have been the family retirement home.

Hoppy's relaxation at the Caleb Mills House was quiet and simple. As I have noted, almost never did the Hopkinses entertain guests at home. But frequently he would have a few college people in for an evening of card playing. The game was invariably "hearts." Mrs. Hopkins never participated, but one or both daughters, Hoppy, and two or three others would play seated around the kitchen table or around a table in his study. It is incredible now that these simple evenings could have been as enjoyable as they seemed at the time.

Increasingly important in Hoppy's later years at Wabash was the companionship of Mildred Roach, his personal secretary. She was the youngest of three daughters of Hank and Dolly Roach. The family had come to Crawfordsville from Logansport, but Mildred had grown up in Crawfordsville. Like many Crawfordsville girls before her, by the time she was an upper class high school student, she had become identified prominently in the undergraduate social life of the college. She was representative of the "flapper" generation in the mid-1920s. Cute rather than pretty, she had a willowy figure, a radiant personality and an infectious laugh. She was a superb dancer. All of these qualities made her popular at Wabash fraternity dances. When I first became aware of her during my student days, she had, like some other Crawfordsville girls, the reputation of being frivolous and pleasure bent.

In the year 1930–31 — perhaps later — Mildred came to work at the college as a secretary assistant in the alumni office. Snob that I was at that time about Crawfordsville girls, I remember being both surprised and vaguely annoyed at her bouncy, laughing presence in Center Hall. But even before I left for England, and certainly after my return four years later, I formed a new appreciation of Mildred. Her frivolity in the late 1920s was mostly sham. She was naturally light hearted and outgoing but she was also highly intelligent and blessed with good common sense about herself and about others. And she was a prodigious worker.

Mildred's office was on the second floor of Center Hall, diagonally across from President Hopkins' office. Little by little in the early 1930s, she began to do extra work for Dr. Hopkins; by the mid-1930s she had become his personal secretary. Hoppy's first secretary was Frances Doane, who came to Wabash with him from Northwestern University. After a year or two, however, Frances married Insley Osborne, whose first wife had died several years earlier. Hoppy's second secretary was Esther Luckett, daughter of Bruce Luckett, a long-time trustee of the college. Esther was a competent secretary, but with the mannerisms of a spinster many years older. She continued to be the president's official secretary, but mostly for routine correspondence. It was Mildred who by 1935–36 worked most closely with the president.

Dr. Hopkins depended on Mildred as an assistant and confidante as well as a secretary. It was she who worked exclusively with him digesting and writing into final reports his data collected as an examiner for the North Central Association of Colleges and Secondary Schools. It was she who took charge, under his direction, of assembling and publishing the annual senior comprehensive examinations. She typed, duplicated, and distributed his reports to the Board of Trustees. No doubt in the process she became a confidential listener and advisor to him.

When Hoppy was hospitalized in the late 1930s for circulatory difficulties at the Methodist Hospital in Indianapolis, Mildred was like a member of the family regularly at his bedside. Occasionally she would visit the family in their summer home in Vermont.

Mildred went with George Kendall, Insley Osborne and me to Vermont in the late summer of 1940 as soon as we learned of Hoppy's sudden death. Through those several trying days, she was cheerful, useful, comforting to the family.

Mildred continued at the college in one capacity or another until her premature death in 1955. After Dr. Sparks became president, she no longer had the prominence she enjoyed in the late Hopkins years. But she was inseparable from the life stream of Wabash, fiercely loyal to it, and a source of strength as assistant registrar. Men continued to fall in love with her. But she never married. I gave the college's eulogy for her at the memorial services held in the Chapel following her death. I found it difficult to do justice to her memory.

Thinking of Mildred Roach touches off in my mind a reverie about the important but largely unacknowledged influence that women have had on the history of Wabash. From the 1830s to the present, in one way or another, women have been deeply involved in the life of the college. Their influence has generally been indirect, finding expression through men with whom they shared their lives, but at times it has been direct and obvious. Now and then it has been troublesome for the college. In the main it has been happy and benign. Often the roles played by women have been self-effacing and sacrificial.

In a men's college it is inevitable, I suppose, that official histories of the institution slight the role of women. Osborne and Gronert have precious little to say about women in *The First Hundred Years*. The same is true of most of us who have had a consuming interest in Wabash history. When I used to dig around in the college archives in pursuit of some passing interest, it never occurred to me to try to identify individual women who out of love played a significant part in Wabash history. I am sure, however, that in those archives and, even more so, in the folklore of the college, there is a fascinating story to be unearthed. It would be a story full of disparate items such as Jenny Blair preserving the records of Beta Theta Pi during the Civil War and being gratefully inducted into the fraternity once the war was over; the prim Hall sisters precipitating the firing of Ezra Pound from the faculty;[27] the second Mrs. Mackintosh raising funds to build a new armory and gymnasium during World War I;[28] Charlotte Kruze shattering forever the ambience of the old Wabash by her ideas for decorating and furnishing the new Campus Center; Mrs. Waldo Stevens making annual springtime pilgrimages to the campus to honor, through an award to a junior, the memory of a beloved only son killed in the line of duty in the Wabash athletic department. It is the kind of stuff out of which legends could arise.

In the nineteenth century women's influence came primarily, although by no means exclusively, from faculty wives. And it was important. Consider, for example, the role of Mary Hovey. Perhaps our most authentic glimpses of Wabash life in the earliest and most difficult years for the college are through her letters and notes. But Mrs. Hovey's role in Wabash history ran far beyond the recorded thoughts she left for us. She may very well have been the decisive influence in bringing to Wabash its second president, her brother-in-law, Charles White. Still more important was her influence on her husband.

Professor Gronert considered Edmund Hovey the most important single individual in the first fifty years of Wabash history. Perhaps Gronert was right. Edmund Hovey was not only one of the founding fathers. He was also a long-time trustee, a teacher, the treasurer of the college, a fund raiser, and the first historian of the college. He was everything to Wabash in its formative years and Wabash became everything for him. He was the original "Mr. Wabash." Unlike his more illustrious friend and colleague, Caleb Mills, Hovey had no other important interests. If Wabash had collapsed and disappeared Mills

27. See *The First Hundred Years,* pp. 291–92.
28. Ibid., p. 304.

would have been saddened but not defeated. He had other equally important ventures to pursue. But Hovey would have been broken-hearted for the rest of his life.

In spite of his extraordinary dedication to Wabash, or perhaps even because of that, Edmund Hovey was, I believe, a moody man, occasionally discouraged to the point of despair. It was his wife who repeatedly revived his hopes and reinforced his resolution. How very different the Wabash story might be if Mary Hovey had not been the cheerful, courageous, and determined woman she was. She deserves to share the honored memory in which Wabash men have enshrined the name of Edmund Otis Hovey.

We know less about other faculty wives in the nineteenth century but Mary Hovey undoubtedly had her counterparts among them. In the twentieth century living memory can recall numerous examples of faculty wives who were prominent and influential in the Wabash way of life. And to faculty wives, especially in the twentieth century, must be added trustee and alumni wives, even a number of one-time sweethearts of Wabash men, whose fondness for Wabash affected the rising fortunes of the college. We must also add that succession of women in recent decades who by working there shared in the unfolding drama of the place.

A hundred years passed before women became important in the day-to-day operation of the college. I doubt that anyone knows who the first full-time woman employee was. I would not be surprised, however, if research revealed that she was the clerk-bookkeeper-typist who assisted Jim Wedding in the college treasurer's office in downtown Crawfordsville. In the early 1920s there were only one or two women working in Center Hall (perhaps Margaret Shannon or Mildred Brown) and even they were part-time. Center Hall, even after its "modern improvements," was obviously designed for men only. Not until after World War II was there a decent lounge and restroom for women in the building.

With the arrival of President Hopkins things began to change. The president's office had a full-time, year-round secretary — first Frances Doanne, then Esther Luckett. Although she did not have the title, Mildred Roach was assistant to the president. Mrs. Frank (Elsie) Davidson became assistant registrar and Mary Johnson Schlemmer (Willis Johnson's sister) began her long career with the college. In Yandes Library, probably to Harry Wedding's dismay, Dr. Hopkins appointed women (Mrs. Robert Lind and Anna Carolyn Crane) as assistant librarians.[29]

It was immediately after World War II, however, that women became numerous and indispensable. President Sparks made sweeping changes in the organization and functions of the college administration, converting Center

29. Dr. Lind was a professor of classics; Miss Crane's sister was Mrs. James J. Paterson.

Hall classrooms into offices, introducing modern business machines, installing a PBX telephone switchboard, etc. His emphasis on public relations, fund raising, student recruitment and alumni cultivation greatly enlarged the amount of paper work to be handled in Center Hall. By the early 1950s I estimate that women staff members comprised from twenty to twenty-five percent of the total faculty and staff.

Some of the numerous women who worked at the college in this dynamic chapter in Wabash history came and went. This was especially true of the veteran student wives who became a part of the Wabash scene after World War II. They provided a ready pool for extra help with the increasing administrative work load. Young women like Carolynne Rudrow, Wanda Sweeney, and Tommye Wright added a bouncy, colorful touch to the college staff in those years.[30] It was a happy time in their lives and they helped in making it a happy time for the college.

The front line among women staff members in those years served the college for long periods of time. For twenty years Adelaide Hayes directed the secretarial pool and was the ghost writer for clouds of letters which flowed from the president's office. For a like number of years Juanita Rutledge was at the nerve center of the college as switchboard operator and receptionist at the Campus Center. For thirty years Frances Scott served as an accomplished secretary, including long stints of duty in the dean's office and in the president's office. For forty years Mary Schlemmer was a key figure in the college's accounting and business services of the college. I could go on and on — Hilda Howard in the president's office,[31] Dolores Diehl in the admissions office, Miriam Stilling in the registrar's office, Gladys Otto and Helen Foley in the library. How can one justly measure the importance of the contributions made by the likes of these women in the history of Wabash?

Wabash College is a college for men. But how many women have there been and how many are there now who could say, "Yes, that is true. But a lot of my life and love went into Wabash. It's my college, too."

However pleasant the day-to-day life within the college may have been in the Hopkins years, the major problems of his administration continued to plague the place. Viewed objectively, it was obvious that the situation of the college was a deteriorating one.

Dr. Hopkins' way of dealing with that problem was to operate the college as economically as possible. In this he was undoubtedly influenced by the Board

30. Wives of Leland Rudrow, Chester Sweeney, and Jack P. Wright, all members of the Class of 1950.

31. Wife of Ralph B. Howard, professor of physics.

of Trustees, particularly its chairman, Governor James Goodrich. In 1935 Governor Goodrich offered to build a new science building provided Wabash would balance its annual operating budget for three consecutive years. Hoppy did this, but only by reducing and then freezing salaries, by avoiding additional desirable operating expenses, by postponing maintenance requirements, and by increasing tuition charges slightly.

The consequences of this austerity were visible to the naked eye. In the summertime the college appeared to be empty and neglected. The grass on the east campus was left uncut until just before college opened in September. The annual painting program was curtailed, with the result that the trim on the older buildings faded and peeled. But there were other unfortunate consequences, too. The younger faculty members became increasingly restive and several moved to other institutions. (For example, Robert Lind to the University of Kansas, Henry Montgomery to Miami University, John Tomlinson to the U. S. Foreign Service.) Student enrollment remained a nagging problem, especially from families that did not need college financial aid. I. C. Elston, one of the wealthiest of the trustees, resigned from the board hoping, he privately explained, to set an example for others whom he termed "dead wood." Nothing happened. Joe Daniels, perhaps out of despair, refused to stand for reelection to the board when his term expired.

In the late 1930s Dick Banta joined the staff part-time to direct the college's public relations program. Dick began at once to improve the "selling" aspects of the college's publications. They became more attractive and more appealing to prospective students, alumni, and friends of the college. More important, he concentrated his attention on student recruitment and on alumni interest. There was initially some carping among older faculty members (especially Osborne) about Banta's having anything to do with admitting students. (He had been a notoriously indifferent student for four years in the "Hell Roaring 500" era.) But Dick was right in breathing new life into the college's admissions program. He had the good sense not to try to deal personally with high schools or with counselling of students, but he was good at enlisting others in these activities and at organizing the kind of off-campus efforts that produced results.

Banta concentrated on the major cities in Indiana and on such centers as Chicago, Detroit, Cincinnati, and St. Louis, which had in the past been sources of Wabash students. He appealed to alumni in these areas to help with banquets for prospective students, and he drafted young members of the faculty to attend these meetings to help "sell' Wabash to alumni as well as to students. Myron Phillips, Franz Prell, John Plummer, I, and later Warren Shearer were put on the banquet circuit. It proved to be a successful program and enrollment rose.

It was in this way that I found myself beginning to speak more and more to groups of disaffected alumni and to experiment with ideas designed to win back the kind of fierce alumni loyalty Wabash had enjoyed in earlier years. I realize now that I then began to toy with the kind of "mystique" about Wabash which I fully developed as president years later. It was also the beginning of a very close and long lasting friendship between the Bantas and the Trippets.

In 1938, or about then, came the final bitter controversy of the Hopkins administration. It was the controversy about the study of religion and the Bible as a prerequisite for graduation. It was initiated by a proposal from Edgar H. Evans, Wabash alumnus and a senior member of the Board of Trustees. Edgar Evans was a shrewd and successful business man who had put together a miniature financial empire centering around the Acme-Evans Milling Company. He was a devout Christian, a pillar in the Second Presbyterian Church in Indianapolis, a staunch Republican, and a devoted alumnus of Wabash as it was in the pre-Hopkins era. Like others, he was convinced that American society was becoming "Godless" as well as socialistic because of the New Deal "insanity" and that a return to a God-fearing, hard working, simple society was imperative if all was not to be lost. To that end, in his later years he devoted much of his time and money to restoring religious studies in the private schools and colleges of Indiana. His crusade met with considerable success everywhere except at his alma mater where, I dare say to his surprise, he met with adamant resistance.

Evans' proposal was simple. He would give $100,000 to endow a professorship in religion, provided the college would agree that all students in the freshman year be required to take — and to pass — a six-hour course in the Christian religion, three hours of which was to be devoted to the study of the Bible. Apparently he first made his proposal to the Board of Trustees, but Dr. Hopkins took the position that this was a faculty, not trustee matter. The majority of the board agreed. But when the proposal went to the faculty, the trouble began. The leaders of the faculty were outraged by the proposal. Osborne, Kendall, and Ormes were especially outspoken and their prestige carried younger faculty members with them. Hoppy, as I recall, really took no part in the discussion of the merits of the proposal, but once the faculty position was clear, he stood firmly with the faculty in subsequent negotiations with Evans and his supporters. It was a disagreeable business.

Some of the faculty regarded Evans as a bigot, narrow minded and intolerant of "non-believers," and, as a rich man, determined to impose his views on faculty and students in disregard of the principles of academic freedom. At the time I shared this point of view, but it was unduly harsh and to some extent unfair. Edgar Evans was a classical puritan with all of the strengths and shortcomings of that way of looking at life. He was a mild-mannered, soft-spoken, even gentle person. But he was tough-minded about what he believed in and remarkably tenacious and resolute. Hard work, honesty, self discipline, frugality, avoidance of even the minor vices of the flesh, faith in the will of God, prayer, repentance of sins — all of these were as important to him as life itself. They were, as he saw it, important also to the fabric of American society, and he took seriously his sense of obligation to do what he could to restore these virtues to their proper place in the minds of people. Education, he decided, was the best instrument to accomplish this end. Somewhere at Wabash, probably in the Chapel, there hangs a good portrait of Evans which captures very well the character I have described. He is wearing a beige jacket and light blue trousers. The intense eye, bony features, and thin lips tell more than words can about the man who caused the controversy of which I am speaking.[32]

As the controversy deepened, various alumni in Indianapolis — friends or supporters of Mr. Evans — interceded in his behalf. Harry Wade, Bas Merrell and Paul Mathews were particularly active. Bas Merrell may have shared Mr. Evans' credo, but the other two were more cynical about it, especially Wade. Their argument was coarse and blunt. "Wabash needs money — lots of it. Here is a man, an alumnus, who is offering the college a hundred thousand dollars. There undoubtedly is much more than that which will follow if the college is sensible about this religion business. The faculty is a bunch of idiots to oppose such a generous offer!" This kind of talk simply stiffened faculty opposition.

In an attempt to resolve the issue, there were, at Mr. Evans' request, two or three long conferences between the faculty and him and his supporters. These conferences were distinctly at cross purposes. I remember one long discussion held after dinner at the Crawfordsville Country Club which, rather than bridging the gap, widened it. Evans himself was conciliatory and gentle, but Harry Wade's remarks infuriated the faculty, and Insley Osborne's gift for withering sarcasm was never more pronounced than it was that night. Apart from these extremes, it was a rational discussion. The faculty's position, best stated by Kendall, included the following: (1) Unlike practically all other colleges in the Midwest, Wabash was, and had been since its original charter in 1832, an independent, not a church-related, college. Its student body was mixed — Protestants, Catholics, Jews, agnostics; (2) It would be a violation of the tradition and spirit of Wabash to "force" students of different religious persuasions to study the Christian religion within a Protestant context; (3) Wabash offered studies in religion but on an optional basis, and that was the way it should be in a college which was "free and independent"; (4) The principle of who determines the academic program of an independent college was at stake. To "succumb" to this pressure would be a loss of faculty prerogative.

It was a hopeless impasse which Dr. Hopkins refused to influence one way

---

32. Painted in 1948 by Ruth Pratt Bobbs, the portrait does hang in the Chapel.

or another, and additional bitter scars resulted among Indianapolis alumni.

Whether the Evans controversy had anything to do with it, I do not know, but the Board of Trustees meeting at commencement time in 1940 was a disaster for Dr. Hopkins. Because he was still having difficulties climbing stairs following his hospitalization, the meeting was held in the Governor's Room in Goodrich Hall rather than in the faculty room on the second floor of Yandes. I attended that meeting as dean of the college, having recently been elected to that position.

The room was too small for the meeting, which added to the tension which developed. There were the usual reports from officers and committee chairmen. Then followed the president's report. This touched off a long and dismal discussion of the future financing of the college, and there was much talk about "bold, aggressive" leadership. Governor Goodrich made a lengthy speech toward the end of the meeting. At one point, I remember his turning to President Hopkins on his right and saying bluntly, "I just don't believe you are the right man for the job that must be done." Nothing could have been clearer. Ten years or so later, Lawrence De Vore told me that, following that meeting, Goodrich had appointed him and Verne Oggel as a trustee committee to inform Hoppy he must resign at the board's request. De Vore decided to wait until September to discharge this disagreeable assignment.

At the alumni banquet that night Hoppy looked pale and haggard. But the commencement weekend program went off pleasantly. At the picnic luncheons in front of Center Hall on Sunday and again on Monday, Hoppy seemed relaxed and in good spirits. I suspect, however, that he was deeply troubled inside. Later that June the Hopkins family left for Perkinsville for the balance of the summer. It must have been early August, perhaps late July, that we received a call at the college that the president had died. The Hopkins family had been at lunch at the Larson home in Hanover. Hoppy complained of feelings of indigestion, excused himself from the table, and minutes later fell dead of a massive heart attack. (Governor Goodrich died later that autumn.)

George Kendall, Insley Osborne, Mildred Roach, and I set out at once by car for Vermont. Taking turns driving, we arrived late the following afternoon. Mrs. Hopkins was composed and dry-eyed. Margaret and Florence were distraught. The funeral services were at the Dartmouth Chapel. I remember nothing of it except the unexpected playing of the Wabash *Alma Mater*. With the playing of this haunting refrain I made no further effort to restrain my tears.

On our first night at the Hopkins' home I remember hearing Margaret say to her mother, "Oh, mama, let's bury daddy in his new black sports shirt! He loved it so!" We buried his body in his black shirt. Insley, George and I were among the pall bearers.

Louis Hopkins will go down in Wabash history, I suppose, as one of the most unpopular of Wabash presidents. I can not dissent from that verdict. But it troubles me that with the passage of time this conclusion will obscure his qualities as a human being and will minimize his very important contributions to the twentieth-century development of Wabash.[33]

If Louis Hopkins is to be remembered as one of the most unpopular Wabash presidents, he also should be remembered as one of its most courageous presidents. A man with less strength of character and less clarity of purpose would have never survived the pressures and the personal attacks which Dr. Hopkins endured for fourteen years. He took criticism, opposition, and sometimes ridicule and insults from students, townspeople, and alumni. His reaction was always temperate and even. Amazingly, he remained calm and objective. There was a particularly vicious issue of the *Scarlet Rash* in 1928 (published in those years by Pi Delta Epsilon on Washington's birthday and at the time of the Pan Hellenic Dance in May). It was so bad that Carroll Black apologized for it to the administration and resigned from Pi Delta Epsilon in protest. Hoppy ignored the attack and I suspect told Dean Kendall to do nothing. It was the same way with some of the scurrilous skits put on by fraternity freshmen on Friday nights at the Strand Theatre before the homecoming football games. They made fun of such things as his short stature and his New England way of saying "idear." Hoppy ignored all such attacks. If he was hurt by this sort of thing, he never showed it. My guess is that as long as he had the solid support of the faculty, nothing in the way of external criticism bothered him.

Dr. Hopkins' contributions to Wabash's twentieth-century development were, in my opinion, substantial, however much they may be slighted because of his unpopularity. Among his contributions the following are worth noting.

It was Dr. Hopkins' fate to become president of Wabash at a crucial turning point in the history of the college. It was the begining of the transition from the "Old Wabash" to the "New Wabash." This included the necessity of breaking with the tradition of Wabash athletic fame. By 1926 it was obvious to any objective observer — but not to Wabash alumni — that the days of Wabash "Wonder Fives" and national basketball championships were gone forever. It was equally obvious that the days in which Wabash could compete in football with Notre Dame, West Point, Purdue, Illinois, Michigan, Iowa, Minnesota, and the like, were irrevocably gone. It was absurd to think that such a small college could continue to play those institutions. The tremendous expansion of university enrollments following World War I and the increasing professionalism of university athletic programs doomed the kind of

---

33. For the Board of Trustees' tribute to President Hopkins, see *These Fleeting Years*, p. 104.

glory Wabash had enjoyed in the first two decades of the twentieth century.

Hoppy, as I have indicated above, met this situation squarely and firmly. He did not try to sweeten the bitter pill for Wabash alumni. He acted quickly and directly on matters such as the control of the finances, scholarships for athletes, and game schedules. This had to be done as a prelude to the rebuilding of an athletic program at Wabash at a sensible level. It was not Hoppy's good fortune to do the rebuilding. This came with his successor, Frank Sparks. But Hopkins cleared the way.

His most important contribution to Wabash was his leadership of the faculty that improved the quality of Wabash as an academic institution of considerable distinction. For the better part of fifty years, the "new" curriculum adopted in 1928 was to remain essentially unchanged. Even after it was substantially modified in the 1970s the central features of the Hopkins curriculum (e.g., comprehensive examinations) remained.

Wabash's nineteenth-century reputation as a good midwestern example of Eastern classical education was enhanced during the Hopkins years. The high standards of earlier years were reinforced by new academic requirements. It is a mistake to think of Wabash, as many people did in the middle of the twentieth century, as an exceedingly "tough place to get in and a tough place from which to graduate," without crediting Hopkins with shaping this reputation.

Had it not been for Dr. Hopkins' urgent and persuasive appeal to me in 1934, I would never have returned to Wabash to join its faculty. I would have been, I trust, an interested and loyal alumnus, maybe ultimately a trustee, but I would never have been first a professor, then dean, and finally president of Wabash. And once I had returned to Wabash, it was Hoppy, more than anyone else, who kept me there. In 1936 Bernard Gavit, dean of the Law School at Indiana University, offered me a position on his faculty to teach the history of English common law. (At Oxford my tutor in English Constitutional History was Sir Gronway Edwards, and in my third year at All Souls my tutor in common law history was Sir William Holdsworth.) The possibility of a new kind of career combining my love of history and my earlier plans to study law appealed to me. I talked this over with Hoppy at length. As usual he was objective and helpful. He didn't try to dissuade me but he sketched for me his view of my potential if I remained in the liberal arts. It included moving into administrative work and some day perhaps becoming a university president. I was fascinated by his thoughts.

Shortly after I said "no" to Dean Gavit, Hoppy made me assistant dean of Wabash. In the year 1939–40, largely due to his influence, I was elected dean of the college, succeeding George Kendall who became dean of the faculty. I was too young for the assignment, but never after that could I be emotionally separated from Wabash and its future possibilities.

FRANK HUGH SPARKS

1941–1956

When the announcement was made that Frank Sparks had been elected the eighth president of Wabash, the reaction of the faculty was muted. The reaction of almost everyone else, however, was one of great enthusiasm and high expectations. The night the story appeared under headlines in the Crawfordsville *Journal-Review,* Marsh Jones telephoned me to express his enthusiasm. (Jones was a prominent Crawfordsville businessman, his principal interest being ownership of the Crawford Hotel. He had been one of the local critics of the Hopkins administration, but despite this our friendship, which began when I was treasurer of the Wabash Beta chapter and Marsh was its alumni advisor, had continued unbroken.) "Byron, at last the college is on the right track," he said. "This man Sparks is absolutely perfect for Wabash. With his leadership Wabash really ought to go places now." And he went on and on about what the college needed and why Sparks could meet the needs.

The attitude of Marsh Jones was typical of townspeople, alumni, and friends of the college in Indiana. Here was a businessman-turned-educator who was "perfect" for the job. For one thing, he was a Hoosier through and through. He was a man who got things done, a real "go-getter." His business career in Indiana had become a legend. He was a "natural born salesman." He stood for all of the values that were then esteemed by the establishment in Indiana, the Midwest, and to a large extent throughout the country. His economics (free market, private enterprise) and his politics (conservative Republican) were "sound." His record for civic enterprises was impressive. And he was a millionaire! What better combination of qualities and attributes could one want for the presidency of an old, prestigious, but nearly bankrupt, Indiana college? It is understandable that his appointment sent a thrill through the rank and file of Wabash alumni. It was an exciting moment full of hope and great expectations.

There were exceptions to this general reaction. Joe Daniels expressed to me misgivings about a "Rotarian" president for Wabash. He was disappointed that the board had not chosen George Kendall.[34] There were others who shared Daniels' misgivings, men who had had Eastern educational experience and who had remained loyal to Dr. Hopkins. But these exceptions were remarkably few, and they disappeared almost completely with the early successes that accompanied the Sparks administration.

It was only the faculty, or at least the Hopkins loyalists on the faculty, who continued to be doubtful about the wisdom of the Sparks appointment.

---

34. Kendall, who served as acting president after the death of Hopkins, had eliminated himself as candidate. BKT.

The very qualities in Dr. Sparks which appealed to the alumni aroused suspicions among the old guard faculty. Sparks was "new rich," an aggresive free market private enterpriser, with no real understanding of liberal arts education, personally ambitious, a doer rather than a thinker, etc. That there would be sweeping changes at Wabash was taken for granted, but there was a fear of the kind of changes that would come. Maybe Sparks would try to convert the college into a university specializing in business administration, a bastion for private enterprise and political conservatism. Maybe he would resurrect the earlier over-emphasis on intercollegiate athletics. Maybe faculty participation in policy formation would be brushed aside. Inevitably Dr. Sparks, because of these faculty suspicions, encountered faculty resistance to early innovations he proposed. As the years went by the "old faculty" gradually felt more kindly toward Dr. Sparks, but to some extent the basic distrust of his philosophy and his goals remained throughout the Sparks years. In spite of their acknowledgement of his remarkable accomplishments for Wabash, there was a disposition among some to sneer in private about the Sparks philosophy and methodology.

I must confess that in the beginning I shared many of these misgivings. In part this was because I was so completely under the spell of the Hopkins-Osborne-Kendall-Gronert philosophy of education. In part it was because I was still highly partisan in my political attitudes. And it was especially because I had not yet grown out of the mentality of the doctrinaire. My doubts about Dr. Sparks continued until the late 1940s. I remember being shocked while I was still in the Navy to read a new, widely-distributed publication coming from the college early in 1946 entitled something like "Private Enterprise and Private Education — Their Identity of Interests." In the text there was a statement to the effect that "at Wabash we make no pretense of presenting both sides." I considered this an outrageous betrayal of pure liberal arts, and I have no doubt this influenced me briefly to pursue opportunities that came to me as World War II drew to a close to embark on careers unrelated to Wabash.

In view of these personal feelings, it is a testimony of sorts to Frank Sparks that, by working with him closely after returning to Wabash, I came to respect and admire him greatly and to share without reservation most of the principles which he espoused nationally on behalf of private colleges and universities. Just as Dr. Hopkins had had a decisive influence on my early years at Wabash, such practical, non-academic success as I may have enjoyed during my own presidency of Wabash I attribute to the tutelage of Frank Sparks. Moreover, when in 1967 I became president of the Independent College Funds of America, Inc., in New York I was really following in his footsteps. As I shall explain later, ICFA came into being as a consequence of the pioneer work done by Dr. Sparks in the 1950s, which led to the formation of state and regional associations of private colleges seeking financial support from corporations. Such success as I had during the six years I was president of ICFA, particularly in

41

my relationships with executives of national corporations, I also attribute to lessons I learned from Frank Sparks.

In order to appreciate fully the enthusiasm with which the news of Dr. Sparks' appointment was greeted and to understand better the methods he used to lift Wabash out of its financial doldrums of the 1930s, it is helpful to bear in mind his life story prior to coming to Wabash. It is a well-known story, often recounted and sometimes exaggerated. My understanding of the story and such incidents in it as I record here came directly from Dr. Sparks. Between 1948 and 1955 I traveled with Dr. Sparks extensively. He often asked me to accompany him to help "sell" Wabash to prospective donors, especially where foundations were involved. These trips together provided wonderful opportunities to talk with him about his experience, his beliefs, and his expectations. Little by little I pieced together his life story and the bases for his convictions. These personal conversations were supplemented by conversations with others — his oldest son, Joe; his stock broker and close friend, Henry Holt; his business associate, "Tommy" Thompson, president and chairman of the board of Arvin Industries; and years later his wife, Abbie.

Frank Sparks was born in a family of small farmers in northern Indiana near Culver and Lake Maxinkuckee. His father, I surmised, was an honest, hard-working farmer, but something of a failure financially. The farm was heavily mortgaged, and Frank told me of his vivid recollections of the family's constant dread that there would not be enough income from crops to meet both mortgage payments and taxes. There was always a shortage of cash, always the pressure to skimp and save, always the specter of mortgage foreclosure. So impressed and troubled was Frank as a boy by this predicament, he early resolved that when he "grew up" he was going to make money and become rich. The evidence of what wealth made possible was all about him at Lake Maxinkuckee, especially during the summer time when wealthy families, principally from Indianapolis, opened their summer resort homes. Their luxurious carriages and even automobiles, their boats, their homes, their servants — all of these customary signals of wealth — made an enormous impression on the poor farm boy.

During the summers he began to work at odd jobs for the summer people In this way he came to know Carl Fisher, who took an interest in Frank. (This was the Fisher whose interests in the infant automobile business in Indianapolis, including the development of the Indianapolis Motor Speedway, made him famous in the early history of the automotive industry. He also pioneered in the real estate boom in Florida and made a fortune in the process.) As soon as Frank graduated from high school, he left farm life forever. He told me it never occurred to him to go to college. He went to Indianapolis and took a job with one of Fisher's enterprises. It was the beginning of what was to become a spectacular business career.

This must have been a few years before World War I. It was an exciting time to come to Indianapolis. It should be remembered that in those years there was some reason to believe that Indiana and Indianapolis rather than Michigan and Detroit might become the automobile capital of the United States. Some of America's finest and most famous cars were then being built in Indiana. The Stutz "Bearcat," the Cole Eight, Haynes, Marmon, Studebaker, the Duesenberg — all of these and others were Indiana products. Thus when Frank Sparks came to Indianapolis, the business atmosphere was heady about the shape of things to come in the automobile industry.

Frank had already begun what was to be his lifelong practice of constructing personal plans and timetables for his future.[35] His private goal when he came to Indianapolis was "to make a million dollars" by the time he was forty.[36] But goals such as this for him were not just vague general aspirations. He made a practice of planning in detail with great care, step by step, how he proposed to proceed and what he would have to do to get ahead. From time to time he modified his plans in the light of his experience, but never did he abandon them. For example, he told me that in his first year in Indianapolis, he worked out a plan by which once a month if possible and certainly once each quarter, he would conceive of an idea that would enable his employer to increase the volume of business, decrease costs, or, in some other way, to realize more profits. He proposed to submit his idea each time to his boss and, if it should be accepted, to ask for a raise in wages. This plan worked quite well for a while, but there came a time when his boss said to him: "Frank, if you would spend more time at your assigned work and less time thinking about how you can get raises you would do better and go further." "Never again after that conversation," Frank told me, "did I ever ask anyone for a raise." He changed his plans in the direction of getting into business for himself. "I early came to the conclusion," he explained, "that while working for someone else might lead to high salary, to become wealthy it was best to be in business for one's self." So he revised his plans. At night and on weekends he studied salesmanship, marketing, accounting, and similar subjects essential for an entrepreneur.

The turning point in this plan came when he formed a close friendship and later a partnership with a like-minded young man who was an inventive engineer, Quintin Noblitt. I do not know exactly when they went into business

35. His ardent faith in the usefulness of planning one's life, in my opinion, was the most important single reason for his introducing, years later, the Wabash Institute for Personal Development. BKT.

36. He met that goal approximately ten years ahead of schedule. BKT.

together to make tire pumps for automobiles. Perhaps about the time of World War I. It was a shoestring operation. They had almost no capital but the Indianapolis Tire & Pump Company was born. Noblitt was in charge of production. Sparks was in charge of sales and finance. "Finance" was an euphemism, because the infant enterprise had to function on a hand-to-mouth basis. Down payments on purchase orders which Frank was able to get covered the cost of starting production to fill the order. The balance of production costs was met when final payment for delivered orders was received. It was a risky thing.

The breakthrough to more healthy operations came as a consequence of Frank's genius as a salesman. After several disappointing tries in Detroit, Frank one day succeeded in convincing Henry Ford's purchasing agent that the Noblitt-Sparks tire pumps were lighter, more efficient, and cheaper than the pumps Ford was then putting in every Model T Ford coming off the new assembly lines in Detroit. Frank came back to Indianapolis with an order for 100,000 pumps to be delivered in a relatively short period of time, a deadline Frank, without any hesitation, had guaranteed to meet. Noblitt was horrified. The company was then operating in an abandoned grocery store (rent $10 a month) behind an Indianapolis drug store. Space for additional equipment and labor was in itself a serious problem. Nor was there any money for quick expansion. It looked like an impossible undertaking. But immediately Frank set out to find the necessary financial backing to make the impossible possible. It was Jim Goodrich (later board chairman at Wabash) who finally responded favorably to Frank's appeal. The line of credit was established at Goodrich's bank. Almost overnight Noblitt-Sparks Industries became a flourishing business.[37]

From tire pumps the company expanded to exhaust pipes, manifold tubes, etc. This constant working with pipes and tubing led to experimentation with products in non-automotive areas. Thus came from Noblitt-Sparks some of the first tubular ("gas pipe") tables and chairs in America. The company built new plants in Columbus, Indiana, and moved its headquarters there. The rest of the story is well known. The company flourished and even made progress during the depression years. It bought up the Arvin patents, changed its name to Arvin Industries, went public for additional capital, became listed on the New York Stock Exchange. Arvin heaters and Arvin radios led the field for a number of years in the automobile industry, but continued diversification of products made it more than just a supporting industry for the automobile business. It was and is a fascinating example of success in American private enterprise.

With the coming of wealth in the 1920s, Frank's life style and his inter-

37. At that time, "Indianapolis Tire & Pump Co." The name Noblitt-Sparks was adopted in the late 1920s. BKT.

ests changed. Much of this amounted to the usual thing in such cases — an impressive home in Indianapolis, club memberships, and travel. Regarded as something of a "boy wonder," he was sought after to participate in other activities, business and civic. He was an enthusiastic Rotarian and became president of the main Rotary Club in Indianapolis. He was increasingly prominent in the work of his church (Baptist), which he took seriously. He was a popular teacher for a men's Bible class.

His business activities widened. A few of these, I gathered from his comments, were disasters. He told me of two ventures that were failures, and in the telling he laughed at himself for having become over-confident. One of these was the grocery business. I assume he invested in what was expected to become a new grocery chain. "No matter what we did," he said, "even weighing our thumbs — we lost money!" So he took his losses and got out. Another was setting up his brother in the chicken business. (His brother had stayed on the farm and apparently had done no better than the father.) Frank offered to finance him in raising chickens for the poultry market. He stressed the importance of volume, and although the brother was apprehensive, they went into business on a big scale. But everything went wrong. Market prices fell or rose at the wrong times. An epidemic of croup swept over the flock, and chickens died by the hundreds. Again Frank took his losses and got out.

Experiences such as these, however, were exceptions in the record of continuing financial success for Frank Sparks during the 1920s. Like everyone else with money to invest, Sparks participated in the surging stock market in New York. According to his son, Joe, he enjoyed New York and spent a good deal of time there.[38] Frank never talked to me about his investments, but when Henry Holt and I flew from Indianapolis to New York together to attend the funeral services for Dr. Sparks in 1965, Mr. Holt during the trip talked at length about various aspects of the Sparks career, including his interests in the stock market. "Some people thought Frank was a plunger in the stock market," he said, "but he wasn't. He was shrewd and prudent about buying and selling, and so was not hurt when the Wall Street crash came in 1929."

In spite of his financial success, as the 1920s came to a close, Frank Sparks was not a happy man. He had set out as a youngster to make money, but, once having succeeded at that, he apparently found it an empty victory. Perhaps he became conscious of his lack of education. Perhaps he uncon-

38. I was astonished to hear Joe say that his father in these years occasionally displayed a quick, violent temper. He told of an incident at a New York hotel when his father flew into a "towering rage" because the quality of the service accorded him was not good. I found this incredible because I never heard Frank Sparks speak sharply to anyone or even raise his voice in anger during his years at Wabash. Instead, he impressed me as being habitually mild-mannered and gentle. If he ever had a quick temper, he had learned how to control it by the time he arrived at Wabash. BKT.

45

sciously felt the need of new and different personal goals. I have sometimes wondered if he had become bored with his life style. He never discussed with me any of his feelings about these questions, but he did tell me that while he was still in his thirties, he began to realize that he was no longer satisfied by the goal of "making money."

Knowing Frank Sparks as I did, I can imagine the private hours he spent reflecting on what to do with the balance of his life — meditating, thinking of alternative new goals, assessing possibilities and finally making a decision. Other impelling influences undoubtedly shaped his thinking. His first wife became seriously ill. His sons, Joe and Duane, were approaching college age. He wanted them to have a good education, something he had considered unnecessary for himself. I believe he had already begun to withdraw from his active role in Noblitt-Sparks and had enrolled for classes in Butler University. I remember being greatly moved when he told me the following story. "One Christmas night when I could not get to sleep, I got out of bed, came downstairs and wrote in my diary a new ten-year plan for myself. Despite my age, I resolved that I would complete my undergraduate education, go on to get a Ph.D. degree and then become a college president. I gave myself ten years to complete the plan." Eleven years later he was president of Wabash.[39]

I have only a very general knowledge of how he accomplished this new plan. He pursued his studies at Butler seriously and ultimately received his bachelor's degree there. At some point, because of his wife's failing health, he moved to Arizona and continued studying at the University of Arizona. When his son, Joe, was initiated into Beta Theta Pi at DePauw University, Frank, because of great interest he had shown in the fraternity, was also initiated. It was an extraordinary thing, requiring, I was told, a quick transfer of Frank's credits from Butler to DePauw and then later back to Butler. After his first wife's death, he completed the requirements for a Ph.D. degree. (in economics) at the University of Southern California. He received his degree in 1940. That same summer Dr. Hopkins died and Frank immediately applied, through friends, for the job. He was the only candidate seriously considered by the Board of Trustees.

It was with this kind of background that Dr. Sparks and his new wife, Abbie (Mann), arrived on the Wabash scene in 1941. To the naked eye alone, it was apparent that a new and decidedly different era in Wabash history was beginning. The Sparkses arrived in a Packard convertible coupe with red leather seats. Later they were to change to a Cadillac sedan (a new car each year) but in any case the elegance of the Sparks car on the then rather seedy Wabash campus made a marked impression on students and faculty alike.

39. I am assuming that the Christmas night decision was made in 1930. BKT.

46

There was nothing formal about the new president's manner. He was friendly, almost folksy, in his relations with everyone. He made no quick moves to "take charge." Obviously he wanted to get acquainted with the faculty and staff. Of everyone he asked a lot of questions, and they were good questions. He was accessible to everyone. His quiet, almost humble, approach to his new responsibilities made a favorable impression. Even his somewhat boyish enthusiasm when he watched intramural sports was disarming. It was a good beginning on campus. Off campus, as I shall indicate later, he moved much more quickly and surely with some of the initial steps he had resolved to take.

The new president was a fastidious dresser. He had an extensive wardrobe. Whether it was sports clothes, street clothes, or formal attire, Dr. Sparks was always well dressed in the latest fashion. It was important to him.[40]

Mrs. Sparks in these early weeks made a more vivid impression on Wabash and Crawfordsville than did Dr. Sparks. Still youthful looking, Abbie Sparks was a strikingly handsome woman with a radiant personality to match her good looks. She had an easy graceful manner with people. Whether it was small talk, business talk, or intellectual talk, she was at ease and secure — and charming. And yet one sensed that behind the friendliness and charm, here was a woman with a mind of her own and great inner strength. Perhaps it was this quality in her that caused most college people to be habitually polite and deferential. Even with the passage of time very few individuals in the college community were close to her. Rarely did anyone call her "Abbie." It was always "Mrs. Sparks." If Dr. Sparks could be aptly described as "perfect" for the president's job, then Mrs. Sparks could with equal justification be called "perfect" for the president's wife.

I later learned that Dr. Sparks, as one might expect, had set himself a plan of objectives for Wabash to be accomplished in ten years. Although we did not know it at the time of his arrival, that plan soon became unrealistic because of America's entrance into World War II in December, 1941. It strikes me as better to think of the "Sparks years" as running from the end of World War II to December, 1955, rather than from 1941 to 1955.

Little of importance took place in that first year in office. As soon as they could, the Sparkses began to remodel the Caleb Mills House into a more suit-

---

40. At an alumni banquet held that fall at the Athletic Club in Indianapolis, Dr. Sparks wore a powder blue dinner jacket that was the subject of much comment and not a little envy. When, after World War II, the trend began for narrow lapels for men's suits and jackets, the first narrow lapels I saw were Dr. Sparks'. In 1963, following a speech I made to the main Rotary Club in Los Angeles, among the men who came up to talk with me was one who introduced himself as Frank Sparks' former tailor. Like so many others, he was a great admirer of Dr. Sparks. "Frank told me," he said, "that he wanted to be just as well-groomed as the best-dressed men in New York or Los Angeles, and that he didn't care what the cost might be." BKT.

able residence for the president. Frank had first tried to persuade I. C. Elston to make the Elston Homestead available for the president's home. But in 1941 Ike was not ready to part with his old family home in Crawfordsville, as he did some fifteen years later. So, at his own expense and with Abbie's planning, the Caleb Mills House was remodeled.[41] It was changed from a rambling New England type farm house into a quite modern, convenient, well-lighted residence with pleasant appointments (terraces on the west and ultimately to the north) for entertaining numerous guests. The important changes were internal. Except for the outside chimney on the north and some more spacious fenestration, the exterior lines remained much the same. Everyone agreed that the results were delightful, and once the Sparkses moved in, the Caleb Mills House became the center for dinner parties, receptions, and a stream of guests that would have been undreamed of in the Hopkins era.

The inauguration was a less splashy affair than I had expected. It was held in the Chapel with a good but not overflowing crowd in attendance. Dr. Bernard von Kleinsmid, president of the University of Southern California, was the principal guest speaker. Herman Wells, relatively new president of Indiana University, spoke briefly and wittily for Indiana colleges and universities. I remember nothing of Dr. Sparks' inaugural address except that, in referring to the students (only a few of whom were present), he used the expression "bless their little hearts." Members of the faculty visibly winced.[42] This was one of the several times, when speaking in the Chapel, that Dr. Sparks used expressions which were natural for him as a Hoosier but, at best, unfortunate, given the prejudices and biases of an academic community. At a chapel speech shortly after the celebration of the 100th anniversary of the Wabash Chapter of Beta Theta Pi, Dr. Sparks with enthusiasm spoke of the Beta song "We are the People, People! We are the People!" in a context that applied it to Wabash as a whole. The Betas in the student body and Beta alumni in the faculty turned crimson in embarrassment. And other fraternity representatives, especially Phi Gams, immensely enjoyed the embarrassment and kept the ribbing going for weeks thereafter. In the early 1950s, when defending the new building program then under way at Wabash, speaking in chapel, Dr. Sparks said at one point, "You can't be a big-shot in overalls!" The student reaction to that remark was predictable. *The Bachelor* and *The Caveman* over-reacted in their sarcastic criticisms, ignoring the sound parts of the Sparks case for new, elegant buildings.

I believe Dr. Sparks was not comfortable speaking in an academic setting. This is understandable. He was at his best with short, snappy speeches,

41. Lee Burns was the architect. He specialized in restoring old homes. BKT.

42. For the text of President Sparks' inaugural address, see "Friends of Wabash" in *These Fleeting Years*, pp. 104–7.

packed with good sense, and always to the point. It was a kind of style best suited for business groups or other college presidents. He also had a gift for sensing the mood of a non-academic audience. At an annual alumni banquet held in the gymnasium on a hot, humid June Saturday night, for example, Dr. Sparks converted a tiresome exercise into a happy occasion. Following numerous short speeches by reunion class representatives and the presentation of the customary awards, Lee McCanliss, chairman of the Board of Trustees, was introduced. He spoke for an hour and twenty minutes. I never heard him speak more tediously than he did that night. The perspiring crowd of men became increasingly restless, but out of politeness stayed in their seats fidgeting, sleeping, or whispering among themselves. At long last McCanliss stopped, and the president of the college was introduced for the final speech, as was customary. The crowd, relieved by the change of pace, came to attention. Dr. Sparks waited a moment and then said, "It has been a long evening and it is hot. Let's go home!" He smiled and sat down. A tremendous cheer went up and vigorous applause. Dr. Sparks had made the banquet a success.

About the same time he achieved a similar instant victory at an annual banquet of the Indiana Society of Chicago. These banquets, one of which I attended and resolved never to attend again, were extravagant, glittery, noisy, and drunken. The programs were invariably too long, too gaudy, and maudlin. On the occasion I am referring to, Dr. Sparks was one of the main speakers. He had prepared a speech thinking the crowd of affluent business and professional men would be an ideal group to which he might present his educational philosophy. As the evening wore on, he mentally discarded his speech. When his turn came, he spoke wittily and to the point for about one minute. It was an instant hit with the crowd and especially with the news reporters and a cartoonist from the *Chicago Tribune*. Dr. Sparks and Wabash received more attention in the press and in the conversational post mortems because of his one-minute speech than they would have received with the longer address.

Following his inauguration Dr. Sparks began to move ahead with the program he had thought out for Wabash in the preceding months. (I shall speak more fully of that program later.) But he had scarcely begun when everything was thrown awry by the Japanese sneak attack on Pearl Harbor and America's entry into World War II.

Dick Banta and I had been in Chicago that weekend on college business. Late in the afternoon of that memorable Sunday, we started back to Crawfordsville by car. We had reached the southern suburbs of Chicago when we began to get by the car's radio the first fragmentary news reports from Honolulu. Like millions of other Americans, we were stunned and appalled. As the full significance of the devastating attack and all that it implied for the future sank in on me, my thoughts about Wabash and the Sparks plans became of secondary importance.

Ever since the outbreak of World War II and especially since the fall of France and the beginning of the "Battle of Britain" in 1940, my Anglophilia had caused me to become increasingly preoccupied with what was going on in Europe and the values at stake in the ghastly struggle. After December 7, 1941, I was committed both emotionally and intellectually to our national effort in the war. I resolved to get into military service as quickly as possible.

My reaction was typical of others at Wabash, both students and staff. The place began to fall apart as a consequence. George Kendall was the first of the key people to leave. On the strength of his military record in France in World War I, his part in organizing and heading the first National Guard unit in Crawfordsville in the 1920s, and with an assist from General Herron in Washington, Kendall was commissioned a lieutenant colonel and left immediately for duty at General MacArthur's headquarters in the South Pacific. Jim Paterson, also a World War I veteran, was in Army uniform by the spring of 1942. I applied for naval service through the Office of Naval Officer Procurement in Chicago, and in the summer of 1942 was commissioned lieutenant (junior grade) with orders to report for training and indoctrination at the Naval Armory in Chicago.

And so it went. Reservists in the student body were called to active duty. Many others volunteered immediately. Upper classmen with a chance for a degree accelerated their studies to "get out" ahead of schedule. No one gave serious thought to long range changes at Wabash. There was no interest in such matters.

All of this threw Dr. Sparks off stride for a short time. But he recovered quickly. Recognizing that his hopes and plans must be shelved for the duration of the war, he threw himself with characteristic energy into efforts to gain some kind of military training program at Wabash which would keep the college intact during the war. His first objective was to win an Air Force training unit. He went to elaborate lengths to make sure our application was approved, including conferences with helpful political friends in Washington. The early responses to these efforts were encouraging, and Dr. Sparks was confident of success. It was a shattering blow to him, therefore, when finally the Air Force rejected the Wabash application. It was the only time I ever saw Frank Sparks visibly shaken and, for a moment, defeated. (I believe one of the reasons for the rejection was the fact that a faculty committee, in discussing details with a visiting Air Force team, characteristically refused to promise that the college would continue the Air Force ROTC unit after the war was over.) But again Dr. Sparks recovered quickly from this surprising disappointment. Later he sought a Navy V-12 unit. This time the efforts were successful, and, not long after I had left the campus, Wabash was converted into a naval training school.

Dr. Sparks tried to persuade me not to leave for military service or at least to delay my departure. I didn't even give his suggestions serious thoughts. I left as soon as I could. Dr. Sparks, after being sure a navy unit was well established at Wabash, went to Washington to be chairman of the Bureau of Manpower Utilization (War Manpower Commission). He turned the management of the college over to a committee (Banta, Ormes, and Harvey) with which he kept in touch.

From the summer of 1942 until the spring of 1946, except for exchanging letters with friends, I had little contact with Wabash.

Dr. and Mrs. Sparks returned from Washington to Crawfordsville in mid-1945. I believe it was shortly after the surrender of Germany in May. The war continued to rage in the Pacific, but it was only a question of time until Japan too would be beaten. President Sparks, knowing this, was eager to get a head start on the post-war development of Wabash.

There was much to be done. The physical plant of the college had suffered during the war years. The fraternity buildings, leased by the college to house Navy trainees, had been badly abused. Settlements with the various fraternity house associations had to be made, including restoration of damages incurred. A faculty had to be reassembled. Preparations for the return of civilian students, especially returning veteran students, were required. In addition, the residue of the Waugh estate required that the construction of a science hall to replace Peck Hall be commenced as soon as possible.[43] To all of these demands Frank Sparks responded with an abundance of energy and relish.

It was late in 1945 when Frank began to talk seriously with me about returning to Wabash as soon as possible. By then I had been assigned to the Great Lakes Naval Training Station as special personnel assistant to Admiral Carpenter, Commandant, Ninth Naval District. This made it easier to communicate with Crawfordsville. Once or twice Dr. Sparks and I met in Chicago and once I came to Crawfordsville to meet with him.[44] Dr. Sparks was per-

43. Following the death on November 15, 1944, of the last beneficiary under the annuity payments established in the will of James D. Waugh, the college had only one year to begin construction of the Waugh Science Hall as a memorial to James M. and Julia D. Waugh.

44. On this visit I was startled by the changes Dr. Sparks had made in the appearance of the president's office. It was still on the second floor of Center Hall, but Frank had refurnished and redecorated it completely. The oriental rug and the quite handsome draperies contrasted sharply with the previous bare and spartan appearance of the room. My eyes must have betrayed my surprise because Frank said to me, "Do you think it is too much for Wabash?" I confessed my surprise, but assured him I liked the change. It gave me clue to the shape of things to come. BKT.

suasive and appealing. He sketched for me his plans for Wabash, once peace was restored. He visualized for me an important role in those plans. At one point he said: "Byron, if you will return, you can run the college academically, and I will cover the place up with money." He proposed a salary of $5,000 a year and promised to "bring you up in salary as fast as possible each year as the college prospers." I was quite impressed by what he had to say and how he said it. But I did not decide right away, as I had when I had received a similar appeal in 1934.

As I have previously indicated, during the war years I began to think of moving along entirely different career lines. To some extent this was a result of my misgivings about where Wabash might be going under the Sparks administration. But more important were new contacts and new friendships I had made in the Navy.

My service in the Navy was about as pedestrian and inglorious as one can imagine. I can smile about it now, but at the time it was a source of great personal disappointment. In my final interviews for a commission in 1942, much importance was attached to my years in Europe and to the fact that I had a good working knowledge of German. I remember being excited by a question concerning possible assignment to Navy Intelligence with overtones suggesting service with the Office of Strategic Services (forerunner of the CIA). When my active duty orders came I was badly let down, therefore, to discover that on completion of an abbreviated training stint, I was to report to the Office of Naval Officer Procurement in Chicago. Later I discovered that Commander Bishop, executive officer of NOP Chicago, had requested the Bureau of Naval Personnel to assign me to his office. Although I finally received orders transferring me elsewhere, never did I escape the tags of Bupers. Wherever I went, it was for an assignment in personnel work. Except for a brief period of detached duty on an aircraft carrier engaged in training pilots, I never came close to sea duty. Instead, I seemed always to be destined to serve as a "thinker" and "planner" for regular Navy staff officers charged with new programs or with troublesome resolution of acute problems involving existing programs (e.g., working with Admiral Farber, Assistant Chief of Naval Operations, on planning redefinitions for land-based naval stations and activities, and with Admiral Carpenter on planning demobilization in the Ninth Naval District).

The point of this digression is to explain how it was that I came to consider seriously breaking my ties with Wabash. In my various naval assignments, I found myself working closely with professional personnel men. A number of them in civilian life were influential in major business enterprises. Reservists also, they were itchy to get back into their own careers. Once Germany collapsed in the spring of 1945, their impatience to return to their civilian positions increased, and I found myself drawn into conversations about work opportunities after the war. Two of these, largely because of close friendships developed in the Bureau of Naval Personnel, I found sufficiently interesting to pursue. One was with a national management consulting firm (Booze, Freye, Allen & Hamilton), and the other was with the personnel division of one of the major banks in Philadelphia. I had gone far enough in conversations and interviews to be close to a decision that would have changed my life when I had the lengthy conversation with Dr. Sparks to which I have referred. His sketch of Wabash's future rekindled the emotional attachment I had developed with the college that I had thought was moribund. I must add that the growing private concern I was experiencing about my wife's emotional problems was also a decisive factor. Dorothy desperately wanted to return to Crawfordsville. We had purchased the old Peter Kennedy place, largely at her insistence. I knew going back to Crawfordsville would be reassuring for her. With these mixed feelings and thoughts, I told Dr. Sparks (in January, 1946, I believe) I would accept his offer.

By March I was out of uniform and back on familiar grounds. Quickly I was involved as heavily as I ever had been and I found it gratifying. There was an air of excitement about the place as Dr. Sparks began to proceed with his plans. In spite of my continuing to be wary about some aspects of the Sparks philosophy, I found working with him stimulating and rewarding. In April, or perhaps it was early May, Frank asked me to speak at a banquet he had scheduled in the ballroom of the Columbia Club in Indianapolis for trustees, alumni, and potential friends of Wabash. It was an excellent crowd to challenge with new visions for Wabash. Dr. Elton Trueblood, whom Frank was then trying to persuade to join the Wabash faculty, was to be the principal speaker. Dr. Duane Roller, new chairman of the physics department, and I were listed for remarks. Dr. Roller spoke first and I followed him.

I worked very hard on that speech, and I felt good about what I planned to say. It could not have been more than ten minutes in length. Against a sweeping background of history, I emphasized that we were then entering a new era in history fraught with great dangers but with enormous possibilities for good also. Whether it would prove to be an era in which the dangers brought catastrophe or an era characterized by a plateau of hope and peace and progress would depend in a large measure on the wisdom and courage with which our country would play its new awesome role. This in turn would depend on the degree of excellence we could attain in education, especially higher education. My last sentence, I remember, ran like this: "I fervently hope that in this crucially important national endeavor Wabash will become a bright and shining star."

I had thought it a good speech, but even so, I was surprised at the response. The whole crowd came to its feet and there was prolonged applause. I was delighted, of course. So was Dr. Sparks and the trustees who were present. Pierre Goodrich, who I am sure prior to that evening had been distrustful of me because of a pro-Roosevelt speech I had made in 1937 that annoyed his father, Governor Goodrich, sought me out afterwards to get better acquainted. This was the beginning of a close relationship with Pierre about which I shall have more to say later. It was also the beginning of newer and closer relationships with President Sparks, which led to better understanding of each other and to rising mutual respect and, yes, affection.

The Sparks strategy for building a "Greater Wabash" in the post-World War II era was exceedingly ambitious. To the "old guard" faculty it was at points barely credible. I would describe the strategy under the following headings:

1. To heal the schisms which had developed between the college and many of its alumni in the 1930s and to restore the spirit of loyalty to and enthusiasm for Wabash that had characterized Wabash alumni in the earlier decades of the twentieth century.

2. To reconstruct the Board of Trustees, making it a powerful body composed of prominent, highly successful, and wealthy individuals.

3. To appoint professors of national distinction.

4. To refurbish and expand the physical plant of the campus and to do so in a style that would result in a plant of distinguished charm and beauty.

5. To attract the kind of financial support capable of sustaining an expensive college operating budget and to finance the construction of new buildings.

6. To give to Wabash a national visibility and reputation which would identify it as a "pillar of strength" in the conservative tradition — independent, self-reliant, and committed to the philosophy of the private sector of American society.

In every one of these objectives, in some more than in others, Dr. Sparks was remarkably successful.

Dr. Sparks started even before the beginning of the war on his first objective. He began, as I have said earlier, with the advantage of almost universal personal popularity among the alumni and with their readiness to respond to his leadership. He immediately began to cultivate the alumni by attending meetings, instituting a massive mail campaign, seeking potential new leaders among the alumni body, opening the college doors to alumni visitors. He spoke their language and for the most part shared their convictions. Their response was immediate and enthusiastic.

Dr. Sparks moved quickly to settle the controversy engendered by the Edgar Evans proposal for required religion in the curriculum. His approach was typical of his way of doing business in such matters. While he was attentive to faculty opinions in the controversy, he made it clear that he considered this matter, as far as decisions were concerned, a presidential and trustee responsibility, not a faculty responsibility. On the other hand, with Evans he was direct and practical. He persuaded Evans to agree to an experiment limited to ten years. During the ten years instruction in religion would be a requirement for graduation. At the end of ten years the trustees, in consultation with the faculty, would decide whether to continue the requirement. To meet student resistance and to make the requirement more palatable to the faculty, it was agreed that the religion requirement need not be met by students in the freshman year. It could be met in any year prior to graduation. Moreover, any Catholic student or orthodox Jewish student who as a matter of conscience objected to the requirement might be excused if he presented a letter from his parish priest or his rabbi requesting an exemption. Finally, Dr. Sparks shrewdly bargained with Mr. Evans for an increase in his proposed gift. $100,000 was not enough to endow the "Edgar H. Evans Chair in Bible and the Christian Religion." He was successful in getting Evans to raise his ante.

All of this was done smoothly and without acrimony. Evans and his supporters were pleased. The faculty acquiesced and the students proved to be indifferent. The college obtained more endowed funds. Rather soon the raging controversy of the late 1930s was forgotten.[45]

With alumni interests in mind, a second front on which Dr. Sparks moved

---

45. The difficulty came in trying to find a professor of distinction to fill the new position. Dr. Sparks first tried for Elton Trueblood, offering him $10,000 a year in salary. Trueblood agreed to help on a part-time basis, but declined a permanent appointment. Fred West, chairman of the Department of Religion at Texas Christian University, accepted, but soon proved to be a disaster. Not until Eric Dean was appointed in 1957 was there healthy continuity in the Department of Religion. At the end of ten years, the requirement was discontinued. Dr. Dean's popularity as a person and as a teacher, nevertheless, drew heavy student enrollment in religion courses. BKT.

promptly was intercollegiate athletics. In 1946–47 Pete Vaughan was replaced by Glen Harmeson, head coach at Lehigh University. Harmeson was a former Purdue football hero who had achieved an impressive win record at Lehigh. Prepossessing and ambitious, he brought to Wabash a new kind of coaching attitude. Recruiting athletes was as important as coaching itself. Dr. Sparks agreed to a policy of athletic scholarships to be controlled by Harmeson. Jobs for room and board were also assured and placed under his control.

This alteration in the policy for college scholarships was the cause of my first serious disagreement as dean of the college with the president. It was a behind-closed-doors disagreement, but it was sharp. Harmeson had requested that athletes nominated by him need not meet the regular academic standards required by the faculty for scholarship recipients (top quarter of high school class). I insisted that all scholarship holders should be treated alike, and that the decisions as to whether a scholarship were granted or not rested in the hands of the faculty committee on financial aid to students, not in the hands of the athletic department. A compromise was reached by which the faculty committee kept control of scholarship awards, but the minimum requirements for tuition grants-in-aid for everyone were reduced to the upper half of the graduating high school class.[46]

Harmeson was a business-like and demanding coach. He had a flair for producing highly-disciplined, smartly-uniformed teams. And he got results. His teams, thanks in part to veteran G.I. athletes he recruited, were impressive to watch. Their win-loss record was good, despite game schedules that included tougher competition. Especially gratifying to students was the beginning of a nine-year winning streak over DePauw. Alumni were delighted.

In basketball and in baseball improvements were also made, although not to the same extent as in football. The appointment in 1948 of Owen Huntsman, long-time coach at Earlham College, as track coach was the beginning of a brilliant record for Wabash track teams that surpassed anything Wabash had known in the past. It was jokingly said at the time of his appointment that the real objective of Huntsman's appointment was to assure Wabash the athletic services of his two sons, both of whom were superb athletes. Jerry, the older son, for two years starred as football quarterback, and Stan, the younger son, became perhaps the greatest fullback Wabash had had up to that time.

The resurgence of Wabash athletic prowess (especially in football) lifted not only the spirits of the alumni, but also of the student body and the faculty. The late 1940s and early 1950s were buoyant years for Wabash. The frater-

46. When I became president I restored the previous higher minimum standards for grants-in-aid and scholarships, thus touching off an argument with Garland Frasier, Harmeson's successor as athletic director and head football coach, which led to his resignation. BKT.

56

nities came to life again and social events such as the Pan Hellenic weekend took on extravagant and colorful dimensions. A majority of the upperclassmen were returning veterans from the war, more mature, more sophisticated and better motivated than their pre-war predecessors. Many were married and the married students quarters ("Mud Hollow," on the site of the present baseball field) were a beehive of activity. There were babies and toddling youngsters all over the place. The spectacle of student wives with their youngsters gathered to watch football practice and to cheer "daddy" was at first strange and disturbing. But it quickly became a natural and a wholesome part of the Wabash landscape. There was more fraternization among professors and students and their wives. At the same time there was more seriousness about the academic routines in the classroom and the laboratories.

These were happy, carefree years for Wabash and they were filled with high expectations for the future. The revival of a colorful athletic program undoubtedly had much to do with that happiness.

Rebuilding the Board of Trustees

Slowly but surely Dr. Sparks succeeded in assembling his "blue chip" board. Through deaths, retirements, and resignations the old Hopkins stalwarts (Bruce Luckett, Chase Harding and others) gave way to new blood. It remained a board of Wabash men. Of the twenty board members all but one, Eli Lilly, were alumni, and they possessed the almost chauvinistic attitude so characteristic of the rank and file of Wabash graduates. It was a board representing considerable wealth, a board of doers, strong minded and influential. Lee McCanliss as chairman was a "take charge man" who practiced what Ike Elston called the "rule of the three G's" for trustees—"Give money, get money, or get off the board." He set an example with his own gifts and pressed others to follow suit.

The quietest, most modest member of the board was Eli Lilly. One of the Americas' wealthiest men, he rarely played an aggresive part on the board but when he spoke, others listened and usually agreed. He began quietly, often anonymously, to give generously to Wabash. It was the beginning of a pattern that was to make him the most important single benefactor of Wabash in its history. If Frank Sparks had done nothing more than winning the interest of Eli Lilly for Wabash, his important place in the history of Wabash would be assured.

Other important new board members also reflected the Sparks touch. Ike Elston rejoined the board. Parrish Fuller from Louisiana had never been involved in Wabash affairs until Frank Sparks "discovered" him and kindled his interest. Ivan Wiles, head of the Buick division of General Motors and later executive vice-president of General Motors had been in the habit of contributing $500 a year to Wabash. Frank went to see him, persuaded him to join the board and to up his contribution to $50,000 a year. Dick Snideman, whom others regarded as a wealthy playboy, became a serious-minded trustee as a result of Dr. Sparks' appeal to him. (Frank told him that a seat on the Wabash board would cost him a minimum of $10,000 a year.) Gene Beesley, president and later chairman of Eli Lilly & Co. (and president of Lilly Endowment), was moved from the alumni-elected section of the board (six members) to the permanent section of the board (fourteen members). So was John Collett, who carried over as the youngest member of the Hopkins board to become the strongest of the post-World War II board. Pierre Goodrich, who succeeded his father on the board in 1940, but who took no real interest in the college until Sparks became president, was one of Indiana's wealthiest men and, in a strange, laborious way of which I will speak later, became one of the most influential trustees in the academic life of the college.

And so it went. By 1950 Wabash had a Board of Trustees of exceptional strength, deeply committed to the task of building a "Greater Wabash" and capable of underwriting the cost of that task. It was a cause of envy among other colleges.

Assembling a New Faculty

At the same time he was rebuilding the Board of Trustees, Dr. Sparks sought to rebuild the faculty by attracting to Wabash as department chairmen a galaxy of stars. He took a personal role in the search and, although he consulted both George Kendall and me, he made the final decisions himself, sometimes against our counsel. The results were mixed. Dr. Duane Roller, head of the physics department at Hunter College in New York, was the first appointment (1944) and it was a very successful one. Brilliant and an inspiring teacher, he gave an immediate lift to the stature of the physics department and was at once accepted by the "old faculty." Dr. Harry Cotton, president of the McCormick Theological Seminary, likewise was an instant hit as new chairman of the Department of Philosophy. He fitted Wabash like an old shoe and quickly became, as he was to remain for years, one of the college's most successful and popular professors. Much the same could be said of Willis Johnson who was lured back to Wabash from Stanford as chairman of the biology department. From then until his retirement in 1968 Johnson was a tower of strength on the Wabash faculty. Dr. Edward Haenisch, chairman of the Department of Chemistry at Villanova University, was appointed chairman of the chemistry department to replace Dr. Howell. Even though this provoked difficulties with

Dr. Howell and his former students, it was an excellent appointment with long-time beneficial results for Wabash.

John Van Sickle, whom Sparks picked after a long search to be chairman of the economics department, came to Wabash from the chairmanship of the department at Vanderbilt. He met Sparks' test for free market economics and was prominently known nationally as a conservative scholar. As a person he was well liked at Wabash and so was his spritely wife, Pat. As a teacher, however, he was disappointing. Tedious and dull in the classroom, he was greeted with waves of boredom. His interests were in writing rather than teaching, and there was something quaint about his philosophical stance. Initially, he was Sparks' "highest priced" appointment. Perhaps for larger considerations, he was worth the "price" — but not as a teacher.

Other similar appointments by Dr. Sparks were less fortunate. Fred West, the new Evans professor of religion was a mistake. He was not an effective teacher and he never seemed really serious about his assignment. He rather quickly developed antagonisms toward Dr. Sparks and became outspoken and harsh in his criticisms. Although it was not clear then, the truth is Fred West suffered from deep emotional disturbances. His paranoia about father-figures became worse and led to increasingly serious conflicts after leaving Wabash, which he did rather soon. He finally underwent a long hospitalization.

Dr. José Gallardo was appointed chairman of the Spanish department. It was a mistake. Everyone liked Joe Gallardo, but he really had no interest in language instruction. Nor was he adept at it. A close friend of Fred West, he began to share Fred's antipathy for Dr. Sparks. After a brief stay he left Wabash.

Another mistake was Dr. Paul Fields, who was brought to Wabash to chair the psychology department from Ohio Wesleyan, where he had held the same position. Highly qualified professionally and a stimulating teacher, he had no interest in liberal education or in the college as a whole. Claiming that he had been assured a free hand by Dr. Sparks in developing a psychological institute, he proposed in faculty meetings curricular revisions to enlarge the role of psychology that were regarded as preposterous by the faculty both new and old. One of the Insley Osborne's last celebrated performances in sarcasm was delivered in a faculty meeting when Fields gave the faculty an "either-or" demand.[47] The following year Fields resigned.

Dr. Warren Roberts, whom Sparks brought from Washington to be chairman of the political science department, was always something of an enigma to me. In some respects he appeared to be a highly creative thinker,

47. Fields had presented to the faculty his personal vision of a completely revised Wabash curriculum, incorporating the most up-to-date psychological methodology and testing apparatus. Professor Osborne concluded his brief but devastating demolition of Fields' proposal: "Good God, man, what would you make of us? A little Ball State?"

59

preoccupied with world political problems and the rearrangements of centers of political power. He talked about his ideas with an air of mysticism and evangelism. But his meaning was obscure and confusing. I was never sure what he was talking about, but my attitude was more charitable than that of others who regarded his views as utter nonsense. In any case he was a popular teacher. Political science enrollments grew rapidly and his major students professed to be enormously impressed by him. But after a few years, Roberts' star seemed to fade with the faculty and students. He never really "fitted" in the Wabash scene. I had the increasing feeling that he was a lonely, frustrated and emotionally troubled man.

The salaries that Frank Sparks paid to bring these and similar men to Wabash now seem to quite modest, but it must be remembered that in the late 1940s and early 1950s, faculty salaries were still at the genteel poverty level. When Sparks offered Elton Trueblood a position at $10,000 a year, even professors who had been plaintive about low salaries were shocked. Van Sickle's initial salary of $8,500 represented an advance of $3,000 a year over his salary at Vanderbilt. All of the new appointees were regarded as highly paid. Although the gap between the "old faculty" stars and the "new faculty" stars was wide, there was a sense of new prosperity throughout the faculty.

In addition to the new department chairmen, there was an influx of second echelon faculty members between 1946 and 1955. Many of these were selections made by George Kendall or me rather than by the president, although he kept the final appointment decisions for himself. This is not the place to comment on these "second echelon" faculty members. But they were for the most part exceptionally good. All of them stayed at Wabash long enough to make a mark there, and several of them are now key senior members of the faculty. One is now dean of the college. Their names without exception touch off in me the warmest feelings of respect and even pride for their association with Wabash — Bredrick (math and Latin), Forbes (history and art), DeLanney (zoology), Williams (zoology), Duston (English), Baker (English), Caplan (English), Powell (speech), Rogge (economics), Wilder (political science), Dean (religion), Salter (physics), Planitz (German), Strawn (French), McDonald (art), Laubengayer (botany), Degitz (accounting and assistant business manager). Several of these came in 1949, one or two before that, and a few came a year or two later. Together with the new department chairmen, it meant an enlarged faculty in a short period of time. There were those (Osborne and Ormes) who worried that the faculty would lose its cohesiveness and that the Hopkins curriculum would be assaulted. Neither worry was justified, as matters turned out. The great majority of the new faculty merged with the old faculty very well and subscribed to the principles of the curriculum with enthusiasm.

Thus, the goal Dr. Sparks set for faculty development was achieved. By the early 1950s I think it could be said that Wabash had a faculty of exceptional strength. Man for man, it was the strongest faculty in Indiana, and it compared favorably with liberal arts colleges nationally.

Plant Improvement

Before I had returned to Wabash in 1946, Dr. Sparks had already changed architects for Wabash. The question of change arose early because of the need to construct a new biological science hall in compliance with the Waugh will. Larson was dropped and Eric Gugler of New York was selected. The choice of Gugler was undoubtedly a consequence of the influence of Lee McCanliss. He and Gugler were close personal friends in New York. McCanliss admired his work and promoted his interest wherever he could. Dr. Sparks liked him, too, but in any case he was inclined to follow Lee's wishes in the matter.

Eric Gugler in my opinion was an artist rather than an architect. To be sure, he had all of the professional qualifications of an architect and was professionally well known in New York and eastern circles. Nevertheless, it was clear that his primary interests were visual concepts — beauty of design, esthetic effects, over-all impressions of proportions and details. He had little patience with mechanical details and perhaps secondary interest in practical problems involving use of buildings. He was also a traditionalist. His buildings at St. Paul's School, his buildings at Wabash, the Anzio Beachhead Memorial in Italy to Americans who were killed there — all of these and others — were in the tradition of the Georgian Colonial style with more affinity for the Williamsburg than the New England expression of that style. (The National Memorial to Theodore Roosevelt on an island in the Potomac River is an exception. That memorial, however, reflects — quite successfully and beautifully — Gugler's feelings and insights as an artist.)

The first time I went to Gugler's office in New York, I had trouble locating it and I was unprepared for what I finally found. It was in the Architects Building, 101 Park Avenue, but it was an exception to the numerous conventional modern layouts for architects' offices. It was something like a converted penthouse, resembling an artist's studio. One entered by going out of the building onto the roof by a canopied walkway, finally reaching a detached set of offices with a bohemian, cluttered atmosphere about them. The dark, small reception room was furnished in battered early American furniture. One had the impression of two or three offices vaguely arranged beyond this; through an unlit narrow corridor one reached a larger room, the principal working space with a large table in the center, windsor chairs and stools, numerous sketches and photographs on the walls, and piles of books and papers. It was disorderly and not very clean but practical for Gugler's working habits. And it was quite pleasant. It was in this room that the style and floor plans for the "Greater Wabash" buildings were conceived. It was here that the innumerable conferences with Gugler took place during which what the college (faculty) wanted in the way of building facilities was transformed into architectural plans. They were long conferences filled with conversational digressions about all manner of matters unrelated to the business at hand. At lunch time there would be a bottle of good wine, hot pastrami sandwiches, potato chips and the like, served picnic fashion around the working table. If the sessions lasted until late afternoon, they concluded with several rounds of bourbon or scotch, followed by dinner in a good restaurant in the neighborhood. It was all quite relaxed and pleasant.

I liked Gugler and enjoyed talking with him.[48] Even though I shared some of the feeling on campus that he sacrificed utility in his Wabash buildings for the sake of beauty, I agreed with Dr. Sparks that he was "right" for us. I also liked Ferdinand Eiseman, who was Gugler's follow-through man for Wabash projects. Gugler's staff was quite small, consisting of two or three senior designing architects who, so far as I could tell, were never involved in Wabash plans. There were no draftsmen. After Eiseman had sketched preliminary drawings for elevations and floor plans at Gugler's direction, the detailed drawings were done by other firms on a sub-contract basis. Once he had conceived the design and internal arrangements, including esthetic details which he personally sketched, Gugler lost interest in the routine work of producing plans. I do not believe he visited the campus more than twice in ten years.

Gugler's overall concept of the future development of the Wabash campus I found quite appealing. He had in mind the development of the plant into a closely knit, compact collection of buildings, easily accessible to each other by foot and surrounded by a wooded, grassy expanse of campus, reminiscent of "nature's unbroken loveliness" in 1832. He visualized the college recovering the private property in Mills Place and finally having a campus bordered by Crawford Street on the west, Wabash Avenue on the north, Grant Avenue on the east and Jennison on the south. He wanted to have Jennison closed and even raised the question of "doing something about those damned railroad tracks." Gugler likened the collection of campus buildings to a "Greek village effect" where only pedestrian traffic would be permitted. Service entrances and parking areas would be hidden away from the central mall. Vistas from the

48. My involvement in the early stages of the planning of new buildings was not only because I was dean of the college, but also because Dr. Sparks asked me to serve as chairman of the faculty advisory building committee to work with the trustee committee and the architects. Dick Banta's role in the planning and actual construction was even more extensive than mine. He functioned as a personal representative of Dr. Sparks and of McCanliss. BKT.

bordering streets, except from Jennison, would provide "glimpses" of the Greek village as well as automobile entrance to the campus. The vista from the east and the relocation of the entrances from Wabash Avenue followed Gugler's plan, but the gate entrances fell considerably short of his concept.[49]

It was not surprising that Gugler became a source of controversy on campus. Almost no one knew him personally. During the actual construction of the Campus Center, the dormitories, the Lilly Library, Baxter Hall — in fact, all the Gugler buildings — he did not bother to visit the campus. He left all on-site inspections to Ferdinand Eiseman. He remained for the faculty generally a mystery man, and perhaps this accentuated some of the sharp anti-Gugler attitudes that developed.

John Forbes, who regarded himself with good reason as an authority on architectural styles, was highly critical of Gugler's designs. He openly disparaged what he called the "warmed over Georgian" style that Gugler invariably proposed and ridiculed Gugler as a designer of personal monuments. Prior to the approval of the plans for the Campus Center, John complained bitterly to the president about being ignored by the building committee insofar as his objections to Gugler's designs were concerned.

Jim Adams was the first chairman of the post-World War II trustee building committee. A down-to-earth practical minded Hoosier with extensive experience with construction projects (he was state highway commissioner under Governor Paul McNutt), Adams took an instant dislike to Gugler. He distrusted "Easterners" and disapproved of Gugler's bohemian tastes. He referred to Gugler's offices as "that rat's nest" and to his architectural designs as "arty" and "extravagant." He used to complain to me privately of his concerns about Gugler. He admired Walter Scholer of Lafayette and went to him on a confidential mission to get his advice. Walter Scholer and Associates were the architects for all of Purdue's new buildings. Scholer was an excellent architect in the conventional, functional mold. His buildings at Purdue look like factories outside but their interiors are pleasant and highly efficient. As a result of Adams' insistence, Walter Scholer became the "associate architect" with Gugler in all Wabash construction, beginning with the Campus Center. Gugler was to be responsible for design and preliminary drawings. Scholer was to be responsible for working drawings, specifications, and work supervision. Gugler was not too happy with this arrangement because it reduced his fee, but Adams

49. Somewhere in the college there must be an artist's rendering of the main north gate which Gugler designed and proposed. It was a handsome thing, but more appropriate for the entrance to the governor's palace at Williamsburg than for a spartan midwestern college for men. It was also frightfully expensive. It was submitted at a time when there was considerable criticism about the lavishness of the new Campus Center. The proposal was indefinitely postponed, and the sketch was tucked away somewhere so it would not be talked about. BKT.

said to Dr. Sparks and Lee McCanliss that he would resign as committee chairman unless Scholer was involved.

A third hard-line critic of Gugler was Leslie Colvin. Colvin was an independent building contractor in Indianapolis with a solid reputation in the Indianapolis business community. He had been a close friend and supporter of Governor Goodrich and this friendship continued with Pierre Goodrich, for whom Colvin built a number of telephone buildings. Perhaps because of this friendship, beginning with the Chapel in 1928, Colvin served as the builder for all subsequent Wabash buildings except, I believe, Martindale Hall.

At this time Leslie Colvin must have been close to seventy. Much of his work was actually in the hands of his son, Burt. He had the manner and the attitudes of a successful man who knew more about buildings than architects did. A big man physically, Colvin had a booming voice and was inclined to pontificate in group discussions. He could barely restrain his contempt for Gugler as an architect. His designs, he said, added unnecessary costs to the buildings and were functionally "stupid." He pointed out that although Gugler managed to include the functional requirements sought by the faculty, he often did so by concealing them. Thus the multi-purpose large lecture room in Waugh Hall was tucked away in the basement partly under the expansive terrace to the west (which leaked). The "look through effect" in the Campus Center, Colvin pointed out, robbed the dining room of space, etc. Outspoken and caustic, Colvin opposed, sometimes successfully, details in the initial Gugler drawings. He complained of Eiseman's being "slow as molasses in January." He also clashed angrily with Dick Banta, who supported Gugler and Eiseman. In the end I believe Colvin was proud of these new buildings, but he was responsible for some of the acrimony their development engendered.

Still another source of opposition to Gugler — or more correctly to Lee McCanliss' and Dr. Sparks' enthusiasm for Gugler — was Oscar (Pop) Welborn of whom I will have more to say under the section on trustees. Garrulous and by nature dyspeptic, Welborn became increasingly critical of the new building program. A long-time trustee, he had become treasurer of the college early in the depression years and was, with good reason, excessively proud of the way he had salvaged the college's mortgage farm loans and had husbanded the college's badly depleted financial assets. This experience, plus his conservative financial nature, caused him to regard rising expenditures of any kind as an ominous threat and unexpected heavy expenditures as something of a personal affront.

Welborn's opposition to Gugler was, therefore, exclusively financial. He could not have cared less about whether the buildings were pretty or ugly, efficient or inefficient. But he questioned the necessity of expensive buildings at all and be blew a succession of fuses at the free wheeling way McCanliss and Sparks went about meeting the cost of the Gugler buildings. The construction of the two new dormitories (Wolcott and Morris Halls), despite building costs several times that of the initial $50,000 gifts, Pop regarded as sheer lunacy. Likewise, the counting of pledges for future gifts as justification for "borrowing" cash from other accounts in order to start construction at once struck him as sinister and potentially ruinous. He said as much with considerable heat and at length in executive committee meetings and at board meetings.

Lee McCanliss, who had little respect for Welborn's business acumen anyway, responded to his complaints and criticisms brusquely and condescendingly, which caused Pop's fury to increase. I do not remember the exact year, perhaps it was 1953, when Welborn heard that a new entrance to the campus from Wabash Avenue had been planned by Gugler. Fearing the worst, he hurried to Crawfordsville to see for himself. Sure enough, there were the stakes carefully planted showing the outline of a grand entrance to the campus focusing on the Chapel. Pop was speechless — almost — with indignation. He demanded from Frank an explanation. I accompanied the two of them to the site of the new entrance and I shall never forget my mixed amusement and astonishment when Pop began feverishly to pull up the stakes. "Frank" he said, "you are not going to spend another dollar on buildings until we have the money in hand as long as I am treasurer!" Frank said nothing but I can imagine his thinking "Well, Oscar, I trust that will not be for very long."

In spite of this kind of opposition to the new plant improvement program illustrated in the foregoing account, Dr. Sparks, with the full support of McCanliss, never wavered in his conviction that a "Greater Wabash" required new dramatic, beautiful buildings regardless of the cost. In this he was supported by the majority of the board and by representative alumni leaders. Parrish Fuller among the trustees was especially supportive of this entire concept. His keen interest in the building of the Campus Center caused him to search in the Louisiana swamps for giant cypress trees from which he had made the spectacular beams for the great hall of the Center. They were his personal gift to the building, as were numerous other items, for example, the pecan flooring for the refurbished gymnasium and the holly paneling for Martindale Hall. Later he became chairman of the trustee building committee. He continued in the post for many years, and he adhered to the Sparks' concept of quality buildings long after Dr. Sparks had left the campus.

Dr. Sparks was also supported and undoubtedly greatly influenced by his wife, Abbie. I believe his notions about "gracious living" came from her. The two new dormitories adjacent to the Campus Center which provided privacy for each student reflected her thinking. So did the quality of the decoration and furnishing of the Center of which I shall speak in a moment.

Little by little the new Campus Center rose to be a reality, with all of its attendant external features, including landscaping. Although Waugh Hall was built first, the Center was the real turning point in the post-World War II building program. It set the stage for all of the subsequent Gugler buildings (the Lilly Library, Baxter Hall, the new gymnasium, the relocation and restoration of Hovey Cottage and Forest Hall, the new entrances, driveways, and walks). Frank and Abbie — others too — regarded it as a jewel marking visibly the transformation of Wabash into a new kind of college. And they were quite right about this. Gugler's personal stamp on the Wabash Campus thereby became as important as it was spectacular.[50]

I have dwelt longer on the building phase of the Sparks plan for a Greater Wabash, not because it was the most important phase, but because it is a monument to the Sparks impact on Wabash which will endure a long, long time.[51] Also, because the process of its achievement was filled with rich human detail, fascinating to the history of the college. This prompts me to continue a little longer with such detail.

When the Center was well along in its construction, Dr. Sparks and Mrs. Sparks began to think of the problem of furnishing it. Why, I do not know, but Frank again turned to me to follow through with his ideas. At a luncheon at the Caleb Mills House one day, I was introduced to Charlotte Kruse, an independent decorator with a shop on North Meridian just south of 16th Street, in Indianapolis. Mrs. Sparks liked her taste and judgment. Mrs. Kruse was a youngish widow, good looking, intelligent, with lots of daring about interior decoration and a gift of sensing what her patrons wanted. Frank gave me a budget figure — $75,000, I believe it was — and asked me to work with Mrs. Kruse in decorating and furnishing the Center. "Work with" was an overstatement. Charlotte Kruse regularly reviewed with me her thoughts and recommendations, but with only a few exceptions (the furnishing of the Scarlet Inn, for example), my role was primarily that of approving what she had already decided.

Financial considerations proved to be the least of Mrs. Kruse's concerns. What she planned and what she bought was for those years quite expensive. Thus the imported hand-embroidered English draperies in the Great Hall cost over $1,000 a window. The large Indian oriental rug for the Great Hall cost between $10,000 and $11,000. Other items — the Japanese silk paper for the private dining room, for example—were correspondingly high. Numer-

---

50. If one looks closely at the Gugler buildings, in each he will see Gugler's personal "G" implanted in the details. Iron lattice grill work usually includes the letter "G." Even the hedge patterns adjacent to the Campus Center and south of the Library (if they are still intact) form the letter "G". BKT.

51. On April 24, 1976, the Campus Center was rededicated and renamed the Frank Hugh Sparks Center. On this occasion, President Sparks' strong beliefs against federally subsidized liberal arts colleges provided the focus for a colloquium on "Independence in Higher Education." Also at this time, portraits by Anthony B. Heinsbergen of the Sparkses were hung in the Center.

ous items of furniture would have been higher still had it not been for Charlotte's tough bargaining ability with suppliers.

The reaction to the Campus Center, when it was finished and completely furnished, was decidely mixed. Visitors to the campus were enormously impressed. Alumni and their wives on the whole were pleased, even proud. On campus the reaction was largely unfavorable. Some thought the Center looked too feminine, too luxurious for a men's college. Some faculty members sneered at the extravagance. But secretly I believe they were pleased. Certainly the quickness with which the faculty began to use the Center and to boast about it off campus belied their criticisms on campus.

The student reaction was in the beginning at least harshly negative. *The Bachelor* and *The Caveman* were cruel and at points devastatingly funny in their criticisms. There were repeated references to "Creeping DePauwism." Don Cole, the leading student cartoonist, did a series of cartoons ridiculing the elegance of the Center. One showed a student sinking into the lush carpets as if they were quicksand, while other students threw him life savers attached to ropes. Another showed campus dogs foraging in the Campus Center garbage cans, one saying to another, "Oh, it's an elegant joint all right, and the food is the best in town." Bill Clark, editor of *The Caveman,* was vicious in lampooning the "millionaires' " college, especially after the unfortunate "you can't be a big shot in overalls" chapel speech by Dr. Sparks.

The swirling controversy about the new Center came to a peak and then subsided in an incident involving the plaster cast of the statue of young Abraham Lincoln in Indiana. Eric Gugler had acquired from the sculptor the original cast of a Lincoln statue done for the Lincoln National Life Insurance Co. in Fort Wayne. It depicts Lincoln at the age of seventeen before he left Indiana for Illinois. Gugler persuaded Lee McCanliss to buy the cast and give it to Wabash to be erected on the east portico of the Center in front of the "Look Through." Lee was delighted with the idea and suddenly, without much advanced warning, the enormous crate arrived on campus. Lincoln was established in the appointed place, and all hell promptly broke loose as far as student reaction was concerned.

"This is a fraud! Lincoln had nothing to do with Wabash! A rich man's whim! Get this atrocious insult to Lincoln and to Wabash off the Campus at once!" And so on and so on. By this time Frank, recovering slowly from a broken hip and distressed by some of the previous student criticism, was on the defensive. He was torn between sympathy with the student point of view and loyalty to Lee McCanliss. He left it to me to reason with the students. I did the best I could, pleading for time to resolve an embarrassing and delicate problem. But my best was not enough for student hot heads. The end came suddenly in the following way.

About that time Herman Wells, president of Indiana University, telephoned me one day to explain that he was hosting a group of distinguished European educators which was visiting a number of American universities. It was a prestigious group including men like the Master of Balliol College, Oxford, the rector of the University of Lausanne, the prefect of the Sorbonne, etc. Dr. Wells had suggested to the group that before returning to Europe, it should take a look at a typical American liberal arts college. He had suggested a visit to Wabash. It was a very kind and gracious thing for Herman to do. I was delighted and we agreed on a date for the visit. I at once alerted the faculty to this rare opportunity for Wabash and gave instructions to the maintenance department to manicure the campus in readiness for our guests.

The morning of the appointed visit I came on campus quite early to be sure everything was in good order. As I passed the new Campus Center I was frozen in sudden horror at what I saw. The Lincoln statue was of heroic proportions (perhaps twelve feet high). Young Abe is standing with an axe under his left arm and a book, presumably the Bible, in his left hand. His right hand rests gently on a massive dog, obviously male, which is sitting on its haunches resting gently against Lincoln's right leg. During the night before the morning of which I speak some students had painted the dog's genitals a brilliant scarlet — just the genitals, nothing else. It had been expertly done. That spot of scarlet was visible from as far away as Yandes Hall! It stood out like a red flare in a black night!

As I say, I was horrified. The bus load of educators was due at ten. What to do? I called the superintendent of buildings and grounds. His men went to work at once with scrapers, chisels and sandpaper. In due time the scarlet was removed but even so this operation was only partially successful. The plaster cast of the statue with age had become a dusty gray in color. This meant that the paint removal operation left the dog's genitals as white as newly fallen snow against a gray background. It was the best that could be done.

A few days later the statue was dismantled and recrated. Thereafter, the controversy about the Center faded into history.[52]

52. In 1956, while attending the Institute for New University Presidents at the Harvard Graduate School of Business, I told this story to friends in the group one evening. There was much laughter. Someone in the group must have related it to Dr. Merry, director of the Institute, for a few months later, he sent a young Harvard case-writer out to talk with me at Wabash. He explained that Dr. Merry wanted to make a "case" out of this incident together with its background for use in future institutes. All of this would be subject to my approval. Weeks later I received a copy of the "case" submitted for my approval. It was well done. All of the names were changed, of course, and Theodore Roosevelt mounted on a rearing stallion had been substituted for Lincoln and his dog. Nevertheless, I declined to approve use of the case. I had in mind Lee McCanliss rather than Frank in making my decision. BKT.

Everything Dr. Sparks wanted to achieve at Wabash required money — lots of it. The building program alone required gift money in quantities hitherto undreamed of at Wabash. But it was not only for buildings that Dr. Sparks sought a flow of gifts at an annual level that initially seemed impossible to attain. The acquisition of a stronger faculty, the upgrading of salaries, the revitalization of intercollegiate athletics, the general enrichment of the day-to-day operations of the college — all of these called for sharply increased annual operating budgets. And because of the loss of four years in World War II, Dr. Sparks was in a hurry. The rate at which he increased operating expenses left carry-over faculty and staff members from the Hopkins years breathless with astonishment and, here and there, filled with serious misgivings. Fergus Ormes, comptroller, for example, was at first overwhelmed. Like Pop Welborn, Ormes by his experience was more conditioned to saving money than to spending it. Fergus had been in the habit of personally turning off lights to save utility bills, rationing the issuance of "blue books" for examinations, salvaging materials and supplies for science laboratories and in countless other ways pinching pennies in the interest of a balanced budget. He was shocked, therefore, at what he called the "clouds of bills" that began to pour into the business office in the years right after World War II.

I often heard Frank Sparks say something to this effect: "I have never known a place which did a better job of making dimes do the work of dollars than Wabash before I came here. But I have no interest in seeing how cheaply Wabash can be operated. If we are going to go anywhere with Wabash, we must spend money. And I will see to it that we have the money to spend." Like all good salesmen, he believed one must spend money to get money. He spent money lavishly, using the "Greater Wabash Fund," which he personally controlled, to cover expenses not provided for in the regular operating budget.[53]

In making such statements, Dr. Sparks was on firm personal ground. Finding the necessary funds was his greatest personal challenge at Wabash and perhaps his most important source of happiness at Wabash. He had an abundance of confidence in his ability to raise money. For him it was a matter of salesmanship, and he brought to bear on all of the college's external relationships his extensive experience in selling and marketing. Fund raising received highest priority in these efforts, but he also applied the same principles to the recruiting of students. The admissions staff he thought of as a sales force. He picked Fred Totten as his first director of admissions because he "organized

---

53. This fund is no longer in existence and should not be confused with the Greater Wabash Foundation.

his sales territory" better than others whom he also considered for the post. He spoke of "pricing" the college correctly for the "market." When the G.I. Bill of Rights was passed by Congress at the end of World War II, providing among other things payment of college tuition up to a maximum of $500 a year, Sparks immediately raised tuition at Wabash to that maximum.

Frank had little interest in endowment money. If it came to the college as a consequence of wills and bequests, well and good. But he did not seek it. He wanted money he could spend at once. Nor did he have much patience with the ordinary concept of an alumni fund. While he cultivated the rank and file of Wabash alumni, he regarded efforts to obtain annual gifts for the alumni fund as a waste of time. One big gift was worth thousands of little ones. To get "big money" one must go where "big money" is to be had. In accordance with this way of thinking, Dr. Sparks concentrated his efforts on wealthy individuals among trustees, alumni, and business acquaintances. And he always went "to the top" in corporations and foundations. He had enormous courage and confidence in this approach.[54]

More often than not he was successful in at least getting an opportunity to tell his story. In the early 1950s this practice led to his close association with American business tycoons such as Irving Olds (chairman of U. S. Steel), Alfred Sloan (retired chairman of General Motors), and Frank Adams (chairman of Standard Oil of New Jersey). He moved with a sure instinct in such circles as these. The Ford Foundation had barely opened its doors in Pasadena, California, when Dr. Sparks made his first call there. He took me with him for that "cultivation call." We did not make a "sale," but the visit led to my being appointed a member of one of the first Ford Foundation committees, the Committee on College Self-Study Programs.[55]

Dr. Sparks had a superb touch with wealthy businessmen. He spoke their language, of course, and had the advantage of his own successful business career in winning confidence. He invariably had an "idea" to propose, something to "try out" on potential donors. If the response was one of interest, then he would talk money — usually "bigger money" than the potential donor had expected. Judging by the results he obtained, it was an excellent technique. He liked to have a *quid pro quo* element in his appeals for gifts. Thus, among

---

54. On some occasions, especially with well-to-do alumni, Frank used a hard sell approach. He returned a check for $500 from an affluent alumnus, for example, with the straightforward statement that he should be giving ten times that much. BKT.

55. There was an interesting sequel to that national committee assignment. The most active Ford Foundation staff member attached to that committee was Elizabeth Pascal. I came to know her well. Years later when I was president of Wabash and Wabash was in the running for one of the first of the Ford Foundation Challenge Grants to Liberal Arts Colleges, it was Elizabeth Pascal, I am sure, who put Wabash "over the top" in that competition. BKT.

his first successful money raising efforts was the "Sponsored Scholarship Program."

The "Sponsored Scholarship Program" involved finding individuals who would agree to "sponsor" (i.e., pay the tuition for) a needy and promising Wabash student. Sparks had printed a series of handsome folio-size books on each page of which appeared the name, photograph, and biographical information of an individual freshman student at Wabash. At the bottom of the page was a line for the signature of the "sponsor" and the amount of money to be contributed each year for four years. I believe he sold this idea first to Kurt Pantzer and with his help as host at a series of dinners, sold the idea to numerous other alumni and friends, principally in Indianapolis.

Later, he expanded this idea to corporations under what he called the "College Industry Program." Indiana corporations and some outside of Indiana (e.g., Florsheim Shoe) agreed to contribute $5,000 each year to support a program designed to encourage Wabash students to go into business. It was a complicated and time consuming program with numerous dinner meetings, usually held in the dreary dining room of the Crawford Hotel, at which top representatives of the sponsoring company would talk about their experience, the challenges of their particular business, the opportunities of young men, etc. The idea was that Wabash students would "sign up" with a particular company, work for that company during the summertime, and then become full-time employees after graduation. Many students took advantage of this program and some went on to realize successful business careers with the companies for which they worked in the summer. But the great majority of the students, for understandable reasons (professional career objectives, for example), did not follow through. This aspect of the program to which Dr. Sparks attached great importance was disappointing. But as a quick money raising device, it was successful, and it served to attract the continuing interest of business leaders.

These efforts were in the late 1940s. In the early 1950s Dr. Sparks helped to influence the development of elaborate national scholarship programs. By that time he was deeply involved in forming state associations of private colleges seeking unrestricted financial support from corporations. (Since the associated colleges movement had much to do with the national image Sparks developed for Wabash, I prefer to speak of it in the following section.) Dr. Sparks was justly proud of the fact that as these early scholarship programs were announced (Union Carbide, General Motors, Sloan Foundation, Baker Foundation, among others), Wabash was invariably one of the colleges included in each program.

His preoccupation with corporate enterprise as a source of financial support for higher education led Dr. Sparks during the middle 1950s to experiment — successfully — with what he termed the Wabash Personal Develop-

71

ment program. He asked me to chair a faculty committee to put together a curriculum designed for young, promising employees of corporations who either lacked a college education or had had a purely technical education. The idea was to "sell" corporations on sending to Wabash each summer for five years young employees who had been identified as probable candidates for top management positions in order that they might obtain an intensified liberal arts education. Personal planning, an area Dr. Sparks reserved for himself, was to be an important element in the program.

This is not the place to discuss the details of this ambitious and — at least as long as his personal influence continued in it[56] — highly successful program. I mention it here only because it too was a "money maker" for Wabash and also served to attract favorable attention to Wabash from the business community generally.

Dr. Sparks' deep involvement in money raising meant that he was away from campus much of the time. Increasingly, in the early 1950s especially, he left the on-campus administrative responsibilities to me as dean of the college. But he was never an absentee president. Despite his travel, despite his incredibly heavy correspondence (he always traveled with his dictating machine at hand), he kept in close touch with on-campus problems, including faculty interests and concerns. But I believe it would be fair to say that he considered money raising his highest obligation as a necessary means to achieving goals he had set for Wabash.

The remarkable results which he attained testify to the wisdom of his decision. Money poured into Wabash at a rate which prior to World War II would have been considered fanciful. Moreover, the tremendous push he gave Wabash in these efforts actually led to even greater sums of new money coming to Wabash in the years that followed.

A New National Visibility For Wabash

Throughout the late nineteenth and early twentieth centuries, Wabash had enjoyed a good reputation as a place with high academic standards and as a colorful, virile college for men. For the most part, however, this reputation was limited to the Middle West. It did not have high visibility nationally. By the time Frank Sparks left the presidency of Wabash, the limited visibility of Wabash nationally had been succeeded by a prominence of quite a high order

---

56. For the record, WIPD continues at Wabash College, alive and well. Its continuing success owes much to the late Ben Rogge, who was able to maintain the effective relationship with the corporate community that Dr. Sparks had begun. For a more extended description of the program, see *These Fleeting Years*, pp. 120–25.

It was a prominence associated with Sparks himself and was almost exclusively identified with concerted efforts to forestall massive federal aid to education.

The process which led to national prominence was not a consequence of any resolution on Dr. Sparks' part to use the issue of federal aid to education as a means to an end. It was rather a consequence of his very deep and serious conviction that massive federal aid to education was an evil threat to the pluralistic society which had characterized America in the past. For him it was a crucial philosophical issue. The prospect of federal aid to education carried with it in his mind the prospect of federal control of education, which in turn would further erode the foundations of a free society in America. This was not a superficial bias on Dr. Sparks' part. He had read and thought a great deal about the issue and he was deadly serious about it. On one of their vacation trips to Europe, Dr. and Mrs. Sparks made a serious investigation of the results of national government financing of higher education, especially in England and in the Scandanavian countries. He found confirmation of his fears in that investigation. It heightened his resolution to do something about the then mounting disposition among American university and college presidents to press for congressional legislation making available massive amounts of tax dollars to both private and public institutions.

I am speaking now of the years between 1946 and 1954. Dr. Sparks early in those years took his concerns to the Board of Trustees. Their response was one of enthusiastic affirmation of the Sparks principles. The board adopted a statement of policy for Wabash which meant refusal to accept government aid of any kind. It was to continue to be a guiding principle for Wabash for years to come.[57]

Dr. Sparks carried his crusade against federal aid to education to the public in numerous ways. But easily the most important of these was the formation of the Associated Colleges of Indiana (ACI) and the subsequent development of similar associations all over the country. Sparks realized that it was not enough just to oppose the concept of federal aid. There had to be a viable alternative which would make federal aid unnecessary. He saw that alternative in corporate aid to education. He believed that if American corporations could be persuaded to contribute even as little as one percent of net profits before taxes to education, there would be no need for tax dollars coming from Washington. The time was ripe to pursue this alternative. The gen-

57. There were some practical modifications made when it came to implementing the policy. Aid to G.I. students was ruled acceptable because it was "aid to students, not to an institution." Research grants for individual faculty members were exempted by the same reasoning. Frank did not want to accept surplus war material being made available to colleges, such as quonset buildings for married student housing. I persuaded him, nonetheless, to accept the housing units which became "Mud Hollow." Except for these departures, Wabash adhered strictly to the new policy. BKT.

eral mood of the American society in the immediate post-war years was highly favorable to higher education. In the value system of post-war America, education stood very near the top in national priorities. As evidence of this mood, corporate support for higher education began to take on dimensions which were revolutionary for American business enterprise. Enlightened business leaders (such as Sloan, Olds, and Abrams), conscious of the national debate on federal aid to education and aware of the serious financial plight of private universities, began to explore the potential of corporate support for education. A friendly lawsuit was initiated (the Smythe case) in federal courts to establish the legal right of corporations to make contributions to education and public welfare causes. It was successful.

But small private colleges were at a distinct disadvantage in appealing for corporate support, especially in the case of major national corporations. A major corporation could justify to its stockholders grants made to a major university where the corporation had an obvious *quid pro quo* interest (research, source for specialized personnel, etc.). For the same corporation a gift to a small liberal arts college posed a different and difficult problem. And to contribute to all or even many such colleges was unthinkable.

Dr. Sparks conceived the idea of meeting this latter problem by a cooperative approach to business. He discussed his idea with Tom Jones, then president of Earlham College, who was excited by the possibilities. Together they made a few test calls on Indiana business firms and in 1948 they received a gift of $15,000 from the Hamilton Manufacturing Company in Columbus to be divided equally between Earlham and Wabash. Encouraged by this experience, Sparks and Jones enlisted the interest of other private college presidents in Indiana and with the backing of a handful of like-minded Indiana businessmen, Associated Colleges of Indiana (ACI) was organized in 1948. The presidents of these colleges agreed to give twenty days a year each to joint solicitation of corporate support.

It was a sure-fire thing and developments proceeded at an exciting pace. An office was opened in the Merchants National Bank Building in Indianapolis. Eb Hastings, a professional fund raiser from the American City Bureau, Inc., was appointed executive director. With considerable publicity, drives were made in the name of Associated Colleges of Indiana. Indiana businessmen generally were intrigued by the novel idea and they liked the anti-federal aid-to-education feature of the cooperative effort. Gift money began to flow into the office of ACI.

This Indiana experiment attracted immediate attention among private college presidents throughout the nation. Quickly similar state associations sprang up elsewhere. By 1952 there were nineteen comparable state associations and one regional association (New England). Seventeen additional associations were formed in the next three years so that by 1955 approximately

500 private colleges in the majority of the states were involved in some kind of cooperative enterprise seeking corporate support.

The mushrooming of this kind of apparatus meant that Dr. Sparks was in great demand in other parts of the country as a counsellor on how-to-do-it problems. A new commission, the Commission on Colleges and Industry, was formed in the Association of American Colleges with Sparks as chairman. In these early years at the annual meetings of AAC, the Commission on Colleges and Industry drew the majority of the attending presidents to its separate meetings. Innumerable state and regional conferences and workshops through the country were organized and held (a) to teach college presidents how to proceed and (b) to kindle good will among local business leaders. Sparks was often a principal speaker.

It soon became obvious that some kind of national coordinating office was necessary to make the work of the various state associations orderly and effective at the national level. Consequently, Sparks took the lead in forming what was known as the American College Fund. For a time it operated in the ACI office in Indianapolis on an additional duty basis. In other states there was some uneasiness about an Indianapolis-based national office and also some differences of opinion about what such a national office should do. In 1958 the Independent Colleges Fund of America, Inc. (ICFA) was established with offices in New York.

The rapid development of these state associations caught the interest of those major national business leaders who were working on a different front to promote corporate support for education. Inevitably (indeed, he took the initiative), Frank Sparks was drawn into the counsels of these men. He had a part, therefore, in forming the Council for Financial Aid to Education, Inc. (CFAE) in New York. He served on the original board of directors and shortly after leaving Wabash became its president. The objective of CFAE was to promote increased corporate support for *all* American higher education, public and private. It carefully refrained from soliciting or receiving gifts except for the cost of its own operations.

Dr. Sparks was, of course, not the only college president to play a prominent role at the national level in this post-World War II phenomenon.[58] But he was the central figure, widely known and highly regarded. Thus Wabash in turn received a kind of instant national visibility identified with rugged independence and adamant opposition to federal aid to education. In addition, Wabash became a beneficiary of the rising volume of corporate gifts to liberal arts colleges. For a number of years Wabash led all other Indiana colleges

58. In addition to Tom Jones of Earlham, the following were among those presidents who were especially active: Coons of Occidental, Baxter of Williams, Blanding of Vassar, Wesel of Tufts, Davidson of Union, Wickham of Heidelberg, Sadler of TCU, and Tate of SMU. BKT.

and most of the colleges nationally in annual gifts received from corporations.[59]

The demands on his time as well as his vast interest in this development by 1954 meant that Dr. Sparks was away from the Wabash campus at least as much as he was there. Gradually there were rumblings of discontent among trustees. For the first time in his administration there were occasional trustee committee meetings held without his being present. He was troubled by this. He confided his misgivings to me in the winter of 1954–55. Unquestionably, it raised a question in his mind about the wisdom of continuing longer as president of Wabash. After all, he had achieved most of what he had set for himself at Wabash. At the June meeting of the board in 1955, McCanliss at one point said, "Well, Frank has gone national on us." The implication was clear.

That same fall Frank began to talk with me about succeeding him. One November night we had a long earnest talk in my office about his leaving Wabash. He pressed me very hard. I was touched by what he said, but also sorely troubled. I confided in him my great concerns about my wife, Dorothy, and my fear of what might happen to her and thus to me if I took on this new responsibility. But Frank was reassuring and persuasive. I finally asked him, "What would you do if I refuse?" He gave me that boyish grin of his and said, "Well, Byron, in that case they will have to carry me out of here with my boots on!"

That December he resigned and at the same trustee meeting I was elected ninth president of Wabash College.

What I have written about the presidency of Frank Sparks amounts only to fragments from a brilliant chapter in the history of Wabash College. Nor does it touch on some of the personal attributes of this remarkable man which would make for human interest reading in a college history. A fascinating book could be written about Frank Sparks in which Wabash College would be only a part. With the approval of Abbie Sparks in 1972–73, I tried to persuade Ed Ziegner (Wabash 1942 and political editor of the *Indianapolis News*) to undertake such a book with my help. But Ed declined. I continue to hope that someone will write such a book.

There were two portraits of Dr. Sparks at the college worth studying by anyone with deep feelings about the years of which I have written. I say "were"

59. In 1973 at the close of my presidency of ICFA, I directed a research study which concluded that in the period 1948–73, the associated colleges' approach for corporate support had resulted in a cumulative total of more than $500,000,000 in corporate gifts to liberal arts colleges. This included gifts direct to such colleges, but generated by the cooperative approach, as well as gifts through state association offices. Despite this impressive figure, corporate support did not prevent the coming of massive federal aid to education. BKT.

because one which hung on the second floor of Yandes for a year or two was removed, I presume at Frank's direction. It should be located and returned to Wabash. Done by a prominent portrait painter, it shows Dr. Sparks in his academic robes, a three-quarter standing pose — almost as large as the full length portrait of President White. Painted about the time he became president of Wabash, it is a quite good likeness. But it always struck me as being somewhat stiff and lacking in the warmth of personality which should be associated with Frank Sparks. He is also pictured wearing rimless glasses, an uncharacteristic detail in later years when he was a devout Christian Scientist.[60]

The second portrait, head and shoulders, hangs on the south wall of the great hall in the Campus Center. Appropriately, it looks across the hall at the portrait of Lee McCanliss. This portrait, done by Harold McDonald, then chairman of the art department at Wabash, is an excellent likeness of Frank in his later years. It also captures to a remarkable degree the warmth of his personality and the shrewdness of his mind. The beginning of a smile in that portrait is typical, and, to anyone who knew him well, it tells much about his strength of character and also his fundamental gentleness.[61]

The train of thought touched off by recalling these portraits causes me to linger a few pages more in my reflections about the personal qualities of Frank Sparks which perhaps were not seen by many who knew him. I recognize that in presuming to judge another man's emotional composition, even when there has been a very close personal relationship, the risk of error in conclusions is ever present. For that reason I write with restraint and care.

To most people Frank Sparks appeared to be a man of very strong convictions and principles and, of course, he was such a man. He also came through to them as a man of action—as faculty members in 1941 put it, "a doer rather than a thinker." It is easy to support this conclusion by repeated documentation from his years at Wabash. But what is not generally recognized is that Frank Sparks was above all an extremely thoughtful person especially in matters of personal relationships, and that down deep he was a profoundly sentimental man.

He had a disposition to see the best rather than the worst in other people and to extend to them the benefit of any possible doubts. Occasionally, this led to problems. He was genuinely fond of and interested in old people and extraordinarily kind to them. I was enormously pleased and touched in May, 1955 when he and Abbie paid a surprise visit to Princeton on the occasion of the fiftieth wedding anniversary of my parents. It was not uncommon for him to have tears in his eyes on sentimental moments such as these.

60. This portrait, painted in 1947 by Ruth Pratt Bobbs, remains in storage at the college.

61. This portrait was given to the college by Mrs. Sparks at a farewell dinner in the Campus Center on January 24, 1956. It now hangs in Kane House.

He was generous toward people involved in emotional quandries. When Fergus Ormes asked about possible problems for the college if he divorced his wife, Emily, Frank said, "Private lives are private lives." He took a similar stand in the scandal in Crawfordsville when Carol Klinger and Trevor Kramer exchanged wives through divorce and remarriage. Iris Klinger, prior to the divorces, was working in the Wabash library. Dick Banta and perhaps others thought she should quietly be dropped from the college staff. Frank declined to act.

Much the same sort of thing was true in matters of faculty appointments and promotions where a clash of political or economic philosophy was obviously present. I do not recall the year, but when George Kendall and I were much interested in appointing Ralph Caplan as an instructor in English, Dr. Sparks interviewed him at length and then said to me, "Well, there's a young man who believes in just about everything I disapprove of, but he is certainly a bright, honest, sincere guy. So if you want to hire him" — and he grinned — "go ahead."

This sentimental, gentle, and thoughtful attribute in Dr. Sparks which I am underscoring was never more pronounced than it was in his great love for Abbie Sparks. There was a theory briefly bandied about when the Sparks first came to Wabash that their marriage was one of practical convenience. Frank as a college president needed a wife and "selected" Abbie as the ideal person. I never took this theory seriously even though, given his commitment to planning, it had a ring of authenticity about it and it became a part of the Sparks mythology. But even if this unlikely story had been true it was obvious to all who knew them well that they were very much in love with each other.

This love in my opinion had a great deal to do with Frank's becoming a devout Christian Scientist. I do not believe for a moment that Abbie tried to persuade her husband to join her in that faith. He did this out of love and admiration for his wife, and once having taken the step, he went all the way. He began by deciding he could get along without using glasses to read.[62]

In the winter of 1954, I believe it was, came an accident that provided the first acid test for his new faith. It was a prosaic accident. While showing

---

62. At the college memorial service for President Sparks in January, 1965, Thomas E. Jones, president emeritus, Earlham College, sketched this anecdote concerning Sparks faith and his decision to do without glasses: "Not long after, I was with him at the annual meeting of the Association of American Colleges in Cincinnati. He undertook to look up a number in the telephone book. Finding that he had forgotten his glasses, he dropped his head and stood in silence. Then, he went into the booth, and, to my great surprise, found his number and made his call. When he came out his face was radiant. He said, 'Tom, that does it. You noticed I dropped my head for a moment before I went into the booth. I said to God, "If there is anything in this eternal livingness, please enable me to read this telephone directory," and He did and I saw it.' Frank never used his glasses thereafter."

a few trustees around a newly-excavated basement area of the Campus Center, Dr. Sparks (having turned off the hanging light in the basement while the others were going up the stairs) missed the first step of the stairway and fell in a twist, breaking his hip. He was only semi-conscious when we took him to the Culver Hospital. As the X-rays were being completed he recovered his mental control and insisted on being taken to the Caleb Mills House.

Dr. Jess Burks, who attended Dr. Sparks, was much distressed by this. He reviewed the X-ray pictures with me and Dick Banta and explained that if the hip bones were not pinned soon, Dr. Sparks might never be able to walk again, and if he did walk it would be with a pronounced "scissors limp." But without further medical attention, Dr. Sparks did walk again in time and with a barely perceptible limp.

For many weeks following the accident, Dr. Sparks remained at the Caleb Mills House. Rather quickly he established a telephone connection with the college switchboard. With his dictating machine and the help of his secretaries (especially of Adelaide Hayes, his executive secretary), he kept abreast of the flow of official paper work. Otherwise, the long hours were devoted to reading with Abbie *Science and Health with Key to the Scriptures* and to meditation and prayer. His first appearance on campus was at the first night of the annual Pan Hellenic Dance that May. He came on crutches, but he was in white tie and tails and his spirits were high. All of us joined in the prolonged applause.

By that autumn Frank was back in the full swing of things, first with a cane and finally without support of any kind. If his damaged hip ever bothered him, he successfully concealed it from others. He never discussed the problem, and thereafter he appeared to live as if nothing had ever happened. In the late 1950s, when they were living in New York, Frank and Abbie took ballroom dancing lessons. They loved to dance. At a meeting at the Homestead in Hot Springs, Virginia, about 1960, with admiration and wonder I watched them dance one night for a long time. I was never able to make up my mind how much of this remarkable recovery was due to Christian Science and how much was simply due to what might be called Frank Sparksism. His was an indomitable will.

One other incident and then I will stop. In the early spring of the year 1950–51, Lee McCanliss arranged a "show down" conference with Pierre Goodrich, Frank and me in New York. That winter Lee had begun to press Pierre very hard for a major financial gift or pledge to Wabash. Pierre, who never liked to give away money and who always sought elaborate continuing controls over whatever he did give, had resisted Lee's importuning. In fact, I think he was angered by Lee's blunt pressure, but he was also troubled. Conferences with Pierre Goodrich were never easy. They were inordinately long and invariably involved with interminable tangential discussions of philosophical questions which were terribly important to Pierre. I presume it was for this reason that Lee arranged for the conference in New York rather than Indianapolis. I was included at Pierre's request because at that time I was working closely with Pierre in his current mania for expanding the study of "Great Books."

Before we set out for New York I was aware that Dr. Sparks was not feeling well. He said nothing about being uncomfortable but he looked bad. One day during a conversation in my office, he suddenly bent over in his chair resting his head in his hands with his elbows on his knees. "Are you all right, Frank?" I asked him. "Oh, yes," he said, "I only have a little problem with my stomach. It will pass." The "little problem" I later learned was a perforated ulcer.

Because he wanted to keep some other appointments he had made, Dr. Sparks flew to New York two days before I did. He kept most of his appointments, but Lee later told me that between appointments Dr. Sparks would return to the hotel to steep himself in a tub of hot water to ease his pain. I arrived at the Gotham Hotel late at night and neglected to ask if there were messages for me. Early the next morning I telephoned Frank's room. There was no answer. After repeated calls I telephoned Lee at his office. "Didn't you get my note?" he asked. "Frank is in the Memorial Hospital. I put him there yesterday afternoon."

With the help of Dr. Norman Treves, Lee had persuaded Dr. Sparks to have examinations at the Memorial Hospital. Those examinations revealed serious internal bleeding and shortly afterward he underwent major surgery. I stayed on in New York for a few days and visited him in his room both before and after Abbie arrived. On my second visit she was there. She was cheerful, even radiant, but I shall never forget the deep distress in her eyes. On the following day when I stayed a little longer with Dr. Sparks before leaving for Crawfordsville I found him at ease but very quiet. At one point he said to me, "Byron, I should never have done this to that girl [Abbie]. And I never will again."

II

THE WABASH FACULTY

There was a Wabash faculty before there was a Wabash president. There was a Wabash Board of Trustees before there was a faculty, of course, but in terms of the mission of the college as defined by that first Board of Trustees, nothing really happened until Caleb Mills reported as the first professor and met the first class of twelve students. Mills was soon joined by two other teachers, Hovey and one of the Thompson brothers. Thus there was a faculty of three at Wabash before Elihu Baldwin appeared on the scene as the college's first president. His first official act was to call a faculty meeting.

This sequence of historical events has often caused me to speculate about the priorities of importance that can be assigned to the basic elements which constitute the continuing life of Wabash. I have never been able to make up my mind whether the faculty or the Board of Trustees is more important as an influence shaping the destiny of the college. But long ago I concluded that these two together are more important than the president, no matter how able or how influential he may be. In a later section I write about my thoughts concerning the importance of the Board of Trustees, especially when the board chooses to exercise its considerable residual powers over the character of the college. But leaving the trustees aside for the moment, there is merit in thinking of the extent to which the faculty by itself can make the college a superior or a mediocre place of learning, a place distinguished for its character and its principles or just an ordinary place without particular distinction of any kind.

Like the Wabash Board of Trustees, the Wabash faculty has been characterized by long periods of service on the part of its members. Wabash presidents come and go. Even counting the exceptionally long tenure of President Tuttle, the average tenure of the first ten Wabash presidents has been a little less than fourteen years. By contrast the average length of time spent at Wabash by associate and full professors has been approximately thirty years in the period 1920 to 1974. For the entire history of the college, the average has probably been longer than thirty years.

Like the Board of Trustees also, or at least the "permanent section" of the board, the faculty has been largely self-perpetuating. Theoretically the reproduction of the faculty through new appointments is the responsibility of the president and the Board of Trustees. In practice, however, new appointments are really in the hands of the faculty. Department chairmen search for candidates, identify those whom they like, and recommend their appointment. In the majority of cases, their recommendations are approved by deans and presidents. Termination of temporary appointments, promotion in rank, award of permanent tenure, and so on, even though officially done by the president, reflect the thinking of senior faculty members. Moreover, department chairmen are decisive in the process of choosing their successors.

There are hazards in this practice which can make for inbreeding and stultification in the faculty. But it insures a kind of unbroken continuity within the faculty not sustained in the office of the president. Such continuity operates as a powerful influence in passing from one set of hands to another Wabash faculty traditions and points of view. Thus, in English a Milford influences an Osborne who in turn influences a Fertig; in chemistry a Garner influences a Howell who in turn influences a McKinney; in speech a Brigance influences a Powell who influences an O'Rourke. And so it goes in department after department over a long span of years. Even when an energetic president shakes up the faculty as President Sparks did by appointing numerous new department chairmen (economics, political science, psychology, philosophy, chemistry, physics and religion), the newcomers have usually been quickly merged into the older faculty and mellowed in Wabash tradition.

The Wabash faculty historically has been a closely knit community, self-conscious and proud. From time to time there have been schisms in the faculty. Probably the sharpest came in the first decade of the twentieth century, when rivalry and antagonism between the departments of science and those of the humanities were deep and bitter. But even then there was a common pride in the exciting renaissance Wabash was experiencing, and there was a common loyalty to the surging fame of Little Giant athletic teams. When, with the unexpected death of President Kane, crisis came, the faculty rallied behind a new president, Dr. Mackintosh. No scientist objected to the fact that the new president was a humanist. In the 1930s, the 1940s, and the 1950s, rivalries among the academic divisions of the college were often keen, but they were healthy and stimulating for the college as a whole. There have been times when faculty leaders had lacked enthusiasm for their president, but there has never been the kind of faculty revolt at Wabash which occasionally has torn apart other private colleges. Nor have the rare collisions of trustee policy with faculty preferences led to the drawing of battle lines which elsewhere has resulted often in institutional censure by the American Association of University Professors. Such disagreements have been orderly and rational, reflecting in part close friendships between individual faculty members and individual trustees. Not all colleges can say the same.

The sense of community and the high *esprit de corps* of the Wabash faculty have in the past been basic sources of the college's strength. As college faculties go, the Wabash faculty has always been small — even now, although it is more than double the size of the faculty in the 1920s. This and Wabash's location in a place like Crawfordsville have served to reinforce the closely knit character of the faculty. The Wabash faculty lives and works closely together to a degree impossible in the case of a faculty numbering in the hundreds or in the case of a college located in a large city where faculty members go separate ways at night and on weekends.

Social life at Wabash has always had an on-campus pattern about it. Those few faculty members who find life in Indiana and Crawfordsville barely sufferable depend on faculty friendships for social diversion and relaxation. The majority who like Crawfordsville and Indiana, nevertheless, tend to socialize primarily with their colleagues on the faculty. Often at faculty parties, there is a refreshing mixture of college administration officers, local trustees, and faculty members and their wives. Such parties are, or at least they were, talky exercises with divergent opinions freely, and often heatedly, expressed about all manner of things. Regularly, arguments about "the college" are generated, and they run on endlessly with a full measure of criticism and disagreement. It is all a part of the informal, haphazard, happy manner by which Wabash consensus has been reached, and the place is thereby "governed." It is, in my judgment, the answer to those who say the unionization of all college faculties and the drawing of hard lines between academic employees and academic management are inevitable.

I am emphasizing faculty pride in Wabash and the faculty's sense of belonging to the place, but instead of using such phrases I believe it would be just as appropriate to speak of the faculty's love of a way of life and of the institution that makes this way of life possible. Those teachers and staff members who stay feel deeply about the place and about what it strives to be. For them, even though they might be embarrassed by my putting it as I do, it amounts to a permanent love affair. This is especially true of Wabash graduates on the faculty or the administrative staff. For them, private life and Wabash life are inseparable.

Myron Phillips was such a faculty member. From the time he entered Wabash as a freshman until he died, he was involved in a Wabash love affair. He once told me, "I really don't care what I am assigned to do here. If they want me to sweep out the place, I will. I just want to work here forever." Myron did almost everything but "sweep out." He taught speech, managed the Scarlet Inn, sold tickets at athletic games, directed Scarlet Masque plays, worked in the admissions office, and finally became director of alumni affairs. Whatever he did, he did with gusto and with every ounce of energy his 101-pound body could generate. Next to his wife and son, Wabash was the most important object for his life.

Warren Shearer was another such faculty member. He began his faculty service almost immediately after graduating from Wabash. Despite interruptions for graduate study, military duty, and a federal government assignment in Europe, it was a service which continued for the better part of four decades. And it was a service of white heat. He taught speech for a time and then, for a longer time, economics. He performed with zeal as chairman of Division III and as noisy captain, coach, and catcher of the faculty's intramural baseball team. In the late 1930s he helped recruit students. For a time he was an office assistant to President Sparks. When I resigned the presidency of the college, he served as acting president until Dr. Cook was appointed, and then served as dean of the college. Cocky and sometimes truculent about Wabash, his private life was for years meshed with that of the college. And he loved what he did.

Dick Banta, although he was not a faculty member, for twenty years served the college in a variety of ways out of love for the place. He would hoot at my use of the word "love," but it is true. Starting on a part-time basis in the Hopkins years, when the college was in serious trouble with its alumni, and continuing throughout the Sparks administration, Dick did almost everything except to teach formally — recruiting students, placating alumni, improving public relations, nourishing athletes, supervising plant construction, publishing Wabash books and magazines, counseling and coddling the chairman of the Board of Trustees. Throughout those years, his salary was a pittance. He didn't care. His reward was his enjoyment of what he did.

Phillips, Shearer, and Banta had almost continuous contacts with the college from their undergraduate years on. It could be said — in fact, it was occasionally said — that they and others like them never outgrew their sophomore enthusiasms. In his droll way, Banta now and then acknowledged this charge when he would introduce himself at alumni meetings as "Dick Banta, class of '25, O.L.S. (Oldest Living Sophomore!). But the kind of intense emotional attachment to Wabash that these three exhibited was deeper and more complicated than that. Nor was it limited to those whose contacts with the college were virtually uninterrupted after their undergraduate years. Repeatedly the same kind of emotional attachment was obvious on the part of Wabash alumni who, after professional or business experience elsewhere, returned to the college in one capacity or another.

There was, for instance, Robert S. Harvey. A year or two before World War II Bob Harvey resigned the state editorship of the *Indianapolis Star* and turned his back on a career of high promise in journalism to return to Wabash as college librarian. His salary was on the order of $1,800 a year. His services to the college were multiple. During World War II he helped to hold the college together by doubling as acting dean. He became registrar of the college, a post he held for years. He taught English, wrote all major college news releases, supervised the college News Bureau, ran the Board of Publications, wrote all the citations for alumni awards of merit, enlivened the ambience of the Scarlet Inn, upped the quality of billiards in the Campus Center, became the college archivist. And he loved it all.

There was, for instance, William B. Degitz. Bill Degitz resigned the treasurership of the Haywood Publishing Company in the early 1950s to return to Wabash as assistant business manager. His move meant a fifty percent reduction in salary. He built the college business office into what it is today. He taught accounting, was deeply involved in the beautification of the campus and in improving its maintenance, served as secretary of the Board of Trustees, did his stint on the alumni meeting circuit, and so on. He had opportunities to leave the college. He never did.

There was, for instance, Carroll E. Black who, after a longer interlude in business far removed from Indiana, came back to Wabash at my invitation in the late 1950s to serve as an admissions counsellor. He told me when I said goodbye to him in 1965 that his returning to Wabash had been the happiest move in his life.

The illustrations I am giving of intense feeling about and devotion to Wabash College could just as easliy and just as validly be drawn from the ranks of faculty members who did not have their undergraduate experience there. Time and again "non-Wabash" men have come to the faculty and, however tentative their thoughts about the place may have been in the beginning, they have stayed permanently. Why? Well, among other things, they liked what they found there, and gradually they fell in love with Wabash and its way of life.

Some of these became in time as gung-ho about Wabash and its myths as any product of the Caveman era. It would be impossible to identify an alumnus more gutsy in the Wabash faith than Bob Mitchum. He adopted Wabash before Wabash adopted him. Others, initially at least, have regarded the Wabash tribal rituals as naïve and provincial. The Wabash sentimentality, so often expressed in one way or another, amused them or it cloyed. They did what they could to modify traditions and to change the rituals. But in spite of that — perhaps even because of that — they themselves became deeply involved emotionally in the college, and they never got over it. They became the creators of new Wabash myths of which they were proud. Imperceptibly they developed their own brand of proprietary attitude toward the college and what happened there. And Wabash is a better, more distinctive, place of learning because they did.

What I have been saying about the attributes of the Wabash faculty makes it clear that inevitably such a faculty exerts a very strong and continuing influence on the life of the institution and on the quality of its possibilities. It is an influence that often runs beyond academic matters. The consequences of faculty academic decisions now and then amount to an intrusion into financial areas which, theoretically at least, are the exclusive responsibility of the Board of Trustees. For this reason, presidents and trustees of private colleges often find themselves frustrated by the faculty when they attempt to introduce changes in the interest of improving the college's fiscal health. No matter how liberal faculty people may be in matters of politics, economics, social behavior and so on, when it comes to their own professional or personal interests, it is hard to find a more conservative, intransigent group of individuals than college professors. The Wabash faculty has been like that.

This constitutes, if not one of the dangers, one of the most difficult problems confronting Wabash and similar colleges. The worsening financial predicament of private colleges cannot, in my opinion, be overcome by continuing forever the traditional procedure of raising tuition fees higher and higher and raising more and more gift money. Sooner or later new and different approaches to the problem of financing private colleges will have to be instituted by boards of trustees. Inevitably such approaches will touch on the most sensitive areas of faculty concern — curriculum, student-faculty ratio, instructional methodology, plant utilization, and the like. It will be a difficult business, perhaps impossible to complete at many places without acrimonious confrontation between trustees and faculty. Perhaps I make wish the father of thought when I say that faculty and trustee history at Wabash is on the side of a rational consensus reached in the best interests of an institution to which both are devoted.

There is a second danger or problem in the faculty way of life at Wabash. As far as I am concerned, it is a minor problem but for those who regard private liberal arts colleges as anachronistic relics of earlier and simpler times, it is a major problem. When Herbert Butterfield, Regius Professor of History at Cambridge University, completed his visiting lectureship in the early 1960s, I asked him to give me his impressions of Wabash. He was quite complimentary in his remarks. He had had experience at several distinguished American universities, but never before had he known an American liberal arts college. He confessed that he was surprised at the high quality of those Wabash professors he had come to know. "Have you no negative comments to make?" I asked him. Without hesitation he replied, "Yes. Life here is too pleasant for your professors. They are complacent. They do not have enough pressure from their professional specialized peers." Sir Steven Runciman told me much the same thing at the conclusion of his lectures at Wabash. Such observations have merit and are worth pondering. And yet if I had to choose between an institution where the "publish or perish" policy takes precedence over teaching and a college like Wabash where teaching has the highest priority, I would take Wabash. Any day!

Whether the consequences of the pervasive influence of the faculty in the on-going life of a college like Wabash are beneficial or not depends on the quality of those who serve as faculty leaders from one generation to another. And faculty quality is not as easy to appraise as the handbooks of accrediting agencies lead one to suppose. For one thing, the criteria for judging faculty quality change from time to time. In the nineteenth century at Wabash, Christian piety and Christian commitment had more to do with qualitative appraisals of the Wabash faculty than did professional pedigrees. In the twentieth century, the possession of advanced degrees, evidence of scholarly attainment, and the like have been more important than Christian piety.

However one chooses to judge faculty quality, the long record at Wabash of high quality in the faculty is quite an impressive one. No doubt Wabash has had its share of mediocre, even shoddy, teachers, but as I read the history of the college, and as I experienced it for many years, there have always been among the faculty more than a few individuals of extraordinarily high quality. In saying "high quality," I am thinking less of the rule book prerequisites for faculty competence than I am of the attributes that make for good human beings. I have in mind men of exceptionally good intellect supported by sound character or men of exceptionally strong character supported by sound intellect. These are the qualities that give enduring value to collegiate experience.

The quality of the Wabash faculty was the decisive factor in winning for Wabash in the late nineteenth century a chapter of Phi Beta Kappa. It was also decisive when Wabash quickly was given full accreditation by the North Central Association of Schools and Colleges after that association was organized early in the twentieth century. Likewise it was among the most important factors which led to Wabash being chosen for one of the first of the Ford Foundation Challenge Grants in the early 1960s. But the faculty's quality has come through in other ways, too. Time and again it has had the courage to stand firm against popular pressures. In the 1850s the Wabash faculty was vocal about its abolitionist sentiments. The first negro student was admitted to Wabash in 1856. The *Crawfordsville Review,* the local Democratic newspaper, was outraged. So, apparently, were prominent parents of some of the current students. The faculty stood firm. In the 1920s, when many people in Indiana and Montgomery County were cowed by the Ku Klux Klan, Wabash professors were outspoken in their criticisms of the Klan and unintimidated by fiery crosses burned on the campus. In the Edgar Evans controversy in the 1930s which swirled about the issue of required instruction in the Bible and the Christian religion, the faculty was adamant despite trustee and alumni pressure. "The principles of the Wabash faculty," said Insley Osborne, "are not for sale." It was not quite a case of saying to outside pressure, "Go to hell!" but it came close to that. This curious mixture of orthodoxy and dissent in the Wabash faculty has had much to do with the college's reputation for rugged independence.

In recent years the faculty at Wabash by objective standards of measurement is a better faculty professionally than Wabash has had in the past. It is a bigger faculty. There is more depth and diversification within individual departments. There are more Ph.D. degrees, more listings in *Who's Who in America,* more evidence of national professional kudos. And yet in terms of dedication to the cause of the liberal arts and to the call of teaching, I doubt that the current faculty is any better or stronger than the faculty of the 1920s, or of the 1910s, or the 1880s, or the 1840s. The impressive repetitive fact that comes through the history of the Wabash faculty is that always there have been, as there are today, exceptional individuals in both intellect and character who have stood for something very much worthwhile to the destiny of the college. And that fact, to a very large extent, makes credible the Wabash claim to being a pillar of strength among private liberal arts colleges.

The attention that I am devoting in these reflections to the importance of the faculty and the Board of Trustees may cause some future readers in the college archives to say, "But Trippet ignored the most important element in the composition of the college — the students." It would be a fair comment. For that reason before concluding this whimsy about the Wabash faculty I should explain my exclusion of students.

If one talks about the college's reason for being at any given point in time, then it is true that its students are of supreme importance. Often when speaking to Wabash students — entering freshmen or graduating seniors — I liked appealing to them in the following way: "As of this moment it is to you that this college belongs. It is for you that this faculty has been assembled. It is for you that the college's endowment has been accumulated. You are the purpose of the whole endeavor that we call Wabash. And it is the promise of your individual lives that makes the endeavor worthwhile."

I believe that kind of thinking now as much as I did when I expressed it in speeches. But the words "as of this moment" are important. Students do represent the purpose of the college while they are students, but they do not control the destiny of the college. The distinction between immediate purpose and long range destiny is an important one. Students often think and act, especially in recent years, as if they, and they alone, should determine what the college should be. This is understandable. It is also fatuous. Students do not and should not determine what the college should be. They do not even determine what is to be taught or not taught. Wabash is a private college in which such matters are determined by the faculty and the trustees. If students do not like the consequences of such decisions they are free to choose another college or university more to their liking. If they choose Wabash, then they abide by what they find there. For me, it is as simple as that.

I realize that what I have just said classifies me as old fashioned, even reactionary, from the point of view of students and probably from the point of view of younger faculty members. But I continue to stick by my guns in such matters. A faculty of quality, dedicated to the liberal arts, is a better judge of what should be taught or not taught than students. Students can influence the faculty's thinking by reacting to the quality of teaching and to the usefulness of course content. They can question the "relevancy" of specific course offerings and curricular requirements. This kind of student ferment can be quite therapeutic for a college that is alive and alert to current issues. The fact remains, however, that the liberal and liberating arts are not well served by a college that tries to offer whatever courses its students demand at any given point in time.

Such Burkeian sentiments are decidely out of fashion now. But the disposition of many colleges in the name of "relevancy" to adjust in response to student demands, whatever those demands may be — black studies, sexual aberrations, basket weaving, or what not — can only lead to steady dilution of intellectual learning. Student interests and student wishes are fickle. They change with changing times. And students come and go at Wabash more rapidly than any other element in the composition of the college. I estimate that in the twentieth century the average length of stay for all students who have entered there is not more than three semesters. The average no doubt is much higher now, but it is still a transient kind of thing on which to define the aims of the college and to build a curriculum to serve those aims.

In 1969 I found myself involved one day in an argument with angry protesting students on a western campus. One of the students challenged some remarks I made by asserting "you can have a college without presidents and professors, but you can't have a college without students." I responded by arguing that precisely the opposite is true. If a college is "a community of scholars" engaged in pursuing the "life of the mind," then you can have a college without undergraduate students, provided there is a faculty intact. Under these circumstances, faculty members could continue to read, study, and write and could continue an intellectual colloquium among themselves. The process would be that of a "community of scholars" engaged in promoting the "life of the mind." For an endowed college, it is a distinct possibility and it might be a good idea to try it now and then. That argument generated considerably more heat than light, but it illustrates the convictions I am expressing. It also explains, whether it justifies or not, my exclusion of students from these reflections.

I am concluding this section with a series of word sketches about a number of faculty members who were in their prime in the 1920s and the 1930s.

By selecting these from the many about whom I could write, I do not mean to suggest that they were the greatest of the Wabash professors whom I have known and with whom I have worked. A few of them fall into that category but most of them do not. I have chosen them rather because they belong primarily to an era before I became deeply involved in the administration of the college, and I can, therefore, be more objective about them than I could if I should write about their successors. Also these men illustrate most of the points I have been making about the Wabash faculty — long service, love of Wabash, and firm convictions about the place. Finally they strike me as interesting human beings.

Early in these reflections, I lamented the fact that the college archives, rich though they are in Wabashiana, are barren when it comes to details of the private lives of early Wabash heroes and heroines. My comments about individual Wabash faculty members constitute a minor step toward diminishing that impoverishment in the future. As I say, these were interesting people. Their lives illustrate the human condition which is as fascinating in the Wabash faculty as it is elsewhere. It is almost all there — achievement and failure, happiness and tragedy, conformity and eccentricity, wisdom and folly. Of greed, malice and meanness there is almost none. Here and there one finds touches of quiet heroism.

ALBERT REIFF BECHTEL

Dr. Bechtel's experience at Wabash exemplifies a common, recurring phenomenon in Wabash history. In 1920, shortly after receiving his Ph.D degree at Cornell University, he was appointed chairman of the Department of Botany by President Mackintosh. Dr. Bechtel and his wife came as young people to Wabash and Crawfordsville, undoubtedly with mixed feelings and undoubtedly wondering how long they would be there. As it turned out, they spent the rest of their lives there. In due time they bought a home on West Wabash Avenue, a stone's throw from the campus. There they reared their children. (The sons graduated from Wabash.) They joined the Wabash Avenue Presbyterian Church and took active parts in its affairs. Year after year Dr Bechtel faithfully met his classes and his laboratories, awakening in most of his students a new interest in science, particularly in botany. Among his numerous major students over the years, more than a few went on to distinguish themselves professionally as plant pathologists, ecologists, or as teachers of botany (e.g., Robert Fulton and his brother Joe). Wabash became a way of life for the Bechtels. They grew old in its service. They died in Crawfordsville and are buried in Oak Hill Cemetery.

It is an experience which can be duplicated over and over in the lives of numerous other professors who came to Wabash as young men and stayed. It was an especially common pattern in the nineteenth and the early twentieth centuries. In the more mobile society which has characterized America since World War II, it is perhaps less common. The incidence of turn-over in the faculty became higher in the 1950s and 1960s. But even so, there are numerous examples of the persistence of the pattern — the Don Bakers, the Ted Bedricks, the Jack Charleses, the Eric Deans, the Vic Powells, the Ben Rogges, the Eliot Williamses, among others. All of these and others came to Wabash young and stayed. Why? It is easy to understand why Wabash graduates might want to spend their lives at Wabash. But for those who came out of different collegiate and university backgrounds, the question is harder to answer. In the earlier period of which I am writing, I suppose some stayed because it would have been difficult to move elsewhere. But these were very few. The majority stayed because they immediately liked Wabash, and their liking deepened into love. Whatever they were looking for in life, consciously or unconsciously, they found it in the Wabash community. And thus I believe it was with Dr. Bechtel and his wife.

He was a superb teacher. He was never flashy, never colorful as was Brigance. Nor was he the kind of conspicuous, attention-getting professor that Gronert was. But he had a kind of quiet solidity about him that grew on students. Above all, his sensitive love of nature, of anything that grew out of the earth, was a contagious quality which the dullest of his students recognized and admired. He was an excellent lecturer, vigorous, enthusiastic, obviously stocked with vast knowledge of his subject matter, but never pedantic. He was even better in the laboratory, patient and helpful with students poring over microscopes, explaining with freshness something he had explained hundreds of times before. He was at his best on field trips in the afternoon, leading a lab section of students over rough terrain in Pine Hills or Turkey Run, gathering specimens of plant life, pausing to give miniature lectures about a tree, or a flower, or a seedling, or a parasite. He painstakingly answered questions and tactfully corrected errors. He made his students look at nature in a new way and to wonder about it.

Because Dr. Bechtel was Pennsylvania Dutch, he sometimes had trouble pronouncing words with *w* in them. Students who were good at that sort of thing used to imitate his speech and his mannerisms, but never in derision, always with respect and fondness. Everyone liked "Doc" Bechtel, as he was commonly called by students.

In my freshman year I included botany, Bechtel's introductory course, in my five-course program. In high school I had studied physics and chemistry, and for that reason I wanted to learn something about the biological sciences. I started with botany rather than zoology because of the good things I heard about Dr. Bechtel from upper classmen at the Beta House. The class, probably a hundred or more, met for lectures in the Old Chapel in Center Hall. Quiz sections and laboratory sections met in South Hall. From his very first lecture I was fascinated by Dr. Bechtel's knowledge and his insights. I can still remember some of his exact comments that struck me at the time as profoundly interesting. They were usually simple truisms that I had never thought of before. They caused me to say to myself, "How true! I had never thought of that." To my way of thinking this kind of student reaction — "I had never thought of that" — reflects the effective influence of a good teacher and his appeal to intellectual curiosity. "A man can move about in search of food and shelter from the elements, but a plant cannot. A plant must depend on its immediate permanent environment," Dr. Bechtel once said. A simple, elementary truth, but I had never really thought of it, and its implications opened an entirely new world of speculation for me. The same thing was true of many similar Bechtel observations. When he introduced us to the mysteries of photosynthesis, I remember he prefaced his technical explanations by a little commonplace talk about the differences between animal and plant life. "A man can walk away from his waste matter. — But a tree must rely on the air and the sun to rid itself of its waste," he said. "How true!" I thought, "How simple, but how true."

As I think about it, I realize that perhaps the most important single thing that happened to me intellectually in my freshman year at Wabash was the awakening of my intellectual curiosity and the quickening of a desire to learn and to know. In high school I had the reputation of being a good student. But it was easy for me. Except by one history teacher, I was never pushed. I had plenty of time for other interests. My lowest grades were in what used to be called "deportment." I attached more importance to my part on the high school basketball team than I did to my performance in class. As I say, my studies were easy for me. At Wabash in my freshman year, all that changed dramatically. The academic demands were severe; the quantitative and qualitative standards were high; the student competition was keen. I realized suddenly how little I knew, and how much there was to know. I found myself beginning to work furiously at my studies and, beyond that, reading my head off on my own in Yandes Library. And I found it both exciting and rewarding. Dr. Bechtel was one of my first professors at Wabash to contribute to this personal revolution. What he did for me I am sure he did for countless others before and later. This is the mark of a great teacher.[1]

Unlike some of his colleagues in the biological sciences at Wabash, nota-

1. In my first semester with Bechtel he gave me a B+. Years later I asked him if he knew he had given me my lowest grade in college. "Yes," he said with his characteristic chuckle, "I became aware of that later and decided it gave me a new kind of eminence on the faculty!" He broke into full laughter and so did I. BKT.

bly Willis Johnson, Dr. Bechtel did not publish books or monographs. Now and then at a state science meeting he would read a paper, but so far as I know, none of these was published in a botanical journal. However, he kept very much alive professionally, particularly in plant pathology. He kept abreast of current botanical literature in his specialty. And he was constantly observing, studying, and classifying obscure plant life in the immediate area of Crawfordsville. In the late 1930s he wheedled some trustee (perhaps Ike Elston) into financing the construction of quite a good greenhouse on the south end of South Hall. When Waugh Hall was built at the end of World War II, he saw to it that the greenhouse was moved to the south side of the new building. It was his private domain, and he spent hours there garbed in a rubber apron, tending his exotic plants, often collecting specimens for microscopic use in his laboratories. He became an expert on foliage and plants in the Pine Hills area.

One day after his retirement, I drove him to Pine Hills to spend a few hours. We hiked about the place as if it were a private field trip. Reaching a particularly rugged area, he suddenly said to me, "You want to see the most ancient form of plant life in this part of the world?" "Sure," I replied, not having the slightest notion what he was talking about. "Well, follow me," he said and with that he took off up a hill, forcing his way through dense undergrowth. (I remember again being astonished at the way he took poison ivy in his bare hands with no concern at all.) Finally, we went up over some quite large boulders and came to a level depressed plot of soil among the granite. He was an old man then and not well, but he scrambled up those boulders at a rate that left me gasping for breath. He pointed to some rich dark green vegetation, a creeping kind of plant hugging the ground. "Those are millions of years old," he said fondling the plants gently. "Older than the ice ages which they survived." And he drifted off into talk about the ice caps that once covered the earth: how the ice had come about as far south as the present city of Terre Haute in Indiana; how it had destroyed practically all living matter; how it gouged out the Pine Hills and Turkey Run gorges; how it had deposited huge boulders in the area, boulders pushed all the way from the Great Lakes area, maybe; how here and there some scrubby plant life, such as that we were looking at, managed to survive the cold and the grinding pressure of the ice and stone. As I listened to the old man talking, more to himself than to me, I was greatly moved.

Following his retirement Dr. Bechtel visibly began to deteriorate, and after the death of his wife, he went down fast. He seemed lost in thought and sometimes would ignore greetings during his walks. He fell quite ill and never recovered. It was a painful, long-drawn-out kind of suffering. George Kendall and I used to visit him briefly in the Ben Hur nursing home on South Grant Avenue. We never stayed long. Dr. Bechtel could not control the violent convulsions in his legs and arms, and it embarrassed him. I was glad when the end came for him.

WILLIAM NORWOOD BRIGANCE

He wrote his books and articles over the name "W. Norwood Brigance." He answered the telephone and among strangers identified himself as "W. N. Brigance." His wife called him "Norwood." So did his professional colleagues. Crawfordsville friends in the Kiwanis Club and the country club often called him "Bill." For generations of Wabash students, however, he was "Briggie." It was a term of affection and esteem tinged with good natured kidding. This student label became his Wabash name. But by whatever name he is remembered among those who knew him, the image called to mind is colorful and dynamic.

In the late 1920s, the 1930s and the 1940s, Brigance was the most widely known of Wabash faculty members. With the possible exception of Gronert, he was also probably the most popular professor among rank and file Wabash students and among the townspeople in Crawfordsville. Brigance came to Wabash as the successor to Professor Cox in the late years of the Mackintosh administration. I suspect that initially he regarded his Wabash appointment as a temporary thing, a stepping stone to better positions at larger institutions. He had numerous opportunities to move to such positions once he had established, as he quickly did, his prominent professional reputation among American teachers of speech. But he stayed with Wabash by choice, and he became one of the most famous of its faculty members in the era of which I am writing. There were leaves of absence. One, in the 1920s, was to complete his work for the Ph.D. degree at the University of Iowa. The longest was to serve as chairman of the Department of Speech at the University of Hawaii. He was there two years. But he always returned to Wabash, where he served under four presidents.

Energetic and ambitious he lost no time making a name for himself at Wabash. Oratory and oratorical contests in collegiate circles were still fashionable in the 1920s, and under Professor Cox's direction Wabash had already attained distinction with national contest winners such as Carleton Gauld. But its fame for producing national oratorical champions and near winners came under Brigance. He coached a string of national champions, among others Leland Ross, Maurice ("Red") Robinson, Ray Ehrensberger, and Bob Goodwin. My personal experience with Brigance, when he coached me in one or two oratorical contests, convinced me that his influence on his oratorical candidates always went much beyond direct forensic instruction. He was adroit at turning phrases and thinking up catchy speech titles. I suspect students speech titles such as "Blood Will Tell," "Inside the Cup," "The Holy Bottle," and others that became famous were really Brigance titles rather than student titles. But he was clever at "inspiring" such things, thereby making his students feel that they rather than he could take the credit.

Brigance's debating teams in his early years at Wabash were always formidable. He demanded of his debaters in-depth preparation as far as facts, statistics, authoritative quotations, reference sources, and the like were concerned. He was also demanding when it came to debate practice. But he gave his debaters more latitude in their style of delivery than he did his orators. Perhaps it was for that reason that I was more comfortable working with him in debate than in oratory. I remember feeling artificial and strained, when I tried to respond to his instruction in oratory. I later realized that his style of public address was simply unnatural for me.

As the years went by and speech fashions changed, Briggie left the coaching of oratory and debate to the second man in the department. Increasingly he devoted his attention to "public discussion." In the process he formed the Wabash College Speakers Bureau, providing a model in student public speaking which other colleges were quick to copy. His flair for publicity helped to make the Speakers Bureau popular and successful. Student speakers were fanned out over Indiana and eastern Illinois, sometimes farther, by Brigance's providing programs for service clubs, women's clubs, church groups, and so on.[2] In the process they netted publicity for Wabash and, of course, for Norwood Brigance.

Student demand for his courses always ran ahead of the rigid limits he placed on the size of his classes. It was not only his popularity as a dynamic teacher that drew the students. "Speech" as taught by Brigance was regarded as a highly practical discipline in the conservative brand of liberal arts which then dominated the Wabash curriculum. A course with Brigance was considered a "must" for pre-law students and for those aspiring to a career in business. But for whatever reason they flocked to his classes, his students felt rewarded by the experience. He got them on their feet quickly and repeatedly to perform in front of the class. He was good at inspiring confidence even in the most timid of his students.

Briggie's own performance before his classes was always something of a show, full of enthusiasm, energy, bouncy good humor, and an overpowering display of miscellaneous facts. A prodigious reader with a retentive mind, he was always abreast of current events, particularly in the political arena. Unlike many teachers of speech, he had no interest in the theater, and, as far as I could tell, he had no interest in literature or philosophy. But in areas such as politics, business, international relations, psychology, and history, he could,

2. The oldest college bureau in the United States, the Wabash College Speakers Bureau is now in its fifty-fifth year. Since 1927, it has supplied speakers to over 3,300 audiences.

and did, talk about anything — always with the manner of one who can give the last definitive word. An ardent Democrat, he was often partisan in his judgments about political figures and events, but he prided himself on his objectivity in such matters. Above all he was an expert in the psychology of persuasion. President Hopkins once remarked that the most useful psychology being taught at Wabash was not in the Department of Psychology but on the third floor of Center Hall.

Nationally, Briggie's professional prominence came from his books and from the active and influential role he played in state, regional and national speech associations. His textbooks were widely adopted by speech departments in colleges and universities throughout the country. The best of these, *The Spoken Word,* was for years probably the leading textbook of its kind in America.[3] In spite of the long hours he spent day after day on the third floor of Center Hall, he found time at night and on weekends to do his writing in his study at home. He was deadly serious and determined about his writing. Even before he obtained his Ph.D. degree one of his articles, "How Good Is Your Speech?" which was published in the *Ladies Home Journal,* attracted wide attention.

His books, articles, and his lecture fees — especially his high school commencement addresses — provided him with an income which for a time exceeded his Wabash salary. His standard of living changed accordingly. When he came to Wabash in the 1920s, he drove a small Starr automobile with a motor that sounded like a sewing machine. As he prospered, he moved up to Buicks and traded for new models frequently. Until the coming of Frank Sparks with his Cadillacs, Brigance drove the biggest car on campus. It was a symbol of his success. His disposition to talk knowledgeably about the technical superiorities of the Buick led to student kidding about the "Brigance wheelbase." He did not mind. All such fun-poking he took in good grace.

He was never at a loss for words in situations that others would have found awkward. Students in the late 1920s repeated a story, probably untrue, of his retort to a Crawfordsville lady at some social function who said, "Dr. Brigance, my husband says you are a supreme egotist." "No, madam," he quickly replied. "I am only conscious of my unusual ability." Once I heard someone in his presence refer to his "genius" in public speaking. He did not deny it. He only commented, "Genius is the capacity for taking infinite pains." In the late 1930s at a long faculty meeting, Briggie proposed and asked approval for a new course which he called "Communicative Speech." His argument ran on at length. At one point Osborne interrupted him in his dry, crisp way, "Is there any speech which isn't communicative?" he asked. A titter ran over the faculty. But Brigance was unruffled. He launched into a technical discussion of different forms of speech. His distinctions may have been some-

3. First published in 1927.

what strained intellectually but his eloquence won faculty approval. His abundant self-confidence meant that, unlike some other prominent members of the "old faculty," Brigance was untroubled when President Sparks began appointing nationally prominent men with high salaries to key faculty positions after World War II. They would not overshadow him. He demanded and received parity in salary and in departmental budget support. Dr. Sparks enjoyed bargaining with him.

Briggie's confidence and his habitual concentration on details carried over to his hobbies. When I first knew him in my student years, he was an avid fisherman. He had an impressive array of rods, reels, lures, hooks and waders. Numerous photographs attested to his spectacular catches, many of them, I presume, in rivers and lakes in the Dakotas where he originally came from. He talked of fishing in general and of his personal experience in particular with the assurance of a professional. When he was in Hawaii, he turned to photography as a hobby, and for a number of years thereafter he produced hundreds of colored slides beautifully and expertly done. Again his discussion of cameras, light meters, film, developing processes, and so on was professional. When he took up golf in later years, he brought to bear on his game the intense concentration of which he was capable. He may not have been the best golfer at the Crawfordsville Country Club, but he was one of the most colorful. His companions used to laugh when he lay down on his stomach to line up his putts, but his putting game was quite good. Toward the end of life Briggie became increasingly deaf. No doubt it was a severe trial for him but he refused to admit it. George Kendall urged him to get a hearing aid, but perhaps out of pride he refused. Instead he worked hard at lip reading, and he did remarkably well at it. He had the "capacity for taking infinite pains."

Brigance was a devoted family man. Perhaps because he kept terribly busy at his professional work, he and his wife, Jane, were less active in faculty social life than were the families of other more relaxed professors. They were not, for example, regular participants in the Pine Hills picnic routines. Many of their close friends, perhaps most of them, were townspeople rather than faculty people. They were active in the Methodist Church, and for years Briggie was a popular and prominent figure in the Crawfordsville Kiwanis Club, an interest which, except for Gronert, most faculty members spurned. At any rate, his family was important to him. I remember being touched by the deference and affection with which he treated his elderly father who often visited Crawfordsville for weeks at a time. He doted on his only child, Shirley. She had her father's sharp intelligence and his self-assurance. When the family returned to Crawfordsville from Hawaii, Shirley for a time often gave exhibitions of Hula dancing. She performed expertly and confidently. Briggie was enormously proud of her on such occasions. They were the only times I can recall his having seemed a little shy.

Dr. Brigance died in 1961 soon after a heart attack he suffered while attending a speech convention in Washington, I believe. There was an unspoken feeling that Wabash would never be quite the same. The record he left behind him at Wabash was impressive. It included the credit reflected on the college by his numerous books. It included the large number of students who went on to distinguish themselves, and thus Briggie and Wabash, as teachers of speech — John Black at Ohio State University, Ray Ehrensberger at the University of Maryland, Jeff Auer at Indiana University, for example. It included his hand-picked Wabash successor, Vic Powell, and the continuation of a tradition of public speaking of high quality. It included the careers of innumerable former students, among whom I count myself as one, who in ways they might find difficult to define were influenced by his teaching.

The portrait of Briggie done after his death by Harold McDonald, which I trust still hangs on one of the walls of Center Hall's third floor, is a remarkably good likeness.[4] For some reason, however, it makes him appear to have been a smaller man than he was. Perhaps it is because his image on canvas is necessarily silent and Briggie in life rarely was.

ROBERT WALLACE BRUCE

I often used to wonder how it was that Bob Bruce came to be a member of the Wabash faculty. Was it because Dr. Mackintosh, on the advice of Professor Tapy, then chairman of the Department of Psychology, believed Bruce to be a brilliant young man of high promise who should be kept on at Wabash? Was it because Bruce didn't know what else he could do? Did he just drift into teaching at Wabash without thinking about it? — the bright, conscientious student suddenly finding that he has stayed on at his alma mater almost as an act of absence of mind? I never found a satisfactory answer to these questions, although it occurred to me that Bob Bruce was a classical example of the old sneer, "Those who can, do. Those who cannot do, teach." But whatever the reasons for his joining the Wabash faculty in the first place, his reasons for staying on until he retired were fairly obvious. For him teaching at Wabash was a pleasant, satisfying way of life. He was, or at least appeared to be, completely contented with his simple routine way of life, year after year, decade after decade.

Bruce began teaching psychology at Wabash the same year he graduated from the college with Phi Beta Kappa honors (1922). I assume he had been a star undergraduate major student of Professor Tapy. From that year until his retirement in the 1960s, except for a year or two in graduate school (University of Chicago) completing the Ph.D. degree, he was never far away from

4. The portrait now hangs in the lobby of the Humanities Center.

Wabash or Crawfordsville. Insofar as anyone came to "know" Bob Bruce, I became well acquainted with him. As an undergraduate I had a one-year course under him, following the introductory course I took with Tapy. I am sure I must have learned something from his teaching but except for his rather quaint method of instructing, I can recall nothing specific. In the late 1930s, I saw much of him, mostly in connection with comprehensive examinations for seniors, and later as dean of the college I worked with him as closely as anyone "worked with" Bob Bruce.

At the death of Professor Tapy in the early 1930s, Bruce became chairman of the psychology department. He continued in this position until in the late 1940s or perhaps the early 1950s, when Dr. Sparks brought Paul Fields (and later George Lovell) to Wabash as department chairman. During much of that time Bruce was a one-man department. He had no professional competition and no professional companionship. Not that he minded. I believe he enjoyed his solitary status. When Dr. Francis Mitchell was appointed in 1952 by Dr. Sparks to add strength to the department and to develop the college's teacher training program, Bruce gave him a completely free hand and made no effort at companionship. The coming of Paul Fields was a distressing experience for Bob. He acquiesced in giving up the department chairmanship, but he was obviously uncomfortable about the sweeping changes Fields made. His routine, comfortable habits were thrown awry. He made no complaint, but he was resentful, and he resisted the changes. When Fields resigned and George Lovell took his place, I believe Bruce was happier, partly because Dr. Lovell, after a number of vain efforts to draw Bob into a unified department structure, let him alone, free to go his own way.

As a teacher and staff member, Dr. Bruce had numerous commendable habits. Except when he was ill, and this was infrequent, he always met his classes punctually. His grades — mid-semester and semester — were always among the first to be turned in at the registrar's office. He was a dependable committee member, always present, always on time — and usually silent. He attended all faculty meetings although he rarely said anything. In oral examinations for seniors, he was a fascinating examiner. His deadpan, Buddha-like expression never betrayed to a student whether his answers were good or poor. Often he led students on until they were over their heads in deep psychological waters, to the vast amusement of other members of the faculty examining committee, especially Ormes.

His class teaching was another matter, pedestrian and repetitive. Few students found him exciting and most of his major students were mediocre in scholarship. I cannot think of a single psychology major who went on for graduate study in psychology while Bruce was chairman of that department. Students generally regarded him as a soft grader. Very few received failing grades. There was considerable student debate about whether Bruce read examination papers. This may have been a hold-over from the Tapy days when students boasted of filling up "blue books" for Professor Tapy with such irrelevant things as the words to "Old Wabash" and receiving their customary grades. That debate was settled when an enterprising student, on a dare, wrote a solid essay in his blue book in answer to one of Bruce's questions, but every now and then inserted in the body of his essay the words "Professor Bruce, if you have read this far, please check here." The blue book came back with each such comment neatly checked. Whether Bruce kept abreast of current professional scholarship in his field. I do not know, but I doubt that he did. Dr. Fields, who was often petulant about Bob, complained to me once he had discovered to his amazement, that Dr. Bruce in 1950 was still using a psychology laboratory manual which had been in vogue at the time of World War I.

After meeting one of his classes, Bob always went home until his next class. He would return to meet the next class, then go home again. It was a practice he repeated throughout the mornings. He was almost never in his office in the afternoon. He was at home (two blocks from the campus on Pike Street). When I was president and there was pressure for office space, which Dean Rogge brought to my attention, I assigned to someone else Bruce's office, which at the time was in the basement of the Chapel near the east stairwell. Days went by before Bob became aware of this. His complaint was mild. His absence from the campus in between classes and in the afternoon was a subject for joking and sometimes remonstrance. "What the hell does Bob Bruce do with all of that spare time?" Fergus Ormes once complained. Dean Kendall, who was present at the time, said with his broad grin, "Well, maybe he's writing an important book in secret." Someone else said, "Oh, forget it! He's madly in love still with Louise."

The latter of these remarks was nearer the truth. Bob Bruce was a devoted family man. Louise (Moon) Bruce and Bob were inseparable. They did almost no entertaining of others in their home and to the naked eye appeared to have no close friends. But they worked together in the Wabash Avenue Presbyterian Church where Bob for years sang in the tenor section of the choir and Louise was the organist, and at such interests as Lambda Chi Alpha, of which Bob had been a member in his student years. Theirs was a happy, self-sufficient kind of life together, and they remained youthful looking much longer than most people do. A few months after the fiftieth anniversary reunion of the class of 1922, during a dinner visit I had with Ivan Wiles in Arizona, Ivan regaled me with his humorous impressions of that reunion. "You know who looked the youngest and least changed at that reunion?" he asked. I had no idea. "Bob Bruce!" he said.

GEORGE CARSCALLEN

George Carscallen had to be seen and heard to be believed. None of Kin Hubbard's colorful Hoosier characters was more picturesque. Seeing him talking with someone at a downtown Crawfordsville street corner, a stranger might have guessed him to be a small-time farmer in town for an afternoon, an idler waiting for a chance call for jury duty, or maybe a hardware store clerk taking a break while business was slow, any number of things but what he really was — an associate professor of mathematics at Wabash College.

George Carscallen looked much the same in the 1950s as he looked in the 1920s. A lean, wiry little guy, he followed a spartan way of life that kept him fit and trim. In his undergraduate years at Wabash, he had been a track man with Cayou as his coach. (Perhaps it was for that reason that Lee McCanliss, a contemporary of Carscallen and also a track man, had a warm feeling toward George.) In the 1920s and the 1930s, he often worked out on the track or in the gymnasium. Even much later one would often see him sprinting across campus between Center Hall and Goodrich Hall. Students regarded him as something of a physical fitness nut.

Carscy was "preachy" about physical fitness and his preaching had moral, puritanical overtones. For years he scolded students about using tobacco and "ardent spirits." Even in his classes he would sometimes harangue students about the evils of "the weed." He was vocal in his distress when President Hopkins relaxed the college rule forbidding smoking on campus. He regarded fraternities as "dens of iniquity" and deplored the way they corrupted the young by promoting get-acquainted freshman "Smokers." This promotion of use of "the weed" also exemplified the exploiting grip of the big tobacco corporations, he insisted. It was all part of the greed of the acquisitive capitalistic society which he assailed from time to time.

It seemed altogether natural that, with such views, Carscallen was an avid student of boxing. "The manly art of self defense," he invariably called it. He could and often did talk at length about famous boxers of the past. Corbett was his greatest hero, but he liked Fitzsimmons, too. John L. Sullivan he considered a dumb clumsy ox by contrast with Corbett. Dempsey he dismissed as a Johnny-come-lately who had only power, no finesse. Gene Tunney was more to his liking, "a real boxer, not just a slugger." With a little encouragement in his younger years he would demonstrate "the art" by shadow boxing for a round or so. He was agile and quick on his feet — and comical.

His agility came out in his fiddle playing. He always said "fiddle" rather than violin and he referred to himself as a "fiddler." It was country music through and through, fast, loud, and simple. He raced through "Turkey in the Straw" as if his life depended on it, "stomping" the time with his right foot and perspiring freely. Often he played with his fiddle propped on his knee rather than under his chin. He loved to play for square dances and lamented the loss of interest in this pastime of his youth.

George had a corn-fed sense of humor. It came out in many ways. In illustration of some point he wanted to make, he often told a folksy story with a humorous twist to it. Whether others found such stories funny or not, he did. He didn't laugh. He cackled. And there was frequent cackling. He loved to talk about almost anything, always with very strongly expressed opinions. His speech was a curious mixture of colloquialisms and octosyllabic words. He was fond of using the word "pusillanimous" in expressing contempt for someone of whom he disapproved or of some idea which he opposed. In political arguments, which he enjoyed, he could be earthy in his comments as he was when he now and then referred to some candidate for office "as a whiskey-drinking, two-bit politician." I am sure George knew he was often the object of amusement and joking among students, but he didn't take offense. Instead, he seemed to enjoy it. For years in the winter time, he wore an ancient bear-skin coat which came almost to his ankles, with an ear-flapped hat to match. The good-natured kidding he received from students when he appeared so attired caused him only to beam with pleasure and to cackle about his own retorts.

Such interests and such attributes were enough to establish Carscy as a colorful adornment on the Wabash faculty for many years, a well known, well liked, eccentric professor, not to be taken seriously outside the classroom. In the 1950s George, in political and economic discussions, ceased to be funny. Newer faculty members especially found him an annoyance and a bore, and they usually alerted guest speakers whom they brought to campus to the probability of being bothered with questions from him. He had always been a Henry George-type socialist, suspicious of big business and critical of most politicians. He became interested in a bookish, superficial way in Communist Russia and in the Cold War period he blamed President Eisenhower and John Foster Dulles; he was outspoken in his criticisms of American foreign policy and belligerent in his defense of Russia. When some visiting scholar spoke in chapel about political, economic, or diplomatic matters, George could always be counted on to ask questions, often launching into a speech of his own. It was sometimes embarrassing for others, but never for George.

Coming from someone else in those tense years, George's comments might have led to serious questions about his being a communist. But no one took him seriously. Ted Gronert sometimes would try to argue with him but never for very long. Other faculty members tended to ignore him, and critics in town thought of him as a "crack-pot." It was all rather pathetic. In his later years this once popular and amusing professor was simply brushed aside.

George Carscallen, I believe, had a barren life apart from Wabash College. He had no close friends off campus. At home I suspect he was henpecked.

Mrs. Carscallen was an unattractive, whining kind of woman full of complaints and resentments. Clyde Rogers, a neighbor of the Carscallens, told me she had a bad temper and on occasion could swear like a fish wife. They had one son, Ernest, who graduated from Wabash but died not long afterward. After that bitterness Mrs. Carscallen became more plaintive about the world in general and I suspect more shrewish at home. George sagged, too, at the loss of his son, but if anything his life at the college became more important to him. His salary, always low, was their only income and their living routines were austere. George was notorious for his penny pinching. He bought his glasses at the dime store, experimenting until he found a pair that "worked." He used to boast about how he saved money with his Model A Ford by turning off the ignition at the top of hills and coasting to the bottom. Clyde Rogers told me that, at George's request, he saved his daily copies of the Crawfordsville *Journal-Review* and gave them to George the next morning. It was a saving of twenty-five cents a week.

How good was Carscy as a mathematician and teacher? I am not sure. Except for his pinch-hitting occasionally for Professor Cragwall, with whom I studied freshman mathematics, I never had a chance to witness Carscallen's teaching methods. He was businesslike, conscientious, and sure of himself. I have no doubt that with math majors he was a good craftsman at teaching in the old traditional style ("Well, gents, let's go to the blackboard to see what we know"). He took a very dim view of the "new math" when it was introduced after World War II, and was scornful of the excitement about "sets," "proportions," and the theory of numbers.

I once asked George why he decided to be a teacher. "Oh, I don't know" he said. "I was always good at figures, even as a little shaver, and at Wabash math was more interesting than all the other studies put together. There's nothing that beats math for finding the truth, you know. About my junior year I got a hankering to teach it. I never got over it, I guess." And he cackled at the thought.

FREDERICK CARL DOMROESE

Herr Professor Domroese was a curious study in contrasts. In the classroom he was a no-nonsense disciplinarian. Freshmen often found his classes in beginning German terrifying. Outside the classroom he was gentle, polite, and somewhat timid. No certified public accountant was ever more fastidious about financial accounting records than Domroese was with student academic records. The permanent record cards for Wabash students in the late 1920s and through the 1930s bear the impeccably neat entries made by Domroese as registrar. He prided himself on his beautiful script no less than on the exactness and accuracy of his entries. Rubrics and curlicues, carefully made, indicated interruptions in a student record or its completion. Accumulative point averages were meticulously compiled and conspicuously noted. Yet in the management of his own practical affairs he was naïve and careless. His close friend Neil Hutsinpillar told me Domroese didn't seem to understand his own personal bank account and was often overdrawn. Strangers encountering him on the streets of Crawfordsville found him formidable in appearance. His carriage and bearing were those of a military man in civilian clothes. His ramrod back, his firm stride, his bristling red mustache, his high stiff collars, his hat rolled to a peak in front and always squarely set on his head — all of this — suggested something straight out of Prussian barracks. But in fact, Domroese was shy, self-effacing and esthetic.

As a teacher Domroese was old-fashioned. His class load was heavy. His work as registrar was on an additional-duty basis. His first- and second-year classes were always fully enrolled in part, of course, because of the foreign language requirement for graduation. His advanced classes were small, but the quality of those students was always quite good. I studied under Domroese three years, and in no courses at Wabash did I work harder. His emphasis was on grammar, syntax, vocabulary, and pronunciation. It was rote learning with repeated oral drills and daily written quizzes. Although he spoke German in his classes often, his objective in class was a reading knowledge of the language. Little time was devoted to simple conversation in German. He loved German literature and especially admired Heine, Schiller and, of course, Goethe. As quickly as he could he led his students into reading German classics in class, moving from the simple stories and poems in the second year to heavy works in the third and senior years. I had reason to smile at this some years later when I found myself in Austria and Germany. I could read *Wilhelm Meister* but I couldn't ask directions for the men's room! Even so, in Austria, where I spent long periods of time, I soon discovered that the basic foundation in German grammar which Domroese gave me was an excellent base for learning to speak the language.

In the Mackintosh and Hopkins years, Domroese was a one-man department. He had good senior assistants such as Art Marr and George Metcalf in the late 1920s. In the thirties he occasionally had part-time help with his beginning classes. For a year or two after I returned to Wabash from Oxford I taught a section of beginning German. And Franz Prell, while serving as director of admissions, was even more regularly involved in assisting Domroese. Nevertheless, the department was a one-man enterprise. Not until Dr. Karl-Heinz Planitz came during the Sparks administration to be chairman did it take on the appearance of a full-fledged department.

Domroese had few major students but an impressive number of these went on to become teachers of German. George Metcalf became chairman of the Department of German Language and Literature at the University of Chicago. Professor Domroese was never self-conscious professionally, never eager to make a record for himself by turning out numerous majors. For him, communicating his love of German to freshmen and sophomores was as important, perhaps more important, than sending major students on to graduate school.

Nowhere did this kind of motivation show more clearly than in the German Club (*Der Deutsche Verein*) which Professor Domroese and his wife nourished and promoted. The dinner meetings of the club at the Domroese home on Meadow Avenue were always well attended and greatly enjoyed. Frau Domroese, a big, bluff, cheerful woman, was a superb cook. Always there were mountains of wonderful German food and, after the repeal of prohibition, an adequate supply of cold beer. There was an invariable program in German, perhaps a recitation, a reading, or even a short play. Always there was the singing of German lieder and a little speech in German by Herr Professor. It was all very *gemütlich* and the Domroeses seemed overjoyed at these simple parties. I smile to myself as even now, almost fifty years later, some of those German songs sung so lustily at the Domroese house come back to me with total recall.

Apart from the study and teaching of German, Domroese had three principal interests in life: (1) his family; (2) Wabash College; and (3) the Wabash Avenue Presbyterian Church. His wife and children were important to him. I have no doubt that within the family circle he was something of an autocrat. At the occasional family suppers when I was a guest, it was quite obvious that he was pater familias. Mrs. Domroese and the two children referred to him as "Professor." "Professor is not here," "Professor is at the college," "Professor is in his study," and so on. He idolized his daughter Charlotte, whom he often called "Carlotabess." She was a bright, cheerful girl, not unattractive, but never sought after by boys. She became a school teacher in Hammond. As she matured her good voice developed into a rich contralto. She was in demand as a soloist, and even after she moved away from Crawfordsville she often returned to sing on special occasions such as Easter or Christmas services at the Presbyterian Church. On such occasions Professor Domroese's face lit up with pride and love. (Charlotte died of cancer while still young.) Ewald, his son, was peculiar, often talking to himself as he stalked about Crawfordsville. He had talent as a painter and did innumerable photographic primitive-type water colors of campus buildings and faculty homes which he sold at modest prices. His father never gave any sign that Ewald was mentally handicapped. He referred to him affectionately as "the boy" and boasted with restraint of his artistic talent.

The Domroeses had no close friends with the exception of Neil Hutsinpillar. Hutsy was extremely good to the Domroeses, often taking them for a drive in his car and once in a while driving them to Indianapolis to visit relatives. It was a self-centered family and Professor Domroese spent most of his spare time at home indulging in one of his several hobbies. He was an avid stamp collector. He also played the violin — not well but with plenty of feeling. Hazel Gronert, who played first violin in the Crawfordsville Symphony Orchestra, once confessed to me that Domroese's playing "set her nerves on edge," and she had arranged for him to sit as far as possible from her in the orchestra. He also dabbled in painting. He studied with Fritz Schlemmer and, probably a little sooner than he should have, began to paint portraits. He took an embarrassed, shy kind of pleasure in showing his paintings to visitors.

Wabash gave Domroese a focal point for his life apart from his family. He loved the place and was enormously proud of it. Although he didn't attend athletic games, he followed closely the scores and admired the current athletic heroes. But he always attended other public functions at the college, usually with Ewald in tow — glee club concerts, lectures, recitals, oratorical contests. The Ouiatenon Club, with its mixture of professors and professional men from the town, never had a more conscientious member than Domroese. He never missed a meeting. Only once did I hear him read a paper to the club. He had obviously worked long and hard on his paper — something about Goethe, I believe — but it was a disaster. It was too long, too involved and obscure, and because of stage fright, I presume, Domroese's voice was even softer than usual. Few club members appreciated what he was reading, but for him it was clearly a performance of major importance.

The church was almost as important to Domroese and to his family as the college was. Every Sunday, rain or shine, hot or cold, they walked the ten or so blocks from their home to the church. If there were a mid-week service or a special meeting such as a Men's Brotherhood dinner, they were present for those also. Mrs. Domroese was an active member of one of the women's "circles." At church dinners and banquets she inevitably would be found in the church kitchen. For many years Professor Domroese sang in the bass section of the choir. He took his part there seriously and he enjoyed it He was always impressive to watch, but in all those years, although I sometimes made a point of straining to hear, I was never able to identify his individual voice.

In the 1920s and the 1930s, Frederick Domroese could correctly be called a prominent and valued member of the Wabash faculty. In the late 1940s and the early 1950s, that could no longer be said. More than most others of the "old" faculty, he was overshadowed by the "new" faculty and by the important changes that took place during the Sparks administration. He aged rapidly and gradually lost his proud erect bearing and brisk step. It was not just that he felt shunted aside. I believe World War II was an emotional ordeal for him. He never said much about the war and there was no question about his American loyalty. All the same he undoubtedly suffered emotionally because of the grisly conflict and the hatred it engendered for his fatherland which he loved At that, he did better than his predecessor at Wabash, Dr. King, who suffered through World War I much more deeply and ultimately committed suicide.[5]

THEODORE G. GRONERT

For more than forty years Ted Gronert was a prominent and popular figure on the Wabash campus. Until the last few of those years, he was an energetic and effective teacher, highly popular with students and greatly admired, even loved, in the Crawfordsville community.

Seeing him in an anonymous crowd a stranger might never have guessed that he was a highly trained historian with a quick, lively mind and a vast store of historical knowledge. He might more readily have been identified as a farmer or a cattle breeder. His ruddy complexion and calloused hands befitted a son of the soil. His full head of hair usually looked like an unkempt haystack and his loping gait, for some reason, always reminded me of newly-ploughed fields. He dressed carelessly in ill-fitting clothes. His trousers were invariably baggy at the knees. He had no sense of color harmony and his neckties, frequently showing food stains, clashed wildly with his shirts. Only his eyes, bright and alert and mischievous, gave a clue to the quality of his mind. When he talked one forgot about his appearance.

Gronert came to Wabash in the closing years of Dr. Mackintosh's presidency from Centre College in Kentucky, where he had been associate professor of history and head basketball coach. I always had difficulty visualizing him as a coach. He seemed to me to be too nervous, too awkward, and much too intellectual to excel as a coach. Nor did he show at Wabash any continuing professional interest in intercollegiate athletics. He rarely went to football games and never to basketball games. But he understood athletes in his classes, and he was always favorably disposed toward the college's athletic program. Moreover, on the tennis courts he habitually exhibited his keen competitive interest and his will to win.

Ted Gronert loved to play tennis and although he had an unconventional, awkward style, he was a formidable player. He specialized in a chopping stroke and in soft lobs which many opponents found infuriating. His left-handedness also seemed to confuse them. Although younger men played against him stylishly, it was hard to get a ball past him. He was everywhere on the court. I remember well my own sense of humiliation at being trounced badly in straight sets the first time I played him. Ted loved winning and often roared with laughter at the embarrassment he caused over-confident young opponents.

Laughter came easily and often for Ted. When he laughed it was not just a hearty chuckle. It was a paroxysm of booming guffaws. His face became crimson, tears came to his eyes. He bent double or sideways, beat his thighs

5. For an account of Dr. King's tragic suicide, see *The First Hundred Years*, pp. 288–89.

with his hands, held his head, and it went on and on. His was a keen sense of humor, sometimes a little corny with his fondness for bad puns, but always it was infectious. People around him felt cheered and carefree.

His happy disposition and enthusiasm came out in his teaching. His classes were always lively and often noisy. He was good at stimulating arguments among his students, arguments which frequently continued out of the classroom. Although he taught all branches of history, his first love was American history. (It was also the area of his greatest professional competency. Gronert did his Ph.D. work at the University of Wisconsin at the time when the American history department there was at the peak of its fame.) His introductory course in American history, given every year, was always crowded. In part this may have been because it was easy to make a grade of C in this course and there were few failures; but, more important, Gronert made the course a fascinating one, even for the dullest of students. Events of the past, the roles of individuals and the sweeping influences of grand developments — all became very much alive again in Gronert's skillful hands.

In his advanced classes for history majors, Professor Gronert was much more demanding. His assignments for library study were sometimes staggering in quantity, and the "research papers" he required were anything but simple. His standards for the grade of A were high and his examinations were tricky. He seemed not to be ambitious about sending his major students on to graduate school for advanced degrees in history. Those who elected to continue in history as a career, Professor Gronert helped. But he was equally interested in those who proposed to become lawyers or businessmen. He regarded history as a useful discipline for everyone, regardless of career objectives.

When I did my junior and senior work with him, Professor Gronert was in the early stages of writing the first half of the college history, scheduled for publication in the Wabash Centennial Year of 1932. He encouraged me and others to engage in research work in the college archives by way of helping him with the undertaking. It was my introduction to the records of the early years of Wabash history. I was fascinated by what I read, and I thus began a study of the history of the college and its people which I continued off and on for the rest of my years with Wabash.

In my senior year Ted asked me to be his assistant, a post annually assigned to a senior history major. In addition to grading quizzes for him, occasionally he asked me to conduct discussion sections for him or to tutor some lagging student in his office. Working with him in this way quickened my interest in teaching as a career, something President Hopkins had already suggested to me. It also led to a closer friendship with Ted and his wife, Hazel, with frequent visits in their home. At that time they were living in the Hovey Cottage, which then stood facing south in the area now occupied by Morris and Wolcott Halls.

It is difficult to imagine a person contrasting more sharply with Ted Gronert's personality than his wife Hazel. Ted was noisy, Hazel was quiet. He was untidy, she was neat. He was outgoing and extroverted, she was introspective and artistic. She was a concert violinist, once of great promise, but in the Crawfordsville years she limited her playing to the college community and that she did only rarely. But in her home she played for her own love of music. Once or twice she played at my request. It was a joy to hear.

Ted Gronert was not a "productive scholar" in the professional sense. He was casual about attending professional meetings and made no effort to write and read learned papers. When he took the trouble, he could write well, but his few publications were colloquial and folksy. (See his *Sugar Creek Saga.*[6]) He didn't pretend to be that kind of an historian. He regarded himself as a teacher both on and off campus. He was an indefatigable reader — newspapers, magazines, books, learned journals. He was particularly interested in current political events and enjoyed interpreting those events to anyone who would listen.

He was in great demand as a public speaker, primarily in Crawfordsville, but to some extent farther afield. Service clubs, women's clubs, study groups, patriotic societies — all such turned to Dr. Gronert for a "guest speaker." He enjoyed this kind of thing and was good at it. He was always teaching and admonishing and never failed to include an inspirational note in his speeches and elements of reassurance. Small town Hoosier audiences were greatly impressed.

No Wabash faculty member has ever done more for good relations between the college and the town of Crawfordsville than Ted Gronert. He had a rapport with townspeople that was wholesome, happy, and instructive. Most faculty members regarded membership in one or another of the town's service clubs as a chore. Along with Brigance, Gronert regarded his membership in the Kiwanis Club as something to be enjoyed and to be worked at whole-heartedly. He was the only faculty member to take an active part in the local American Legion Post. He served as post commander one year and was highly respected and esteemed by his fellow Legionnaires. He once told me that he regarded his work in the Legion as both enjoyable and important. "Most faculty members sneer at the Legion and what it stands for," he said, "But these [Legion members] are good people and I can help them in their prejudices. They listen to me." And he did help them and thus Wabash, too.

Ted Gronert in many ways was a "typical college professor," often lost in thought, forgetful about practical matters, and "absent minded." He now and then burnt out his automobile engine because he forgot to check the oil.

6. *Sugar Creek Saga; a History and Development of Montgomery County* (Crawfordsville: Wabash College, 1958).

He was not infrequently the butt of jokes about such matters.[7] But he had a kind of shrewdness and foresight that belied this reputation. Although his income was never large, he was prudent with his money. He never bought anything unless he could pay cash for it, including his house on Kennedy Place. He always had savings. At the height of the Great Depression, he bought General Motors stock at its lowest price level and held on to it as the economy recovered. When he died he left to Wabash a respectable, tidy estate gift.

After the death of his wife in 1959, Ted was a lonely man. The uproarious laughter subsided. He devoted more and more of his time to gardening, at which he was always successful. He kept his neighbors supplied with green vegetables from spring to early fall. It was a characteristic pattern for a very warm-hearted, kind and generous man.

LLOYD B. HOWELL

Of the several Wabash professors about whom I am writing, none had a larger or more devoted following among his former major students than Lloyd B. Howell. From the time he became chairman of the Department of Chemistry, late in the Mackintosh administration, until he was succeeded as chairman by Dr. Edward Haenisch about 1950, "Doc" Howell turned out an outstanding stream of chemistry majors. In impressive numbers they went on to obtain their Ph.D. degrees and then to important careers in chemistry. They became research chemists in industry, several rising to become top executives in their respective companies (e.g., Tom Mastin at Lubrizol; Bill Haines at Johnson & Johnson; Dick Schreiber at Upjohn) or they became university professors or administrators (e.g., Dick Byerrum, academic dean at Michigan State University). In addition to these, there were any number of medical doctors who as premedical students at Wabash studied with Doc Howell.

The record achieved by Wabash in science in the twentieth century is one of the college's claims for national distinction. Considering the college's size, it is an amazing record worthy of the national recognition it won in studies dealing with the undergraduate origin of doctorates in science. Quite apart from that, the strength of the Wabash science departments and the graduation

7. One fall night in the late 1930s when my wife and I were living at 414 West Wabash I heard a crash on Wabash Avenue, and at the same instant all our lights went out. I rushed out on our front porch, but could see nothing. I could hear an automobile starter grinding away fruitlessly. Finally, I made out a car stacked up against an electric light pole on the campus side of the street. It was Ted's car. He had come out of the campus drive, turned right and, not correcting his steering, kept moving to the right, crashing into the utility pole and dislocating the neighborhood transformer which was attached to it. "I was a little late for a speaking engagement," he explained to me lamely. It was small wonder people didn't like to ride with Ted when he was driving. BKT.

requirement of two years of laboratory science had much to do with the reputation Wabash enjoyed as a rigorous place of learning. For almost three-quarters of the century, there was no "soft option" in science for Wabash students as there usually was at other colleges. (It troubled me when I learned that in the 1970s the faculty had finally relaxed this tough requirement.)

In all of this Lloyd Howell for years played an influential role. As an undergraduate at Wabash he studied under Garner, a faculty hero of an earlier era. Garner undoubtedly made a deep impression on Lloyd Howell. He used to refer to Garner with great respect. Perhaps he also inherited from Garner some of the attitudes that came out of the bitter schism in the Wabash faculty between the scientists and the humanists in the first decade of the twentieth century. For Doc Howell the discipline of science, especially chemistry, was on a level which could not be approached or even comprehended by the more commonplace disciplines of the humanities.

After graduating from Wabash and staying on for a year as an instructor, Doc Howell completed his Ph.D. studies at the University of Illinois. He was an instructor there briefly and then moved to Rice Institute in Houston. He was appointed chairman of the Wabash Department of Chemistry by President Mackintosh in 1924. No doubt it was like coming home. He never dreamed of leaving Wabash thereafter. With his family, his work at Wabash, and his interests in Crawfordsville, he appeared to be a supremely contented man.

Doc Howell ran the chemistry department with an iron hand. In old Peck Hall and later in Goodrich Hall it was tacitly understood that the chemistry area was a private Howell kingdom. No one dared to trespass or interfere. Subordinate chemistry teachers came and went during the years of Howell's chairmanship. They were always clearly subordinates with nothing to say about departmental policy. To some extent Doc Howell exercised the same kind of influence throughout all science departments, especially in the physical sciences. Until the coming of Dr. Duane Roller in 1944, the Department of Physics played second fiddle to chemistry. In 1928 with the adoption of the "new" curriculum, Howell was made chairman of Division I. He was very much in command of the division throughout the 1930s. Dr. Bechtel, Dr. Paul Scott (zoology), Dr. Polley (mathematics) and George Horton (physics) were generally quite deferential to his chairmanship. When Dr. Willis Johnson returned to Wabash after World War II to head the biological sciences, Doc Howell's domination of the science division began to be diluted somewhat. Johnson, another towering figure in the history of Wabash science departments, had a very sturdy mind of his own. In due time he succeeded Howell as chairman of Division I.

Howell's reputation as a ferocious teacher was the most formidable on campus in the 1920s and the 1930s. The quantitative and qualitative demands he made on his students were staggering. His department was no place for the casual, easy-going student. He was a ruthless grader. Students in beginning chemistry flunked the course in large numbers, often in the first semester. Doc Howell showed no mercy. He was polite but unyielding to all special entreaties. He flunked his own son, Gilbert, in his first year in chemistry. His major students understood that their obligations to the study of chemistry came ahead of all other study obligations. If something had to yield in a student's schedule of classes, it was never chemistry. If some subject had to be slighted in class preparation, it better not be chemistry. Chemistry majors in the senior year often had to forego participation in intercollegiate athletics or had to decline attendance at the Turkey Run Senior Study Camps. They were too busy in the chemistry laboratories.

This way of running the chemistry department led to frequent student criticisms, not from Doc Howell's majors but from others. Premedical students especially complained of Doc Howell's unreasonable requirements. Again and again a promising pre-med student found himself in trouble because of failing grades in chemistry. He had to take chemistry a second time in summer school elsewhere in order to qualify for entrance to medical school.[8]

The allegation was made that Howell discriminated against a student unless he intended to major in chemistry. It was an unfair criticism probably, but it was abundantly clear that Doc Howell's primary interest was directed toward future chemists, not to future medical doctors and least of all to the general student who simply wanted some exposure to chemistry. Faculty leaders outside of the science division became increasingly restive about this situation.

When I returned to Wabash as dean of the college in 1946, this was one of the first major academic problems I began to brood about. The returning veteran students were less docile than their predecessors and the complaints of the pre-medical students among them could not be ignored. Much as I admired and liked Doc Howell, I concluded that the time had come to change the department chairmanship. It was a conclusion I reached after much thought and consultation with others, including Dean Kendall and Willis Johnson. When I discussed the problem with President Sparks, his response was characteristically decisive. He said in effect, "O.K., let's find a new chairman from outside the college." He set to work at once to locate candidates.

On one of our trips East together, Dr. Sparks and I arranged a get-acquainted visit with Dr. Edward Haenisch, then chairman of the chemistry department at Villanova University. We talked with him at length in a hotel in Philadelphia. We both liked him and he obviously was interested in coming

8. While dean, I made a study of the records of successful young doctors who had done their pre-medical work at Wabash. The number who, while doing well in all other studies at Wabash, had failed or barely squeezed by in chemistry was shockingly high. BKT.

to Wabash, notwithstanding the touchy situation the relieving of Dr. Howell would entail. I reviewed that situation with Haenisch at considerable length. What had been intended as a purely exploratory conversation concluded on a definitive note. Dr. Sparks and I came back to Crawfordsville to inform Dr. Howell. That conference took place in my office with Dean Kendall joining Frank and me for the lengthy discussion. Dr. Howell, while reluctant to give way to a newcomer, was milder in his resistance than I had expected him to be. His sourest note was struck when Frank told him he proposed to increase his salary substantially. I believe Doc Howell regarded that announcement as something of a bribe. But he seemed actually to like the idea of devoting his time in the future exclusively to major chemistry students.

This change unquestionably hurt Doc Howell's pride, and there was a flurry of resentment expressed by his loyal alumni. Thereafter, he tended to be more withdrawn from the center of college life, and although he cooperated politely, he never fully accepted Dr. Haenisch. Haenisch deserves a chapter in someone's memoirs about Wabash, if for no other reason than his amazing courage and cheerfulness in the face of terrible physical suffering he endured some years later. His professional pedigree was more impressive than Doc Howell's, and he had a wider, more generous view of the role of chemistry in a liberal arts college. Little by little he won the support of the Howell men and he began to establish his own record for turning out Wabash chemists of distinction. He was more accommodating to pre-medical students and to general students who had no interest in majoring in chemistry. It was a happy appointment for the college, and yet I never got over feeling somewhat sorry for Doc Howell.

In spite of his devotion to chemistry *über alles,* Doc Howell was another example of Wabash alumni faculty members who forever ran an "Old Wabash" temperature. He was an enthusiastic follower of Wabash athletics, all sports. He was proud of the tough reputation of the college and in a way identified with the "Hell Roaring 500" image of the college. He took a keen and continuing interest in his fraternity chapter, Lambda Chi Alpha. He enjoyed speaking in chapel and at student meetings of one kind and another. He was a puritan in his habits and his moral attitudes. His speeches were full of old-fashioned, paternalistic advice — hard work, honesty, moral rectitude.

His wife, Ione, was prominently associated with him in this aspect of Doc Howell's role at Wabash. A warm-hearted, outgoing person, she loved to chaperone fraternity dances, to entertain students informally in the Howell home, to serve as something of a mother confessor for students in trouble. Strait-laced about moral conduct, she nevertheless was tolerant of "weaknesses" of youth and fretted like a mother hen when her favorites were in trouble. She was enormously busy and helpful in women's activities at the college, at the church, at the Masonic Temple. She was popular with students and, in the post-World War II period, with the student wives. She died suddenly of a heart attack while attending a meeting of student wives in the upstairs south room of the Campus Center. I remember rushing from my office to the Center that night and being amazed by Doc Howell's calmness and his steadiness despite the great shock.

As was the case with so many other Wabash faculty members, the Wabash Avenue Presbyterian Church was important to Doc Howell. He was a senior elder and he took his responsibilities seriously. For years he was a familiar figure as an usher, as a collector of contributions, as a Sunday School teacher, as a key figure in meetings of the Session, and as a member of the Board of Trustees. He also was a serious-minded participant in the Masonic Lodge.

Perhaps it was his religious faith or his Masonry or both that made him seem serene and at peace during his retirement years. After the death of Mrs. Howell, he continued to live at Mills Place, virtually on the campus, with his youngest daughter. When I last saw him he was working in his garden, pausing now and then to smoke his pipe.

NEIL HUTSINPILLAR

I encountered Neil Hutsinpillar as a teacher in the second semester of my freshman year at Wabash. My impressions of him as a person and my opinion of him as a teacher were quite unfavorable. And I said as much in a theme I wrote for Insley Osborne, either that semester or perhaps the first semester of my sophomore year.

Part of the difficulty, I am sure, stemmed from the fact that I was first exposed to Osborne as a teacher of English. As is clear from what I have written about him elsewhere, I idolized Insley Osborne. From the first class meeting when I studied under him, my attitude toward him was one of great admiration mixed with awe. The contrast Hutsinpillar presented I found shocking. His precise mannerisms and his monotonous, dry-as-dust instructional methods irritated me. Even his occasional witticisms seemed pedantic to me. He methodically arranged that first class alphabetically. The back row ran (Al) Steele, (Harold) Stick, (Joe) Stone, Trippet, (Ken) Wood. When he called the roll it was obvious that Hutsy enjoyed the Steele, Stick, Stone, Trippet, Wood sequence. "Too bad your name isn't Tamarac or Turpentine or something like that," he would occasionally remark to me with pleasure. I found it excessively boring.

I do not remember what I wrote in that theme for Osborne. No doubt it was a brash, immature criticism of Hutsy and, as I later concluded, very unfair. But whatever it was, it troubled Osborne. When I had my next "theme conference" with him, he made no criticisms of my sentence structure or of my choice of words as he usually did. Instead he went immediately to the heart of the matter. "You are writing about Hutsy, aren't you?" he began. (I had not used Hutsinpillar's name in my paper.) "Yes," I said, half afraid of what was coming next. Osborne went on to talk quietly at some length about Hutsy. I was surprised and pleased by the intimacy of the talk. He acknowledged that Hutsinpillar was often considered a dull teacher, especially by good students and especially in the freshman year. He made it clear that he and Hutsy had talked about the problem and that Hutsy had even suggested that perhaps he should give up teaching and go back to his family business in Ohio. But Insley also stressed Hutsy's good points as a teacher — his good training in linguistics, his conscientiousness and fairness, his sympathy for the plodding student, his willingness to go to extraordinary lengths to help students who wanted to improve. He ended up by saying something to the effect, "And Hutsy is a good person to have around, a very fine person and a gentleman. I hope you will suspend judgment on him for a little while longer."

I was wrong about Neil Hutsinpillar and Insley was right. He *was* a "good person to have around." With the passage of time, I came to appreciate the good qualities in Hutsy's work and the excellence of his attributes as a human being. In a way it was something of a lesson for me. I learned that the effectiveness of a faculty member cannot always be judged by his performance in the classroom nor by the "results" he achieves in the short run. More important is his impact over a long period of time, the judgments expressed years later by those who were once his students. Many times as dean and later president, I thought of Hutsy when it came to evaluating the effectiveness of individual professors. Thinking of him helped me to appraise others.

I never modified my opinion that Neil Hutsinpillar was a pedestrian kind of teacher. But notwithstanding that, I came to regard Hutsy as worth his weight in gold to Wabash in other ways. His rub-their-noses-in-it way of teaching English composition unquestionably led a long line of Wabash freshmen to speak and to write English a little better than they had. For some advanced students his survey of English literature, while perhaps never exciting or inspiring, opened new and wider doors to the enjoyment of reading. But this sort of thing was less important than the countless little things Hutsy did for students. He had a quiet, friendly way with students in trouble. The lonely, the discouraged, the misfits, often sought his counsel and his companionship. I doubt that he did much counseling, but he was an excellent listener and by sympathetic questions led such students to unburden themselves to him. It was good therapy. Although he took pains to conceal it, he often helped by "advancing" a little money to those in need, forgetting, I have no doubt, the repayments.

Returning alumni who had studied with him invariably asked about him and often went to spend an hour with him. I was pleasantly surprised when I learned that among such alumni it was common to find the toughest of former athletes and the playboys as well as the "poor souls." It would be difficult to imagine a faculty member less inclined toward athletic endeavor than Hutsy. He didn't coordinate well physically and was always a little dainty in his movements, but he took more than passing interest in athletes and athletics. He attended home games regularly for many years. He never cheered, but his Wabash bias was nonetheless unmistakable.

Neil Hutsinpillar had a memory like an elephant. Especially where Wabash events and Wabash people were concerned, his powers of specific recall were amazing. Names, dates, places, events, quotations — for all such things Hutsy was a living, dependable memory bank. "Ask Neil. He will remember," became a stock phrase around campus when something out of the past was being uncertainly discussed. Years after the facts, Hutsy, when talking with returning alumni, could tell them exactly where they sat in the classroom with him. He remembered their home towns, their fraternity affiliations, the positions they played on the football team or the baseball team. Often he remembered members of their family and asked about them. In the middle 1930s he and John Tomlinson spent a long weekend with me at my parents' home in Princeton. Years later he recalled for me exactly what we had done, the places we visited in Evansville, the first names of my mother and father, and so on.

Now and then the chapel committee would ask Hutsy to speak in chapel. Especially in later years his chapel speeches, which he wrote in a college blue book and methodically read, had to do with what Wabash was like in the 1920s or the 1930s. They were always matter of fact, routine accounts intersperced with droll observations. I found them fascinating and so did most of the faculty, although many students slept through his remarks.

Hutsy's habitual kindness to students extended to faculty members. Everyone liked him. He was a welcome dinner guest whenever a faculty party was given. He was regularly called on to make up a fourth at bridge when a fourth was needed or to squire some lady temporarily without an escort to a party or a Dramatic Club play. At the faculty picnics in Pine Hills or at the numerous dinner parties at the Kendalls, Hutsy was always present, always a willing helping hand. Yvonne Kendall was very fond of him and took delight in teasing him in one way or another. He responded always with good nature and frequently with dry wit.

Although he was socially a member of the "in" group, he was on close friendly terms with those in the "out" group. He was thoughtful about people like the Bechtels and the Carscallens, who never mixed with the faculty socially. He was enormously kind to the Domroeses, perhaps their only close friend in the community. After Hazel Gronert died, I tried to spend time with Ted Gronert in his home once a week. He seemed increasingly withdrawn to

116

me and he began to have health problems of his own. Once he said to me, as if sensing what was on my mind, "Don't worry, Byron. Neil Hutsinpillar calls me every morning just to check up on me." It was characteristic of Hutsy.

Including his retirement years, Neil Hutsinpillar spent more than a half century on the Wabash campus. It was his home and the most important thing in his life. But he was not as provincial as this may sound. He had independent private income from a family hardware business in his home community near Gallipolis, Ohio. His Wabash salary, even after World War II, was low. But he never lacked money. His tastes were simple and he lived prudently but he indulged himself when he chose to do so. For many years he always had good cars — once or twice a convertible coupe — which he drove sparingly and gingerly. He traveled widely and frequently in the summer time — throughout the United States, often to Europe, a little in Latin America. He was a confirmed bachelor by plan. He told me once the responsibility of a wife and children, when he had thought of such things, scared him. He made careful blue chip investments and prospered modestly. He was conservative by nature and a quiet Republican in the midst of liberal Democrats. He refused to take retirement pay when the time came to retire. He said he didn't need it and didn't believe in such things. Instead he made gifts now and then to the college. Characteristically, the most important of these was a fund he established after talking with me in the early 1960s to provide travel grants to long-time women employees of the college.[9] "The college tends to forget people like Mary Schlemmer and Frances Scott," he said, "but they are important, too."

Such insights as I have into the personality and character of Neil Hutsinpillar came not while I was a student at Wabash, but later. In the year 1930–31, when I stayed on to fill John Tomlinson's post while he completed his Ph.D. degree, Ted Henshaw, Jim Paterson and I shared an apartment upstairs in Neva Chapman's house at 513 South Grant Avenue. We invited Neil to take his dinners with us. It was the beginning of a new appreciation of this man. In 1934–35 and 1935–36 Hutsy, John Tomlinson and I maintained an apartment (the east side of a duplex) on West Jefferson Street. Without anyone planning it, Hutsy became the house manager, keeping the accounts, managing the cook-housekeeper, and generally running the place. It was a happy household, sometimes a little boisterous for Hutsy but lots of fun for him. John Coulter often ate the evening meal with us, after which there were long hours of bridge or belote. Hutsy, an excellent but exceedingly deliberate bridge player, made John Coulter, who played with verve and dash, restless. "My God, Neil," he once exclaimed, "I could run down to the Silver Dollar for a

9. Since his death, the Hutsinpillar Fund has provided recreational and travel monies for the college staff.

117

beer and be back before you make up your mind what to play." Hutsy was absteemish and old maidish about his drinking. But there was one memorable exception brought on by Hutsy's innocence about alcohol. One cold winter evening Tommy and I came home from a Division III meeting to find Hutsy in his favorite chair reading or trying to read his customary *Time* magazine, but obviously quite tight. "What the hell happened to you, Neil?" one of us said. "I don't really know," said Hutsy obviously troubled. "This beer seems awfully strong. The bottles on the back porch were almost completely frozen and I had to pour from several to get just one stein of beer." He had been drinking straight alcohol!

Sometime after both John Tomlinson and I were married, Hutsy moved into the Hovey Cottage when the Gronerts vacated it for their home on Kennedy Place. When Hovey Cottage was moved to its location just west of the old gymnasium to make room for the Campus Center and the two dormitories, Hutsy moved with it. When Hovey Cottage was moved from that location to the cluster of original college buildings near the Caleb Mills House, Hutsy again moved with it. And there, as I write this account of him, he continues to live, a revered figure at Wabash. He must be ninety.

Neil Hutsinpillar, after an interview with Doc Mack in Chicago, came to Wabash in 1920 without ever having seen the place. He fell in love with Wabash and Wabash with him. It makes me wonder. How can you have a story book college without a "Hutsy" every fifty years or so?

WILLIS JOHNSON

I am illustrating my general observations about the Wabash faculty by writing profiles of specific professors all of whom were appointed by President Mackintosh and all of whom continued at Wabash until their retirement.

Strictly speaking, Willis Johnson does not fall into this category. His lengthy service as a faculty member was broken by a decade at Stanford University. But I like to think of his years at Stanford as an interlude of preparation for his final long stint as a Wabash professor. Moreover, during his years at Stanford he was really never out of touch with the college. He took with him to Stanford some of his Wabash associates — Dr. Joe Oliphant, for example. He regularly returned to Crawfordsville to visit his family, and on such trips he invariably spent time with faculty friends on campus. Emotionally his ties with Wabash were never broken. I can identify with that kind of deep personal attachment to the college, and I therefore include him in the small band of Wabash teachers whose memory I am honoring in these pages.

Willis Johnson was appointed a Wabash instructor by Dr. Mackintosh in 1925. Except for a year's leave of absence to complete his graduate work at the University of Chicago, he continued as a faculty member under Dr. Hopkins. When Dr. Graves resigned in 1928, Hopkins made Johnson, despite his youth and despite his not yet having a Ph.D. degree, chairman of the Department of Zoology. In the mid-1930s he accepted an appointment at Stanford University, where he organized and directed an experimental basic course in the combined biological sciences. At the close of World War II President Sparks persuaded him to return to Wabash as chairman of the Department of Zoology and administrative head of the biological sciences. The appointment was made in time for Willis to play an important role in planning the internal arrangement of Waugh Hall. As I write this, he is still teaching at Wabash although semi-retired, and he continues to be an influential senior faculty member.

Willis Johnson's involvement with the Wabash faculty thus spans a half century. He has served under six Wabash presidents and two acting presidents (Shearer and Misch). This in itself must be something of a record in the history of the college. More important than that, however, is the very considerable impact on the life of the college which he made by his strength of character and by his dedication to the teaching of science as an essential part of the liberal arts.

Willis grew up almost in the shadow of the college. His parents were not college people but through their children Wabash became something of a way of life for them. Willis was the first to become involved in the college. His brother, David, followed him as an undergraduate. He too became a zoologist and for years was chairman of the Department of Zoology at Indiana State University. His sister, Mary Johnson Schlemmer, became a member of the Wabash staff in the early 1930s. She began as secretary to Ted Henshaw in the alumni office. In the closing years of the Hopkins administration, she became assistant to Fergus Ormes in his role as comptroller. As the business office expanded after World War II, Mary's responsibilities grew. When she retired, she had worked for Wabash for more than thirty years.

Willis was a student at Wabash at the peak of the "Hell Roaring 500" era. He was not prominent as an athlete but he was a sturdy competitor and at the Lambda Chi Alpha house, which throughout the 1920s boasted the largest collection of football and basketball heroes in the college, he was the close companion of athletes. Small wonder it is that he was an avid supporter of the college's athletic teams. For years he regularly attended home games and usually saw football games with Butler in Indianapolis and with DePauw in Greencastle. He was less noisy in his Wabash partisanship than Myron Phillips or Warren Shearer, but he felt no less deeply about Scarlet victories and defeats than they did. He believed in and was proud of the robust traditions of the college.

It was the academic life of the college, however, which held the greatest appeal for him and the greatest challenge. He had an enormous respect for his principal teachers not only in science but also in the humanities and the social sciences. He was graduated with Phi Beta Kappa honors and was awarded the John Maurice Butler prize for scholarship and character. He and I never talked about it, but my guess is he must have felt as I later did that joining the Wabash faculty was a matter of personal destiny.

His work at the college was a totally consuming interest. He and his wife, Elizabeth, lived quietly in the college community and took little part in the social life of the faculty. They built a pleasant home on South Grant Avenue, raised two children — the son, John, graduating from Wabash — and they attended strictly to their own business. So far as I could tell Willis had no hobbies other than gardening. Like Ted Gronert, he had a "green thumb" and his vegetable garden was envied by his neighbors. Unlike Ted Gronert, he also was devoted to and successful at growing flowering plants and shrubs. He spent hours maintaining an immaculate lawn.

He faithfully attended services at the Wabash Avenue Presbyterian Church, but unlike Howell, Bechtel and other professors, he played no active role in the affairs of the church. He continued his interest in Lambda Chi Alpha and repeatedly gave counsel and assistance to the chapter in routine fraternity problems. In the 1950s and the 1960s he was regarded by undergraduate members of the chapter with a respect that bordered on awe. I suspect there was a mixture of apprehension in their respect. As one chapter president put it to me when we were discussing some chapter crisis in the dean's office, "For all of his preaching at us, Doc Howell never bothers us. But when Dr. Johnson lets loose at a chapter meeting, he scares the pants off of us!"

However quiet and simple his private life may have been, his life as a faculty member was exceedingly full and diversified. In the Hopkins years and even more so after World War II, he was one of those hard working dependable faculty members who could be called on by the administration to help with all manner of college affairs and college problems — attending alumni meetings and banquets for prospective students, entertaining visiting lecturers or candidates for faculty appointments, working with ad hoc committees on policy questions or institutional problems, courting potential donors, conferring with trustees, and so on. All such assignments were in addition to the demands of regular faculty committee duties, of which Willis always bore a heavy share.

Willis readily accepted such additional duties and invariably he performed well. He was particularly good with trustees, who regarded him highly and attached importance to what he had to say. He, John Collett and Frank Misch had been classmates at Wabash, and he and Allen Saunders had been young faculty members together. He thus had a rapport with these and other Wabash trustees which most faculty members did not have. They felt they could "level" with Willis about college problems and that he would "level" with them. His friendship with Norman Treves, as I have noted elsewhere, had much to do with the substantial bequest Dr. Treves left to the college.

It is remarkable that, notwithstanding such numerous and time consuming services as these, Willis Johnson managed to meet his teaching obligations and keep his professional standards at an extraordinarily high level. He put severe demands on himself in his teaching and his academic administrative responsibilities. In addition he engaged in continuing research projects as an example to those who worked with him, as well as for the sake of keeping professionally alert and alive himself.

He ran the Department of Zoology and Waugh Hall with a very firm hand. He was courteous and thoughtful about it, but there was never any doubt about who was in charge. Dr. Richard Laubengayer, chairman of the Department of Botany, was often plaintive about the situation, but once when he and I were discussing his grievances he conceded that Willis was fair and just, as well as firm. When he succeeded Dr. Howell as chairman of the science division, Willis was equally businesslike in "running" the entire science program at Wabash.

The attitudes of mind and standards of performance which characterized his administrative work were reflected in his teaching. He was methodical, thorough, and patient. He was also tough. His courses were meticulously well-organized and tightly scheduled. His successful textbook for introductory college courses in biology (written in collaboration with DeLanney, Laubengayer, and Williams) gives a good indication of his orderly approach to the teaching of biology.[10] Some students found his lecturing voice strident, and others considered the work load he demanded unreasonable. But even those who chafed at the required course in biology respected him for his competence as a teacher and for his fairness. For major students in zoology, and there were many, he was an inspiration.

The general student reaction to Johnson as a teacher was one that I fully shared. In my sophomore year I began the study of zoology. For the most part my work was with Dr. Wiley Crawford, but now and then Willis would lecture to the class in connection with laboratory experiments we were about to undertake. He was at the time a very young teacher, yet I remember how my interest quickened when he talked to us, while demonstrating the purpose of the newly assigned experiments. There was an intensity about his instruction that impressed me greatly. When he took us step by step through demonstrations that "ontogeny recapitulates phylogeny," I was fascinated. It was his influence that spurred me to read Darwin's *Origin of Species,* which in turn caused me later to audit Johnson's course on evolution.

10. *Essentials of Biology* was first published in 1969 by Holt, Rinehart, and Winston (New York).

On the place of science in the Wabash curriculum, he was a "hard liner." He believed that some basic knowledge of both the physical sciences and the biological sciences as well as some solid experience with the scientific method were essential in liberal education. He took a dim view of "soft options" in the science requirement for graduation. But unlike Dr. Howell, who was impatient with and sometimes rude to "non-science" students in chemistry classes, Willis was tolerant and understanding with such students in biology, and he went to extraordinary lengths to help them. I dare say it was a bitter blow for Willis when the Wabash faculty recently diluted the science requirement for graduation.

In the never-ending faculty discussions about curriculum issues in the 1950s and '60s, Johnson's "hard lining" was not confined to science. His initial experience as a faculty member coincided with the time when young faculty members, led by Osborne, achieved a complete renovation of the Wabash curriculum. He probably took little part in the lengthy exercises that led to the adoption of the "new" curriculum in 1928. But, judging from his later role on the faculty, he was deeply impressed by the educational philosophy which undergirded that curriculum. Thirty years and more later he could be counted on to resist strenuously any curriculum revision proposals which in his judgment circumvented the rigors of the now "old" curriculum.

He opposed relaxation of distribution requirements. He fought against the introduction of "cross over" options in divisional concentration — combining a major in one division with a minor in another division. He resisted efforts of new faculty members to make the required freshman course in Contemporary Civilization optional. For several years in the 1930s, he had taught a section of that course, and he was a staunch believer in its objectives. He successfully opposed the proposals to permit students to "postpone" one or another of the regular freshman requirements.

Restless new young faculty members often despaired of such conservative influences as Willis Johnson's in faculty debates. "He simply wants to embalm the old curriculum," John Forbes used to complain. But Willis over the years probably supported more proposals for updating the academic program at Wabash than he opposed. His educational conservatism was rooted in his dislike of whatever he regarded as superficial, faddish, or frivolous. Against these he was a defender of the Wabash faith.

Generally Johnson was quiet at faculty meetings, but on the academic and moral questions that from time to time came before the faculty, there was never the slightest doubt about what he stood for and what he stood against. And when he spoke his logic and his earnestness were often decisive. His remarks lacked Osborne's incisiveness, and they were unrelieved by Osborne's flashes of wit and humor. Nevertheless, it might be said that Johnson was Osborne's successor as "the conscience of the faculty."

The record of Wabash students who majored in the biological sciences and who went on to distinguish themselves in education, in research, and in medicine has been an impressive one throughout the twentieth century. But never has it been more illustrious than in the decades associated with Willis Johnson's tenure as a faculty member. He would be the first to disclaim personal credit for the brilliance of this record. He would point, instead, to his colleagues in both botany and zoology, and with good reason he would attribute to their teaching and their example in research the astonishing flow of biology majors from Wabash to graduate and medical schools in the 1950s, the 1960s, and the 1970s.

The faculty in the biological sciences in these years was a remarkable group of dedicated teachers — Eliot Williams, Lou DeLanney, Tom Cole and others in zoology; Dick Laubengayer, Paul Romberg, Bob Petty and others in botany. But it was Willis Johnson who brought these men to Wabash — or, as in Tom Cole's case, brought them back to Wabash. They were at Wabash primarily because of him, and they stayed as long as they did in part because of their attachment to him and to what he stood for.

The strength of the Wabash faculty has been to a large extent in faculty leaders of exceptional character and sound intellect, dedicated to the cause of Wabash. I can think of no finer example than Willis Johnson.

GEORGE VALENTINE KENDALL

George Kendall was the most civilized man I have ever known. Much as I would like to, I cannot do justice in words to the character and personality of this man, to say nothing of the quality of his mind. Nor do I trust my judgment when it comes to appraising the importance of his place in the history of Wabash College. In part I realize this is because my association with George Kendall and his wife was such that I am even less objective in writing about him than when I write about others who were his contemporaries at Wabash.

George Kendall had a profound and permanent influence on my life. In saying that, I do not have in mind matters of instruction, advice, and assistance, although there was much of that sort of thing. I have in mind, rather, the example he provided for me and for many others in how to think about life and how to face up to its realities with dignity and grace. The point I made about the educational power of example when writing of Dr. Mackintosh is equally apt in the case of George Kendall. For generations of Wabash students and for a succession of younger men on the Wabash faculty, he set a standard of thought and conduct by which they could measure their own strengths and weaknesses. In the process of emulation they became a little better and a little stronger. Certainly he did this for me. Even though I usually fell far short of his standards, his example was imbedded in my conscience.

Where George Kendall acquired the habits of mind and traits of character which I am ascribing to him, I have no idea. He came from a prominent, well-to-do family in St. Louis with relatives on both sides of the Mississippi. No doubt his up-bringing had much to do with the sturdiness of his character. Yet when I came to know his brother, Harry, and his sister, Alice, for all their similarities in appearance and, to some extent, mannerisms, I was struck by their differences from George. He completed his undergraduate education at Brown University. Following graduation from Brown he studied at Columbia University, where he obtained his master's degree in English literature. His graduate work was interrupted by America's involvement in World War I. George immediately volunteered for military service and with a second lieutenant's commission he soon went to France. He was attached to an artillery unit on the eastern sector of the Western Front. I never heard him talk about his war experience but obviously the most important thing that happened to him was his meeting and falling in love with an Alsatian lass from Thann, Yvonne Gehyer. He brought her with him to the United States as his bride.

His quick enlistment in the army in 1917 was a characteristic expression of his abiding love of country and his deep sense of duty. There was nothing Fourth-of-Julyish about his patriotism. He never preached Americanism. The flag waving editorial policy of the *Chicago Tribune* and that of the *Indianapolis Star* amused him. He never hesitated to speak critically of national policies of which he disapproved, and he poked fun gently at American foibles and prejudices. It was in the style of *The New Yorker*. But he accepted with respect American society as he found it, including what he regarded good naturedly as its follies and its absurdities. Throughout the years of Prohibition, for example, he never drank. To do so was against the law of the land, and that was that for George Kendall.

He had no interest in such organizations as the Sons of the American Revolution, the American Legion, or the Veterans of Foreign Wars, in all of which he could have been a card-carrying member. And yet when duty called he was quick and total in his response. When, after World War I, National Guard units were being activated all over the country, George helped to organize the unit at Crawfordsville and served for a time as its first captain. Pete Vaughan, who served as his executive officer and who succeeded him as captain, told me once of the striking figure George Kendall made in uniform on his horse. "But Dean Kendall was really too much of a gentleman to be a Guard captain," he said. "The kids didn't know how to take him."

Immediately after the Japanese attack on Pearl Harbor, George, although he was then fifty-two, began to think of what he might do in military service. He wrote to General Herron in Washington. With his help he was commissioned a lieutenant colonel with orders to report immediately to the South Pacific where he was attached to General MacArthur's general headquarters

124

staff. He was the first of the permanent Wabash faculty members to leave for military service. In later years I never heard him speak of his four years in service during World War II. As in the case of his experience in World War I, he was reticent about recounting his military service. Perhaps he considered it bad taste to do so. More likely he felt there was nothing worth talking about as he had simply done his duty. In spite of this reticence, in the year 1947–48, I believe it was, he read a fascinating paper at a Ouiatenon Club meeting describing the South Pacific in wartime. There was nothing in the paper about himself but his accounts of others, including General MacArthur, whom George greatly admired, were superb.

George Kendall, in my opinion, was the greatest dean of the college that Wabash has had so far in the twentieth century. He came to Wabash as Milligan Professor of English in the early 1920s, from Columbia University where he was an instructor following World War I. His friendship with Insley Osborne, whom he had met in graduate school before the war, and with whom he had shared a room, undoubtedly influenced his decision. So did his friendship with John Coss, whom he also met in graduate school. But my guess is the really decisive influence was Yvonne's unhappiness in New York. She wanted to be nearer the countryside. Within a year, possibly two years, after arriving at Wabash, Dr. Mackintosh appointed George dean of the college to succeed Dean Cowles, who moved to Wooster College. From then until 1939, when he resigned the deanship and I succeeded him, he was "the Dean." Students referred to him this way — "I have to see the Dean." "I have the approval of the Dean to change course." "The Dean announced in chapel . . . ." "The Dean broke up the fight." And so on.

It must be borne in mind that until 1956 when I created the office of dean of students to share the work of the dean of the college, Wabash for years had had only one dean. He was the central operating administrative officer of the college. He was the academic leader for the faculty. He worked with the president in the formulation of institutional policy. He was in charge of all student housing, student health, and student activities, He, and he alone, was responsible for student discipline. He sat with the president at the front table at all faculty meetings. He had a chair to the president's right at all chapel services and daily read announcements following the opening hymn. During the Hopkins years especially, he was thought of by trustees as an integral part of the college administration and as such was frequently consulted. He attended all meetings of the Board of Trustees.

Dean Kendall brought to bear on these multiple responsibilities his remarkable character and his extraordinary, good common sense. His "presence" had much to do with his success. He was a prepossessing man, tall and straight. In his youth he was a good-looking blond, but by the time he became dean, he was bald. If anything, his baldness added to his stature in the eyes of students.

He wore thin rimmed glasses to read, sometimes half moon rimless glasses, and for many students who for one reason or another found themselves in his office, his lively blue eyes peering at them over his glasses became an unforgettable experience. Habitually composed and even stern looking, he frequently broke suddenly into a wide grin which became famous at Wabash. When he laughed it was a full hearty laugh. I suppose it was his independent personal income that enabled him to dress well and expensively. He dressed conservatively and casually. He had a Brooks Brothers look about him and in fact often bought his jackets and slacks at Brooks Brothers. He was fond of Burberry overcoats and rain coats, which caused people in Crawfordsville occasionally to remark, "he looks English."

The influence of such a man as dean would have been substantial at any men's college. At Wabash it was overwhelming. His deanship spanned the "Hell Roaring 500"-Caveman Era. It began when Wabash football and basketball teams under Pete Vaughan were still tough and formidable for Purdue. It was a time of convertible Stutz Bearcat coupes, coonskin coats, hip flasks, bathtub gin, lavish Pan-Hellanic Dances with flaming flapper coeds imported from Butler, DePauw, Indiana University and elsewhere. It continued through the depression years, when a more bedraggled student body with corduroy slacks patched with adhesive tape had less money to spend, but were equally resourceful at raising hell, and when "The Raggedy-assed Cadets are on Parade" was one of the more modest Wabash songs. Far from seeming to be out of place in such an ambience, Dean Kendall had only to appear to quell a riot at the Strand Theatre, to break up a fight between halves at a DePauw football game, or to throw a hush over a raucous fraternity bash of some kind. It wasn't quite that simple, of course, but it appeared that way. He always addressed students collectively as "Gentlemen" and individually as "Mister." Some students were afraid of him, some were awed by him, all respected and admired him, and those who graduated felt real affection for him.

Day after day, week after week, he read in his crisp booming voice daily announcements in chapel. Invariably they concluded with the request that the "following gentlemen please come to my office at their earliest convenience and in any case by not later than noon tomorrow." He stood erect while hymns were sung but he never sang, not even "Old Wabash" and *Alma Mater*. No one commented on this. It was understood and in a strange way students took a kind of pride in the fact that alone among all those singing lustily in chapel, the dean never sang. He did not enjoy giving public speeches, and he rarely did. But when he spoke, for example, at Insley Osborne's memorial services and at the chapel service for my inauguration as president, he was good. There was never a false note, never hyperbole, never emotion.

One winter day driving to Princeton for a holiday I picked up a freshman hitch hiker at the edge of Crawfordsville. We talked about his experience at Wabash. Much of his enthusiasm centered on Dean Kendall. "Boy, does he give this college a front!" he exclaimed. Jack Scott, a colorful cheerleader from Philadelphia in the middle 1920s and later vigorous president of the National Association of Wabash Men, who as an undergraduate had had frequent brushes with Dean Kendall, was fond of saying, "I'd rather be kicked out of Wabash by Dean Kendall than admitted by another dean to any college I can think of!" Such tributes as these reflect the respect, admiration, and affection which Wabash students had for George Kendall.

In my final annual report to the Board of Trustees in May 1965, I discussed what I regarded as the several distinctive sources of strength of Wabash. One of these was the philosophy of the college toward its students, particularly toward their lives outside the classroom and the laboratory. It was a philosophy which presupposed that students were adults, not children, that they were able to distinguish between right and wrong, and that they were aware of their responsibility for the consequences of their behavior. It thus gave wide latitude and freedom in the choices students could make in their private lives. It was an institutional policy more akin to European university policy than to American. And among private liberal arts colleges, especially in the Midwest, it was exceptional. At most private colleges there were numerous rules and petty prohibitions, at Wabash there was only one rule of conduct: "Students are to conduct themselves as gentlemen at all times, both on and off the campus." On the whole Wabash students responded well; in fact their pride in the general policy made them more loyal to the college and more mindful of its good reputation. I believe this is one of the reasons for there having been only minor difficulties at Wabash in the late 1960s and early 1970s, when student rebellions swept over most American universities and colleges. Wabash students already enjoyed the freedoms then being demanded elsewhere.

George Kendall was the principal architect in the development of this policy structure. He did not believe in wet-nursing students. He was contemptuous of the growing body of literature having to do with student guidance and counselling. He rarely attended state and regional meetings of deans, and when he did, he said he found most deans "crashing bores." He relied on repeated personal conversations with individual students and on occasional informal discussions with student leaders to make the Wabash philosophy work well in practice. When breaches in the code occurred, he dealt with them quickly, firmly, and consistently. There were no half-way measures. Suspension from college was the only disciplinary action resorted to. But Dean Kendall did no preaching in such cases, no petty scolding. He was matter-of-fact and business-like, and rarely was there student whimpering. There was no appeal to higher authority from his judgments.

The emphasis I am giving to his role as dean of the college is a proper emphasis from the point of view of Wabash alumni. But it tends to obscure his very important role as an academic leader for the faculty and his role as a teacher. In the Hopkins years George Kendall was a steadying influence in faculty meetings. He could gently impose his will and that of the administration on the most petulant arguments that occasionally arose. He was the faculty's best spokesman in those rare instances when there was disagreement with the trustees (such as the Edgar Evans controversy). Even after he had resigned the deanship and had been given the largely honorary title Dean of the Faculty, he continued in the late 1940s and early 1950s to be a powerful influence in shaping academic policy. When Dr. Hopkins died, George Kendall almost automatically became acting president. He was one of the few faculty members (and for a time, the only one) who called President Sparks "Frank." In 1952 when Insley Osborne died, George became chairman of the Department of English. He was surrounded in the department by younger men whom he for the most part had selected, Walt Fertig, Owen Duston, Don Baker, Ralph Caplan, and others. They were good. Often they were restless about what they regarded as the stodgy, old-fashion posture of the department. But they were devoted to George as a person and accepted his conservative attitudes cheerfully.

While he was dean of the college, he had a half-time teaching load consisting exclusively of advanced courses. He made no pretense of being a scholar in the sense of research, writing, and publishing. He wrote a great deal of poetry, much of it for Yvonne. But he was almost secretive about his poetry and never tried to publish anything he wrote. But, if not a scholar, he was certainly scholarly and brought to bear on his teaching his extensive knowledge of English literature and, more important, a kind of special wisdom about life. Because of schedule conflicts, I could never take his most popular course, Shakespeare, but I took his course on the development of the English novel.

Like Osborne, he did practically all of the talking in class. Occasionally he would ask a question, but for the most part he talked. It was not a lecture. It was more like a series of soliloquies, analyzing characters, pondering the human predicament, speculating about moral dilemmas. His novel course began with Fielding and, according to the catalogue statement, was to conclude with twentieth-century writers. But in the year I studied with him, we never progressed much beyond Charles Dickens. We read our heads off for him, but the value of the course for me was not what we read. It was listening to George think aloud about life—tragic, comic, and humdrum life. His skeptical, stoical, tolerant way of looking at life came through with great impact. Ecclesiastes could have been his favorite Old Testament book — "there is nothing new under the sun," "Vanity, Vanity — all is Vanity." Seneca could have been his favorite philosopher. The life of the mind is all that really counts. If the quality of the life of the mind is good, then disagreeable hardships, disappointments, and pain can be endured, not cheerfully perhaps, but with courage and dignity. It was George's personal philosophy which came out in these soliloquies. It was a good philosophy for young men to hear and to ponder.

Harold McDonald's excellent portrait of George, which now hangs in the deans' reception room in Center Hall, captures the personal qualities of George Kendall which I have underscored. I never understood why Harold used the almost beet red color for George's face, but the treatment of his facial expression with the friendly quizzical eyes and the beginning of his tolerant but skeptical smile is really extremely good.

No account of what George Kendall meant to Wabash in the decades of which I am writing would be complete without a comment about Yvonne Kendall. For those among the faculty, trustees, and alumni who were close to the Kendalls, it was impossible to think of George without thinking simultaneously of Yvonne. This was true, although by choice Yvonne officially stayed in the background as far as the college was concerned. She rarely came on campus except when it was a matter of protocol or duty. An exception to this practice came while George was away during World War II, when Yvonne for a time worked as the college's switchboard operator. There were no Kendall children, and I suspect Yvonne worked at the college during those years primarily to fill the lonely days.

Her practice of staying in the background meant that, unlike some other faculty wives, she was never really well known personally in the Wabash community. For the majority I suspect she had an aura of mystery. To strangers she appeared to be shy and somewhat aloof. She and George came to Crawfordsville while she was still quite young. On her rare appearances at student functions, she invariably attracted admiring glances from students. She was good looking with light red hair, a very fair complexion, wide blue eyes, and a full sensuous mouth. She spoke little and softly, with a slight French accent. Other such young faculty women might have evoked an occasional student whistle, but there was something about Yvonne's bearing and air that caused students to react with a "Yes, ma'am" attitude. Only those who came to know her well, and I count myself among those, realized that the shyness and aloofness were largely a façade, a kind of protective coloration for a French girl transplanted suddenly to a strange American land.

Yvonne's formal education was limited but her native intelligence, her lively intellectual curiosity, and her love of reading gave her cultural resources and intellectual perspectives which impressed those who knew her well. No doubt George had much to do with her self-education. But it was far from another instance of Pygmalion and Galatea. As closely as she was identified with George, she was very much a person of strength and individuality in her own right. She had an uncanny way of sizing up people correctly, and she had a disarming kind of candor in conversation. Once when she and I were discussing Phillip Sassoon's *Memoirs of a Fox Hunting Man,* I told her I would like to write something like that and asked her if she thought I could. "No," she said, "I don't believe you could. You have not had enough experience with life." I remember feeling abruptly deflated, but she was right, of course. She was almost always right in her judgment of people.

Yvonne had an innate sense of beauty. It was reflected in the charm of the Kendall home. When I entered Wabash in 1926, they lived in the west side apartment of the Ben Crane home, diagonally across Wabash Avenue from the Beta House. Shortly after that, they bought and rebuilt an old faculty home on Crawford Street directly across from the west end of the old gymnasium. (When he retired George gave the house to the college, subject to a very modest annuity for ten years.) From the first time I entered that home in my senior year, I loved the place. So did others. There George and Yvonne did their part of what little college entertaining of official guests that took place during the Hopkins administration. There frequent small faculty dinner parties were held through the depression years. It was a beautiful home, always immaculately clean. Yvonne loved gardening and was good at it. Thus the flower garden and the vines became a part of the house. She was an excellent cook. Her dinners and suppers for guests were different and invariably good. In later years there were many of Yvonne's paintings here and there throughout the house. I believe she began painting seriously under Fritz Schlemmer's direction, but I could be mistaken about that. But certainly she worked hard with Harold McDonald, who thought highly of her painting.

Far from the shy, somewhat aloof person she appeared to be to strangers, Yvonne Kendall was by nature a warm, fun-loving woman. She liked to dance and she danced well. Often she was frivolous in conversation and something of a tease for close companions like Neil Hutsinpillar, Fergus Ormes, and Jim Paterson. She kept the faculty picnics in Pine Hills lively and amusing and skillfully diverted conversation among the men away from shop-talk. To people she liked she was enormously generous and good.

Her goodness to me and the tactful guidance she gave me in matters of manners and social etiquette and in ways of thinking about the world, especially about Europe, I later realized were a valuable part of my education. Years later when reading Lord Chesterfield's letters to his son, I thought of Yvonne with a smile when I encountered Chesterfield's advice to complete one's education by cultivating the acquaintance of a somewhat older woman of culture, wise in the ways of the world. In 1930 she, Tommy Tomlinson and I sailed together to Europe, and she and I returned on the same ship in September. It was my first trip to Europe and I felt all the excitement customary for an untraveled Hoosier youngster in such an adventure. It was the beginning of a close companionship for the two of us. Thanks to long conversations with Yvonne on those two Atlantic crossings, I began to look at Europe in ways other than as a tourist. In 1933 she accompanied my mother, of whom she was very fond, to England to visit me in Oxford. She escorted her as far as London, before going on for one of her periodic visits with her own family in Thann. It was an extraordinarily kind act of friendship, the kind of thing, among others, which caused me to love her.

When George retired from the Wabash faculty, the Kendalls moved to Duxbury, Massachusetts. It was a move in accordance with a plan carefully worked out long in advance. Why Duxbury? Because George's life-long friend from his years at Brown, Dr. Carrie Bumpus, had a home there and urged George to join him. Because also New England and the Cape Cod area appealed to George and Yvonne. I suspect also that the move so far from the Wabash campus reflected George's way of thinking about such things. I can imagine his saying to Yvonne, "Our work and life here at Wabash are finished. We should get out of the way of others now." They were happy at Duxbury. They bought and rebuilt a large eighteenth-century barn with plenty of space around it. Like the smaller home on Crawford Street it had a distinctive charm about it, and under Yvonne's direction the gardens became a joy to behold and a haven for song birds. It was the kind of place befitting the retirement years for a couple like George and Yvonne. And yet, I have some reason to believe that they occasionally regretted having left the Crawfordsville area. The numerous Wabash people who made pilgrimages there I suspect made the Kendalls nostalgic.

I last saw George Kendall perhaps a year before his death. Lorenza and I drove up from New York to visit briefly with them. I wanted Lorenza to meet George and Yvonne and to have them meet her. George was obviously in physical difficulty. He was in pain and walked slowly with the help of a cane. But he was still erect, still alert and lively mentally. His warm grin was still as flashing as ever. He made no complaints about his health. As Yvonne took Lorenza around the garden to admire the plants, George and I followed more slowly behind them. We chatted casually about what I was then doing in New York, about how things were going at Wabash, about old friends, and about my new wife. "That's quite a fetching looking woman you have, Byron," he said, "I am happy for you. And for her, too!"

A few days later, there arrived at our apartment in New York a small handsome antique oriental rug which we had admired in the Kendall home. Sometime later came a silver antique English fruit basket. Gifts from George and Yvonne. How characteristic, I thought.

CLARENCE E. LEAVENWORTH

At the time I entered Wabash as a freshman, Clare Leavenworth was already in point of service a senior member of the faculty. Of the faculty members then teaching only Tapy (psychology), Chapman (physics), Cragwall (mathematics) and Graves (zoology) had had longer periods of service at Wabash. Leavenworth was appointed to the Department of Romance Languages by President Mackintosh shortly before World War I. He served as chairman of that department through the 1940s. From 1928 on he also was chairman of Division II. His undergraduate work was at Hamilton College, with which he often compared Wabash. His master's degree was from Yale and his Ph.D., I believe, was from the University of Chicago.

Throughout the Hopkins years, Leavenworth was one of the pillars of strength on the faculty. He was among the "Young Turks" on the faculty in the early 1920s who pressed for sweeping changes in the curriculum. Once those changes were accomplished under Dr. Hopkins' leadership, Clare, along with the other "Young Turks," became staunch defenders of the status quo. This stance fitted in well with his economic and political philosophy, which was quite conservative. A Republican, he was one of the few faculty members who was troubled by Roosevelt's New Deal. He was, therefore, enthusiastic about President Sparks when he arrived at Wabash, and he supported him in his policy decisions in spite of the apprehensions of most of his old faculty friends. But Clare Leavenworth was never the faculty influence in the early years of the Sparks administration that he was during the Hopkins years. The 1940s were declining years for him.

Clare at one time or another taught Spanish and Italian, but his forte was French. It was also his first love. He prided himself on his French accent and devoted much attention to pronunciation in working with his students. Like Domroese, his teaching objective was to help students obtain a reading knowledge of foreign language. He was less eccentric in his teaching methods than Domroese. A prodigious worker himself, he insisted on solid work from his students, and he relied heavily on repeated daily drills on grammar, syntax, and vocabulary. He had few major students but hundreds of Wabash students studied with him in their freshman and sophomore years.

Partly because his upper divisional teaching load was light and partly because of his own interests, in the 1920s and the 1930s he developed courses in art history and art appreciation. Until Dr. John Forbes joined the history department shortly after World War II, Clare was a solitary proponent of an enlarged place for art in the Wabash curriculum. He gave increasing emphasis to his art appreciation courses and they were popular, in part because they were regarded by students as being easy. Clare also pushed for the inclusion of studio art in the curriculum. He was not successful in those efforts, but he managed to get approval for Fritz Schlemmer to open a studio on campus and to give instruction in sketching and painting on a non-credit basis. (Later Dr. Forbes, with my support as dean, won this objective with the faculty, and under Harold MacDonald studio art became permanently established and continues to flourish.)

Clare Leavenworth's temperament and mannerisms were those of an esthete. His manner of speaking, his tastes, his judgments about things were discriminating and precise, even prissy. Some students regarded him as effeminate and excessively sensitive. He had a nervous kind of laugh which often came out tentatively when he was talking, and he frequently was rather apologetic in manner, especially when disagreeing with someone. His interest in art led him to take up painting as a hobby. He admired Fritz Schlemmer's paintings and studied with him off and on. He was as dilettantish about his painting, however, as about other outside interests. Occasionally during vacations he would go to the southwest or to Mexico on "painting trips," but I am not aware that he really worked at his hobby. In spite of these personal aspects, Leavenworth could be firm and tenacious about matters of academic policy and quite influential in faculty debates.

It sometimes used to occur to me that Clare was a frustrated *bon vivant*. His general posture was that of a conservative, rather staid person, but now and then he betrayed an attraction for a very different view of life. I was struck by this at a chapel program in the late 1930s. In the Hopkins years, the Friday chapels always consisted of musical programs. On this occasion a trio of Indiana University coeds performed, singing numbers representative of the period's most popular jazz forms. They were attractive, cute girls. They swayed and wiggled and gestured as they sang in very close harmony. The students loved it. They howled and cheered with delight after each number, demanding more and more until chapel time was in fact extended. I was sitting next to Clare in the back of the room. After about the second encore, above the din of the student applause, he leaned over toward me and with his apologetic laugh exclaimed, "Isn't this grotesque!" But I noticed that his face was flushed with excitement, and his applause after each number was vigorous. I also noticed after performances of the Dramatic Society, Clare loved to dance. He was especially fond of dancing with Mildred Roach. But Clare had never gone beyond the "finale hop" in popular dancing, and his style in dancing was, therefore, a little quaint in the late 1930s.

It is impossible to think of Professor Leavenworth without thinking also of his wife, Annie. Annie Leavenworth was the more forceful of the two. Where Clare was tentative, Annie was decisive. Where he was hesitant and equivocal, she was positive and firm. She was a fascinating person in her own right. A graduate of Smith, she had traveled widely and had studied for a time in France. In the late 1920s and off and on in the 1930s she taught French part-time. Along with Neva Chapman, who taught German, she broke the tradition of an all-male faculty at Wabash. They both were discreet about their membership — never attending faculty meetings and generally maintaining low visibility. They were both good teachers, much respected and loved by their students.

But Annie Leavenworth was more than a good teacher. She had a fine, quick mind, a keen sense of humor, and an abundance of nervous energy. She talked a mile a minute, crisply and often sharply. She kept well-informed about what was going on in the world and took seriously the troubles and ills that swept over America in the depression years. She was a flaming do-gooder, but she was practical about what she did and said. She became an ADA-type Democrat, probably to Clare's dismay, but she never became involved in party politics. Instead, she became a moving spirit in the local chapter of the League of Women Voters. She was an early champion of local negroes, helping to establish the first local chapter of the NAACP. She admired Harry Freedman and his wife Sophie and supported Harry in his heroic work with the Crawfordsville Community Chest, later the United Fund. She was impatient of women's social activities. She did her part in faculty wives' social programs, but she seemed clearly bored by it. She had "no time to waste" with the Women's Circles at the Presbyterian Church. "Those biddies just meet to gorge and gossip!" she said bluntly and perhaps unfairly. Always she was incredibly busy working at something "worth-while." People sometimes disagreed with her, but she was highly regarded and, among those who knew her well, greatly loved.

The Leavenworths had one child, a son. Bill grew up in Crawfordsville, a bright attractive blond with an engaging smile. He was a source of pride and joy for Clare and Annie, but he was unspoiled. After studying a year or two at Wabash, he transferred to Hamilton and was graduated there. He married a stunning brunette, Martha, whose intelligence and charm won her an immediate place in the hearts of the Leavenworths and of those who came to know her at Wabash. The prospects for these two undoubtedly brought great happiness to Clare and Annie. In World War II Bill joined the Army Air Corps. Late in the war came the telegraphed news that he was "missing in action and presumed dead." His plane had been shot down somewhere over France. I was not there at the time, but Dick Banta later gave me a full account. Annie was alone at the time in their home at 1000 South Grant Avenue. Clare was on a painting trip in Mexico. Annie was staggered by the news, but recovered quickly and set about doing what had to be done with her remarkable good sense. "Do you want me to locate Clare, Annie, and give him the news?" Dick asked. "Oh, heavens no!" she said. "Clare will go to pieces about this. Anyway, there is nothing he can do. We'll notify him later."

The loss of Bill was a terrible thing for the Leavenworths, but they went on in the years that followed as best they could. Following an operation for a prostate tumor, Clare's health declined seriously. When he died Annie arranged for a brief funeral service which was held at the Bright Funeral Home just across the street from the campus. It was a closed casket service. Annie buried Clare in an old Wabash T-shirt and khaki slacks stained with paint.

"No point wasting good clothes," she said, "I'll give Clare's suits to the Good-will people."

FERGUSON R. ORMES

Fergus Ormes joined the Wabash faculty early in the 1920s. Following his undergraduate education at Colorado College, he did graduate work at the University of Chicago and at Yale where he obtained a master's degree. He went from graduate study to New York where he worked in an accounting firm. It was from there that he came to Wabash. I never learned the details of this move, but apparently Fergus and his wife, Mabrie, did not like life in New York City and as a way out sought a teaching position. His move to Wabash and Crawfordsville proved to be his last. He stayed until he retired some forty years later.

President Mackintosh appointed Ormes as assistant professor of economics with primary responsibilities for teaching accounting and money and banking. When President Hopkins dismissed Joy Luther Leonard, Fergus was made full professor and succeeded Leonard as chairman of the Department of Economics. When the curriculum was reorganized in 1928 and the divisional system was instituted, Ormes became chairman of the Division of Social Sciences (Division III). He held the post of department chairman until the late 1940s, when President Sparks brought Dr. John Van Sickle to Wabash for that position. He served as chairman of Division III until the middle 1950s, when Dr. Warren Shearer succeeded him. Dr. Hopkins also made Fergus college comptroller and later business manager. He and Mary Schlemmer constituted the entire business office for years. In the early 1950s, at my recommendation, Bill Degitz was lured from his promising career in business to strengthen the college business office. Ormes, however, kept the title of comptroller until his retirement.

I did not become well acquainted with Fergus while I was an undergraduate. He seemed remote and somewhat forbidding to students. I was also prejudiced by a remark made by a senior at the Beta House at the first chapel service I attended in my freshman year. Chapel was then being held in the upstairs of the gymnasium. As the faculty assembled for that first chapel, coming in one at a time, my senior companion remarked at the entry of Ormes, "There comes the most disliked member of the Wabash faculty." I paid little attention to the remark at the time although it no doubt sank into my subconscious mind. Years later I wondered about the basis for the remark. It then seemed groundless to me. Apparently it reflected Fergus' reputation as a tough and rough teacher in the classroom. Like Dr. Howell in chemistry, Ormes was a terror for many students.

He was not a prepossessing man. He walked with a slight limp, the result of infantile paralysis in his childhood. His teeth were badly stained by tobacco. A chain smoker, like Pete Vaughan, he rolled his own cigarettes with Bond Street tobacco. He was deft and quick at the chore. As I have indicated, to those who did not know him, he appeared to be a dour, forbidding kind of person. It was a grossly erroneous impression. Fergus Ormes, although he often was brusque and cutting in his remarks (especially when he was annoyed or angry), was really a very warm, friendly kind of man. He had a wide range of intellectual interests, a quick sense of humor, and a knack for telling stories. He loved the out-of-doors and was habitually nostalgic about Colorado, which he visited regularly during vacations. He was an avid promoter of the faculty picnics in Pine Hills. As I shall make clear in a moment, he loved to play his guitar and to sing. For the few who were close to him, Fergus Ormes was an excellent companion.

In my senior year (1929-30) I had a course with Ormes in advanced economic theory. I found nothing in that experience to confirm his reputation as a terrifying teacher. He was obviously tough and demanding. His reading assignments were heavy. He gave ten-minute written quizzes daily and full hour examinations once a month. He had what Insley Osborne called "considerable facility at writing the letter F." There were always a number of failing grades each semester. But his conduct of class discussions was relaxed and gentle. He used the Socratic method, almost never lecturing. He directed questions not for factual answers, but for reasoning. He followed a student's reasoning wherever it went. Often it led to a blind alley from which there was nowhere else to go. And the student, to his embarrassment, recognized this. Rarely would Fergus make comments. Instead, he would lead others over the same route, but with improved turnings on the students' parts. Some students found this then unconventional method of instruction baffling, but the better students found it stimulating.

He was fond of setting up hypothetical situations and then by questions dissecting the situation in great detail, in the process reinforcing conceptual definitions in economics — capital, labor, rent, return on investment, profit, loss, fixed costs, and so on. A favorite gambit in this connection was Robinson Crusoe on his island. (Did he have any capital? Did he make a profit? What difference economically did it make when his man Friday arrived? And so on.) It was micro-economics exclusively, but it was extremely well done. In his accounting courses his method was more straight-forward and conventional with great emphasis on practical accounting problems, using actual cases taken from annual corporate reports.

Ormes was an excellent Division III chairman. He organized the division's work efficiently. He held frequent division meetings, often at night in his home, for the purpose of reviewing problems in the senior reading course or for planning the written comprehensive examinations, or for tinkering with the Division III curriculum from time to time. It was not all work. He contributed to high morale and good fellowship within the division by organizing in the fall and the spring division picnics, usually held in Pine Hills. Good steaks, potato salad, some green vegetables, plenty of cold beer and hot coffee, a cheerful fire and bracing cool evening air — all this made for very pleasant stag evenings. The picnics were well attended by everyone in the division, and by invitation came also a few kindred spirits from outside the division such as Dick Banta, Myron Phillips, and Neil Hutsinpillar, sometimes, George Kendall, and Insley Osborne. After the "cook-out" there followed singing around the fire.

Fergus Ormes played the guitar expertly. At the Division III picnics and also at the faculty picnics which I mentioned when writing about Dr. Hopkins, it was Fergus who invariably led off the singing. The songs were somewhat different at the faculty picnics from those at the Division III parties. At the former it was a long series of old familiar standbys — "Down by the Old Mill Stream," "School Days," "My Darling Clementine," "Someone's in the Kitchen with Dinah," and the like. But at the Division III stag parties the songs were more earthy. Fergus would lead off with something like "The Man Who Drinks His Whiskey Clear and Goes to Bed Right Mellow," or " 'Twas Friday Morn When We Set Sail," or "Roll Me Over in the Clover." Others would join in or take the lead in some personal favorite. I introduced in the mid-1930s the "Ball of Kerrymuir," a ribald ballad in Scot dialect which I had learned from Scottish friends at Oxford. I understand it became something of a legend after I became president and no longer went to Division III picnics.

In the late 1930s Fergus and I gradually became close friends. When I became assistant dean and even more so after I became dean of the college, he and I had occasion to work closely together. Also his wife of those years, Emily, was a friend of Dorothy and the Trippets and the Ormeses were often together. Fergus' first wife died about 1932 or 1933. Soon after that, so soon in fact that in the more staid circles of Crawfordsville eyebrows were arched, he married Emily Schlemmer, a sister of Fritz Schlemmer. Emily must then have been in her forties. She had plain, angular features but she was attractive nonetheless. Bright, pleasant and talented, her marriage to Fergus, though something of a surprise to everyone, pleased her friends and his. Emily was a brilliant musician at both the organ and the piano. Her performance of Gershwin's *Rhapsody in Blue* was a breath-taking thing to watch and to hear. But although they had some happy years together, it was a marriage filled with increasing tensions and, toward the end, acrimony. Perhaps the difficulty Emily experienced moving into a family with three rather young children (Robert, David, and Emily) so soon after the death of their mother had much to do with their troubles. But I suspect more important were the great differences in the personalities and interests of Emily and Fergus. In 1946 they separated and shortly afterward were divorced. It was a traumatic experience for both of them, more so for Emily than for Fergus.

In the late winter of 1946–47 (it may have been later) Emily came to our house at Kennedy Place one afternoon, terribly despondent and distraught. Normally a moderate drinker, she had begun to rely heavily on that most ancient of tranquilizers, alcohol. She wept much and lamented her disappointments in life. She regarded her life as a waste and upbraided herself for her troubles. Her state of mind bore all of the tragic symptoms of melancholy, self-pity, and suppressed hostility. I was alarmed and so was my wife. We persuaded her to stay the night with us.

The next morning early I telephoned Dr. Vernon Hahn, a distinguished brain surgeon and psychiatrist in Indianapolis. He agreed to see Emily late that morning. We drove her to Indianapolis for the appointment and waited for her. When she rejoined us I was delighted with the change in her spirits and her thoughts. It was miraculous. She was jovial and confident again and most grateful for the introduction to Dr. Hahn. She looked forward to her second appointment later that week. But Emily never kept the appointment. Late the next morning Doug Ostrom, a veteran student at Wabash who with his wife lived in a part of Emily's house, became concerned when Emily made no appearance. Finally he investigated. He found her dead in bed. She had carefully done her nails, put on her make-up, combed her hair, donned her best nightgown, gone to bed and then taken a massive dose of sleeping pills.

Emily's suicide left Fergus badly shaken. I suspect it was the beginning of a final decline for him, barely perceptible at first but increasingly apparent to his friends. After his divorce he moved into the Hovey Cottage with Professor Hutsinpillar. That was his home for the rest of his days at Wabash. He recovered some of his previous spirit but he was restless and a little lost. He and President Sparks never got along well together. Frank regarded Fergus as negative and obstructive in his attitude. Fergus, who for years had slaved to keep college expenditures down, was overwhelmed by Frank's free spending habits. Like Pop Welborn, whom Fergus admired, he was increasingly apprehensive about the rush of changes taking place at Wabash — especially about their cost. Bill Degitz, whom Fergus liked, tactfully began to expand the staff of the business office and to introduce modern business machines and methods. (Fergus was accustomed to adding long columns of figures with pencil and paper.) Gradually, Fergus felt "out of it." The same thing was true with his faculty role. When Van Sickle, Rogge, and other newcomers joined the faculty Fergus felt that he was on the sidelines.

In some ways he adjusted quite well. He seemed terribly pleased and proud at my election as president. He presented the college with a desk made by the Virginia Craftsmen for my office. It was an exact copy of my desk at Kennedy Place, which he knew I loved. He visited his beloved mountains in

Colorado more often. And to the surprise of many, he began to study seriously dramatic acting. He had always enjoyed amateur acting in the Crawfordsville Dramatic Club. But now he turned to it with deadly seriousness. He enrolled in a summer dramatic school in upstate New York. He played summer stock for a while and took a new and prominent part in the Dramatic Club's productions. He frequently took principal roles in plays and he performed well. Now and then he directed other plays, and they were good.

In addition to these interests, Fergus edited the copious notes he had taken over the years in long hand at faculty meetings, trustee meetings, and at special events of the college. He left a large box full of such notes at his death marked for my attention. On one of my infrequent trips to the campus in the early 1970s, Gladys Otto, who was working with Bob Harvey on the college archives, told me she was holding the box for me. "Don't you want to read these papers, Byron?" she asked. "They are marked for you." At the time I couldn't bear the thought of reading them. "No," I said, "Keep them in the archives. They will be valuable someday for a college historian."

Sometime before I left Wabash in 1965 Fergus' health broke badly. Ultimately he was taken to Kansas where his daughter Emily and her family were living. In 1967 he died. I was living in Denver at the time. I joined his children, Robert and Emily, and a handful of his Colorado relatives to bury his ashes in a cemetery in Colorado Springs. It was one of those gorgeous Colorado days. After the very brief graveside services I looked west at the spectacular mountain landscape. "How Fergus would love this!" I said to myself.

JAMES INSLEY OSBORNE

Of all my teachers at Wabash, Insley Osborne was the nearest to a personal idol. For sheer brilliance of mind I rated him at the top of the faculty when I was an undergraduate. I see no reason now to modify that youthful appraisal. Before I had even seen Professor Osborne, I had received from Wabash alumni in Princeton an exaggerated build-up of his intellectual attainments. "Doc" Anderson, Dale Eby, and Ben Watt barely knew Insley Osborne. He preceded them as a student at Wabash, and he had not yet joined the Wabash faculty when they were undergraduates. But they knew of his reputation, and they boasted about his being a Wabash Beta. In the spring of 1926 when I was a guest at the Beta House, I heard the same kind of hushed praise of Professor Osborne from Beta upperclassmen. I was later to learn that this was a standard practice during freshman rush week. At any rate, my advanced notices concerning Insley Osborne were such that I regarded him as a great man before I ever met him.

My first experience as a student under Osborne, far from shattering my early illusions about him, actually deepened them. I was "placed" by orientation examinations in his section of freshman English composition. I found myself tongue-tied in his presence, but that one semester with him as a teacher was a thrilling experience. Thereafter, I enrolled for every course I could possibly take with him. When in the second semester of 1928–29 Osborne took over from John Tomlinson a course in recent European history, I remember rearranging my schedule to hear what he had to say about the coming of World War I and its aftermath. Along with others I was spellbound by his grasp of details of that dramatic period. His detailed account of the assassination of the Archduke Franz Ferdinand at Sarajevo in the summer of 1914 and all of the grim consequences that flowed from that event, is still quite vivid in my memory. He had us sitting on the edge of our chairs. These were events through which he had lived, and they had a special fascination for him. The same thing was true of his discussion of the Paris Peace Conference in 1919, in which he had been a participant. It was heady stuff we listened to.

I even took his course in Anglo-Saxon and Middle English, which for a long time he offered in alternate years. There were only three of us in the class, which meant there was precious little time to coast while others did the reciting. (We took turns reading aloud, then translating into modern English.) Moreover, it was an early afternoon class, perhaps the worst time of the day for heavy mental concentration. After an introduction to the mysteries of the Anglo-Saxon alphabet and sentence structure, we struggled through excerpts from the *Anglo-Saxon Chronicle,* writings of the Venerable Bede, *Beowulf,* and God knows what else. It was rigorous mental exercise. Today I could not read a sentence in Anglo-Saxon if my life depended on it. Nevertheless, I regard that year's course as a valuable one. The intellectual discipline required to read Anglo-Saxon was in itself a confidence-building experience. More important, with Insley's help it gave me a new insight into the origin of the English language and its uniqueness among modern languages. After that experience, Chaucer's Middle English was easy and Elizabethan English was a joy.

Not everyone felt about Insley Osborne's teaching as I did. Some found him utterly incomprehensible. I remember my first roommate at the Beta House, Maury Rush, burly fullback on the football team, coming home for lunch early in the fall of 1926 and lamenting his enrollment in one of Osborne's courses. "Jesus," he said, "I've got to get out of that English course but quick! I don't know what the hell Brother Osborne is talking about." Others found his style boring. Such students often fell sound asleep in his classes. Insley never seemed to mind. But most found him interesting and stimulating, even if they didn't always understand him. A minority found him an inspiration. Among these a high percentage went on to make a career out of teaching English, Jimmy Clifford, Tom McCormick, Bob Frank, Russ

Ames, Walt Fertig, Gene Lawlis, Sheldon Vanauken, and David Hopkins to mention a few. Others became writers or publishers like John Koffend (associate editor of *Time* magazine), Frank Barnett, and Jim Goode.

Insley's teaching technique appeared to be haphazard and disorganized. He did not exactly lecture. He never used notes. He rarely asked a question. He simply began talking as soon as the class assembled and he kept talking for fifty-five minutes. One had to listen carefully to follow him and to avoid missing his frequent sallies of dry humor. His favorite classroom was on the ground floor of Center Hall where the deans' and registrar's offices are now located. He would take his seat on the raised platform, pull out his gold watch on a chain, lean on the pulpit-like desk in front of him, and begin to talk about whatever reading assignment the class was currently studying. As he talked he looked over the heads of his students, out of the windows, played with his gold watch chain, twirled his Phi Beta Kappa key, and generally broke every rule in Brigance's book, *The Spoken Word*. He had a peculiar inflection often ending a sentence on a rising note of emphasis.[11] Usually the rising inflection included the punch line, the central point of the discussion. But for all these oddities, what Insley Osborne had to say, more often than not, was pure gold.

It was impossible for Insley to change his style. In the early years of the experiment with the "Colloquium on Important Books" in the late 1940s, I regularly co-led with Insley the discussion of Aristotle's *Ethics*. It was a disaster for Insley. He could not overcome his habit of talking to the point rather than simply asking questions. Even is his freshman composition class, there was little student recitation. But there was plenty of student work assigned — a theme each day. Although there were weekly individual "theme conferences" with Osborne, he made a practice of reading aloud and criticizing student themes in class. The writer of the theme was never identified and the criticisms, while often devastating, were courteous and polite.

In addition to criticizing points of grammar and sentence structure, Insley regularly gave miniature lectures about specific words, explaining the Greek or Latin or Anglo-Saxon derivation of the word, its shades of meaning, its synonyms, its common misuses and so on. I once used the word "utopian" in a freshman theme that Insley chose, apparently at random, to read in class. Insley talked for ten minutes or more about the word — how it was derived from two Greek words, "ou" meaning "not" and "topos" meaning "place"; how it, therefore, literally meant "not a place" or "no place" or "nowhere"; how and why Sir Thomas More coined the modern word "Utopia" as a title for his famous book; how since More's use of the word its meaning had been corrupted; why it was really an absurdity to say something like an "utopian

11. Dick Ristine in informal short speeches often uses the same inflection. There are times when his manner of speaking causes me to shiver with recollections of his illustrious uncle. (Dick's mother was Insley's sister.) BKT.

idea," in other words a "no place idea." By the time he had finished his dissertation, both the word "utopian" and I had been wrung dry. Ever since then I have been wary of using the word "utopian."

Such exercises in philology were not limited to his freshman composition class. Again and again in advanced classes, he would digress to engage in critical analyses of words, phrases, and colloquial expressions. He was fond of pointing out that, depending on the situation, or the writer's intention, or the context of connotation, it is often better to use simple words derived from Anglo-Saxon than more "elegant" words derived from Greek or Latin. He illustrated by reading passages from Hemingway's *Farewell to Arms*. He liked the way when, speaking of battle wounds, Hemingway wrote "His guts were hanging out." He could have written "His intestines were exposed," Insley said but the imagery would not be the same. With reference to the Declaration of Independence, he discussed the power of the word "freedom" as contrasted with the word "liberty." In a different context he underscored the absurdity of changing "Naked came I from my mother's womb," to "Nude came I from my mother's womb." On the other hand, he said just the reverse holds true in other concepts. To refer to a painting by Matisse as "Naked Young Woman," instead of "Nude Young Woman" makes for obscenity in a work of art where none is intended.

In such intricate discussions as these, there was nothing pedantic about his method or his purpose. His interest was simply the promotion of clear, precise, and correct use of the English language. Not all of us who studied under him learned to write as well as he could write but he drilled into us a respect for the English language we had never had, and he gave us a taste for discriminating carefully in the choice of words we used. For me he opened intellectual doors, the existence of which I had never even dreamed.

If Insley Osborne had never done anything but teach, his fame in the twentieth-century history of Wabash would still be secure. But Insley was much more to Wabash than an influential teacher. As with others, Wabash was a central part of his life. He was born in Crawfordsville and grew up virtually on campus. His father, Pat Osborne, had been associate principal of the old preparatory department in Kingery Hall, associate professor of Latin and mathematics, and for an even longer period secretary of the Wabash faculty. Insley was graduated from Wabash in 1906. He stayed on for a year or two as an instructor. Scholarly though he was, he must have had all of the ferocious Wabash spirit that emerged with the athletic glory of the Cayou years. His chapter entitled "The Little Giants" in the *First Hundred Years* is a masterpiece in the re-creation of those exciting years. But Insley was not an athlete. Moreover, he went through a touch-and-go bout with rheumatic fever which left him with a permanently bad heart. In spite of this, once recovered, he won a Rhodes Scholarship to Oxford. (He was the second Wabash Rhodes Scholar,

Claude Peiffer being the first.) Insley regarded his Rhodes Scholarship as something of a fluke. "It was only because I knew Greek, and Greek in those years was a prerequisite for Oxford," he once explained to me. It was a characteristic Osborne understatement. At Oxford he won the Matthew Arnold Essay Prize.

Returning to America just before the outbreak of World War I, he began his graduate work at Columbia University where he ultimately won his Ph.D. degree. It was there that he met and formed a life-long friendship with George Kendall. George was really his only close friend and companion at Wabash. (He was the only faculty member to call Insley by his undergraduate nickname, "Steely." He sat with "Steely" when he was dying in Culver Hospital.) Not being able to qualify for military service because of his heart, in 1917 Insley entered government service in Washington, but later was commissioned a first lieutenant in the intelligence service. Precisely what he did I do not know, but whatever it was it must have been good. He was picked as a member of President Wilson's staff when plans were made for the Paris Peace Conference in 1919. Student speculation about the Osborne role at the Paris Peace Conference took on the wildest kind of exaggeration, including the suggestion that he was the real author of Wilson's celebrated "Fourteen Points." Such imagining ran far apart from the actual facts, no doubt, but though Insley himself never talked about his experience, a rich experience it must have been.

It was with a background such as this that Insley in 1919 accepted President Mackintosh's invitation to return to Wabash as Yandes Professor of English. Until he died thirty-three years later, he never was far from Crawfordsville and Wabash, or for long. Almost immediately he became a power within the faculty. He was one of the leaders of the "Young Turks" among the faculty who pressed for a thorough revision of the curriculum. President Hopkins appointed him chairman of the committee that produced the new curriculum which went into operation in 1928. Insley thereafter became a champion of the status quo and beat off such later efforts as were made by new young faculty members from time to time to tamper with the "new curriculum." He had a quick temper, and when it flared his tongue was exceedingly sharp. He was a master at civilized invective. In such cases — arguments in faculty meetings, conferences with trustee committees, and so on — he often wounded people with his biting sarcasm and he meant, at the moment, to wound. Later he might — or might not — apologize. Young faculty members learned to tread warily around him during faculty controversies. Ben Rogge once said, describing his first impressions of a Wabash faculty meeting in which Osborne was in good form, "It was clear to me that young faculty members are to be seen, not heard!" Kendall called him "the principal in the thought of the college." Brigance called him the faculty's "voice of conscience." In intellectual and academic matters, he stood rigidly on his principles. He would not compromise with whatever he considered to be expedient or mediocre.

Students of the late 1940s undoubtedly remember Osborne as a haggard, drawn-looking man. He was then failing rapidly in health. But in the 1920s and early 1930s he was still handsome. He rarely laughed aloud, but he chuckled often, and he had a smile that lit up his whole face. He was a homebody. His first wife, Elsie Walkup, died within two years of their marriage. They had a son James (Jimmy) who after two years at Wabash went on to M.I.T. for a degree in engineering. In the late 1920s Insley married Frances Doane, President Hopkins' secretary whom he brought with him from Northwestern University. Frances, who was then in her late twenties, was an attractive woman with the soft brown eyes of a doe and a smile like the sunrise. It had all of the appearances of a happy marriage. They had one child, Deborah, a beautiful but strange girl.

Except for his family and the college, Insley had no consuming outside interests. The Wabash Avenue Presbyterian Church was important to him. So was the Crawfordsville Public Library, where for years he served as chairman of its Board of Trustees. But except for these, he did not mix much with townspeople. Unlike Gronert, Brigance, and others, he spurned the town's clubs. He made an exception of the Ouiatenon Club which he regularly attended and where once in a great while he read a paper, always brilliantly written. In spite of this aloofness from his native town, he was full of amusing stories about town characters and local interests. He avidly read the Crawfordsville *Journal-Review* as well as the *New York Times*.

Insley Osborne was a truly brilliant man, who had extraordinarily high promise in his youth. His writing had the marks of future greatness. His book, *Arthur Hugh Clough,* written while he was a young man, is still considered the definitive work on Clough.[12] His introduction written for a late edition of *Barchester Towers* was a subject for discussion among specialized scholars.[13] Anyone reading *The First Hundred Years* without advanced warning can tell where Gronert's writing stops and Osborne's begins. His amusing account of Ezra Pound's short stay on the Wabash faculty had been quoted in biographies of Pound. When he succeeded his father as secretary of the faculty, the minutes of Wabash faculty meetings took on a crispness that future historians of the college will find fascinating and amusing. With such native gifts for writing, why did he not write for publication and possibly for fame? After his book about Clough, he published nothing. Ted Gronert told me Insley procrastinated with his part of *The First Hundred Years* and in the end wrote it rather hurriedly. A paper he wrote for the Ouiatenon Club in about 1938, called "To

12. *Arthur Hugh Clough* (London: Constable and Co., 1920).

13. Anthony Trollope, *Barchester Towers* (New York: The Macmillan Co., 1926).

Keep the Peace," a lucid and persuasive criticism of the policy of appeasement then being followed by England and France, was a moving, prophetic thing. Verne Oggel (minister of the Wabash Avenue Presbyterian Church and a Wabash trustee) insisted that Insley should send the paper to *Harper's Magazine* or to the *New York Times*. Insley did nothing about it.

Some thought Insley's failure to write for publication reflected his conviction that he did not have long to live. He was not a hypochondriac, and yet, judging by occasional remarks he made, he was undoubtedly mindful of his faulty heart. Perhaps he did not write because he did not have to, as he would have had if he had continued at Columbia under the pressure and competition of his faculty colleagues. Neil Hutsinpillar said Insley was too much of a perfectionist to write for publication. Perhaps there was truth in all of these surmises. Closer to the truth, I believe, is the fact that Insley was simply devoid of ambition and he was indolent. He as much as confessed this to me in a long conversation we had in the late 1930s when, probably at Hoppy's suggestion, he urged me to continue at Wabash rather than moving to Indiana University. He put heavy demands on himself as far as his teaching and his committee assignments were concerned. But apart from those obligations which he enjoyed, he was an idler. When he was not in the classroom or his office, he was at home in his study. He was a prodigious reader. But often he played solitaire or dealt poker hands by the hour, no doubt meditating to himself as he relaxed with the cards. Sometimes I thought of him as an Achilles-like figure, withdrawn from the fray and preferring his own company to that of others.

My sense of indebtedness to the memory of Insley Osborne continues to be fresh as well as deep. His influence on me was not the continuing growing influence of George Kendall, but it nonetheless was a very important influence, at points quite decisive as far as my life experience was concerned. Although we were friends after my graduation from Wabash I never felt as close to Insley as I did to George Kendall, Fergus Ormes, Ted Gronert, and others. He was the only faculty member who called me by my undergraduate nickname, Trip, but in spite of that, there was no close companionship. Perhaps I was never able to overcome my student-master feelings about him. In any case, he was a hard man to know intimately.

To Insley I owe exclusively my years of study at Oxford. Never would I have thought of applying for a Rhodes Scholarship had it not been for him. I was speechless with surprise and disbelief when one day, interrupting a tennis match I was playing, he said, "Trip, it is time to submit annual applications for Rhodes Scholarships, and I think you should try." Later we talked about it at length. He explained that the competition would be more difficult now, because the Rhodes trustees had discontinued the system by which each state in alternate years elected two Rhodes Scholars. Beginning that year, the nation

145

was being organized into eight districts of six states each, and each district would select four scholars from among the winners in each of the six member states. But he added, "I think you will have a good chance and I want you to try." It struck me as preposterous but if Insley wanted me to try — "well, okay," I said to myself, "I will try." After the final district committee interviews in Chicago, I came back to Crawfordsville thinking, "Well, it was an exciting experience. I am glad Insley insisted that I go through it even if I didn't win." Then came the telegram from Frank Aydelotte, American secretary of the Rhodes Trust, — "I am happy to inform you . . ." et cetera. I took the telegram to Insley at once and his whole face lit up with a prolonged smile. I have never seen him look more happy.

Insley Osborne died on a bleak day in January, 1952. George Kendall told me Insley knew he was dying when the end came. He could not speak, but he put his hand in George's and faintly squeezed a "good-bye." Frances Osborne lay critically ill in Culver Hospital at the same time. In a matter of weeks she too died. The whole college mourned.

ROBERT E. VAUGHAN

This section about faculty members in the 1920s and 1930s would be incomplete without a few words devoted to Pete Vaughan. If Wabash continues to be a storybook kind of college, the day will come, I predict, when Pete Vaughan will be regarded in much the same way that the legendary Indian, Francis Cayou, has been regarded in Wabash history.

In his prime Pete was a great hulking man with broad shoulders and a head like a Greek god. He was all meat and bone, with no fat. Even when an old man he still walked with the lithe gait of the natural athlete. And a superb athlete he was! He grew up in Crawfordsville where he starred as a clever member of the high school basketball team which, I believe, won a state championship. Being from a staunch Catholic family, he went to Notre Dame where he became a bone-crushing fullback on the football team. Legend has it that in a game with the University of Michigan, Pete plunged for a touchdown with such force that his head broke off one of the wooden goal posts. He won All-American recognition. After two years at Notre Dame he transferred to Princeton, probably with inducements from Princeton alumni. He played football there for two years, again winning All-American recognition. After that he coached here and there, including a stint as basketball coach at Purdue, and then entered military service. Like George Kendall, he went into action rather soon in France, and like Osborne he had a brief tour of military duty at President Wilson's headquarters in Paris. These facts I learned from Pete himself in a series of conversations I had with him in the 1930s.

President Mackintosh brought Pete to Wabash as head coach of football and basketball in the fall of 1919. From then until President Sparks replaced him with Glenn Harmeson, as football coach and director of athletics right after World War II, Pete was a towering figure on the Wabash campus. His early years at Wabash — from 1919 until about 1928 — were years in which more glory was added to the Wabash athletic tradition.

Like Cayou's football teams, Pete's teams played a rugged schedule year after year. As late as my freshman and sophomore years, Wabash was still playing universities like Purdue, Indiana, Illinois, Iowa, Northwestern, and Minnesota. In the years just before then Army and Notre Dame were sometimes on the schedule too. The last game with Notre Dame, in the era of Notre Dame's famed Four Horsemen, was played, I believe, in 1924. Usually Wabash lost these games, but until the curriculum and the entrance requirements were changed by President Hopkins, the scores were respectable, and now and then Wabash managed to beat Purdue. Wabash teams were regarded as colorful and scrappy, a pleasure to watch. Always there were a few outstanding and spectacular individual stars — men like Pete Thorn and Lon Goldsberry. Wabash was still good copy for the sports pages of newspapers then, often winning headline attention. In the fall of 1927, I cut out of the *Indianapolis Star* and posted above my desk a banner headline which read, "Wabash Launches Burning Attack to Defeat Colgate 14 to 7." We were all thrilled by and cocky about that victory. I was especially proud because Clayton Weist, my close friend from Princeton, made the winning touchdown.

The same thing was true of Pete's basketball teams in the early 1920s. Their schedules were long and arduous. And they won more than they lost. Pete produced another "Wonder Five" built around men like Chadwick, Goldsberry, Burdette, and "Cat" Adam. The run of basketball glory was still strong my freshman year, with a team full of stars like Red Robinson, Benny DeVol, Theron Coffel, Tootie Thornburg, and others. Invariably the gymnasium was packed for home games, and a rowdier, noisier student cheering section never existed at Wabash. Late arriving freshmen were tossed head over heels by upper classmen into the top bleachers. Young faculty wives and Crawfordsville girls on arrival were greeted with shrill whistles and ribald cheers. The girls blushed, but they loved it. When the pep band broke into "When Wabash rips them up again — Hurrah! Hurrah!" the place went mad. And when it played "Old Wabash" the rafters all but shook with the thunderous chorus of singing. It was a very exciting time to study at Wabash.

Pete Vaughan was at the center of this excitement but he himself was an unflappable, laconic, gruff kind of guy who always stayed in the background. He spent long hours at the gymnasium and on the gridiron. Until I was president and occasionally asked him to come to my office, I cannot recall seeing him in Center Hall. He appeared to be a silent, somewhat shy man, avoiding

147

the spotlight always. He hated public appearances and almost never spoke in public. In 1947 (perhaps it was 1948) on the occasion of his retirement, Indianapolis alumni organized a testimonial dinner for him at the Indianapolis Athletic Club. It was a big crowd with many of his former great players back for the occasion. After the banquet there were numerous fulsome speeches, presentations of resolutions, memorial gifts, and so on. Pete at the speaker's table seemed embarrassed and uncomfortable. When it came his time to speak everyone rose and there was prolonged applause. Pete stood there smiling and shifting from one foot to another. Finally, when quiet came, he mumbled a few words ending in "Well, thanks a lot," and sat down.

But although he disliked public speaking, he loved telling stories to his "kids" — stories about athletes, famous games, his wartime experiences, and the like. When I became well acquainted with Pete in the 1930s I found such stories, interspersed with his rippling chuckle, fascinating. I gained a better understanding of why it was that his "kids" loved him. Often as I traveled around the country in the late 1950s and early 1960s meeting alumni groups, one or more of his former players would ask me, "How's old Pete?" often adding some such remark as "Ah, what a man!" or "There was a great guy!"

I am sure the academic changes made in the early years of the Hopkins administration became a bitter pill for Pete to swallow. But, unlike Harry Scholler, director of athletics and baseball coach who, as I have explained elsewhere, was loud and outspoken in his opposition to the changes, Pete, so far as I could tell, never voiced his disappointment. He was too good a soldier for that. Nor did he lament the austere budgets assigned to him in the depression years. He did the best he could, and his best was often quite impressive as far as results were concerned. The game schedules were vastly different and so were his teams, but they played with spirit, sometimes way above all reasonable expectations. Pete improvised from one year to the next, making adjustments to suit his material. When he had a big powerful man like Earl Dowd in football, he built his offense around one man. When there was no big man, he concentrated on a passing attack. In basketball he experimented with the fast break and the full court press long before these became standard practices. In spite of all this, in the late 1930s he came in for frequent alumni criticisms. Some said he was "dumb." It was unfair. But fair or unfair Pete seemed untroubled. When Dr. Sparks decided changes in the athletic department should be made, Pete cheerfully stepped aside. He left the college to manage the local Coca-Cola plant, which was a family business. For some years he rarely came on campus.

Pete was a confirmed bachelor. He never dated girls and he shunned social parties. His recreation in Crawfordsville was at the Elks Club, where he might have a bottle of beer and an hour or two at the billiard table. Regularly after retirement he went to Notre Dame for the big home games. Otherwise he stuck to business. His friends and acquaintances, therefore, were astounded when without warning he married Esther Luckett, President Hopkins' long-time secretary. It was not the most natural of marriages. Both were well along in years. Each was very much set in routine habits and interests. Esther's father and mother were staunch conservative Presbyterians, suspicious of Catholics. Pete's sister (Mrs. Eldon Riggs) a widow by then, was jealous of "Robert," whom she idolized. But the marriage was a good one. Unhappily, not long after the marriage, Esther fell seriously ill. She became progressively worse, losing the use of her legs and finally speaking only with difficulty. Pete cared for her with remarkable tenderness. The sight of the big man daily carrying Esther out to their car for an afternoon ride was touching. After she died, Pete took care of Esther's mother until her death with the same kind of tenderness.

My friendship with Pete Vaughan was a late development for me at Wabash but it was a good one. I admired him and enjoyed talking with him. In 1959 following my break with Garland Frazier, Harmeson's successor as football coach and director of athletics, I began to search for a new man to revive a spirited athletic program within the new academic framework of the college. I asked Pete to help me and he did. He talked with all candidates we seriously considered. At the suggestion of Norman Moore (dean of students and former football player and assistant dean at Princeton), I investigated Ken Keuffel, head football coach at Lawrenceville Academy. I immediately liked Ken. The idea of appointing a Ph.D. in English as football coach appealed to me and so did the notion of seeing the single wing style of football instituted at Wabash. After Ken's visit to Crawfordsville I asked Pete what he thought. He chuckled. "Well, he's sure different," he said. "But he is a very smart student of the game and, brother, does he have enthusiasm! The kids would like him. I think he would be pretty good." We appointed Ken Keuffel football coach, and at the same time I persuaded Pete to come back for a few years as athletic director. He was then seventy-two. He jumped at the offer, and I think he loved being back in the Wabash gymnasium again. I never made an appointment while president which pleased me more.

Somewhere in the college there must be a photograph of Pete Vaughan, taken during a football game in the middle 1920s. It should be enlarged and hung alongside a similar enlarged photograph of Cayou, in an appropriate place on campus. It appeared in the 1930 yearbook. Pete is down on one knee on the sideline watching intently the development of a play. His cap is pulled down. His mouth is open. He is unconsciously rolling a cigarette. It is an excellent study of Pete's total absorbtion in the game. And that is a fitting way to remember him at Wabash.

Such, as I remember them, were fourteen of the long-time faculty members who, between World War I and World War II, made Wabash a good place of learning. They all came to the college as young men during the presidency of Dr. Mackintosh and they grew old in its service. All but one of them went through the sixteen Hopkins years, and all of them continued well into the Sparks years. A few were still in active service through most of my own administration. They were in their prime during probably the most austere era in the financial history of the college. Their average individual salaries during those years was less than $200 a month. There was no retirement plan, and there were no sabbatical leaves of absence.[14] They may have been conscious of this penury, but there was very little complaining. They were happy with their way of life, and they made the morale of the faculty remarkably high.

As a group they lacked the kudos of another generation of long time faculty members who succeeded them. Nor as a group did they have the brilliance and versatility in teaching later exemplified at Wabash by men like Jack Charles, Harry Cotton, Eric Dean, and Ben Rogge. But in dedication to a cause, neither their predecessors nor their successors surpassed them. Their cause was Wabash College.

14. The Board of Trustees adopted the first retirement plan in 1948. Sabbatical leaves were not granted before 1963.

III

WABASH TRUSTEES

The pages of college histories are filled for the most part with accounts of the achievements of presidents and faculty members. Relatively little space is given to boards of trustees. Individual trustees from time to time appear in these narratives, sometimes prominently. Almost always, however, their roles are limited to matters of finance. Thus they appear as benefactors or as saviors of the college in moments of financial crisis. Rarely in college histories does the board of trustees come through as an integral part of the college on an equal footing with the faculty and administration.

Superficially this can be explained by saying that college histories are usually written by faculty people who understandably are disposed to attach highest priorities to what happens on campus. Inevitably this means focusing attention on presidents, deans, professors, and students. A more important explanation, in my judgment, is embedded in the subtle changes which gradually took place in the early twentieth century in the relationships between boards of trustees and the institutions for which they were responsible. This in turn touches on a subject that is far more important than college histories.

For a long, long time the role of trustees in the life of a college (I am speaking of small private liberal arts colleges) was closely identified with the role of the faculty. Often professors also served as trustees, or trustees also served as professors. In a sense they were interchangeable parts in the early development of the institution, united in a common purpose and a common commitment. Professor Gronert in his part (the first half) of *The First Hundred Years* makes this abundantly clear. Edmund Otis Hovey, for example, was as important as a trustee as he was a professor. Trustee meetings, as Gronert speaks of them, frequently sound like faculty meetings, concerned with academic policy, curriculum details, rules of conduct for students, etc. Not only were trustees "interchangeable" with faculty members; they also occasionally moved from trustee roles into the full-time responsibilities of the college president. Thus, Dr. Kane moved from the presidency of the board to the presidency of the college and for a time served concurrently in both

151

positions. Dr. Mackintosh was perhaps an even better example of the point I am making. He served Wabash first as a trustee, later as trustee and a part-time faculty member, and finally as president.

This close identification of trustees with the on-campus life of the college was characteristic of practically all small private liberal arts colleges throughout the nineteenth century. Early in the twentieth century, however, important changes began to take place in the respective roles of the faculty and the board of trustees. As a consequence of the rising professional self-consciousness of college faculty members and primarily at the insistence of newly-formed professional associations (e.g., the American Association of University Professors), new concepts and new definitions of faculty rights and responsibilities were advanced and gradually accepted by college administrators and trustees. Thus, by the 1920s, it was generally understood that matters of educational and academic policy were the exclusive domain of the faculty. Trustee responsibilities correspondingly were limited to the financial and business affairs of the college. The growing importance of academic freedom and faculty tenure as essential safeguards against tyrannical administrations and boards of trustees served to reinforce the new definitions. So did the growth of educational accrediting associations which in the twentieth century became powerful influences in the development of individual colleges.

This entire process in the early years of the twentieth century without question served to improve the quality of higher education in America and to strengthen the academic integrity of individual institutions. But it also sowed the seeds for new institutional problems which emerged toward the middle of the century and which became increasingly acute in the 1960s and the 1970s. For one thing, it contributed to the widely shared view among faculty members that they and they alone should decide what was in the best interests of their institution. Put in the most crass form, this amounted to faculty assumption of complete control over what a college might or might not do as a place of learning. The function of the president and the board of trustees should be above all else that of providing, in ever increasing quantities, the money required for operating purposes and for capital improvements. But this function in no way implied a residual power on the part of trustees to determine the content of the curriculum, faculty-student ratios, class schedules, instructional methodology, and the like. At least such was the typical faculty point of view by the middle of the twentieth century. In general, trustees acquiesced in this division of responsibilities.

This clear-cut separation of trustee and faculty responsibilities sounded good in theory, but in practice it led to problems. The problems stemmed from the fiscal health of the institution. Educational policy decisions made by the faculty often meant in reality financial decisions which were the domain of the trustees. The proliferation of academic course offerings, size of classes and number of teachers required; promotions in professorial rank; decisions about faculty tenure — all of these were matters for faculty decisions, but they directly affected the cost of operating the institution, a matter for trustee decision. The financial predicament which most private colleges had to contend with in the post-World War II era thus led to second thoughts about the separation of trustee and faculty responsibilities.

In the early 1950s Beardsley Ruml, a long-time trustee of Dartmouth who took an active part in promoting corporate aid to education, brought his creative mind to bear on the problem I am speaking of. With the help of Sidney Tickton, his research assistant, he wrote a little book which he called *Memo to a College Trustee*.[1] Briefly, his argument ran like this: The fiscal problems of private colleges will not be solved in the long run simply by obtaining more and more money, through tuition revenue and gifts, to meet constantly increasing operating budgets. The practice of repeatedly increasing tuition fees leads to the danger of pricing private colleges out of the market. Increasing student aid to preserve enrollments also becomes self-defeating in the long run, because increased unfunded student aid is in reality an added operating expenditure. Finally, desirable and gratifying though successful drives for increased gifts may be, there is a limit to what may be expected from philanthrophy. Reasoning this way, Ruml argued that, in addition to mounting fund drives, private colleges would have to operate more efficiently. This, of course, involved the very heart of the college's academic program and methodology. He concluded, therefore, that college trustees must take back into their hands the responsibility for academic policy which by default had gradually been given exclusively to the faculty.

I was enormously impressed by Ruml's reasoning and I remember being puzzled that Frank Sparks was only mildly interested in his prescriptions. I made a point of attending meetings where Ruml expounded his theories. In this way I became acquainted with Sidney Tickton and formed a friendship with him which led us to work together years later in New York.[2] From Tickton I learned much of the statistical detail which supported Ruml's theories. For me, even though I was still dean of the college at Wabash, this was the beginning of a new way of thinking about college finance which led to my being classified nationally as a "conservative" college president a few years later.

In his ideas for reconstructing the control of academic programs, Ruml was ahead of his time. The 1950s were lush years for American colleges and

1. *Memo to a College Trustee: a Report on Financial and Structural Problems of the Liberal Arts College* (New York: McGraw-Hill, 1959).

2. My acquaintance with Tickton may have had some bearing on the $2 million challenge grant Wabash won from the Ford Foundation in 1960. Tickton by that time had become a consultant for the Foundation and was involved in the process of selecting colleges for those grants. BKT.

universities. Public attitudes toward higher education were almost universally good. The rising birth rate and the rising percentage of high school graduates going on to college made full student enrollment for years to come seem a certainty. The booming national economy gave a strong impetus to philanthrophy. Multimillion dollar fund drives for private colleges and universities became commonplace. Against all of these favorable signs, Ruml's caveats about financial limitations and about the need for more efficient college operations fell on deaf ears.

In spite of this, I continued to think along the lines Ruml had proposed. When I became president of Wabash, I bought and distributed copies of *Memo to a College Trustee* to all Wabash trustees and Wabash faculty members. The reaction of the faculty was predictable — no comment. The reaction of the trustees to my surprise was almost as disappointing. Except for John Collett and Ivan Wiles, I don't recall any trustee interest in even discussing Ruml's recommendations. In 1956 or 1957 I was invited to speak at the annual state meeting of the Association of University Professors. I was assigned the topic, "the role of the faculty in college administration." I do not know what they had expected me to say, but what I in fact said won undivided but also quite unfavorable attention. I made a direct attack on the policy pronouncements of Committee T of the national AAUP.[3] I described much of the current faculty role in the management of college affairs as a usurpation of power from boards of trustees, and I spoke at some length of the vast residual powers still inherent in these boards, if they should choose to exercise them, regardless of what the faculty might think. It was, I admit, a cocky speech, and I had fun needling my audience. I was surprised when the speech was published by AAUP and amused by the indignant responses in the form of letters to the editor. I did nothing further to follow up on this argument. I was too busy by that time helping to raise money for Wabash. (Not until I was president of ICFA in New York did I return to an active role in encouraging more efficient academic operations through trustee action.) But I continued to investigate the history of the importance of boards of trustees, especially at Wabash, and my conviction deepened that the destiny of a good college depends more on the quality and dedication of its board of trustees than it does on any other single element in the make-up of the institution.

In the late 1960s and the early 1970s, the crushing problems that overtook all institutions of higher learning in America, especially private colleges, brought about a reaffirmation of the crucial importance of boards of trustees. The rosy glow that had characterized colleges and universities in the 1950s gave way to the bleakest kind of forebodings and fears. Student activism, black power demands, faculty paralysis, shrinking enrollments, mounting bud-

3. Committee T was a standing committee of AAUP charged with studying faculty participation in college administration. BKT.

get deficits, a decline in philanthropy — all of these and more — combined to present colleges and universities with their most severe crises in the twentieth century. The disappearance of the private liberal arts college as a species in American higher education became a possibility. Under these circumstances boards of trustees again became more nearly what they were in the beginning, the decisive influences in the governance of their colleges. This reaffirmation at many places was not without considerable tension and acrimonious resistance on the part of faculty members and students. Nor was the action of boards of trustees always wise and statesmanlike. It is a tribute to the quality and strength of the Wabash Board of Trustees and to the traditional character of the college itself that these turbulent years passed with minimal confrontations at Wabash and without the angry clashes between faculty and trustees which were common on many campuses. It is another reason for my believing that when the history of Wabash in the twentieth century is written, the role of its Board of Trustees will emerge in heroic dimensions.

The personal thoughts I have been expressing about trustee-faculty relations provide an appropriate frame of reference in which to judge the effectiveness of the Wabash Board of Trustees in the middle decades of the twentieth century. In my appraisal I include the trustees of the Hopkins years, although I knew few of them personally and had only limited opportunities to observe their roles. I am on surer ground as far as trustees for the period 1946–65 are concerned. As dean of the college I attended all board meetings and occasionally executive committee meetings. I also worked closely with the trustee building committees. Thus, before I became president I knew every board member quite well, and with a number of them I had developed close friendships. In the years 1955 to 1965, I worked at least as much with trustees as I did with Wabash faculty members.

Relying on the memories of these personal experiences, I rate the role of the Board of Trustees from 1926 through the 1960s as the most important single influence in the preservation, the strengthening, and the enrichment of Wabash College. In saying this, I do not mean to down-grade the importance of the contributions made by either President Hopkins or President Sparks, or, for that matter, whatever good may have resulted from my own presidency. Nor do I mean to minimize the importance of the quality of the faculty or the significance of the faculty's influence in making Wabash what it was in those years. The fact remains that the Board of Trustees selected the presidents in that almost half a century period. It was the Board of Trustees who responded to the different brands of leadership those presidents offered and who provided them with the support, financial and otherwise, for their constructive and enduring contributions to the college.

In performing this central role, the Wabash Board of Trustees deserves exceptionally high marks in the history of the college and also in comparison with liberal arts college boards in general. The individual members of the board were not always equal in prominence, individual abilities, or financial resources. In several respects the board membership in the 1920s and 1930s was undistinguished and unimpressive by comparison with that in the 1950s and the 1960s. But in both periods the majority, if not all, of the board members made a very deep personal commitment to their trusteeship, and they had a sense of dedication to the best interests of Wabash as they conceived them. These characteristics of Wabash trustees unhappily are not always present in boards of trustees. I have had personal experience with college boards whose members took their trusteeships lightly and who, therefore, tended to leave to the president, once he was selected, the working of miracles. No matter how able the president may be, under these circumstances, it means mounting troubles for the college; if the president is mediocre or weak, it means disaster sooner or later. The histories of America's strongest private colleges, over and over, reveal the presence of able and dedicated boards of trustees. The Wabash Board of Trustees has been that kind of board, especially in the years of which I am writing.

Another happy characteristic of the Wabash Board of Trustees is that, no matter how forceful or opinionated its individual members, no matter how extensive its disagreements with faculty positions, no matter how severe its disapproval of individual faculty members' points of view, the board has never acted arbitrarily or tyrannically with respect to the faculty. There have been numerous instances when one or several trustees were annoyed by some faculty position or political or economic opinion. But in these instances, trustee remonstrance was properly made to the president. Never was there the kind of trustee action aimed at repressing freedom of opinion which at many other institutions led to AAUP censure. In the rare instances when trustee decisions ran counter to majority faculty preferences, the process was a rational, deliberate one, with plenty of time allowed for give-and-take discussion with faculty representatives.

The early twentieth-century redefinition of faculty and trustee responsibilities which I have discussed applied at Wabash as it did everywhere else. President Hopkins had much to do with establishing Wabash precedents in support of this division of responsibility, and yet, in a peculiar Wabash way, there was never any hard and fast formalization of this division. There was never any printed proclamation or published institutional manual, so common elsewhere, spelling out the powers of the faculty and those of the trustees. Through all of these years the rapport between individual trustees and individual faculty members was quite remarkable. Much of the credit for this happy circumstance goes to the faculty, at least to those faculty stalwarts whom

156

each generation invariably produced. But much of the credit also goes to the good sense and statesmanlike qualities of individual trustee leaders.

This "peculiar Wabash way" left in the hands of the Board of Trustees residual powers which were (and are) limited only by the State of Indiana as the source of the college's charter and its amendments. I used to speak of this residual trustee power as amounting to exclusive responsibility for "the fundamental character of the college." I liked that concept when I announced it, and I like it still. Whether it was consciously applying this concept or not, the Wabash board on a few occasions has not hesitated to act in accordance with it. A celebrated precedent was established by the board in the closing years of the nineteenth century when, despite the recommendations of President Burroughs, backed by the majority of the faculty, and despite noisy pressures from within Crawfordsville (including a lawsuit brought by Peter Kennedy) — in spite of all this — the Board of Trustees adamantly refused to make Wabash a coeducational institution. A second instance was the board's affirmation in the 1950s of complete independence from federal aid to private colleges, despite faculty wishes and the general trend among other colleges. A third instance came in the early 1970s when, repeating history, the board reaffirmed its intention of keeping Wabash a men's college. This kind of resolution and courage on the part of its trustees has had more to do with the distinctive image for rugged independence Wabash has enjoyed for almost a century and a half in Indiana than is generally acknowledged.[4]

How can one explain these remarkable qualities of the Wabash Board of Trustees? Perhaps they cannot be explained. But I believe there are two or three points worthy of reflection.

In the twentieth century, at least, the Wabash Board of Trustees has always been predominately composed of Wabash men. Most of these received degrees, but even those who did not (e.g., Ike Elston and Parrish Fuller) had spent enough time at Wabash to fall permanently under its spell. It has long seemed to me that "outsiders" on the Wabash board never played the significant roles in Wabash affairs that "outsiders" frequently played in the history of other good colleges (e.g., Laird Bell at Carleton College). In fact, most "outside" Wabash trustees have been disappointments, and their stay on the board has been brief and perfunctory. The most illustrious trustee that Wabash has ever had was probably Henry Ward Beecher. But apart from his lending a prestigious name to Wabash, I was never able to discover a single instance of

---

4. The starting point for this tradition of trustee courage and resolution was not the celebrated "kneeling in the snow" act in 1832. As far as I am concerned, it was the trustee decision a few years later, following the destruction by fire of the newly constructed South Hall (it was not called South Hall; it was Wabash College), to rebuild the college and to persevere with its purpose. How many other infant colleges closed and disappeared in the face of disasters less severe! BKT.

157

his making a significant contribution to trustee decisions. Certainly the handful of "outsiders" who came and went in Wabash trusteeship in the twentieth century were largely supernumerary (e.g., Francis Dean of Cleveland, Evans Woollen of Indianapolis, Hjalmar Johnson of Chicago). The two notable exceptions to this kind of experience were Governor James Goodrich and Eli Lilly. But those two are important exceptions proving the rule. Year in and year out the main trustee load was carried by a succession of Wabash men.

There are dangers in this kind of board membership. The numerous handbooks for college governance, written usually by college professors, prescribe elaborate mixtures in board membership — a sprinkling of professional educators, a certain percentage of "outsiders," and so on. These involve precautions against inbreeding, against an excess of "old-school-tieism," against the disposition of alumni to embalm the college in forms dear to them from their undergraduate years, against excessive political or economic conservatism. These may be theoretical dangers for an institution, but, generally speaking, I could never detect their manifestation on the Wabash board. Despite their common sentimental allegiance to their alma mater, they represented different life experiences, different life styles, different geographical areas, different philosophical points of view. (It is hard to imagine two individuals, for example, more widely separated in value systems and life styles than Ike Elston and Edgar Evans). The Wabash board traditionally has been regarded, correctly, as politically conservative but almost always there has been a healthy amount of dissent in this context (Pete Edson, for example). My final report to the Board of Trustees was a tribute to them, stressing the board's diversity and varied creativity. This diversity was (and is) a built-in safeguard against the kind of unimaginative, stereotyped posture professional educators so fear. And the common unifying emotion and interest that animated the board was love of Wabash. Again I use the word "love" deliberately. Wabash and what happened there, Wabash and its triumphs and failures, Wabash and its dreams for the future — these were all terribly important to practically all Wabash men on the board. This is a matter of love. These rich and deep emotions in my judgment explain the remarkable devotion and the inordinate amount of time, energy, and money given to Wabash by its trustees.

Closely allied to this characteristic many individual Wabash trustees have always had a variety of other particular interests in campus life. These included close friendships with some faculty members, especially with Wabash alumni faculty members who shared with their counterparts on the board what I used to call the "Wabash mystique." Especially important were the affiliations trustees had with the various fraternity chapters on campus. The extremely important influence exercised by fraternities on the life and character of the college in the twentieth century, at least up until the late sixties, is in itself a subject worthy of a separate book. My point here is that the traditionally close continuing interests of Wabash alumni in their respective fraternity chapters gave Wabash trustees ready access to Wabash student leaders. It also provided a continuing source of information about changing undergraduate attitudes and interests. This acted as an antidote against the danger of trustees "embalming" the college. Moreover, Wabash trustees were usually regarded by undergraduates in their fraternity chapters as heroes to be listened to and emulated. (I shall never forget the thrill I experienced at the Beta House in the late 1920s when Beta members of the board would visit us, take part in our meetings, discuss college problems with us, ask us what we thought about this or that matter under consideration by the board.) This relationship in subtle ways contributed to good *esprit de corps* within the college.

By and large, Betas and Phi Gams — because they were more numerous on the board — played the principal roles in this kind of relationship. But practically all fraternities had similar contacts. Edgar Evans, Roy Massena, and later Marshall Pipin maintained contacts with Delta Tau Delta. Will Hays, Lawrence De Vore, and Will Hays, Jr., did the same with Phi Delta Theta, Parrish Fuller and Byron Hollett with Sigma Chi, Harry Moses with Lambda Chi Alpha, Dwight (Pete) Green (Governor of Illinois) with Kappa Sigma, and so on. How does one properly appraise the valuable by-products which came from such relationships?

A final point I would make is that the Wabash board in those decades had great strength in its leadership. The presidents of the board were very different from each other, as I shall point out later, but each of them in his respective time was responsible for board action of the highest importance. Each of them had vision for the future and each set an example in service and gifts to the college that was inspirational to others. How different the Wabash history of these years might have been had the presidents of the board been hesitant, timid men, only half-heartedly committed to the Wabash cause.

College presidents come and go. In the twentieth century, Wabash has already had seven presidents and three acting presidents for short intervals. Except possibly for my succession of Frank Sparks, each of these changes meant a break in continuity and a change in administrative style. But in the Board of Trustees, as in the faculty, there is a kind of continuity, an overlapping of stewardship, a passing of the torch of Wabash faith from one set of hands to another. This provides for a consistent level of leadership and service and comes close to accounting for Wabash's secret of success. I had this in mind in 1973, when I agreed to serve as an interim president for La Universidad de las Americas in Mexico. Speaking at the first meeting of that university's Board of Trustees and faculty leaders, I said in part, "If a university has a strong and dedicated board of trustees and a capable and dedicated faculty, it really is not very important who becomes president of the institution."

It is possible that I have overemphasized the importance of the emotional attachment between Wabash members of the Board of Trustees and the college as a motivating influence in the stellar service they rendered in its behalf. I am sure my own emotional attachment to Wabash operates as a strong bias in such judgments. Nevertheless, I stick by my conviction that this emotional quality comes as close as any single thing can come to explaining the secret of the success of Wabash.

Strong feelings of pride in and allegiance to alma mater are characteristic phenomena in the history of American higher education. But it is generally recognized that in a few institutions this common characteristic reaches extraordinary and exceptional levels of reality. Thus, all of the Ivy League colleges are famous in part because of the remarkable devotion they elicit from their alumni, and some — Princeton, Dartmouth and Yale, for example — top the others in this respect. Intercollegiate athletic rivalries often provide the most visible and audible form by which this alumni spirit is expressed. But it is not limited to athletics. It extends to the total being of the institution, its history, its traditions, its academic fame, its financial resources, its promise for the future. It has, in fact, the elements of a religious faith — love, reverence, and a sense of duty.

It must have been clear from the speeches I used to make to Wabash friends and alumni, just as it must be clear from what I have written in these reflections, that I believe Wabash is another example of the few institutions in which pride in and allegiance to alma mater reach "extraordinary and exceptional levels of reality." Among private colleges west of the Allegheny Mountains and certainly in Indiana, Wabash has been for years and continues to be a little different. It is not just another typical liberal arts college. There is something distinctive about it. And this "something distinctive" has been enormously appealing to the vast majority of those who have studied there. Even those who stayed for only a year or two and then went elsewhere to graduate often kept Wabash for their first allegiance (e.g., Ed Ball, Wabash and Yale; and Carroll Ragan, composer of "Old Wabash," Wabash and the University of Illinois). Why? The answer is a matter of mystique.

Not infrequently this Wabash distinctiveness has been acknowledged in non-Wabash circles. Ford Wilkinson, then president of Rose Poly (now Rose-Hulman Institute), at a dinner meeting of the presidents of Associated Colleges of Indiana in the late 1950s, embarrassed me (and pleased me) when he spoke of Wabash as the one member college of ACI which enjoyed an "Ivy League image." Melvin Hyde, while president of Evansville College (now the University of Evansville), frequently expressed publicly his admiration of and curiosity about the "amazing Wabash alumni spirit." Russell Humbert, dynamic president of DePauw, which has its own body of highly loyal alumni, paid Wabash a bank-handed compliment once when he complained of the "chauvinism" of Wabash alumni. At an exploratory conference of twelve midwestern college presidents and deans in 1961 when Landrum Bolling, president of Earlham College, and I took the lead in forming the Great Lakes Colleges Association, Jim Dixon, president of Antioch College, half-jokingly remarked at one point, "I did not know that Wabash would cooperate with anyone!" In the winter of 1954–55 William Cadbury, academic dean of Haverford College, in supporting my nomination for the chairmanship of the American Conference of Academic Deans, referred to Wabash as a "distinguished Eastern college which happens to be located in Indiana." Bish Thompson, popular columnist for the *Evansville Press,* in one of several columns about Wabash, praised its "ferocious alumni spirit" and called it his "adopted college."

Whether Wabash still enjoys this kind of image, I do not know. Nor do I know if the Wabash community still is self-conscious about and proud of its distinctiveness. But I believe there can be no question that in the twentieth century — up to the late 1960s, at any rate — Wabash enjoyed and prospered from an almost fabled reputation. And this reinforces the observations I will shortly write about individual members of the Wabash board in the period, 1926–1965. The one quality they have in common is this emotional attachment to Wabash.

I have elected to write about only a handful of the trustees whom I knew well in these years. But the same central point I make about them could be made about practically all Wabash alumni trustees who served in those years. Men like Will Hays, Ned Ames, Roy Massena, Mark Brown, Lafe Lafollette, Ed Ball, Allen Saunders, Frank Misch, Marshall Pipin, and others would be equally worthy of similar tributes. Nor do I mean to imply that the few trustees about whom I make brief comments were the most important trustees of this era. Several of them fall into that category, but others do not. Neither am I suggesting that I was personally closer to the individuals I write about than I was to others. Richard O. Ristine and Will Hays, Jr., for example, befriended me in moments of personal crisis in ways I shall never forget; to them as close personal friends I owe debts I can never repay. The truth is that I feel unequal to the task of writing about all trustees whom I knew well and who meant much to me. In a sense, therefore, those whom I have elected to write about amount to a random sample by which I can illustrate the general points I have been making.

JAMES D. ADAMS
Wabash 1908

Jim Adams' membership on the Board of Trustees in the late 1940s and early 1950s was not a lengthy one. Except for serving as chairman of the trustee building committee right after World War II, which I have discussed earlier, he had no important trustee committee assignments. A well-to-do rather than a really wealthy man, he gave modestly, though regularly to the college. Nevertheless, Jim Adams impressed me as a first-rate trustee, thoughtful, conscientious, and always dependable. A soft spoken, modest man, he was usually quiet at board meetings, but when he spoke it was with great good sense. Occasionally he could be tough about his convictions as he was when he insisted that Walter Scholer be associated with Eric Gugler as the college's architects. In a way he represents the numerous alumni who, during relatively short tours of duty as Wabash trustees, have taken their responsibilities seriously and have functioned well. Such trustees, unlike "permanent" members of the board, rarely receive much credit in the official college history. I suppose that is one of the reasons I decided to write about him.

But there are other and better reasons to remember Jim Adams. Earlier in this section I spoke of the healthy diversity that existed traditionally among Wabash trustees. Jim Adams is a case in point. As an undergraduate he had no fraternity affiliation. Like Lee McCanliss and later Frank Misch, he, therefore, brought to a Board of Trustees composed predominately of fraternity men a different perspective on the life of the college — the point of view of the "have nots," so to speak.

Adams was a Democrat (Jeffersonian), which also meant a slightly different set of presuppositions in a board made up principally of Republicans. Jim had been increasingly active in Indiana Democratic politics in the 1920s and was appointed state highway commissioner by Governor Paul McNutt in 1932. In that post he was credited with several innovations in the state's labor force which helped in the common attack on the "Great Depression." It reinforced his reputation for being a champion of little people.

Finally in a board made up largely of city men (Indianapolis, Chicago, New York, Toledo, Detroit), Jim Adams was essentially "small town." He loved Columbia City and its people and people like that all over Indiana. His successful business enterprises — newspapers, banking, farming, and a small manufacturing plant—were close to the people of small towns. He was Hoosier to the core, and all of this was reflected not only during his Wabash trusteeship, but for years before as an alumnus.

Jim Adams was an undergraduate at Wabash in the era of the original Little Giants. It was a chapter in his life that remained forever dear and important to him. He was a good athlete at Wabash and a star baseball player. Years later when I knew him, his lean, rugged frame made it easy to imagine what he was like at the age of twenty. Like most of his contemporaries, he regarded Francis Cayou as a hero and felt a great sense of loss when Cayou was fired by Dr. Mackintosh. I used to be spellbound by Jim's recollections of Cayou and his Little Giants in the long conversations he and I occasionally had. A popular chapel speech I made in 1953 and later repeated at a Homecoming Chapel for alumni which I called "Francis Cayou and the Little Giants" was full of insights given to me by Jim Adams.[5]

But Jim also regarded most of his Wabash professors as heroes, too. Bodine, he told me, made an enormous impression on him, so much so that he felt a sense of shame when he did not come up to Bodine's expectations. Professor Milford in English literature was also apparently a powerful influence. I will never forget the thrill I experienced when Jim told me how, when he was playing baseball for Wabash, he used Shakespeare to bolster his courage and his resolution. Before taking his stance at the plate as batter and waiting for the first pitch, he would say to himself, "Cowards die many times before their deaths; the valiant never taste of death but once." "That never failed to help me then and it never failed to help me in later life when I was up against serious difficulties," he told me.

Over the years Jim Adams communicated his enthusiasm for Wabash to innumerable youngsters who, as a consequence, became Wabash students themselves. More often than not they were athletes and poor. Jim quietly put up the money for their college costs. One of these (Bob Fahl) became a star football player for Glenn Harmeson and later married Jim's older daughter.

EUGENE N. BEESLEY
Wabash 1929

Gene Beesley and I were fraternity brothers and close friends at Wabash in the late 1920s. He was a year ahead of me, but we early discovered that we had common interests which caused us to work together on fraternity chapter matters and to share social diversions customary for fraternity brothers. I succeeded Gene as treasurer of the Betas at Wabash and a year later followed him as chapter president.

This undergraduate friendship has continued for a lifetime; of all the trustees I am writing about I know Gene Beesley best. Curiously enough, however, until the closing years of my presidency at Wabash I saw less of Gene than I did of other key trustees, notably John Collett. In part this was because Gene's spectacularly successful business career meant that he was an inordinately busy man. His brilliant performance with Eli Lilly & Co. led to his presidency of the company while still relatively young. Later he became chairman of the board at Lilly and continued as chief executive officer until he was sixty-five. Inevitably, his record at Lilly led to his involvement in numerous other major business enterprises in America. He became a director for such corporations as Uniroyal, Procter & Gamble, and General Motors. Above all he became a power in the national and international pharmaceutical industrial

5. See *These Fleeting Years*, pp. 75–80.

community, frequently drawn into federal governmental affairs at both the congressional and the presidential levels. He also inevitably became involved in many civic, charitable, and religious enterprises, both local and national, which meant heavy demands on his time. The most important and time consuming of these was Lilly Endowment, Inc., the second largest philanthropic foundation in America, where he served for years as a member of the Board of Directors, later as president, and finally as chairman of the endowment.

In view of this kind of career, the remarkable thing is that Gene Beesley found time to serve his alma mater as a trustee for many years and to take that assignment seriously. He was without question one of the members of the Wabash board in the decades following World War II who contributed to its reputation as a "blue chip board." For years he served faithfully and efficiently as chairman of the board's executive committee. In moments of crisis he was as steady as granite. His annual financial contributions to Wabash were modest for a man of his means. But this bothered Frank Sparks more than it did me. I never underestimated the importance of Gene's personal closeness to Eli Lilly, nor his key influence in Lilly Endowment. Moreover, in the early 1970s Gene gave to Wabash a half million dollars as a personal gift.

Gene Beesley came to Wabash as a green youngster from Thorntown, Indiana. He was a protégé of "Lafe" LaFollette, also from Thorntown, who also served for years on the Wabash Board. Although I believe Beesley earned a law degree by the night school route in Toledo in his early years with Eli Lilly and Co., Wabash was really his only alma mater. His experience there was a turning point in his life and, as for countless others, his Wabash years were happy and rewarding. In his freshman year he starred in the Scarlet Masque's production of *Merton of the Movies*. He went on from one such triumph to another as an undergraduate. He played a lusty first trombone in the Wabash "Sea Going Band," worked his way up to senior manager of the last of Pete Vaughan's great football teams, was an outstanding president of the Beta chapter, and a power in campus politics. "Big Man on Campus" though he was, he also achieved a good scholastic record. And for all his eminence in national and international business circles and despite his commitments to other worthy causes, Gene Beesley never forgot what Wabash had meant to him in his youth.

JOHN P. COLLETT
Wabash 1924

Since 1955 John Collett has been the most valuable single trustee on the Wabash board. Moreover, the quality of his trusteeship since he joined the board in 1939 as a young man makes him one of the truly great trustees in Wabash history.

In saying this I am mindful that this distinction might be accorded by some to Eli Lilly. In view of the many millions of dollars Eli Lilly has given to Wabash, it could be argued that he deserves to be called Wabash's most valuable trustee. But Eli Lilly — for all of the magnificent financial support he has given to Wabash and for all of the years he has been a trustee — functioned on the board as something of a bystander and an onlooker. Occasionally he would speak his mind about some important issue and his views frequently were decisive, but many times I have heard him say with a smile, "Well, I think that's a question for you Wabash fellows to decide!" Furthermore, Eli Lilly's continuing interest in Wabash reflected his great confidence in and high esteem for those officers and members of the board who were most directly involved in managing the college's affairs. This included John Collett as well as Gene Beesley.

The considered judgment I have expressed about John is no disparagement of the value of other important trustees in these years; not at all. I am reasonably confident that the consensus of all trustees serving Wabash in the past twenty years, if it were sought, would confirm my conclusion.

I first became acquainted with John shortly after he became a member of the board when we served together on a joint faculty-trustee committee to review the athletic situation at Wabash. I was immediately attracted by his good judgment and by his strong feelings that competitive sports were especially important in a men's college. These were feelings which I shared. (I had already begun to use the adjective "robust" in talking about the Wabash way of life.) Later, after World War II when I attended trustee meetings in my capacity as dean of the college, I was increasingly impressed by John's good sense about the college and by his obvious dedication to its best interests. I remember saying as much to Dr. Sparks and Lee McCanliss following a board meeting in the late 1940s and being deflated by Lee's rather airy dismissal of John's thinking. It was not until later that I realized Lee was habitually condescending toward Indianapolis trustees in general with the exception of Eli Lilly.

In these same years John Collett, I believe, developed some interest in me and we found ourselves frequently talking about the college and its possibilities. Following the speech I made at the Indianapolis Columbia Club in May of 1946, which I mentioned earlier, John was especially warm in his congratulations and in the encouragement which he gave me. For me it was the beginning af a friendship which deepened with the passing years and on which, once I was president, I relied heavily.

In December, 1955, following the board meeting when I was elected president of the college, I confessed to John my fear of following Frank Sparks, especially in the matter of fund raising. I will never forget his saying to me, "Don't worry. I believe you will raise more money than Frank has. And I can help you." It seemed incredible at the time but John was as good as his word. He did help; together in the next ten years we did raise more money than Frank Sparks and Lee McCanliss had raised for Wabash. John and his wife, Mary (Hamilton), were generous with their personal gifts to Wabash. Furthermore, his extensive business and financial acquaintanceship meant that he knew where money was. His shrewd appraisals about potential givers were almost always right. And he had courage and confidence when it came to asking for major gifts. I am speaking principally of Indiana sources for gift money.

My last fund-raising act for Wabash was prompted by this Collett talent. In the summer of 1965 after I had resigned, at John's suggestion I went with him to talk with Mr. H. J. Reade in Indianapolis. John was convinced that Mr. Reade, an elderly and wealthy man, was a good candidate for a major gift to Wabash, notwithstanding his close association with Butler University, and he believed the state of Mr. Reade's health made it imperative to talk with him at once. Our visit with Mr. Reade went well. I proposed that he make a substantial gift to Wabash to help with our plans for a new gymnasium, but that he retain the income from this gift for life. He liked the idea and later that summer, with Byron Hollett's legal help, a formal contract was signed. In a matter of weeks after that Mr. Reade died, and Wabash applied the entire gift to construction of the new gymnasium.

Another area in which John Collett's service to the college was of exceptional value was the management of the college's investment portfolio. Here he brought to bear his professional knowledge and business experience. This is not the place to dwell on his private business and professional accomplishments. I would like to underscore the fact, however, that John Collett had the courage in the height of the "Great Depression" to form his own investment company while he was still in his early thirties. From that audacious beginning Collett & Company went on to achieve in later years brilliant success, including participating frequently with important national investment houses in the public sale of major financial underwriting programs.

For years John was a key member of the trustee investment committee while Oscar Welborn was treasurer. In 1957 he succeeded Oscar as treasurer of the college and he served in that capacity until he became president of the board in the winter of 1965–66. When he accepted the treasurership he specified that he wanted authority to act in the purchase and sale of securities without prior reference to the investment committee. He coupled this request with the recommendation that the board retain the services of an outside investment counsel who could check and advise him on investment policy and on specific purchases and sales. The executive committee of the board was to become the overall supervisory committee for the treasurer.

John's proposal was approved without question, and he began to look for the outside counsel. What I knew about investments was next to nothing, but as a matter of courtesy John asked me to go with him to Boston for conferences with several prospects. He arranged a luncheon meeting with Paul Cabot, treasurer of Harvard and member of the Harvard Corporation, to get his advice. As a consequence of several conferences in Boston, we (i.e., John) decided on Loomis Sayles, Inc., as the right counsellors for Wabash. A formal agreement was finally made and for a series of years thereafter Loomis Sayles was involved in the management of the Wabash portfolio. I was favorably impressed by the officers of Loomis Sayles and by their account men assigned to Wabash, especially the second of these, Jos Lambie. And yet I was increasingly struck by the fact that Loomis Sayles never made any policy or specific transaction recommendations that John Collett hadn't already thought of. My limited amateurish knowledge of such matters simply increased my respect for John's financial acumen. I continue to believe that the healthy growth of the market value of as well as the rising yield from Wabash investments in these years were almost exclusively the fruit of John's knowledge and experience.

Particularly after 1958, it was John Collett to whom I turned for guidance and help on all manner of college problems. The fact that Ivan Wiles, who succeeded Frank Sparks as chairman of the board in 1958, was invariably a long way from Indiana made it natural for me to consult more frequently with the treasurer than with the board chairman. I could always count on John's thoughtful attention to any problem, no matter how inconsequential, about which I sought his advice. Often he took the initiative in calling me.

As I have made clear in another section of these recollections, I attached great importance to the opportunity which came to Wabash in 1960 to win one of the first of the Ford Foundation Challenge Grants. Several trustees were very helpful in winning that grant, but none more so than John Collett. In the spring of that year, after Wabash had obviously emerged successful from the preliminary winnowing process applied to some 100 colleges, Elizabeth Pascal from the Ford Foundation came to Indiana for an in-depth inspection of the college. For reasons I have alluded to elsewhere, I was sure of my own standing with Miss Pascal, but this, I knew, would not amount to much in her mind if she did not come away with a good impression of the faculty and the trustees. Her visits with the faculty went off quite well. She then asked if she could meet some trustees. I turned to John for help. He and Mary arranged a dinner meeting in their home in Indianapolis, which I am confident had much to do with Elizabeth's going back to New York with high marks for Wabash. Mary Collett's part in that evening's discussions was more important than she realized. As a Smith graduate she talked Elizabeth's language.

Some weeks later, when it was clear that Wabash was going to get a grant, but the amount remained to be determined, James Armsey, who was in charge of this grant program at Ford, came out to meet with trustees and with me. I arranged a luncheon at the Columbia Club with as much "brass" from the

167

board as I could assemble. Mr. Lilly was present, but for understandable reasons said almost nothing. Lige Martindale for other reasons was also quiet. Ivan Wiles was helpful but a little too tentative for Armsey. Gene Beesley, as he sometimes could be, was a little cool and aloof, and to my dismay expressed skepticism about the ability of Wabash to meet on a $2-to-$1 matching basis the maximum grant available to us — $2 million.

That night we again had a dinner meeting at the Collett home. As far as I am concerned, this dinner meeting and John's part in the discussion put us over the top. After dinner Fred Hadley and I excused ourselves for a while to permit Armsey to talk alone with the trustees present. It was John Collett who said in effect in that closed session, "What the hell! Let's go for broke! Let's accept the $2 million challenge. We can meet it." Driving Jim Armsey back to his room at an airport hotel that night, we reviewed the evening's discussion. At one point he said, "Tell me more about your man Collett."

The factor of emotional attachment to Wabash as the principal motivating influence for trustees which I have emphasized was never more pronounced than in the case of John Collett. His family's connection with Wabash went back to the earliest years in the college's history. He was proud of this. His undergraduate years at Wabash were happy years that reinforced his pride. He was an avid Phi Gam, serving as president of the chapter in his senior year. Phi Gamma Delta at Wabash continued to be important to him. He rarely missed the annual "Pig Dinner" and in numerous ways, not the least of which had to do with fiscal matters, he continued to be a guiding influence in the chapter's history. But like other avid fraternity member trustees, he put the college ahead of his fraternity.

John Collett identified with the athletic prowess of Wabash in the early 1920s. It was a life-long identification. He regularly attended Wabash athletic games, especially football. He was exhilarated and buoyed up not just by victories but by valiant effort, win or lose. And he was troubled and depressed when occasionally Wabash teams or the Wabash student body fell short of his standards. All of this was important to him. It had to do with the basic character of the college as he visualized it. His persistent interest in tennis, a sport he continued to play many years, led him to give to the college its excellent tennis facilities, both indoor and outdoor.

John's identification with the academic life of Wabash and with its leading professors was correspondingly strong. He took a personal interest in the lives of numerous faculty members and he shared their concerns even when he disagreed. In January, 1952, John and I sat together in the Chapel at the memorial service for Insley Osborne. It was a moving service. When Dean Kendall finished his remarks, I turned to John. There were tears in his eyes which made me feel better about my own tears. When Owen Duston of the English department died in the early 1970s after a long illness, it was John who called me in New York to tell me the news. He spoke sadly but with pride and appreciation of Owen's courage in the face of death. This too was important to him. I really believe next to his family — possibly next also to his business — Wabash was the greatest love in John Collett's life. He gave of his time, talent, and money to other worthy causes, but these were the palest of shadows compared to his great love of Wabash.

Recently the Board of Trustees presented to the college a portrait of John Collett. I have not seen it but, judging by a photograph, it is a superb portrait. For me in a way it symbolizes so much of what is good in the modern Wabash. The patrician face, the confident cheerful disposition, the suggestion of inner strength of character — they are all there. Even the boutonniere in his left coat lapel is right.[6]

JOHN J. COSS
Wabash 1911

John Coss is the only alumni trustee in Wabash history to be removed from the Board of Trustees by the concerted voting action of the Wabash alumni body.[7] This dubious distinction is less important than another distinction which was the cause of his repudiation by his fellow alumni. As I have explained in my comments about the Hopkins years, John Coss was the trustee primarily responsible for Louis Hopkins' becoming the seventh president of Wabash College. He and Hopkins had become acquainted during World War I, when they were both involved in a testing program for candidates for army officer commissions. Coss also knew Walter Dill Scott, who became president of Northwestern University after World War I and who took Hopkins there with him as director of personnel. As chairman of the trustee presidential search committee, Coss plugged hard for the candidacy of Louis Hopkins. His prestige among his fellow trustees undoubtedly influenced the board's decision. It is not surprising, therefore, that Hoppy was closer to John Coss than to any other trustee after he became president, and this in turn explains Coss' influence in the curriculum revision that occurred in the late 1920s.

My information for these observations is second-hand, but the source of that information, Insley Osborne, was quite reliable. Insley and John were close boyhood friends and fraternity brothers (Beta Theta Pi). Although Insley was slightly older, they formed a lifelong companionship. In fact, I am convinced

6. The portrait by C. J. Fox hangs at the right of the entrance to the Goodrich Room, Lilly Library.

7. In using the term "alumni trustee" here, I am referring to those members of the Board of Trustees (six) who, according to the college charter as amended, are elected for specific terms of office by the alumni. BKT.

that John Coss should be credited with influencing Osborne's return to Wabash from Columbia University where he was an instructor and for George Kendall's decision to join forces with Wabash, too. Osborne, Kendall, and Coss were good friends and associates at Columbia in the years before and after World War I. Thus, Coss played a role in bringing to Wabash two towers of strength on the Wabash faculty in the early decades of the twentieth century.

Coss himself continued his career at Columbia, a career of considerable distinction. He became full professor of philosophy and a popular teacher there. His greater prominence, however, was as director of the summer school which in the 1920s became famous. This position meant that he worked closely with Nicholas Murray Butler, famed president of Columbia. Butler, who presided over Columbia in the post-World War I era as if it were the Court of St. James, had enormous prestige in American higher education. John Coss was, therefore, in a position to exert useful influence in behalf of Wabash and he did so in a variety of ways.

In the summer of 1930 John arranged for President Hopkins to participate in a symposium at Columbia called "Five College Plans." It was a distinguished set of colleges, including, as I recall, Dartmouth and Swarthmore. It won kudos for Wabash in the East and in educational circles generally. In the early 1930s John Coss was also responsible for sending to Wabash a number of lecturers and visitors. The most important of these was Irwin Edman, who developed a great liking for Wabash and its people. In his well-known book, *Philosopher's Holiday,* he spoke of Wabash and Crawfordsville favorably and with affection.[8] John also took a keen interest in young Wabash men who came East for graduate study or, as in Bill Howard's case, for employment. Jimmy Clifford, who became a celebrated authority on Samuel Johnson, was among those Wabash graduates with scholarly aspirations whom John befriended and assisted.

It is interesting that much of this sort of thing Coss did after he had been humiliated by the Wabash alumni vote in 1930.[9] He did not sulk about this, as lesser men would have. When that vote was announced in June, 1930, although his friends — Joe Daniels, for example — were depressed about it, John was cheerful and stoical. I know this because of conversations I had with John at the Beta House following his last meeting as a trustee.

John Coss exemplifies another kind of diversity which Wabash alumni trustees have from time to time brought to the Wabash Board. Unlike many colleges, Wabash has never made a point of seating on its board as a matter of

8. *Philosopher's Holiday* (New York: The Viking Press, 1938).

9. The John J. Coss Memorial Fund is additional testimony to his strong and enduring interest in the college. Following the death of his sister, Miss Millicent Coss, part of his estate became an endowment, the interest from which has been used for faculty recreation or travel. The first award was given in 1953.

principle a "professional educator." But occasionally such professionals have been elected to the board by Wabash alumni, not because they were educators, but because they were respected alumni. Thus in the post-World War II era, Worth Frank, president of McCormick Theological Seminary in Chicago, and Frank Ristine, dean of Hamilton College, served on the board for a time. Later Cleon Foust, former dean of the I. U. Law School in Indianapolis, was elected. Of all of these, in my judgment, John Coss was the most distinguished and the most influential. Even the required freshman course, "Introduction to Contemporary Civilization," which became a long-time familiar feature of the Wabash curriculum, operated as a continuing testament to Coss' personal influence.

Did John Coss have an emotional attachment to Wabash? He grew up in Crawfordsville virtually on campus (Mills Place). He told me once that he could not remember anything of his earliest childhood that wasn't somehow related to the Wabash campus. Coming back to Wabash for John Coss was literally coming home.

I presume the portrait done of John Coss in the late 1920s by Fritz Schlemmer still hangs in the Caleb Mills House where I personally hung it (over the fireplace in the living room) when I lived there. It came to the college along with the collection of antique furniture John willed to the college. An excellent likeness of John when he was a trustee, it is one of Schlemmer's best portraits.[10]

JOE DANIELS
Wabash 1911

In the late 1920s and through most of the 1930s, Joe Daniels of Indianapolis was one of the stronger members of the Wabash Board of Trustees. Following his graduation from Wabash (with Phi Beta Kappa honors), he went on to Harvard Law School where he also had a distinguished record. In time he became senior partner in the law firm of Baker & Daniels. He was a brilliant lawyer, generally acknowledged as such throughout Indiana.

At the time I first became well-acquainted with him during my early years on the faculty, he was a decisive influence on the board. As I have recounted elsewhere, he masterminded the belated counterattack on the anti-Hopkins forces among the alumni in 1930–31. Much of the credit for the fact that Russell Byers, when up for re-election that year, did not go down to defeat as John Coss had, was due to Daniels' strategy and tactics. Later in the 1930s I believe he lost confidence in Dr. Hopkins, and he finally declined to be re-elected a trustee. But his interest in Wabash continued and, from time to time, often in connection with Beta Theta Pi matters, I had a chance to

10. The Schlemmer pastel remains in the Caleb Mills House.

visit with him. Always it was clear to me that his interest in the college was undiminished.

My admiration for the quality of Joe Daniels' mind was such that when I became president, with the approval of Ivan Wiles and John Collett, I persuaded him to rejoin the board. Perhaps as a courtesy to me he agreed to do so but only for a four-year stint of duty. He was then sixty-six. He served conscientiously until the early 1960s, but in part because the Board of Trustees in those years was a far stronger board than in the 1930s, his trustee contributions were less important than they were during the Hopkins years. Nevertheless, it meant much to me to have him back on the "first team."

Joe was especially helpful in the conferences with Elizabeth Pascal of the Ford Foundation the night John and Mary Collett gave a dinner party for her. And he never failed to try to do whatever I asked him to do for the college. One such response is worth recording as a tid-bit of human interest.

In the late 1950s I began to talk with Fred Stark of Princeton, Illinois, about a fanciful idea he had for making Wabash rich. Fred's son (also Fred), had graduated from Wabash in 1956, majoring in chemistry. He had done well as a student and had taken on all of the usual enthusiasm characteristic of Wabash men. His father, who had never gone to college, was overjoyed with his son's experience and developed his own enthusiasm for Wabash. He had become a close friend of Myron Phillips, and Myron, who was good at "smelling money," saw to it that the elder Stark and I got well acquainted.

Mr. Stark was an eccentric cookbook kind of chemist, forever tinkering with chemical experiments, most of them having to do with synthetic rubber products. But he had had, or claimed he had had, shabby treatment at the hands of lawyers. Just when he would be ready to patent some new process, he would discover that his lawyer had double-crossed him to the benefit of some major firm, such as DuPont. When I got involved with Stark, he was not only engaged in lawsuits with a former lawyer, but had no confidence in his new lawyer. He moved his operations to Minneapolis, partly to get away from the spying he was convinced he was up against in Illinois.

Mr. Stark had discovered a new formula for producing butane rubber at about one-tenth of the then common production cost. He was sure it was a money-maker, and he wanted an absolutely reliable as well as competent lawyer. I told him about Joe Daniels and asked Joe to help. My motive in this was money for Wabash. Stark wanted to put the patents then pending for his new formula in hands where DuPont couldn't possibly tamper with them. His idea was to create a not-for-profit corporation into which all royalties were to be paid. He proposed to give this corporation to three educational institutions: Wabash (45%), St. Louis University (45%), and Brandeis University (10%). He estimated "conservatively" that Wabash's annual income from this corporation would amount to $400,000. It had the ring of fantasy, and

172

yet I saw the primitive laboratories in operation, saw the products being sold to Montgomery Ward, and I had our maintenance department successfully try some of the "rubber" to stop leaking roofs. It was a case of saying "Who knows?"

Once Joe Daniels investigated, he told me he thought it was pure "pie in in the sky," but he added, "Nevertheless, for the possible good of Wabash I will do what I can." We went to Minneapolis together. Joe took Byron Hollett of his firm with him. We spent a couple of days in conferences with Mr. Stark, who took an immediate liking to Joe. He called him "Little Joe." As a consequence of those conferences, Rubber Research, Inc., was formed, wholly owned by Wabash, St. Louis University, and Brandeis.

It was indeed "pie in the sky" partly, however, because Mr. Stark's health failed and in due time he died. But my point in telling this story is Joe's remark about "for the possible good of Wabash." It was a manifestation of the "emotional attachment factor." Joe Daniels had it.

I always had a feeling that after the death of his first wife, an attractive and gifted woman, Joe was inwardly a terribly lonely man. Maybe not. But at any rate I have wondered about his insistence that he would only come back on the board for one term. It was as if he foresaw his decline. He suggested Byron Hollett as his successor on the board, and he was in time elected and went on to become, as Joe Daniels had once been, a tower of strength for Wabash. But that is another story that belongs to the years after I had left Wabash.

LAWRENCE DE VORE
Wabash 1911

Ever since 1832 leading citizens of Crawfordsville have been prominently involved as trustees in the life of Wabash. In the twentieth century they were less numerous at any one time on the board than they had been in the nineteenth century, but they continued to be important, some more so than others. Men like T. H. Ristine, long-time treasurer of the college, and Judge Albert Thomas, for a while president of the board, were carry-overs from the nineteenth century. In the 1920s and 1930s there were men like Chase Harding, Bruce Luckett and Frank Davison. Harding, the town's leading lawyer, was especially prominent. And after World War II came Dick Ristine and Bill Hays. Both were exceedingly active and useful trustees, Bill Hays being in my opinion a better trustee than his illustrious father had been.

To this company of Crawfordsville trustees belongs Lawrence De Vore. He was a prominent businessman in Crawfordsville (partner in the Evans-De Vore Company, chairman of the board of the First National Bank, and a director in other enterprises). He owned rich farmland north of Crawfordsville near New Richmond and prided himself on being a farmer. He was a pillar in the First Methodist Church, but also a senior spirit in the Crawfordsville Country Club set. His wife, Mabel, was an active club woman and something of a power in the town's conservative social life. The De Vore home on East Wabash was often referred to as "elegant."

During his student days at Wabash, Lawerence De Vore earned the nickname "Count." Maybe it was his careful and expensive way of dressing. Perhaps it was his — for Crawfordsville — somewhat aristocratic manner. While an undergraduate he and a fraternity brother, Walter Linn (Phi Delta Theta), both being active in college forensics, founded Tau Kappa Alpha, the national honorary society for forensics.[11] Lawrence did not keep up his interest in T K A, but he maintained close ties with Phi Delta Theta. He had much to do with the extensive remodeling of the Phi Delt house shortly after World War II.

De Vore was a quiet, almost passive trustee at board meetings. Between meetings of the board, however, he was consistently helpful to the president of the college, first to Dr. Sparks and then to me, especially on matters relating to Crawfordsville. He took a keen interest in the post-war building program and for a brief time served as chairman of the building committee. He was helpful in the acquisition of real estate adjacent to the campus.

Lee McCanliss regarded Lawrence as an unproductive lightweight on the board and apparently wanted him to relinquish his seat to someone who would be helpful to the college financially. I say "apparently" because of a conversation between Ike Elston and Lawrence which I could not help overhearing. We were riding back to Crawfordsville together following a winter board meeting in Indianapolis. It must have been 1953, perhaps earlier. Ike was in a truculent mood. As he was getting out of the car at the Elston Homestead, he said forcefully to Lawrence, "Don't you dare let McCanliss push you off the board! If you go off the board, I go too! Don't forget it!"

Lawrence De Vore continued on the board. In the late 1950s and early 1960s I saw much more of him than I had before. He would often drop in my office for a casual visit. Increasingly he talked with me about his family and his personal affairs. He had one daughter, Margaret, who was an epileptic. He worried about her future "after Mabel and I are gone." He explained a trust fund which he had established for her future care. In some of these conversations, I was astonished by his sentimentality about the college and fascinated by accounts he related of earlier figures in the college history whom he had known. Twice I went with him to inspect his lush farmland. It was a beautiful sight. Each time he said to me, "Well, Byron, you had better get acquainted

11. See *The First Hundred Years*, pp 316–17. In 1963, the society merged with Delta Sigma Rho to become a men's and women's honorary society for forensics.

with this land because someday Wabash College will have to manage it." Death was on his mind.

About 1962, maybe 1963, Lawrence discussed with me his will. It provided for an endowment fund for Wabash to support the De Vore Chair of Economics. He was deadly serious in these conversations. One afternoon he brought the will with him to the office and we went over it together. Later that year or perhaps the following year, Lawrence fell seriously ill, but there was no reason to believe that he would not recover. All Crawfordsville was shocked when news of his sudden death was announced. In a moment when his nurse had gone downstairs, he got out of bed, took his shotgun and put an end to his life. His will was never found. Perhaps he destroyed it. Perhaps it was lost.[12]

ISAAC C. ELSTON, JR.
Wabash 1894

I doubt that Wabash will ever have a more colorful trustee than I. C. Elston. Part buccaneer, part *bon vivant,* part gracious gentleman, Ike Elston from the 1920s until the early 1960s was a splash of color on the Wabash board. His service as a trustee was broken for a period when he resigned in the late Hopkins years, but his connection with Wabash was never broken.

I never took the trouble to verify from the college records how long Ike had studied at Wabash, and it was impossible to tell from Ike's verbal accounts. They varied from time to time. It must have been a short period, but it was long enough for him to become a member of Phi Kappa Psi. Ike boasted that he had been kicked out of Wabash. He explained that that is why one of his first gifts to the college was three sets of campus gates. The college in the early 1890s had "given him the gate," so he returned the compliment threefold.

Ike was a descendant of one of Crawfordsville's oldest and most famous families. He acquired, by purchase from another branch of the family, the beautiful Elston Homestead in Crawfordsville, which was built in 1835 by his grandfather. But Ike spent most of his time in Chicago where he increased his inherited wealth. He was a senior partner in the investment firm of Paul H. Davis & Company, which in the 1950s was taken over by Hornblower & Weeks. I presume Ike made his money in the securities and also the commodity market. I am not sure how, but he made money, lots of it. He rode very high in the roaring 1920s with the usual trappings of the American rich, including a yacht which he kept in Florida waters. Like countless others, he was badly hurt by the stock market crash in 1929. But he was by no means ruined. John Coulter, who was close to Ike, used to laugh about his losses. "Poor I. C." he said, "He is

12. De Vore left his estate to his widow, who, in turn, through her will, established the Lawrence E. De Vore Chair in Economics.

175

despondent because he was worth $9 million and now he has only $2 million!"

Like the *Chicago Tribune,* Ike had an acute Chicago bias. He loved Chicago, and he was inclined to sneer at New York. He distrusted Eastern bankers and lawyers and the "liberal" Eastern Republicans. A McKinley type Republican, he hated Franklin Roosevelt and all New Dealers with a passion. He never left any doubt about his feelings. He turned over to the college his government farm checks received in accordance with federal regulations on crop control. He said it was "tainted money." He used to ask me in the 1940s, "How many Reds are there on the faculty? Tell me the truth." Or he would say, "Tell me, is that fellow Paterson really a Communist?" (Jim Paterson taught labor economics at Wabash.) At the height of the furor created by Senator Joe McCarthy's campaign against communism, a campaign which made McCarthy's name anathema on college campuses, Ike proposed that Wabash give McCarthy an honorary degree. I often suspected that he made such comments partly because it amused him to see his more liberal friends squirm. Once when he was castigating Democrats on the faculty, I said to him, "But, I. C., I am a Democrat too." "Yeah," he replied, "but I've checked you out. You're the same kind of Democrat my grandfather was." By that time (the late 1940s), I was on good terms with Ike Elston. For reasons I never understood, he took a liking to me and to Dorothy too.

In Chicago Ike was regarded as the "grand old man" among Wabash alumni. Now and then he would pick up the balance of the check for an alumni party at the University Club, covering all costs above a nominal price paid by each alumnus for the dinner. I expressed my thanks to him once for this kind of anonymous contribution and he said, "Well, I have to do this sort of thing now and then to ease my conscience. I am really not qualified to be a member of the club, you know. They [the Club] think I am a Phi Beta Kappa." He had a Phi Beta Kappa key which he flaunted now and then, saying he had won it in his freshman year at Wabash. God knows where it came from.

During the depression years Ike kept the Elston Homestead in Crawfordsville closed, with only a caretaker there. When the country's economy improved, he opened the house again and began to spend more time there each spring and fall. During these seasons, he entertained frequently and graciously, and my wife and I were often included in these parties. In this way I met his first wife, Pearl, a charming person but an invalid. Following Mrs. Elston's death shortly after World War II, Ike lengthened his stays in Crawfordsville and increased his entertaining. Florence Woelfel of Chicago was his companion and hostess. Considerably younger than Ike, she fitted well into the Crawfordsville and Wabash scene and was accepted warmly and sincerely by Ike's friends. She was devoted to Ike and later to his memory. In the middle 1950s they were married in the Elston Homestead. It was a simple, rather touching ceremony with Dr. Harry Cotton presiding. Dorothy and I and a handful of local friends attended. Ike, I believe, was a little tight at the wedding and had trouble with his few lines, but he seemed content and natural about the marriage, which had all the appearances of being quite a happy one.

Each Memorial Day Ike gave an all-day party at his house with the 500-mile race in Indianapolis as the excuse. The guests on those days were similar. Two or three couples, old friends from Chicago, were house guests. Oscar Welborn, an old Elston crony, came over from Indianapolis. A few couples from Crawfordsville, perhaps Lawrence and Mabel De Vore, Binford and Mary Miller, Herb Morrison, president of the Elston Bank, and his wife, Gordon and Julia Beamer, Dick and Carolyn Banta, and others. Always there was a sprinkling of younger couples, too. (Ike enjoyed having young people in his home). Dorothy and I were regular guests. So were Ed and Katie Gullion for a time. Later Dick and Lou Ristine and Bill and Ginny Hays were there. The routine was always the same. A betting pool was formed for the race, which was followed casually by radio. The drinks came early, together with good things to nibble. Guests relaxed in the screened-in porch to the east or strolled in the gardens. Finally came an excellent buffet lunch followed by general sleepiness.

Ike's parties were always a little bibulous. Until his doctor forbade it late in life, Ike enjoyed his drinks. Following smaller dinner parties, the men would "retire" to the library for coffee and brandy. Occasionally Ike would fall asleep in his favorite chair and would snore noisily. The conversation among the others continued as if Ike were not there. Finally he would waken with a start and with some irrelevant remark such as "Lawrence, let's have another cup of coffee."

Ike Elston was full of interesting stories about people, Crawfordsville, and Wabash. I regret that I paid no more attention than I did, but I never knew when he was telling the truth and when he was fabricating. At a dinner at the Columbia Club in Indianapolis, when the first edition of *Indiana Authors and Their Books* was being presented with a flourish, there were numerous toasts made to different authors.[13] Whoever spoke about Lew Wallace made a point of the Sultan of Turkey having presented to Lew Wallace a portrait of a beautiful woman in appreciation of Wallace's work as U. S. Minister to Turkey. Ike, who was present, said in a loud voice, "Hell, that was no gift from the Sultan. It was a portrait Lew had painted of one of his concubines!" (Wallace married one of Ike's aunts in Crawfordsville.) His account of his grandfather calling his sons and his son-in-law (Lew Wallace) together in the Elston Homestead at the outbreak of the Civil War for the purpose of announcing gold deposits he was making in Montreal banks in the name of each was a fascinating bit of history which I should have pursued.

13. R. E. Banta, compiler, *Indiana Authors and Their Books,* 1816–1916 (Crawfordsville: Wabash College, 1949).

In the early 1960s Ike suffered a severe stroke and lingered a long time in his bedroom in the Elston Homestead. Florence was heroic in the love and care she gave to him. I visited him a few times during his last illness. Florence said he recognized me, but his incoherent babbling depressed me. I came away once again impressed with the indignities of old age.

I have no idea how much money Ike Elston gave to Wabash over the years. Many of his gifts were almost surreptitiously made and often for pedestrian purposes not appealing to the average donor. (He paid for new boilers for the campus power house, for example.) Together with Will Hays, he was credited with a blitz to raise the funds required to build the Chapel in the late 1920s. There were other less spectacular gifts over the years. Perhaps his most meaningful gift to Wabash was that of his beloved Homestead.

The portrait of I. C. Elston in the Elston Homestead belongs to a period in his life before I knew him. The mustache always bothered me. It seemed strangely uncharacteristic. Apart from that, the portrait, in my opinion, fails to catch Ike's tremendous vitality.[14] I like better the portrait done for the Elston Bank and Trust Company by Lee Detchon. It is from a photograph, but Lee knew I. C. and he brought out in the eyes, the mouth, and the ruddy complexion much of the character of this unreconstructed Falstaff.

PARRISH FULLER
Wabash 1915

In the decades immediately following the World War II no Wabash trustee was prouder of his trusteeship than Parrish Fuller.

Wabash was not the only educational institution with which he had such an association. In Louisiana he was a member of the Board of Overseers at Tulane University. He was an active trustee on a state board for Negro colleges, and he served on the Board of Advisors for the Ochner Medical Center in New Orleans. He liked the kudos that came with such positions, but for him they were more than mere honorary designations. He worked hard at the responsibilities they entailed. Proud as he was of such positions in Louisiana, none of them meant as much to him as the trusteeship at his alma mater.

Parrish Fuller was a student at Wabash only one year. He came to Wabash from Shelbyville, Indiana. I never heard him speak of his brief experience as a Wabash student. But, in retrospect at least, it was a happy year in his youth, especially his experience at the Sigma Chi House. The death of his father caused him to drop out of college and to go to work. While still quite young, he made his way to Louisiana. Ambitious, energetic, and shrewd about ad-

14. This portrait, painted in 1926 by Walter Russell, hangs in the front parlor of the Elston Homestead.

justing to Southern attitudes and mores, he was almost immediately successful. He went into the lumber business, and with partners he helped to develop what were to become the largest soft wood mills in the South. It was a highly profitable enterprise.

The company's home offices and principal mills were in Oakdale, Louisiana. There Parrish and his wife, Hester, made their home and reared their family. When I visited him for the first time in the late 1950s I found the town smaller and sleepier than I had expected. But there was nothing small or sleepy about the lumber mill, the town's dominating industry. On that first visit Parrish took me on a brisk inspection tour of the entire operation. He told me it was his practice to make weekly walking inspections of the yards, the storehouses, and the mills. He wore a pedometer on such tours and measured the distance covered as something like two miles. In no time at all his fast pace on that hot summer day left me dripping with perspiration and gasping for breath. It was an impressive lumber center, but I was relieved to get back to the Fuller home, a spacious, charming white house in the Louisiana tradition, surrounded by well-groomed gardens.

His success in lumber led to other business interests. He was a director of one of the leading banks in New Orleans. He acquired extensive real estate interests, including timberlands, and he put together something he called Fuller Forests, Inc. Nationally he had interests in companies allied with the lumber industry in one way or another, such as Celotex. As he became well to do and prominent, he was drawn into a variety of civic and public enterprises. He was a Louisiana Democrat with economic views somewhat to the right of many northern Republicans. On the fringes at least, he was involved in Louisiana politics. Thus, although a northerner by birth and upbringing, he became part of the Louisiana Establishment.[15]

Throughout these years of growth in Louisiana, Parrish kept in touch with Indiana. He apparently lost all interest in Wabash, however, and no one from the college bothered to try to revive it. It was Frank Sparks, with his uncanny instinct about such matters, who rekindled his interest in the college and persuaded him to become a trustee. Once back in the Wabash fold, Parrish embraced the college and its possibilities with his characteristic energy and enthusiasm. It became one of his consuming, happy interests, and, although I never heard him say as much, I dare say he ranked his recovered love for Wabash close to his love for his family.

15. In 1967 I flew to Louisiana from Denver, where I was then living and working, to attend the celebration of Parrish's seventy-fifth birthday. I was astonished at the number of guests and well-wishers who assembled at the Fuller home — Oakdale neighbors, politicians from Baton Rouge and New Orleans, former governors, university presidents, industrialists, bankers, sportsmen, young socialites, old people. It was a lavish, colorful celebration with much to eat and drink, and it went on and on. Parrish loved it. BKT.

From the beginning he took his trusteeship seriously. He almost never missed a board meeting. He spoke up frequently and freely at board meetings about virtually all matters that arose, even when, it occasionally seemed to me, the item under discussion was beyond his experience and his knowledge. He was invariably deferential to Eli Lilly, but with others he never hesitated to disagree if he thought it important to disagree. He was, especially as long as Dr. Sparks was president, a consistent and fulsome supporter of whatever the administration proposed. As time went by his earnestness about his trusteeship took on a somewhat proprietary attitude. He came to expect as a matter of course a college car and driver to be put at his disposal when he made the train trip from Louisiana to Champaign, Illinois, en route to Crawfordsville. But his earnestness about his trusteeship never flagged. If anything, it became stronger as the years went by.

His annual gifts in cash or negotiable securities were modest for a man of his means. And for reasons I never understood, for years such gifts came in the name of his daughter, Mary Margaret, and his son-in-law, James Voorhees, in Denver. (Later, while living in Denver, I enjoyed a close friendship with Mary Margaret and Jim. They were delightful, interesting people, but it was clear their interest in Wabash was at best only casual.) But if his gifts in cash were modest, his other contributions to Wabash were as substantial as they were numerous.

Parrish Fuller's greatest interest in the college had to do with its buildings and its grounds. It was an area in which he felt a special competence, and he responded whole-heartedly when Dr. Sparks outlined for him his dream of achieving for Wabash an entirely new plant of unusual charm. Lee McCanliss, probably at Dr. Sparks' suggestion, appointed Parrish to the trustee building committee shortly after he became a trustee. After Parrish succeeded Jim Adams he was constantly at the center of all the major plant projects at the college. The magnificent plant which Wabash now enjoys is a monument to Frank Sparks, whose imagination and courage inspired the post-World War II building program. But in a way it is also a monument to Parrish Fuller, and some of its most unusual features — the cypress beams in the Great Hall of the Campus Center, for example — testify dramatically to his personal influence.

Nor was his interest limited to new construction. Repeatedly he expressed his concern about old buildings on the campus and about the importance of first-rate maintenance. He regarded old South Hall as a likely source of a catastrophe, and he was responsible for severe restrictions on the uses to which it could be put long before the decision was finally made to tear the building down. It was he who discovered that the east wing of the old gymnasium was gradually pulling away from the fieldhouse portion. His dire predictions about the problem led to major repairs and to renovation long before

180

the hopes for an entirely new gymnasium were realized. He worried about such unglamourous but vital details as the heating plant and the maintenance shop, and he was responsible for their move upward on the priority list among plant improvement projects.

Above all, he gave special and continuing attention to the campus trees. They were a passion for him. He insisted on a contract with specialists at the University of Illinois which resulted in semi-annual inspections of the campus trees, and a systematic program in tree pruning and remedial care, as well as the institution of a tree planting schedule. The beauty of the east campus a hundred years hence will be a tribute to his foresight.[16]

Unlike Jim Adams, Parrish liked and got along well with Eric Gugler. He defended Gugler's "artiness" and the high cost of the buildings he designed. Gugler for his part responded warmly to Parrish's pleas for using more wood than customary in new buildings. With Leslie Colvin he frequently disagreed. He took a dim view of the "cost-plus, agency-fee" contract arrangement the college had with Colvin & Son. Parrish wanted competitive bids for all new construction. Colvin, supported by personal friends on the Wabash board, successfully resisted Parrish's demand.[17] The two men also disagreed about building materials. Fuller pressed hard for using heat pumps in individual buildings and laminated wooden beams instead of steel. Colvin airily dismissed such suggestions as impractical and amateurish. Although he felt strongly about such matters, Parrish chuckled good naturedly about their disagreements.

The post-World War II buildings at Wabash, when one looks closely, have a remarkably high amount of wood in them, thanks to Parrish Fuller's influence. And much of that wood he gave to the college or provided at very low cost. There was, for example, the pecan flooring in the renovated fieldhouse, the parquet floors in much of the Campus Center, flooring in parts of Baxter Hall, the holly paneling in Martindale Hall, the wood in the new Sigma Chi House, and so on. Especially there were the cypress beams and paneling

16. From 1970 to 1980 Fuller contributed approximately $500,000 to create the Hester Porter and Parrish Fuller Arboretum Fund, the income from which is dedicated to grounds maintenance. This has made possible a well-planned and extensive seven-year planting program, adding coniferous trees and shrubs to the entire campus and giving it a touch of color during the winter months. In recognition of this gift, as well as Mr. Fuller's other contributions as a trustee, in 1977 a permanent educational display, named the Arboretum Center, was dedicated. It is located on the concourse between Waugh Hall and the Mason B. Thomas Laboratories.

17. In the late 1950s, when Leslie Colvin had relinquished to his son, Burt, the major role in their firm, Parrish finally won his point about competitive bids. This was in connection with the construction of Martindale Hall. As Parrish had predicted, Colvin's bid was high, and the contract was therefore awarded to the Dunlap Construction Company in Columbus (Jerry Dunlap, Wabash 1927). BKT.

for the ceiling of the Great Hall in the Campus Center. He personally selected the giant trees to be cut in the bayous of Louisiana. He followed the logs through the mills in Oakdale as they were cut and dressed into enormous beams. He supervised their drying and curing, and he kept a watchful eye on them as they were finally loaded on railroad flatcars for shipment to Crawfordsville. He included two extra beams beyond Gugler's specifications for "contingency purposes in the future," he said. It was a labor of love.

After the Campus Center was completed and in use, almost every time Parrish was in Crawfordsville he took at least a few minutes to look at his beams. He liked to admire them and to talk about them. But he also took a professional interest in the way they aged. In the earlier years he was constantly on the look out for signs of accumulating moisture. He was concerned about the flat composition roof over the Great Hall. On one such visit, following a prolonged period of rain, he detected evidence of water seepage. A long conference with Finis Burkhardt, superintendent of buildings and grounds, followed immediately. On his next trip to Crawfordsville, he, Finis, and I together inspected the roof and the beams. Parrish was pleased with the corrective measures that had been taken. "With proper care," he said, "these beams will last for centuries!"

For Parrish it was a proud, confident observation. But for me suddenly it was a sobering thought, full of awe about the passage of time. I found myself wondering not so much about the beams as about the college itself. "How long will Wabash endure?" I wondered.

PIERRE F. GOODRICH
Wabash 1916

Pierre Goodrich was the most complicated man I have ever known. I could write a book about this man, but I despair of doing justice to his multi-sided personality and his amazing range of interests.

I was never sure whether Pierre Goodrich was an inarticulate genius or just inarticulate. I was sure only that he was terribly time-consuming. His business and financial accomplishments supported the speculation that he was a genius, financially anyway. He had the Midas touch. His interests included public utilities (Winchester Telephone Co., Indiana Telephone Co., Indianapolis Street Railways), banks (Winchester) and investment companies (Cities Securities), farms, Republic Coal and Coke Co. (Chicago), and Ayreshire Collieries (strip mines in southern Indiana and Illinois). In all of these Pierre either had the controlling ownership interest or, in combination with associates, was in a position to exercise control. He was as much interested in capital growth as he was in income, perhaps more so. When he finally sold Ayreshire

Collieries to Ashland Oil, the sale package was on the order of $40 million. He surrounded himself with able operating lieutenants — Dwight Peterson for Cities Securities, Bill Sheidler for Indiana Telephone Co., and Norman Kelb for Ayreshire Collieries, for example — but he kept his hands very much on the overall controls.

Ostensibly he was a lawyer. After graduating with Phi Beta Kappa honors from Wabash, he obtained his law degree from Harvard. But he never really practiced law personally, and I find it incredible to think that he could have. He was too much like Hamlet. But he always had able lawyers associated with him. When I first became well acquainted with him, his firm was known as Goodrich, Campbell & Warren, with offices in the Electric Building on the Circle in Indianapolis. Later, until his death, it was Goodrich & Warren, with offices personally designed by Pierre in the 3500 block on Washington Boulevard. As far as I could tell, the bulk of the legal work done by the firm related to the Goodrich empire. Pierre himself did no legal work, although regularly and for long hours he was in his office whenever he was not traveling.

Shortly after Governor Goodrich died in the fall of 1940, Pierre was elected to succeed his father as a trustee. At the same meeting Lee McCanliss was elected president of the board. Although he never said so, I am confident that it meant a great deal to Pierre to succeed his father on the Wabash board. He obviously had great respect and admiration for his father. The father and the son were very different individuals. Judging by what little I saw of him at Wabash board meetings and more by what people told me about him, James Goodrich was a hard-hitting, decisive kind of man, quick to analyze a situation and then to act. He could not have been such an imposing governor of Indiana without such qualities. He dominated the Wabash board in the late 1920s and the 1930s by force of personality and by his prestige. Pierre Goodrich by contrast was, or appeared to others to be, laborious and tedious in arriving at decisions, often ambivalent and equivocal, sometimes mysterious. He worried and stewed about problems, consulted others, disregarded their advice once given, explored alternatives, checked and double-checked his own tentative conclusions. It was an exhausting process for those who worked with him. But when he acted finally, the results, for him at least, were almost always beneficial.

Pierre served as a Wabash trustee from 1940 to 1969. During much of that time he was a vice president of the board. He was always a trustee who had to be reckoned with in major decisions and the reckoning had to be done before formal meetings. He was quite fond of Frank Sparks and Frank "handled" Pierre well. Lee McCanliss, on the other hand, was too brusque and short with Pierre. In the 1950s and 1960s, it was often John Collett who dealt most effectively with Pierre, partly because they had the common bond of Phi Gamma Delta.

While Pierre could usually be counted on to support the policies of the president (when he had been consulted in advance), he was something of a loner on the board, interested primarily in things he himself wanted to do. He had the disconcerting habit during board meetings of wandering around the room talking *sotto voce* with some individual trustee or often with me, losing contact with whatever general discussion was taking place and distracting attention from that discussion. It was not intended rudeness. Rather it was absent-mindedness or perhaps just intense preoccupation with some personal thought which he felt impelled to review with someone else.

Despite his great wealth, Pierre was a stingy giver. I believe he never made an unrestricted gift to the college. Always there were strings attached. A gift of a block of Ayreshire Collieries stock, for example, was accompanied with the unwritten understanding that that stock was not to be sold by the college without Pierre's approval, the income was to be retained and added to the principal, and the ultimate uses of the fund were to be subject to his direction. Other gifts for specific purposes he equally controlled. The truth is, I believe, Pierre, like others before him, wanted to control his wealth from the grave. He went to extraordinary lengths to insure that the private foundation he set up (The Liberty Fund) would forever be concerned with purposes of which he approved. Twice the Internal Revenue Service refused to approve the conditions that he submitted for the fund. But even in the end it was a closely directed philanthropic foundation. (Ben Rogge, in whom Pierre had great confidence, helped in designing the controls for this fund and served as one of its trustees.) Pierre resisted numerous entreaties for a major gift to Wabash during his lifetime. He and he alone determined when, how much, and for what purpose he would give.

In fairness to Pierre, it should be remembered that he was a prudent, almost puritanical steward of his money. There was nothing religious or sanctimonious about his puritanism. It reflected simply his own notions of how wealth should be conserved and used. There was nothing ostentatious or frivolous about his life style. He dressed carelessly and casually in conservative taste. His home on Central Avenue was rather modest in a deteriorating neighborhood in Indianapolis. The interior had an antiseptic, austere kind of beauty about it, but nothing lavish was displayed. He stayed at expensive conservative hotels in New York and elsewhere but there was no "partying" on such occasions. His second wife, Enid, was a simple quiet woman with great good sense and the patience of a saint. (Pierre's first marriage ended in divorce.) Enid, I believe, met Pierre when she was his nurse in a hospital. From the life style of Pierre and Enid Goodrich, no one would guess that Pierre was a multimillionaire.

Pierre's interest in Wabash was almost exclusively limited to its academic, intellectual, and artistic life. He had none of the gung-ho Wabash spirit about athletics. When he spoke to me of his undergraduate years at Wabash, it was always in terms of what he had learned there intellectually. He had great respect for Professor Cragwall, who was apparently at his best when Pierre studied under him. Pierre was critical of the conventional pattern of liberal education, impatient with textbooks and with professorial lectures. He saw no reason why a college needed a library of more than about 5,000 books, provided they were the right books. By the end of World War II, Pierre was deeply committed to the effort to promote the reading of "Great Books," on and off campuses, and to the Socratic method of discussing those books. It became for a number of years an obsession with him.

I am not sure how I came to be so deeply involved with Pierre in his immersion in "Great Books," but I did. Perhaps when Pierre first began to discuss his ideas with Frank Sparks, Frank suggested that he work with me as dean of the college. At any rate in 1946–47, I found myself drawn into numerous and lengthy conversations with Pierre about education. After overcoming whatever initial reservations and suspicions he may have had about me, he drew me increasingly into his interests. For the better part of the next ten years, we worked closely together. Despite the endless, lengthy long-distance telephone calls at all hours of the day and night, despite the frequent interminable conferences, despite the rigors of traveling with Pierre, I acknowledge that I learned a great deal from this man, and in the process I learned to respect and admire much of what he stood for.

It was in this way that Pierre Goodrich really exerted a profound influence on the intellectual life of Wabash in the post-World War II era. I drew Jack Charles, Harry Cotton, and others into the Goodrich circle. The "Colloquium on Important Books" for juniors and seniors at Wabash was born this way, and the trend away from textbooks in a number of courses also resulted.[18] Through Pierre I became acquainted with Robert Hutchins and Mortimer Adler at the University of Chicago. With him I visited St. Johns College in Annapolis, Maryland, where I came to know well Stringfellow Barr and Dean Klein. It was an important chapter in my own education.

Pierre's interest in "Great Books" led naturally to his idea of constructing what came to be known as the Goodrich Room in the Lilly Library. I really liked Pierre's idea and worked very hard with him to see to it that the room unfolded exactly as he wanted it. I defended his concept against criticisms of the faculty and especially of the librarian. Some called it "Goodrich's Folly," but I continue to think of it as a distinctive gem in the Wabash plant. The process of working with Pierre on this room was exhausting, time consuming, and at points comical.

Hours and hours went into discussing the design of the room, its precise

18. The first "Colloquium" was offered in 1946 and continues as an attractive option for juniors and seniors.

dimensions, the quality of the limestone, the texture of the wood, the layout for the great table, the kind of chairs. The inscriptions on the walls and their exact locations involved long debates. A final hang-up was the first inscription — the first known use of the word "liberty."

After consulting with experts in the Oriental Museum in Chicago, in the University of Pennsylvania, and elsewhere, trying to find exactly the right process for the clay tablet which bears the Sumerian symbols for the word "liberty," with the help of Harold McDonald (then head of the Wabash art department), I found an artisan at Veedersburg who said he could do the tablet. Pierre finally was delighted with the results.

Among the incidental things which Pierre Goodrich did in his desire to improve the intellectual life of the campus was to bring to the college prominent scholars for lecture purposes. They were invariably of a conservative stripe but there was never any doubt about their intellectual credentials or their intellectual integrity. Among these visitors were Roscoe Pound, dean emeritus of the Harvard Law School; Felix Morley, former president of Haverford College; and prior to that newspaper pundit and editor, William Buckley, author of *God and Man at Yale* and later controversial newspaper columnist.[19] The lectures by Pound and Morley were published in book form.[20] All of this was financed, of course, by gifts to Wabash from Pierre.

The most celebrated of these visitors was Ludwig Erhard of West Germany. It was in June, 1959. Erhard at that time was vice-chancellor and minister for finance in West Germany. Later he became chancellor. Pierre had become acquainted with Erhard at an annual meeting of the Mont Pelerin Society in Switzerland. After elaborate maneuvering over a period of months on Pierre's part, Erhard agreed to give two lectures at Wabash on the European Common Market and to accept an honorary degree from Wabash. (By working hard on my rusty German I managed to give Erhard's citation in German, which surprised and pleased him.)

This was a terribly important event for Pierre, and he attended to all of the details with, even for him, unusual care. Especially important to him was a reception to be given for Erhard and his party at the Elston Homestead. Ike and Florence cooperated fully and cheerfully. But Pierre fretted about the drinks to be served. He wanted the best Rhine wine to be had, the best imported German beer, the right glasses, and so on. He harassed his importer in Indianapolis, sampled, rejected, and changed beers, and fussed around with

19. *God and Man at Yale: the Superstitions of Academic Freedom* (Chicago: Regnery, 1951).

20. Roscoe Pound, *The Development of Constitutional Guarantees of Liberty* (New Haven: published for Wabash College by Yale University Press, 1957); Felix Morley, *The Foreign Policy of the United States* (New York: Knopf, 1951), and the same year as a pamphlet by the American Enterprise Association.

the arrangements at the Elston Homestead. Finally, Ike somewhat testily said, "My God, Pierre, why don't you just serve some good cocktails. I have all the makings here." But Pierre would have none of this. Finally, the appointed hour arrived and Pierre, nervous as a kitten, was anticipating Erhard's enjoyment of Pierre's labors. After the introductions Ike said, "Well, Doctor, what will you have to drink?" Through his interpreter, after a cursory glance at the wine and beer, the good doctor replied, "I'd like a double Scotch on the rocks." Ike was hilarious. So was everyone else — except Pierre Goodrich.

I wrote a tribute to Pierre Goodrich on the last page of a booklet Wabash printed describing the Goodrich Room at the time the Lilly Library was dedicated. It was a fitting tribute I believe, including the phrase "he is a discontented man."

LEE McCANLISS
Wabash 1907

Like Jim Adams, Lee McCanliss came out of the original Little Giant era of the first decade of the twentieth century. He entered Wabash a poor boy from Parke County, Indiana, in the fall of 1903. It was at a time when, under the vigorous guidance of President Kane, Wabash was once again emerging from unhappy years and entering one of its "golden ages." A great faculty, a growing, lusty student body, and above all, the blazing record of Cayou's football teams made it an exciting time to be at Wabash. Like Adams also, Lee had no fraternity affiliation. He was an independent and proud of it. He won letters on the college track team and began a lifelong practice of daily physical workouts.[21]

Lee McCanliss was enormously proud of Wabash as it was in his years as an undergraduate. At commencement time in 1957 my wife and I gave a dinner party at the Campus Center for the returning members of the class of 1907 and their wives, celebrating their fiftieth class anniversary. (It was a practice which we continued annually and which is still observed.) At that banquet Lee spoke at length. He was in good form — light-hearted, cocky, and at points inspirational. It was really quite a touching expression of Wabash love and pride.

Lee McCanliss ran a temperature for Wabash all his life. His professional life and successes during his many years as a resident of New York never dampened his Wabash enthusiasm. Graduating Phi Beta Kappa from Wabash, he went on to law school at Columbia University and then stayed permanently

21. Every day of his life in New York up until a few weeks before his death, he ran a mile around the indoor track of the New York Athletic Club. His weight at seventy-two was the same as it had been at twenty-two. BKT.

in New York. He was a successful Wall Street lawyer. I presume his great personal breakthrough came when, while still relatively young, he represented the J. P. Morgan interests successfully in a piece of complicated litigation. It was the beginning of close connections with the Morgan Bank. I have sometimes wondered if this experience, gratifying though it undoubtedly was for Lee, wasn't in a way a hazard for him later on. As someone — who, I cannot remember — once told me, "Lee McCanliss was right in predicting the Wall Street crash of 1929 but he has been wrong about everything important ever since." Certainly Lee, by the time he became president of the Wabash Board, had an abundance of confidence in his own judgment and an *ex cathedra* manner toward those who disagreed with him.

His private life — much of it anyway — was unhappy. His wife suffered severe emotional disturbances which led to permanent hospitalization. His only son committed suicide. Lee made his permanent home at the Gotham Hotel. He had a simple but large room there with a view down Fifth Avenue to the south. He always seemed cheerful and outgoing in the company of others, but I have wondered often if he were not very lonely. Perhaps this is another reason for his increasing devotion to Wabash as the years went by.

Lee's performance as a trustee in the 1930s I knew of only by hearsay. But it must have been of high quality for him to have been elected president of the board when Governor Goodrich died. I regard him as one of three great board presidents in the decades covered by these reflections.

In some ways as chairman he dominated the trustees more than Governor Goodrich did. A short man, Lee would always rise from his chair when he addressed the board or when he put motions to a vote. He had a high-pitched voice and spoke emphatically and directly. Except for Mr. Lilly, whom he invariably treated deferentially, he was often sharp with individual trustees, occasionally rising during the discussion to cut off further debate. He often stopped Oscar Welborn in the middle of some caveat about expenses. His way of putting motions was somewhat arbitrary. He usually did not call for votes. "Any objections?" he would ask and then without pausing he would add "I hear none. Unanimously carried."

Lee pressed individual trustees hard for gift money both in and out of meetings. I remember his habit of rising at some point during board meetings to talk about gifts. He had a set speech which he gave at the December meeting about money requirements for the coming new year. Frequently in this speech he would say, "I'll start things off by pledging right now $100,000. Now what will you do?" He shared Dr. Sparks' lack of interest in gifts from the rank and file of the alumni, but unlike Frank, who always expressed appreciation for such gifts, Lee could be openly disparaging. John Farber in the late 1940s made a gift to the college of $5,000 to support an annual essay contest. Farber attached importance to the contest and kept tinkering with the details. He wanted to discuss his concerns with Lee, who, on about the second visit, brushed Farber aside by saying, "Well, it's only $5,000. Why worry about it?" John was hurt and angry.

These methods, even if sometimes a little brusque, got results from most of the trustees. But in time there was subdued resentment at Lee's methods. I. C. Elston called him "the little dictator" and Pierre Goodrich mumbled increasingly about what he called Lee's "harassment." Lee became a very close friend of Dick Banta and relied increasingly on Dick's thinking about the college. Dick's blunt way of expressing his conclusions sometimes influenced McCanliss and led to his making sweeping statements about this or that college matter which simply were not correct. It was a McCanliss habit which annoyed people.

The Sparks administration in a way was the Sparks-McCanliss administration. The two men worked closely and extremely well together. Lee regarded Frank as a great Wabash president, which he was, and gave Frank unflinching support. I am sure Lee regarded my election as president as falling action, but he probably would have felt the same about anyone else. Frank and Abbie were very fond of Lee and devoted to him. It was an excellent team, therefore, and Wabash benefited greatly as a consequence.

In view of this, it is a happy circumstance that Lee's portrait and Frank's face each other from opposite ends of the Great Hall of the Campus Center. Lee's portrait always seemed to me to be a little too impressionistic but the penetrating gaze from his eyes and the characteristic pince-nez glasses are good.[22]

DAVID W. PECK
Wabash 1922

David Peck merits a niche in Wabash history not unlike that I have assigned to John J. Coss. In saying this I have in mind the fact that David Peck, more than any other trustee, was responsible for the selection of the eleventh president of Wabash, Thaddeus Seymour. When Paul Cook left Wabash after his short term as president in 1968, Judge Peck was appointed chairman of the presidential search committee. He took his assignment seriously. He knew what Wabash needed in a new president, and he set high standards in fulfilling that need. He was good about consulting other members of his committee, both trustee and faculty, and he also consulted with others. But Dave Peck from the beginning of this search had a candidate in mind who he thought would make an ideal Wabash president.

Whitney Seymour (Sr.), Thaddeus' father, was a close friend of Dave

22. Painted by C. J. Fox.

Peck. He was a distinguished New York lawyer, who once was president of the American Bar Association. Through him Judge Peck came to know and to think highly of Thad Seymour and his wife, Polly. He had recommended Thad for the position in 1966, but at that time Thad, who was just well into his work as dean at Dartmouth, was not interested. This time he was.

I write with some assurance about these matters because Dave asked me to help with advice in the search committee's work, and I gladly responded. It soon became apparent that an awkward problem was to complicate the selection process. A vigorous ground swell had developed among alumni and faculty members to make Richard Ristine president. And there was much to be said for that thought. Dick's family had been associated in one way or another with Wabash almost from the beginning. His knowledge of Crawfordsville and his friendly relations with the faculty made him a popular choice. His political career in Indiana, including being a state senator, lieutenant governor and unsuccessful candidate for governor, had made him well known throughout the area. After being defeated for the governorship, he landed on his feet as vice president of L. S. Ayres and Co. in Indianapolis. He was a young, but prominent member of the Wabash Board of Trustees. His wife, Lou, was an attractive, able young woman well-liked throughout the Wabash community.

These were all potent influences in behalf of Dick Ristine's candidacy for the presidency of Wabash. And he wanted the position. He had the support of important trustees such as Gene Beesley. I was aware of these developments and thought well of Dick's prospects, but when I first talked with Dave Peck after he called me one day to help his committee, it was clear that Peck was not going to be pressured into selecting Dick Ristine. It was not an easy decision for him. Dave liked Dick and thought highly of him, but he believed Wabash should have a "professional" — someone with solid college administrative experience — as president. He had the courage of his conviction, and this says something about the character of Dave Peck, faced as he was with the choice of a friend or someone he knew far less well. He was fully supported in this position by John Collett and others.

At Judge Peck's request, I met Thad Seymour and talked with him at length in my office in the Empire State Building. I liked Thad and although earlier I had recommended and introduced Dave to John Logan, president of Hollins College, I agreed that Thad Seymour appeared to be an excellent candidate for Wabash. Later the search committee recommended and the board approved Seymour's election. But had it not been for Dave Peck's chairmanship of that selection committee, it might have been a quite different story.[23]

23. It was because of the tension produced by this selection of Seymour rather than Ristine, I believe, that John Collett urged me to join the Wabash Board in 1970. He thought

This account of Judge Peck's role in the selection of one of the presidents of Wabash perhaps obscures his much greater contributions to Wabash as a trustee. In fact, it was only one of innumerable services he has performed. His presence on the board, his keen analytical mind, his stature in legal circles, his gifts and those he influenced — all of these — have made him a source of strength for the college. And what he did, he did out of continuing affection for the college where he had studied.

Dave Peck grew up in Crawfordsville, the son of a prominent merchant there. He was an active member of Phi Gamma Delta while an undergraduate and he made a brilliant academic record ending with Phi Beta Kappa honors. Graduating from Wabash in three years, he went on to achieve an equally brilliant record at Harvard Law School and then entered the practice of law in New York City. For a number of years he served with distinction as a New York appellate judge and was active in New York Republican party politics. He was talked of as a candidate for governor of New York.

It was while he was at the height of his career as a judge that I became acquainted with him. I heard him speak at a New York alumni banquet and was greatly impressed by what he had to say. I suggested to Dr. Sparks that Peck ought to be a trustee and Frank agreed. Lee McCanliss, when consulted about this possibility, gave one of his off hand "dismissal" remarks. In effect he said, "Well, Dave Peck is a fine fellow and a good judge, but he has no money." Nevertheless, Dave Peck was elected a trustee in 1955.

Subsequent events proved Lee wrong. Peck gave up his judgeship and became a senior partner of Sullivan & Cromwell in New York. In that famous law firm he became a star. One of the partners told me that David Peck was their number one barrister and that he was perhaps the finest barrister in the entire New York bar at that time. It is not surprising that he became affluent as well as famous. (In 1973 Peck was one of the three lawyers considered as a successor to Archibald Cox as special federal prosecutor in the Watergate scandals.)

Among other things, Dave Peck was a writer of considerable talent. His *The Greer Case* reads like an exciting novel. "Playhouse 90," the famous TV program of the 1950s, picked up this book and presented it as one of its most

my filling out Pierre Goodrich's unexpired term would be helpful to Seymour and reassuring to the alumni. I was touched by John's personal appeal and my wife, Lorenza, who heard John's reasoning at a lunch the three of us had together at the St. Regis Hotel, agreed with him. I accepted and returned to Wabash briefly as a trustee. It was a mistake. I found it difficult emotionally to return to Wabash, and at the few meetings I attended I felt reticent about expressing my thoughts. Moreover, it was quickly evident that Thad Seymour and his wife, Polly, had winning ways with Wabash alumni and needed no reassuring symbols to make their way into the heart of the college. I declined, therefore, to continue when that partial term ended. BKT.

popular features. Peck's *Decision at Law* was equally well done, although not as widely read as *The Greer Case.*[24]

Here, then, is another man who by his fortunes in life and their demands on his time might very easily have ignored his Indiana alma mater. But he didn't. Wabash is a better, sturdier place because of that.

DR. NORMAN TREVES
Wabash 1916

Like David Peck, Norman Treves was a native of Crawfordsville. His family, the Tannenbaums, was old and prominent in Crawfordsville, with interests in retail stores, real estate, and the First National Bank. At Wabash during his student years, John Farber told me that Norman was regarded as a "whiz kid." He was not just a good student. He was a prodigious reader and a restless exploring kind of scholar. He received his Phi Beta Kappa key in his junior year. His major studies were in the most rigorous subjects at Wabash — the sciences. Years later he spoke to me with obvious deep respect for his professors in those years, especially Dr. Garner in chemistry and Dr. Mason B. Thomas in biology. He told me that they changed his whole life. Instead of carrying on in the family businesses, he resolved to become a medical doctor and scientist.

After serving briefly as an instructor in zoology on the Wabash faculty, he completed his medical studies at Johns Hopkins University. He did his intern work at a New York hospital, and thereafter New York was home for him. He specialized in cancer and became in time one of the country's leading authorities on breast cancer. He was not only a great diagnostician and surgeon; he was also a productive research scholar in the area of breast cancer. A long time senior staff doctor at the Presbyterian Memorial Hospital in New York, he served as head of its breast cancer division. He was a lecturer at the Cornell University Medical Center in New York and from time to time read and published monographs on breast cancer at medical and scientific association meetings in both the United States and Europe.

Norman prospered financially as a consequence of his medical practice and his wife, Rebecca, came from a wealthy Eastern Jewish family. They owned a charming apartment in Sutton Place in Manhattan, and both were discriminating collectors of antiques and objects of art. They had no children. Rebecca in later life fell victim to multiple sclerosis and became an invalid. Perhaps because of this, particularly after her death, Norman often seemed melancholy and detached.

24. *The Greer Case, a True Court Drama* (New York: Simon & Schuster, 1955); *Decision at Law* (New York: Mead, 1961).

I first became aware of Norman Treves at an alumni banquet held in the Masonic Temple in Crawfordsville in the early 1930s. There Norman unveiled and presented to the college the portrait of Dr. Mackintosh about which I spoke early in these recollections. He and John Farber, shortly after Dr. Mackintosh's death, commissioned a well-known artist to paint the portrait. I do not remember precisely why, but I was electrified by Dr. Treves' quiet and short speech in tribute to "Doc Mac." What he said was full of insights on the permanent influences exerted by the old on the young.

It was not until Dr. Treves became a trustee in the early 1950s that my casual acquaintance with him deepened into a close friendship. At trustee meetings he rarely had much to say. Nor did he have any important committee assignments. But the questions he would raise were always penetrating. Usually they had to do with the quality of the academic program of the college. I noticed that Lee McCanliss appeared always to be respectful of Norman's thoughts. He was a faculty-minded trustee. He made it a point to get acquainted with faculty leaders, especially scientists. He took advantage of the faculty-trustee luncheons and of the Phi Beta Kappa breakfasts to do this. But he did not limit his interests in the faculty to these superficial contacts. Occasionally he would sit in on class discussions and he often visited laboratory sections. He became well acquainted with Willis Johnson and encouraged him with gifts for special projects.

While I was president Norman came to Crawfordsville a day or two before trustee meetings and usually stayed on a day or two afterward. We invariably had long talks about the college and its possibilities. I found him a helpful critic of my dreams for the place. He loved the campus and was proud of the plant additions. He especially loved the campus trees; and on our walks about the campus he often referred to their "nobility" and of what they had "seen" in the life of the college. He took a keen interest in landscaping details and helped with various planting projects by gifts. He made me a bet that the holly tree I planted in front of the Campus Center would not endure. "We are too far north, Byron," he said. I hope that tree continues to live and to prove him wrong.

We began to talk seriously about what he could do in his will to help Wabash. I suggested a set of really major scholarships for science students to be endowed in his name. He preferred a "chair" in the biological sciences reflecting in part his admiration for Willis Johnson. Thus was born the idea of the Norman Treves Professorship. He never told me how much money he had in mind. He only asked me what it would take to endow such a professorship. I suggested a minimum of $250,000. When he died his gift to Wabash for this purpose was on the order of $600,000.

Lee McCanliss and I rode together after Norman's funeral services to the cemetery in New York where Norman's ashes were interred. "Norman was a great man," Lee said, "But he killed himself, you know." I was startled and asked him to explain. "Why, he didn't take care of himself! He ate too much, smoked too much. Took no exercise. Went off to his country home alone instead of going to a hospital when he knew he was in trouble. It is ridiculous that such a gifted doctor who prolonged the lives of so many others was so careless about his own life." That remark tells more about Lee than it does Norman. And yet I have reason to believe that Norman was ready to die and looked forward to the end.

OSCAR ("Pop") WELBORN
Wabash 1896

To those who knew him only casually during the many years of his trusteeship, Oscar Welborn appeared to be a crusty old bachelor with no great interest in anything other than matters of finance. In those matters he was regarded as something of a wizard.

There was much in Pop Welborn's personality and life style to support this impression. He was a loner in the way he lived. He had few intimate friends. Among his fellow trustees only Ike Elston appeared to be a close companion. All of his adult life in Indianapolis he lived alone, for part of that time at the Old University Club and then for years at the Indianapolis Athletic Club. His rooms at the Athletic Club were pleasant, but plain and simple. Ascetic in his tastes and habits, he never used tobacco and rarely took a drink. He avoided large social parties, including Wabash alumni meetings. Although well to do, with no dependents, he spent money sparingly, and if he indulged himself for personal enjoyment, it was never apparent to the naked eye. He dressed neatly, but conservatively, and his automobiles were always in the moderate price range. In his undergraduate years at Wabash, he had been a prominent member of Beta Theta Pi, but in all my years at Wabash, I never saw him enter the Beta House, nor did I see him at Beta reunions. Also as an undergraduate, he took an active part in promoting athletic teams, and as student manager of the football team in the middle 1890s, he was credited with having kept the team in business as far as finances were concerned. In later years, however, he seemed indifferent to the college's fortunes in intercollegiate athletics. I never saw him at a Wabash football game.

By the time he became a trustee, his consuming interest was financial investments at which he had achieved a reputation in Indianapolis and in Indiana for uncanny shrewdness. Following the stock market crash in 1929, his reputation was enhanced. Governor Paul McNutt in 1933 put him in charge of liquidating state banks which had failed in the early years of the Depression. His efficient administration of this unpleasant and difficult task won him high praise in financial circles. It also probably reinforced his disposition in later years to speak in an *ex cathedra* manner about good and bad financial practices.

With experience such as this, Oscar Welborn was a natural to be comptroller of Wabash during the trying decade of the 1930s. He was treasurer from 1941 to 1957, when he was succeeded by John Collett. During much of that time he also served as secretary of the board. The severe financial problems of the college, coupled with his reputation for financial acumen, made Pop's management of the college's investment portfolio and his general supervision of the operating budget of the college something of a law unto itself. Governor Goodrich, as president of the board, always treated him with respect, and President Hopkins was somewhat awed by his frequent discourses on the state of the college's finances.

When I first began to attend trustee meetings, Oscar was probably at the height of his prestige. I remember being enormously impressed by the way he put a stop to trustee discussions about proposed modest increases in expenditures by saying bluntly, "What are you going to use for money?" or "Where's the money coming from?" or, simply, "We can't afford that! It's out of the question." Invariably the board meeting turned meekly to other safer topics on the agenda. I also remember, then and later, being completely lost by his lengthy explanations of various college accounts. His querulous comments about "overdrafts on the operating account, covered by advances from the foundation account which in turn has overdue credits against the plant account" overwhelmed me. For a long time I attributed my confusion to my naiveté about finance. I was much encouraged and relieved, therefore, when in the early 1950s I heard John Collett remark that he did not know "what the hell Pop is talking about half the time."

Perhaps it was his blunt way of talking about finances at trustee meetings that led people to speak of him as "crochety" and "peevish." Or perhaps he was simply true to his character. John Coulter, who knew Oscar as an undergraduate at Wabash, laughingly told me once, "Oh, Oscar, is just by nature dyspeptic. He turned sour in a disappointing love affair in his youth and never got over it." Following a board meeting in the early 1950s, at which Oscar had made serious difficulties for one of Dr. Sparks' proposals, Ivan Wiles quoted his father, who had worked with Oscar at the Fletcher Bank, as saying, "Oscar Welborn was hard to get along with. He was always cantankerous."

Cantankerous or not, Pop Welborn deserves more praise from Wabash College than has ever been fully expressed. He became a trustee in the middle 1920s, and for the next three decades he was unexcelled in his conscientious devotion to his trustee responsibilities. From the beginning he took an active interest in the college's finances. He became treasurer of the college at one of the bleakest periods in its financial history. He brought to bear on the Wabash investment portfolio his considerable knowledge and experience, and little by little he transformed the portfolio from the shambles in which he found it following the crash of 1929 into a healthy income-producing collection of stocks and bonds. The investment committee of the board in the 1930s shared the credit for this transformation. But with the steady backing of Ike Elston, it is clear that Pop dominated that committee for years.

By comparison with the current Wabash endowment, the endowment fund of the college in the years of which I am speaking was relatively small. But then as now it was the largest endowment per student among private colleges in Indiana. Moreover, its importance to the operating budget of the college was greater then than now. Annual giving by alumni for operating purposes was virtually nonexistent, and the concept of corporate support for education was years away. The operating budget at Wabash was dependent almost entirely on revenue from tuition fees and endowment income. Thus, the improvement in the performance of the Wabash endowment fund in the 1930s and early 1940s is an impressive tribute to Oscar Welborn's service as a trustee. (He received a modest salary as college treasurer, but his frequent gifts to the college, always made without fanfare, more than made up for his salary.) His accomplishments at Wabash impressed outsiders, too, and led to his being retained for a number of years by the DePauw Board of Trustees as an investment counselor.

One of the thorniest financial problems confronting the college in the depression years was the liquidation of foreclosed farm mortgages. During the last years of T. H. Ristine's treasurership and during the treasurership of his protégé and successor, Jim Wedding, the college perhaps unwisely had ventured into the farm mortgage business. With the collapse of the economy in the early 1930s, most of these college loans went sour and foreclosures followed. The consequent problems for the college were acute. There was ill will toward the college because of the foreclosures. There was no market for the farms the college possessed, and there was no apparatus for managing their operations. Especially sticky was the uncertainty (under the amended college charter) about the college's legal right to own and to operate the farms. Pop Welborn tackled this problem with the same zeal with which earlier he had liquidated Indiana banks that had failed. He persuaded the Board of Trustees to transfer title to the farms to the newly-created Wabash College Foundation. He entered the farms on the asset side of the foundation account at almost nothing in dollar value. Gradually he "worked the college out of the farm business." As cash came in from the sale of farms, he bought securities of his own choosing. In time the foundation's portfolio amounted to several hundred thousand dollars. Pop resisted all occasional proposals thereafter to transfer back to the college the assets of the foundation. Instead of that, he arranged for the foundation to pay what amounted to foundation dividends to the college.

Whether the Wabash Foundation was the brain child of Pop Welborn I

196

do not know. It could well have been. I believe both Governor Goodrich and Joe Daniels had a hand in drafting the enabling legislation that brought the foundation into being. The language used was beautiful from the point of view of the college. The Wabash Foundation was and is empowered to do almost anything in the best interests of the college. It thus became a useful instrument for handling questionable securities or property rights willed or given to the college.[25]

But whether or not the foundation was Oscar Welborn's brain child, he managed it as if it were his private corporation. He served officially as its secretary-treasurer. Its Board of Directors met once a year in Crawfordsville. The meetings were brief, with Oscar doing most of the talking. The Wabash alumni members of the board from Crawfordsville, businessmen like Herb Morrison, Fred Daugherty, and H. E. (Bud) Greene, made up the majority of the board. I suspect they were only dimly aware of what Oscar was talking about. Official business consisted of re-electing officers and passing technical resolutions prepared in advance by Welborn.

Pop Welborn's influence within the college Board of Trustees waned in the early Sparks years. He was distressed by what he regarded as the free-wheeling financial methods used by Dr. Sparks and Lee McCanliss in the new building program. He protested particularly the use of gift pledges as security for money borrowed from the college endowment for plant improvement purposes. Dr. Sparks had little to say when such angry protests came, but Lee pooh-poohed such outbursts and cut short the discussion. Quite apart from this kind of disagreement, Pop's age and his declining health made it obvious that he should relinquish the treasurership of the college. I have no doubt he was saddened by this, but outwardly he was cheerful and cooperative when he turned his responsibilities over to John Collett, in whom he had great confidence.

What I have written about Pop Welborn I realize makes him appear like a curmudgeon. But there was another side to Oscar Welborn which perhaps few people saw as I did.[26] The fact that he came from Princeton, Indiana, as I

25. A good example of this usefulness concerned Roger Wolcott's legacy to the college. When he died, he left a sizeable estate, much of which went to Wabash. Among other things, he left to Wabash highly speculative "rights" to oil royalties in the United States, to uranium royalties in Canada, and property interests in a gambling casino. All such items went into the foundation account. BKT. (*Editors' note:* After the passage of the tax reform act of 1967, the foundation was disbanded. It had served its purpose and the new law made its continuation too cumbersome and expensive.)

26. The person who perhaps knew Oscar Welborn best was Anna Carpenter. She moved to Indianapolis from Crawfordsville as a young woman, and for years worked with him, first as a secretary, then as an assistant, and in the end as his guardian angel. Pop was enormously fond and proud of Anna. He taught her all he knew and encouraged her in a career that brought her considerable distinction in her own right as an investment analyst. BKT.

197

did provided something of a bond of friendship between us which became more important after I became president of Wabash. He seemed genuinely pleased at my election and his was the first gift ($1,000) I received for Wabash when my presidency began. The Welborn family in Princeton was an old, distinguished family, but Oscar appeared to have lost all interest in the family and the community. I was surprised to discover in conversation with him that he was really quite proud and a little sentimental about Princeton. I was not surprised, therefore, when sometime later he gave to Princeton the money which made possible the construction of the new Gibson County General Hospital.[27]

His sentimentality about Princeton gave me a clue to his devotion to Wabash. In spite of his crustiness he was really very much in love with Wabash and emotionally committed to its best interests. In his final illness I used to visit him briefly at the Methodist Hospital in Indianapolis. He was often quite confused. Once he called me "Dr. Burroughs." But confused or rational, it was of Wabash that he talked continuously on those occasions — of his student days, of Beta Theta Pi, of "Tubby" Tuttle, of Dr. Mackintosh, of football heroism, and, yes, of the financial problems of the college.

There is no good portrait of Oscar Welborn at Wabash. It is a pity.[28] For those who knew him well, it should be a portrait catching his bright blue friendly eyes and his gentle smile. He should be remembered not only for his toughness in college finance, but also for his quiet and generous spirit.

IVAN L. WILES
Wabash 1922

It is the proud boast of liberal arts colleges that their graduates with only the A.B. degree can go to the "top" in their life's work with no further formal education. Qualifications are usually added, of course. In some cases, medicine and law for example, some additional professional training is required. Nevertheless, especially in business, there are enough examples of going to the "top" with only the A.B. degree to give credence to the boast. There have been numerous such examples at Wabash. Frank W. Misch (long-time trustee and acting president of the college in 1968–69) is one impressive example. Starting at the bottom rung of the ladder after graduating from Wabash, he rose to be vice president for finance of the Chrysler Corporation. Allen Saunders (also a long-time trustee) is another. Few cartoonists can boast of three comic strips

27. I was asked to speak at the dedication of the Princeton hospital on Oscar's behalf, and I also gave the eulogy at the memorial services held for him at the First Presbyterian Church in Princeton when he died. BKT.

28. The only portrait in the college's collection was painted by Irwin Lee Detchon and hangs in the lobby of the business office, Center Hall.

internationally syndicated and running simultaneously, as Allen Saunders could boast if he were a boasting man.

But among all such Wabash examples that of Ivan Wiles is probably the most spectacular. Starting at the bottom with General Motors, as Misch did a few years later at Chrysler, Ivan had a meteoric rise to the managership of the Buick Division of General Motors. While Ivan was the head of the Buick Division, it had an incredible growth in sales, nudging Chevrolet for the top sales position in the entire General Motors system. Nor was this record-setting pace and Ivan's position merely a matter of coincidence. Ivan had the reputation of being a "killer" at General Motors, hard driving, imaginative, inspirational to his subordinates. It did not surprise those who knew him when he was selected to become executive vice president of General Motors, and there was open talk about his succeeding Curtis as president. I am hazy about the exact years of these events, but at one point *Business Week* did a feature article on Ivan Wiles with his picture on the cover and speculated about the likelihood of his heading General Motors soon.

Whether this would have happened or not, there is no way of telling. In any case, it ceased to be a realistic possibility when on one of his physical check-ups at the Mayo Clinic, required by the corporation of its top executives, it was discovered that he had a duodenal cancer. It was a shattering blow for him, his friends, and all of us at Wabash. The surgery and subsequent treatments were successful, but Ivan had reached the zenith of his career. Although he continued thereafter for some years as executive vice president of General Motors, he lived under the shadow of a recurrence of cancer.

It was Frank Sparks who persuaded Ivan Wiles to become a trustee after World War II and to take an increasingly active role in the exciting developments at Wabash in the 1950s. Acting on his theory that any alumnus who gave $500 a year to the college, without being solicited, merited attention and cultivation, Frank had a series of visits with Ivan in Flint which resulted in Ivan's gradually increasing his annual gifts to $25,000 a year and for a while to $50,000. Busy and constantly under pressure though he was, he found time to attend board meetings and to participate positively in its work.

When Lee McCanliss retired from the presidency of the board in December, 1955, Dr. Sparks, by prearrangement, became his successor. In theory it made good sense but close as he and I were, it proved to be an awkward arrangement. Neither of us was completely at ease. Early in 1958, after his short-lived campaign for the Republican gubernatorial nomination for Governor of Indiana, Frank resigned his position on the Wabash board. Ivan Wiles occurred to several trustees as a logical choice for president of the board, and somewhat later he was elected to the post. He certainly was my preference at that time, and I helped to persuade him to accept.

Ever since my undergraduate years when I first met Ivan at the Beta

House, I had admired him. Good looking, urbane, with a ready laugh and an easy, relaxed manner with people, he became something of a hero for generations of undergraduate Betas. He became something of a hero for the college, too, after becoming head of Buick. The admissions office of the college over and over talked of him, along with other alumni, to prospective students as an example of what Wabash could do for its sons. The example of a Phi Beta Kappa English major rising to the top in General Motors was too good not to include in such sales talk.

This acquaintanceship of the late 1920s became a friendship later on. Ivan married Mary Louise Wyatt of Rushville. Her brother, John Wyatt, was a classmate and one of my closest friends at the Beta House. It was a natural thing, therefore, for me to have a chance to visit with Ivan within the Wyatt family circle. My point in mentioning this friendship is to explain the great enthusiasm and high expectations I had about Ivan's becoming president of the Wabash board. And yet as matters worked out, he was not the active board chairman I had expected, and, as I have explained elsewhere, I found myself working more closely with other trustees, particularly with John Collett.

In making this observation I am not faulting Ivan's interest in the college or his seriousness of purpose as president of the board. But circumstances worked against his involvement in the affairs of the college to the extent I had visualized. He was not close at hand. His homes were in Flint and Walloon Lake, Michigan, and in Arizona. Second, after his long siege with cancer at Mayo's, he lived under the specter of recurring cancer. Finally, his wife, Mary Louise, developed health problems of her own, including a complete emotional dependence on Ivan. She resisted his traveling alone and became a source of concern and worry for Ivan.

Even so, while Ivan was president of the board, there were numerous pluses. Perhaps the most important of these was the beginning of more substantial gifts to Wabash from Eli Lilly. Mr. Lilly thought very highly of Ivan and was personally fond of him. Ivan joined me in a final conference with Mr. Lilly at his home at Lake Wawasee to talk about a new library building at Wabash. Ivan's participation in these conversations was decisive. He also had much to do with persuading Mr. Lilly to let us use his name on the building. Ivan was also quite important in winning the Ford Foundation Challenge Grant in 1960 and in helping to meet that challenge once we had it.

But the truth is, I believe, that Ivan Wiles did not enjoy being president of the board. Nor did he really want the position. He accepted it out of a sense of duty in response to entreaties from others, including me. He was pleased when he could turn that responsibility over to John Collett, which he did shortly after I resigned in 1965. He continued on the board, however, and provided more strength to the college in the difficult years in the late 1960s and early 1970s than he had when he was president.

When he was an undergraduate, Ivan Wiles founded the Scarlet Inn. He never boasted about it, but in a long sentimental conversation we had at his cottage on Walloon Lake one summer, it was clear to me that he was really quite proud of this. I wouldn't be surprised if Ivan would rather be remembered as the founder of the Scarlet Inn than as a one-time president of the Board of Trustees.

Such, in brief and in part, were a few of the numerous Wabash men who in these four decades guided the destiny of Wabash College. Such they were as I saw them and knew them. They are representative of the rich diversity of talent, experience, and points of view which has characterized the Wabash board in the past fifty years. Above all, they exemplify in different ways a deep commitment to their alma mater. Four of these men are still living and active as trustees. I have written of all of them in the past tense, however, because what I have to say about them is already a part of the history of the college.

The extent to which the lives of these men, and others like them, were intertwined with the life of the college, is an indelible part of what I used to call the poetry of Wabash. In the early 1960s I made a speech at a Homecoming Chapel about the poetic quality of Wabash history. Omer Foust, then director of alumni affairs, liked that speech and later had a portion of the speech printed and hung in the corridor of Forest Hall. Perhaps it is still there.[29] I do not remember exactly how I put it, but in substance it was something like this.

> The poetry in the life of a college like Wabash lies in its history. It lies in the almost miraculous fact that for a long time here on these familiar grounds students and teachers as real as ourselves worked and studied, argued and laughed, and worshipped together. Now they are gone, one generation vanishing after another, as surely as we shall shortly be gone. But if you listen you can hear their songs and their cheers.

When I wrote those lines I was thinking primarily of students and student life. But I apply the sentiment equally to trustees and professors. There is, indeed, something poetic about the history of Wabash when thought of in this way. And it becomes a source of inspiration and strength for those who have in their hands the stewardship of the college at any given present moment.

To some this way of thinking about a place like Wabash is sentimental drivel. Maybe so. But for me, and I believe for many others, there is a kind of reality about the past which cannot be denied. The past is always there, influ-

29. This now hangs in the Arnold Admissions Center.

encing the present and thus the future. The present moment always seems more real and more important, but the present is so very fleeting. It is constantly, irrevocably receding into the past. The quality and the value of an institution like Wabash and what it has to offer for the future are rooted in its history. The strengthening or weakening of that offering depends above all else on the trustees. As far as I am concerned, in the period since 1926, and especially since 1946, the trustees of Wabash in this respect have never been found wanting.

IV

STUDENTS AND ALUMNI

In one context or another I have often heard the term "typically Wabash" applied to Wabash students and Wabash alumni. For students it was usually prompted by behavior patterns. For alumni it usually referred to expressed attitudes of mind about their alma mater.

Whether such comments are still made I have no idea, but in my years of association with the college they were commonplace, and I have no doubt they were commonplace for many years before then. Occasionally, especially in Crawfordsville, the term "typically Wabash" carried overtones of disapproval and contempt. Since the earliest years in the history of the college, there have been in Crawfordsville those who looked upon the college with distrust and dislike. For such people recurring student behavior patterns were regarded as a public nuisance, and they often provoked comments of disgust and resentment. In the 1920s a riot touched off by a student effort to "crash" the Strand Theatre, or a prolonged water fight at night between fraternities on West Wabash Avenue, or alleged orgies following student dances were indignantly tagged "typically Wabash." But for others the same kind of behavior patterns were a source of amusement which added color and zest to life in Crawfordsville.

Away from Crawfordsville the term "typically Wabash" usually signified approval mixed with admiration, even affection. In the 1910s the annual "Wabash invasion" of Indianapolis prior to a Butler football game was good newspaper copy. On those occasions the rowdy behavior of Wabash students and the occasional indecency of the signs they flaunted were greeted with good-natured indulgence and were dismissed as "typically Wabash."

Earlier, when I recorded my thoughts about Wabash trustees, I spoke of tributes paid by non-Wabash men to the Wabash alumni spirit. It was this kind of Wabash image which made the term "typically Wabash" commonplace. I recall fragments of an afterdinner speech made in the late 1930s by a Franklin College alumnus which illustrates the point. He was speaking of the years when there was an intense basketball rivalry between the "Wonder Fives" of Franklin and the "Wonder Fives" of Wabash. Recounting the events of one memorable game between these rivals, he spoke of the pre-game tension in the crowded bleachers. "It was a typical Wabash crowd," he said, "noisy, cocky, and deliriously happy."

It was not only groups of Wabash alumni or Wabash students who drew the tag "typical." The same kind of remark was often made with respect to individual Wabash men. Now and then while participating in Rhodes Scholarship selection committee meetings, I was pleased when some committee member would comment favorably about a "typically strong" Wabash candidate. In the late 1950s, while calling on a northern Indiana business executive on behalf of Associated Colleges of Indiana, I was amused by his enthusiastic comments about "typical Wabash men." Just a day or two earlier he had had a conversation with Dave Mathias, who I presume had come to his office as a salesman. My business friend had been favorably impressed. "Oh, I knew he was a Wabash man before he told me," he said. "He was typically Wabash! I can always spot them." And he went on to mention other Wabash men by name whom he considered "typically Wabash." Jokingly, I told him that he ought to make an annual corporate gift to Wabash. To my surprise I later learned that he had done precisely that.

Has there ever really been a typical Wabash student? A typical Wabash alumnus? A typical Wabash man? Anyone who says "yes" to these questions would be hard pressed to support his answer with facts. Such generalizations as he might make or such statistical averages as he might present would apply equally well to almost any private college in the Middle West. Moreover, to every generalization he might make about "Wabash types" there would be such numerous and, at times, sharp exceptions that only a kind of Wabash mythology would remain.

The basic composition of the Wabash student body has changed from time to time. Throughout the nineteenth century and in the early years of the twentieth century, Wabash students were predominantly white, Anglo-Saxon, protestant, and Hoosier. The great majority were Presbyterian and, prior to the Civil War at least, religion was the central influence in their being at Wabash. In the twentieth century this early profile of the Wabash student body changed steadily. The majority of the students continued to be Hoosier but the student body was less homogeneous. By the middle decades of the century there were more Roman Catholics in the student body than Presbyterians, and Methodists were the most numerous single group as far as professed church affiliation was concerned. Religion as a central influence in the total life of the college declined in the early decades of the twentieth century. The vestigial structures and symbols of the early religious character of the college which continued became more and more ecumenical.

For many years, beginning in the post-Civil War period perhaps, Wabash attracted students from prominent, well-to-do if not wealthy families in Indiana. They came from Indianapolis and other cities in the state, but especially they came from county seat towns. Wabash was "the place to go" for the sons of such families. The enrollment records of Wabash are studded with prominent Indiana family names whose sons habitually went to Wabash. Three generations of Wabash students from such families were not uncommon. In notable instances — the Ristine family, for example — the family name appears over and over from the earliest years to the present.

To some extent this pattern of the family origin of Wabash students has continued in the twentieth century, and it is still evident today. But during the depressed years of the 1930s and in the more affluent years following World War II, it became less conspicuous and less important in the composition of the student body. As American society became more mobile and as youthful notions of "collegiate life" changed, young men from Indiana families who might earlier have entered Wabash as a matter of course tended to go to eastern colleges or to large universities. At the same time, other sources for new, entering Wabash classes became more significant. Lake County in Indiana, for example, toward the middle years of the twentieth century became numerically as important as Marion County. Enrollment of students from outside Indiana also rose during those same years. Chicago, Peoria, St. Louis, Detroit, Cincinnati, Cleveland, and other mid-western cities became increasingly prominent in the geographical origins of Wabash students. Often the influence of a single alumnus far from Indiana accounted for an influx of Wabash students quite different from earlier student types. In the 1930s and 1940s there was an astonishing run of excellent scholars from Winona, Minnesota, thanks to the influence of Ed Davis. And in the late 1940s and in the 1950s there came a series of impressive athletes from western Pennsylvania, thanks largely to the influence of James A. Price. These changing influences affected the composition of the Wabash student body to such an extent that a cross section of Wabash students in the 1950s or 1960s would have contrasted sharply with a similar cross section in the first decades of the century.

From the very beginning scholarships and financial assistance have played an important role in determining the composition of the Wabash student body. But like other influences which have accounted for the kind of students who have come to Wabash, the college's policies with respect to financial aid have undergone subtle changes. In the earliest years and continuing through most of the nineteenth century, Wabash was generous with scholarships to poor but promising students who proposed to become teachers or Presbyterian ministers. The record of Wabash alumni in the nineteenth century and early in the twentieth century who became teachers or preachers or foreign missionaries is an impressive one. These same men during their undergraduate years undoubtedly influenced the mores and behavior patterns of the Wabash student body. One has only to look at the titles of papers read or resolutions debated by the college's literary societies in the nineteenth century to appreciate the extent of their influence.

With the turn of the century, beginning with the administration of Dr. Kane and continuing through the administration of Dr. Mackintosh, the college's policies with respect to scholarships took on an athletic cast. For a time, especially during Harry Scholler's years as director of athletics, athletic scholarships and most college jobs for students were administered by the athletic department. Although scholarships for excellent students who needed financial assistance and who were not athletes continued during these years, the bulk of the college financial aid program went to athletes. During my four years as a student at Wabash, my father paid my tuition fees and all of my expenses. The same thing could be said of practically all of my fraternity brothers at the Beta House except those who were prominent athletes. For most non-athletes only student loans were easy to obtain.

As might be expected, such policies of financial aid to students for the first two decades of the twentieth century had much to do with the rugged, tough way of life which became characteristic of Wabash during those "Little Giant-Caveman" years. With the coming of Dr. Hopkins as president, however, this policy of financial aid to students was drastically changed. Coupled with the introduction of a new curriculum and the tightening of both requirements for admission and requirements for graduation, the Hopkins policies for aid to students inevitably affected the composition of the student body. Wabash student traditions developed earlier in the century continued, but there were obvious differences between Wabash students of the 1930s and their predecessors in the 1910s and the 1920s.

The post-World War II era saw equally marked differences in the character of the student body. From 1946 until early in the 1950s, it was a student body in which veterans of the war predominated. Older, more mature, and more sophisticated than their predecessors, they provided a new tone to student life. Many of them were married, and their wives and children made the college a different kind of place. Some were battle scarred and indifferent about earlier traditions. Gene Burks, his vocal chords shot to ribbons in the Battle of the Bulge, harangued the student body as its president in his hoarse whisper trying to reinstitute student traditions he remembered from before the war but it was an impossible undertaking.

President Sparks again changed the college student aid policies. In part the changes were intended to revive earlier athletic glory and this objective was reflected in the spectacular success achieved by Glenn Harmeson's football teams and by those of his successor, Garland Frazier. But Dr. Sparks also instituted a new program for Honor Scholarships. With funds contributed first by the Volker Fund and later from other sources, Wabash launched an annual selection process, including both written and oral examinations, designed to attract exceptionally able students. They were, for the times, lush scholarships, paying full tuition plus a cash stipend of $500 a year; financial need was not involved. It was frankly a device to increase the number of brilliant students enrolling at Wabash each year. It was also hoped that it would broaden the geographical base of the student body, so the scholarships were widely advertised. By the late 1950s the consequences of this new scholarship program were evident in the composition of the student body and in the intellectual life of the college. By the 1960s a cross section of the student body would again have revealed a quite different breed of students from those in a similar cross section ten or twenty years earlier.

Bearing in mind the kind of changes I have summarized, to say nothing of individual differences from one student to another, how can one speak of a "typical Wabash student?" And since alumni emerge from changing student generations how can one speak of a "typical Wabash alumnus?" Moreover, when one stops to think about it, the differences among alumni as far as their feelings toward the college are concerned are more pronounced than those among students while on campus. Consider, for example, the boast that Wabash alumni are enormously proud of and intensely loyal to their alma mater. Well, yes and no.

Many alumni—in some geographical centers, practically all—are proud of and enthusiastic about Wabash. But judging by their silence, their absence from alumni meetings, their disregard of appeals for annual gifts to the alumni fund, many Wabash alumni are also indifferent to the college. It was always a disappointment to me, as I am sure it continues to be to others, that substantially less than one half of all living Wabash alumni contribute regularly, however modestly, to the annual alumni fund. The average percentage of those contributing annually at the highest point in the 1960s was between thirty to forty percent. By comparison with places like Dartmouth, Yale, or Princeton it is a disappointing record, softened by those few Wabash classes from earlier years which attain records of ninety or occasionally even one hundred percent in annual participation.[1]

1. Since the disappointing 1960s, alumni participation has greatly increased. In 1976 the *New York Times* described the Fund for Continued Independence and Excellence as "the most successful fund-raising campaign of any small college in the history of American higher education." This campaign ran from December, 1973, through December, 1976, and raised $32,199,067. Alumni participation reached 38.7 percent, the highest in Wabash history. The percentage of participation today is still consistent with the campaign figure, in marked contrast to the 25 percent participation in the late 1960s. In 1965 the Greater Wabash Foundation was founded by Frederic M. Hadley, then the vice president of the college. Its membership has grown from 87 to 959. In December, 1981, the Caleb Mills Society was established. The society is made up of contributors of $1,000 or more each year to the college. Membership through February, 1982, is forty-six.

More troublesome still is the fact that some alumni appear to have turned their backs on the college completely. They are not numerous but they include men whose success in life should reflect favorably on their alma mater. Now and then such an alumnus, weary of receiving appeals for contributions or annoyed by some development at the college, writes the alumni office to demand that his name be removed from the college mailing list. More often, however, they simply ignore Wabash or play down their connection with it.

Not long ago I heard a Wabash alumnus speak condescendingly of the college when he was explaining to an eastern professional colleague how he happened to attend Wabash. "I went there as a student because I was bought!" he said laughingly. He had indeed come to Wabash as an Honor Scholar, but the choice had still been his. His record at Wabash was a brilliant one and, as far as I could tell, he had had a happy experience as an undergraduate. His scholastic record and the enthusiastic support of his principal Wabash professors won for him a fellowship in graduate school where he obtained his Ph.D. degree. Today he is well launched on a promising career as a faculty member at a distinguished university.

In the first year of our efforts to meet the Ford Foundation Challenge Grant, I identified perhaps twenty-five alumni whom I knew personally and who were in high income brackets but who had not been active supporters of the college. For the most part they were off the beaten Wabash paths with no Wabash companions nearby. They were out of touch with the college. I resolved to call on each one personally. It was a most gratifying, reassuring experience. I found the majority warm and enthusiastic about Wabash and its possibilities, and they were eager to be helpful. There was one exception, however, which left me humiliated and depressed. After several attempts I managed to talk by telephone with an alumnus who was then an associate editor of a famous weekly national magazine. He had graduated from Wabash with Phi Beta Kappa honors in the late 1930s. I remembered having heard him pay a moving tribute to Insley Osborne in his senior year in which he acknowledged his sense of "permanent indebtedness" to this great teacher. But he had never returned to the campus since graduation, never attended alumni meetings, never contributed to the alumni fund. When I talked with him by telephone, he explained it was a terribly busy day for him, but if I could come right away he could "squeeze out" a few minutes. He met me in the ground floor lobby of his building. He did not ask me to his office. He did not introduce me to associates who greeted him coming or going through the lobby. He was polite but cool and obviously impatient. After a brief stand-up conversation, we shook hands and I left. I wrote him a follow-up letter later to which I received no reply.

On the other hand there are repeated instances of major gifts from individual alumni which are unsolicited. Often they come from men who were at

Wabash briefly. A good example of such is the handsome gift recently made by Fred Lowey and his wife, Lois, through the Wabash Deferred Giving Program. Fred Lowey came to Wabash in the fall of 1941, a refugee from Hitler's Austria. He had never heard of Indiana, let alone Wabash, when friends of his in New York arranged for him to come to Crawfordsville. When I met him at the bus station in Crawfordsville, I could see the hurt and apprehension still in his eyes. He had no money and few clothes. Fred Lowey was at Wabash only one year, perhaps less. He was quick to enter the military service, when the United States became involved in World War II. He won his citizenship in service in the South Pacific battle arena. After the war he returned to New York where he gradually rose and prospered in the financial jungle of Wall Street. Wabash College represented an important turning point in his life, and the friendly hands extended to him there he never forgot.

Repeatedly I used to ask myself "Why are there such differences among alumni?" I was never able to answer that question. But the process of thinking about it helped me to clarify my notions of the relationships between the college and its students and alumni. The college has a right to expect and at points to demand certain things from its students. It has a right to expect students to make a serious effort to use well the educational opportunities Wabash provides them and to acquit themselves creditably in whatever they do while they are there. It also has the right to demand respect for the good name of Wabash, the value of which students often underestimate. But when it comes to alumni the college has no right to expect or to demand anything. It can only hope.

The college can hope that whatever its former students gained in self-development at Wabash will be put to good use in their individual lives. It can hope that their affection for their alma mater will continue and deepen and that they will do what they can to help the college remain strong and vibrant. But whatever they may say or think or do about Wabash is a matter of choice for them. It is not a matter rooted in some kind of implied contract between college and alumnus. The college is right in forever seeking financial support from its former students and it is important that it do so. If the alumni, who are the immediate beneficiaries of what the college has to offer society, do not support the college, there is precious little reason why others should support it. But whether alumni choose to respond to such appeals and the nature of their response when they do are not the criteria by which the success of the college should be measured. The success of Wabash should be measured in terms much larger than these, and it can only be measured over a long period of time.

What I have been saying about students and alumni may seem to contradict the fulsome observations I have made elsewhere in these reflections about the spirit of Wabash and the importance of love of college in making it a storybook kind of place. But for me there is no contradiction. The image of the never-ending tapestry with which I began these reflections comes to my mind again. The colors change and reappear and change again. Figures of individuals are often indistinct and shifting themes of action are ambiguous in meaning. Nevertheless, there is a kind of unity and coherence in the unfolding drama and for one who admires it there is an appeal which outweighs disappointment.

I underscore my faith in the Wabash mystique when I express thoughts such as these. If there is no such thing as a typical Wabash student or a typical Wabash alumnus, there are, nonetheless student and alumni attitudes toward the college which can be called typical. And they have been manifested for a long, long time. Their expression takes different forms. They are not always vocal. They are not always gung-ho. The love of college exemplified by an Oscar Welborn or a Reg Sullivan, who were students in the 1890s, is a quiet, mild kind of thing compared with that of a Charlie Logan or a Jack Scott or other Wabash men who came out of the Roaring Twenties. But who can say that the one is less or greater than the other? When speaking about what Wabash means to them, a "Doc" Elliot or a Homer Showalter may appear poles apart from a Frank Mullen or a Vaino Grayam forty years or more their junior, but emotionally they have an obvious common bond in Wabash. If there are examples of Wabash alumni who have won distinction and prominence in life but who seem to have forgotten Wabash, there are many more examples of such men from whom Wabash continues to claim allegiance, men like Tom Marshall, Arthur J. Brown, General Charles Herron, Will Hays, Byron Price, Pete Edson, Allen Saunders, and numerous others.

The involvement of alumni in the affairs of the college as counsellors, student recruiters, and financial supporters has a long history. President Tuttle probably had this partly in mind when he referred to alumni as the "glory" of the college. In the earliest decades, non-Wabash men were the principal benefactors of the college, but in the decades following the Civil War individual Wabash alumni became increasingly important in enlarging the college's financial resources. In the earliest decades Presbyterian ministers and teachers were probably the most important influences in student enrollment. But gradually they were replaced by alumni as the most important single influence on youthful decisions to enroll in Wabash. Until after World War II when the college instituted a full-time, professional director of admissions with traveling assistants, the role of alumni in the recruitment of students was vital to Wabash.

Since World War II the involvement of alumni in the affairs of the college has become more extensive and more highly organized. The presence of alumni on campus has become more frequent and the numbers in attendance have become larger. Directors of the National Association of Wabash Men, class agents, trustees, administrative officers of the college, and faculty members frequently mingle together. Major policy decisions at the college almost always reflect alumni judgments and advice. Always there are moving spirits among such returning alumni who for years give generously of their time, energy, and money to make such an enterprise a continuing success. They obviously enjoy the experience. It is important to them as well as to the college. I am tempted to list names of alumni from all over the country, influencing in this way younger alumni who gradually take their places with their devotion to Wabash. But the list would be too long and even then only representative of countless others not named. It is the likes of these who give credibility to the public recognition of something called "typically Wabash."

Is the college spirit of those Wabash men an unusual and distinctive thing? What I have already said in one way or another elsewhere in these recollections must make it plain that I believe it is. I cannot prove it. No one can. It is like enumerating reasons and submitting proofs for loving one's wife or one's parents. It is something felt and something expressed in countless ways. Love of college and loyalty to college can be found at practically all colleges and universities, but they are more pronounced at some than at others and at a few they have a fervent quality about them. I believe Wabash is one of these few.

How far back in the history of Wabash this kind of student and alumni emotional commitment goes is difficult to say. There is good reason to believe it runs quite deep. Professor Gronert used to be fond of quoting a letter from a student written to his father from some distant Union Army encampment during the Civil War. In effect he told his father, "If I should be killed in battle or die in service, $100 of my back pay should be sent to Wabash in care of Professor Hovey." There are in the college archives other similar signs of devotion to Wabash recorded by early students. At one or two annual alumni banquets at the Masonic Temple in the late 1920s or very early 1930s which I attended, I remember being thrilled by impromptu speeches given by elderly alumni. They were like testimonials rendered at a religious revival meeting. There was, for example, an alumnus from the 1880s who dramatically recounted the glories of his undergraduate years. The climax came when he held aloft his right hand and, waving his gnarled, crooked fingers, he vouched his pride in these visible reminders of injuries he had received while playing baseball for Wabash. The crowd roared its approval. And Billy Martin's set speech at those banquets about how Wabash chose its colors was a familiar ritual. When he reached his punch line the crowd joined him in unison — "HELIOTROPE, HELL! WE WANT BLOOD!"

Notwithstanding the evidence of strong feelings about Wabash in the nineteenth century, I believe it was in the first quarter of the twentieth century, and especially in the first decade, that what students and alumni have called "the Wabash Spirit" fully flowered. No doubt the evangelical Wabash gospel as preached by President Kane had something to do with it. Even more, probably, the fame won by Wabash athletic teams, especially in football, and the gift from outsiders of the nickname "Little Giants" accounted for a new surge in self-conscious Wabash pride and confidence. But it was both deeper and more subtle than that. It amounted to a perhaps sub-conscious recognition that Wabash among colleges and universities in the Middle West was — well, different and therefore special. And after 1900, as a liberal arts college exclusively for men, it was indeed different. In a way it was threatened by the educational trends of the times. A kind of clannishness, a kind of tribal ritualism, at points naïve and defensive, developed among Wabash students which they carried over into their alumni years. It attached priority importance to traditions. It exalted into legends, well-known incidents and episodes in the history of the college — the founders kneeling in the snow, the burning of South Hall, the marching off to war of the "entire" student body in the 1860s, the bloody class fights on Washington's birthday, and so on. It was a ritualism encouraged by revered faculty members and highly respected presidents. It was a ritualism which stuck. With deletions and additions it has been passed from one student generation to another ever since.

When Carroll Ragan and Ted Robinson introduced the song "Old Wabash," they captured the new sense of confidence and pride that enveloped the college at the turn of the century. But without knowing they were doing so they also launched what was to become in itself an increasingly influential cause of the sustained Wabash spirit in the twentieth century. The times are different now and perhaps "Old Wabash" has less appeal and less meaning for the current generation of Wabash students. Between 1900 and 1965, however, no student who came to Wabash as a freshman forgot the high emotion tinged with terror he felt when his class first sang "Old Wabash." Thereafter, he sang it and heard it sung lustily over and over and over again. It thus became a cause as well as an effect of the rise of the "Wabash Spirit."

In my senior year at Wabash I met Carroll Ragan when he returned to the campus to see the "new" Beta House. Those of us who visited with him for perhaps an hour were greatly impressed, not by anything he said or did, but simply because we knew that when he had been our age he had composed the music for that stirring college song which for us was as much a part of the college as Center Hall. He said nothing about "Old Wabash" or about *Alma Mater*. And we did not ask him questions about them. I now regret that. I would like to have asked him if he was surprised at the way the two songs had endured. Especially I would now like to have asked him if he had discussed with Ted Robinson the lyrics for "Old Wabash" while Robinson was writing them. When Robinson wrote the words for "Old Wabash," like Ragan, he was still a Wabash student. And yet he expressed poetic sentiments which are appropriate for an older alumnus who looks back on his college days through rose colored glasses.

If representative alumni of the college who were students between say 1910 and 1960 were to be asked what words from "Old Wabash" come most immediately to their minds when they think of that song, I dare say the great majority would reply "From the hills of Maine to the western plains." But if they were asked to think more carefully about it and then to identify the phrases which now mean most to them, their answers would include such phrases as ". . . there's a name held dear and a color we cheer . . . ," ". . . praise it in song and story . . . ," ". . . long in our hearts we'll bear the sweetest memories . . . ," and so on. Gross sentimentality? Perhaps it is, but it says much about the deep feelings most Wabash men have toward their college.

Much the same can be said of that other song, less well known to the public, but cherished by students and alumni — *Alma Mater*. If the word "stirring" is the right adjective for "Old Wabash" "haunting" strikes me as the right adjective for *Alma Mater*. There is something about it, both the words and the music, which for most Wabash alumni is acutely nostalgic. Sung by the college glee club on special occasions or as a solo by someone with the voice and feeling of a George Littell, it never fails to touch the emotions of returning alumni, in some cases to the point of tears. And as in "Old Wabash" the poetic phrases in *Alma Mater* pluck at the sentiments and myths which are a part of the Wabash Spirit: ". . . at thy shrine of cherished memories, the hosts of Wabash meet to pledge . . . ," ". . . these fleeting years we tarry here," "beguile us with their subtle charms . . . ," ". . . grant now thy benediction," "that worthy we may follow . . . ," and so on. It too is both an expression of and a reinforcing influence in the twentieth century spirit of Wabash.

"These fleeting years we tarry here. . . ." How true it is. Even those Wabash alumni who have the closest and longest ties with the college are only transients in the long line of Wabash men. We are here today, gone tomorrow. But the "fleeting years" really do "beguile us with their subtle charms." It is difficult to say why. One alumnus takes one thing with him from his student days; another takes another thing. For some it may be an influential memory of professors or of one professor in particular. For others it may be the influence of a great coach. For still others it may be primarily a fraternity or student friendships formed which grow stronger as years go by. For some it includes the town of Crawfordsville, Sugar Creek, and Pine Hills. An astonishing number of Wabash students over the years have made Crawfordsville their lifelong home after graduation. They become businessmen, doctors, lawyers, public school teachers, government employees. Often they marry Crawfordsville girls. Their sons usually become Wabash students. Their daughters often go to DePauw. They become prominent leaders in the civic and social life of the community. Most of them keep close personal ties with the college. It is a permanent part of their way of life.

Whatever it is that different men take with them from their Wabash experience, there is an emotional overtone that endures and it often becomes richer with the turning years. Even when time and distance may make it ap-

213

pear that all such feeling is dead or forgotten, a chance encounter with an old Wabash friend, a class reunion, suddenly hearing the strains of "Old Wabash," and the like, revive the latent feeling. It is as if there were something about Wabash that casts its spell on those who spend a part of their youth there which they can never break — not all, to be sure, but most. And it is this intangible "something" that explains what is meant by the phrase "typically Wabash."

V

1956–1965

The confidence with which I wrote about people and events in the Hopkins years and the Sparks years deserts me now that I begin to think about the years 1956–1965. It is not the accuracy of my memory that I distrust. It is the quality of my judgments about my memories. I am not sure I can distinguish between what was important and what was not.

In part, I suppose, this difficulty stems from my having been too near the center of things at Wabash during these years to have observed with any sense of detachment what was taking place. More important, these were increasingly strenuous and unhappy years for me. The inevitable resurrection of those feelings of strain and unhappiness I fear will color whatever thoughts I may record. This is not a reliable state of mind out of which to write history, even personal history, and I find myself reticent about trying to write anything having to do with this period. For all of these reasons I shall be briefer in recording recollections and reflections for these years than I otherwise might be.

I was pleased and proud to be elected ninth president of Wabash in December, 1955. In a way, it seemed to me to be the logical culmination of my experience as student, teacher, and dean at a place which I deeply loved. Moreover, I believed at that moment in its history I had something to offer Wabash as its president which could be good and enduring. And yet from the very beginning, those private positive feelings were clouded by apprehensions and misgivings. They were to become more pervasive and more complex as time went by. Although I did not appreciate it until much later, a deepening internal conflict of personal loyalties provided the elements for a classical Greek tragedy of minor importance.

My election as president was an almost perfunctory thing. The only serious conversations I had about the prospect were with Frank Sparks in the fall of 1955. My conversations with Parrish Fuller, chairman of a newly appointed trustee committee charged with recommending a reorganization of the Wabash administration, were brief and superficial. Among other trustees it was only with Pierre Goodrich that I discussed the matter at length. I came away from that conversation with the feeling that Pierre very much wanted to become president of the Board of Trustees.

The Fuller committee did its work so casually that George Kendall had to remind Parrish shortly before the December meeting of the Board of Trustees that the faculty must be consulted. This was hurriedly done, and the faculty, I understood from George, quickly approved the trustee committee proposal. The trustee meeting was an almost routine meeting. More discussion was devoted to Dr. Sparks' proposal for the establishment of the Wabash Institute for Personal Development with himself as its free-handed director than was devoted to the Fuller committee report. Lee McCanliss resigned the presidency of the board and Frank was elected to take his place. I was elected to succeed Frank as president of the college. It was a cut and dried process more akin to top management changes in a business corporation than to electing a new college president.

Undoubtedly there must have been ambiguity in the minds of Wabash people about these changes. The fact that Dr. Sparks moved from the presidency of the college to the presidency of the board probably caused some to wonder who was in fact to be the chief executive officer of the college. He moved into a separate office in Center Hall, and he and Mrs. Sparks continued to live in the Caleb Mills House. To the naked eye it must have appeared that no real change was being made. Small wonder it was that outsiders were confused. Marsh Jones, for example, in his direct and innocent way, asked me if it was true that I was "only an interim president." It was an awkward situation. Had Frank and I not been understanding friends, it might have led to friction between a new president and his predecessor.

But in spite of the perfunctory nature of these administrative changes and despite whatever speculation they may have engendered, as far as I could tell my becoming president of Wabash was greeted with an abundance of good will, perhaps even enthusiasm, among students, faculty members, and alumni. I could not have asked for a more encouraging beginning. Shortly before the official transfer of authority, following Dr. Sparks' farewell remarks to the student body and faculty in the Chapel, the college conferred on me the honorary doctorate of humane letters.[1] I was stunned and touched by the honor.

The inauguration ceremony weeks later was at my request a simple Chapel service lasting no more than twenty minutes.[2] It was strictly a college

1. The degree was conferred on February 1, 1965.

2. The inauguration was actually held during the Homecoming Chapel, Saturday morning on October 13, 1956. Trippet requested a simple ceremony, in part, because of plans for celebrations on a larger scale scheduled for 1957, the 125th anniversary of the college's founding. Part of Trippet's inaugural address, "A Symbolic Act," is included in *These Fleeting Years,* pp. 125–28.

family affair with no representatives from other institutions. The glee club sang. There were short prayers. George Kendall spoke for the faculty. Dr. Sparks as president of the Board of Trustees administered the oath of office and handed to me the original charter of the college and Elihu Baldwin's diary. My response was brief, a repetition of thoughts I had often expressed before about the educational primacy of the liberal arts.

The transition from being dean of the college to being president of the college was uneventful. I furnished the president's office with early American things which, except for the desk which was a gift to the college from Fergus Ormes, my wife and I had collected over the years. It was a plainer office than it had been in the Sparks years, but it had a warm feeling about it and for me, at least, it was right. Whatever awkwardness there may have been because of Dr. Sparks' continuing presence on campus gradually diminished as he pursued his own off-campus interests. In 1958 he decided to try for the Republican nomination for governor. When he failed to win the nomination he resigned the chairmanship of the Board of Trustees. With the approval of the executive committee of the board I persuaded Ivan Wiles to become the new president. At the next trustee meeting he was elected to that post with enthusiasm. Dr. Sparks accepted the presidency of the Council for Financial Aid to Education and he and Abbie moved to New York. These changes, rather than the changes made in December 1955, really marked the beginning of a new administration at Wabash.

Once it was vacated by the Sparkses, Dorothy and I began to arrange the Caleb Mills House for our official residence. For the most part we furnished the Caleb Mills House with college-owned furniture. The John Coss collection of early American antiques, which he had willed to the college but which had never been properly displayed, at last was put to good use. When Helen Condit, Caleb Mills' granddaughter, died in Terre Haute, we bought some of her antique furniture to add to the collection in the Caleb Mills House. Dorothy persuaded Roger Wolcott to give to the college for use in the Mills House numerous pieces of furniture as well as silverware, glass pieces, dishes, and various objects of art, all from the family's home in Wolcott, Indiana. Other gifts for the Mills House were helpful, especially a Hamilton family dining room suite given by Mary Collett. The Caleb Mills House, while less elegantly furnished than it had been in the Sparks years, had a great deal of charm about it, and for that Dorothy deserved the full credit. We spent much of our time there and found it useful for official entertaining. It was never "home" for us, however, especially not for Dorothy, who much preferred the quiet isolation of our Kennedy Place home. We kept Kennedy Place intact and used it as a retreat.

In the early weeks of 1956 I rebuilt the on-campus administrative structure to my own liking. I wanted Ben Rogge as dean of the college. To my surprise, when I proposed his election to the faculty there was opposition from

217

some of the younger faculty led by Owen Duston. I suspect the fact that I wanted Ben as dean carried the day with the majority. At the same time I appointed Stephen Kurtz to a new position I created, dean of students. Thus, the heavy burdens of the dean's office were divided between two exceptionally able officers. To Bill Degitz, who until then had worked in the shadow of Fergus Ormes, I gave full responsibility for the business office. Warren Shearer, who, had he not been a Wabash alumnus like myself, might very well have been a logical candidate for dean of the college, I appointed chairman of Division III. To Myron Phillips I gave enlarged responsibilities as director of alumni affairs. I made no effort to replace Dick Banta, who resigned his position as assistant to the president when Dr. Sparks left the presidency. Instead I gave increased responsibility to Ed Gullion who had also served as an assistant to Dr. Sparks. He became director of development. Later, for a brief time, that title was to be changed to vice president for development. The rest of the administrative apparatus I left unchanged.

This top administrative team was a very good one, I thought. There were to be changes later, but initially I regarded it as a permanent team in which I had confidence. We began a practice of weekly breakfast meetings for the purpose of exchanging information and planning. On the whole it worked well. Much of the credit for such accomplishments as I was able to make for Wabash as its president rightfully belongs to Rogge, Degitz, Kurtz and Phillips. Others who came later, notably Fred Hadley as vice president for development and Norman Moore as dean of students, deserve a large measure of that credit also.

These preliminaries were not as time consuming as they may sound. Almost immediately after assuming the presidency of the college I plunged into the work that goes with that office. I didn't need the time that a stranger would have to get acquainted with Wabash and its people. In a way it was simply a matter of continuing what I had already been doing for a number of years. And that first year went extremely well. In 1956, for the first time in its history, Wabash attracted more than a million dollars in annual gifts. I had nothing to do with that happy achievement. It was a harvest reaped from seeds sown by Frank Sparks and individual trustees. Nevertheless, that success bolstered my confidence in an area where I had been doubtful — money raising. I began to believe in my dream of leading Wabash into a brilliant era in its history.

My ambitions for Wabash were simple. Often new college presidents announce bold plans involving sweeping changes and exciting innovations. And there was much of this kind of fermentation in higher education in the late 1950s. I had no such plans. But I had firm convictions about what I would try to accomplish for the college. I wanted to lift Wabash to a new, extraordinarily high level of excellence on all fronts. And I wanted to win for Wabash national recognition for that excellence. I wanted to accent the intellectual and creative possibilities of the college and at the same time to reinforce its distinctive, spirited character with new expressions of the traditional pride which for more than a century had animated the history of Wabash. This amounted to breathing reality into what I often termed the "Wabash mystique." It also involved a subtle shift of emphasis. Without retreating from the principle of independence from government aid which, as preached by Dr. Sparks, had given to the college a special and perhaps controversial kind of national identity, I intended to enhance its national visibility as a sturdy place of learning in the finest tradition of the liberal arts.

It could be said — as indeed it was said — that such ambitions as these added up to nothing more than a desire to make an already good college still better. Many of my friends and colleagues in college and university circles throughout the country regarded such a desire as commonplace and pedestrian. The times, they said, called for extensive changes in education relevant to the great issues then confronting American society. They argued that higher education should take the lead in bringing about urgently needed reforms in American society. Furthermore, they reminded me, just doing the same old thing but doing it better had no appeal to philanthropic foundations. Blazing new trails, shaking off traditions, introducing novel experiments — this was the sort of thing that attracted "big money."

I was unimpressed by such arguments. Much of the feverish experimentation among colleges struck me as faddish and transitory, related hurriedly and sometimes even cynically to whatever educational slogan happened to be the "in" slogan of the moment. And as far as the reconstruction of society was concerned, however desirable that might be, this was not the business of a college like Wabash. Wabash should be truly apolitical. Its only partisanship should be its commitment to the cultivation and communication of those intellectual disciplines and those bodies of knowledge which comprise the liberal arts. What individual members of the faculty or student body thought or said or did as responsible private citizens was their private business. But the college's contribution to whatever changes might take place in American society should be limited to its educational influence on the lives of its students.

This admittedly conservative way of looking at the mission of the college I frequently defended in public. At an institute for new college presidents at the Harvard Business School in 1956 I was virtually alone in presenting this point of view. At the annual National Conference on Higher Education in Chicago in 1960, I was invited to address one of the general sessions as a spokesman for the traditional philosophy of the liberal arts. This in turn led to my participation in numerous other forums at which I took the same stance. As chairman of the Commission on Liberal Education of the Association of American Colleges from 1958 through 1962, I espoused the same point of view in its annual intellectual life conferences for college presidents in Nova Scotia, Colorado, and elsewhere. It was a process that clarified and strengthened my personal philosophy of liberal education. Perhaps it also gave a slightly new sense of direction to the college community. Now and again it served to protect the academic freedom of the faculty and to defend student behavior and student credos which would have been regarded as reprehensible at more "liberally minded," "action oriented" institutions. Instead of repelling the "big money," I have reason to believe it actually helped Wabash to attract it.

In 1956 I had no concrete plan for achieving these goals. I must confess that I banked heavily on chance opportunities which I hoped rather than believed would develop and to which the college could respond advantageously. But, although I had no specific plan to pursue, there were quite specific step-by-step objectives which I thought must be achieved somehow if my ambitions for Wabash were to be realized. Apart from steadily enlarging as well as improving teaching and learning resources for both students and teachers, these objectives included additional plant construction and strengthening the financial underpinnings of the college.

The highest priority for plant construction I assigned to a new, first-rate library. If this could be achieved, it occurred to me that Yandes Hall could be converted into a Humanities Center with a new emphasis on art, music, and drama. High on the list also was the construction of a new building for the social sciences. Slightly below that came construction of improved physical facilities for student living, both non-fraternity and fraternity. This would mean building a new dormitory more conventional and more functional than Morris and Wolcott Halls. It would mean also that the college should acquire title to the fraternity houses to facilitate financing of new construction or remodeling by gifts to the college restricted for such purposes. Finally it seemed desirable to expand and improve the college's facilities for both intramural and intercollegiate athletics.

As far as strengthening the financial underpinnings of Wabash was concerned, the objective was to double the Wabash endowment funds and at the same time to operate the college with gradually increasing efficiency in order to reduce the per student cost of operations. Achieving these two objectives would, I believed, reduce the "gap" between budgeted expenditures and stable revenue (income from endowment and from student fees) and would thus make the college less dependent on annual gifts and grants required to operate with a balanced budget. As I have related elsewhere in these reflections, I had become fascinated with Beardsley Ruml's prescriptions for improving the fiscal health of private colleges. Long before I became president of Wabash, I was convinced that sound financing of private colleges required more than repeatedly increasing tuition fees and raising larger and larger amounts of gift money.

The increase in endowment funds was a hope rather than an objective.

I had no idea how the Wabash endowment might be doubled. Nor was the idea of augmenting endowment a popular one at the time. Dr. Sparks had had minimal interest in gifts for endowment. He wanted new money which could be spent immediately, both for operating purposes and for plant construction. Given the needs of the college in the 1940s and early 1950s, he was right about this priority. But the predicament of the college in the late 1950s was no longer a desperate one. It seemed to me that the time was right to press for major gifts for endowment purposes. It might be a slow business, but in the years to come it could lead to solid and highly beneficial results. The Wabash endowment did in fact increase significantly in the years 1956–65 but perhaps the long range benefits from seeds planted in those years are yet to be realized.

The improvement of efficiency in operations I expected to come by gradually increasing student enrollment to perhaps 1,000–2,000 without a corresponding increase in staff. Although enrollment did increase slightly for a time, the goal I had privately set for an increased student body was never met. What little progress we were able to make toward more efficient operations reflected changes brought about by Bill Degitz with my full support.

Such, in brief and in a general way, were my aspirations for Wabash when I became its president. I believed those aspirations could be achieved in ten years. In 1959 for personal reasons I privately concluded that I would have to settle short in the pursuit of these aspirations and do what I could in five rather than ten years. The coming of the Ford Foundation Challenge Grant in 1961 made me disregard that decision of 1959.

In writing about the pursuit of these aspirations, I intend only to touch on a few matters. This means omitting much that might be of human interest to some future reader of these reflections. It also means foregoing personal appraisals of numerous individuals whose roles in all that took place at Wabash in these years were more important than mine. I regret this omission. I should enjoy expressing my continuing feelings of gratitude and indebtedness to those men and women who did so much for Wabash in that decade and especially to those who befriended me personally. But it occurs to me that such a digression, much of it entirely personal history, could better be done in a separate piece which I may write later for the college archives.

The Lilly Library. The new library came faster and more easily than I had expected. In the summer of 1956 at his resort home on Lake Wawasee I had the first of several long visits with Eli Lilly. I did not ask Eli Lilly for help with the library project. (In fact, during my years as president, I never asked him for a contribution of any kind.) I only related to him my dreams for Wabash in that first visit and asked for his advice and whatever help he might choose to extend. Our lengthy conversations at Wawasee were relaxed and pleasant. Apart from Wabash, our only common interest was our mutual love of history. That became something of a bond between us. I learned much from him about Indiana history, to which he was devoted. In response to his rather shy suggestions, I became active in the Indiana Historical Society, serving as a member of its executive committee and finally for a few years as president. I went with him and others now and then to Angel Mounds near Evansville, which at that time was one of several consuming historical interests of Mr. Lilly. I also became involved in the excavations at the site of the old fort just north of Vincennes. He was pleased.

Except for this common interest in Indiana history, I was never close to Eli Lilly. I often wondered if anyone was really close to him. One of America's richest men, his modesty, his preference for anonymity, his shrewdness about people and business, his dry sense of humor — all of these attributes, it seemed to me, kept him at arm's length from others. In those early conversations with him, he asked many questions. My heart jumped, I remember, when he asked me why I gave such high priority to a new library and about what I thought it might cost. He also seemed seriously interested in my conviction that a substantially larger endowment for Wabash in the future would be essential for its continuing independence. But he did not at any time suggest what he might do personally to help.

It was Ivan Wiles, I believe, who was decisive in persuading Eli Lilly to build a new library at Wabash. Others no doubt were helpful in this, including John Collett and especially Gene Beesley. But it was Ivan who joined me at the crucial point in the early conversations with Mr. Lilly. He had great admiration and affection for Ivan. Ivan's easy, gracious manner made continuing conferences with Mr. Lilly almost like casual small talk.

One day Ivan flew to Lake Wawasee in a General Motors seaplane to join Mr. Lilly and me in discussions of long range plans for Wabash. Shortly after that Mr. Lilly called me to his office in Indianapolis to say that he would give to Wabash Lilly Company stock with a value of approximately $1 million for the purpose of constructing a new library, *provided* the gift would be treated anonymously and *provided* his name would not be associated with the building. I quickly agreed to the request for anonymity but hedged on his request about associating his name with the building. I asked if we might not discuss that request at a later date. With a smile, he brushed my request aside.

As the building later slowly became a reality, Mr. Lilly seemed increasingly pleased. Characteristically, he took only a minimal part in developing the actual plans for the building. Pierre Goodrich, on the other hand, was deeply involved with even the tiniest details of planning and constructing the handsome seminar room which his gift made possible in the library. With Pierre I spent countless hours on such details. But with Mr. Lilly, even when I showed

222

Byron K. Trippet, Dean of the College: 1939–42, 1946–55

Assistant to Dean George Kendall, 1936–39

After graduation, 1947.
Dean Trippet is at the far right; President Sparks stands second from the left.

Dr. Spark's view of the major building project of his presidency, the Campus Center,
(dedicated October 30, 1954).

GEORGE TILFORD

At a pre-inaugural party in Indianapolis, January, 1956.
From left to right: Dean-elect Ben Rogge and his wife Alice, Abbie and President Sparks,
Dorothy and President-elect Trippet.

The faculty's surprise farewell dinner for the Sparkses, January 24, 1956. At this table (*clockwise from the lower left*): Crawford Polley, Mrs. Van Sickle, Willis Johnson, Mrs. Sparks, Dean Kendall, Mrs. Polley, Dr. Sparks, Mrs. Kendall, Harry Cotton, Mrs. Johnson, John Van Sickle, Ted Bedrick, Mrs. Williams, Dean Rogge, Mrs. Gullion, Dick Banta, Mrs. Trippet, Ed Gullion, Mrs. Banta, President Trippet, Mrs. Rogge, Eliot Williams, Mrs. Bedrick. At the far left is a cake decorated with a few bars of "Old Wabash."

The inauguration of Byron K. Trippet as the ninth president of Wabash College, October 13, 1956. Dr. Sparks prepares to hand President Trippet a copy of the college's charter.

Following the ceremony, Dean Kendall, President Trippet, and Dr. Sparks chat together.

President Trippet attaches the new sign on the door of the Center Hall office.

The new president at work

President Trippet delivers the first lecture to a new group of WIPD students on the impact of education on the problems of the modern world.

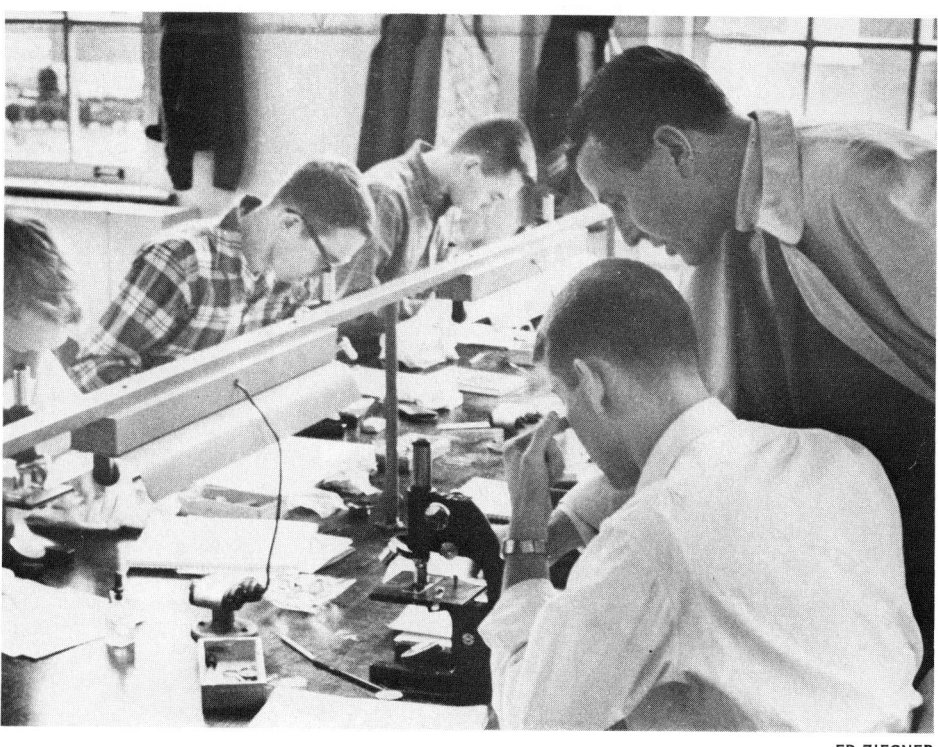

President Trippet stops to talk with students in laboratory, while showing reporters around campus.

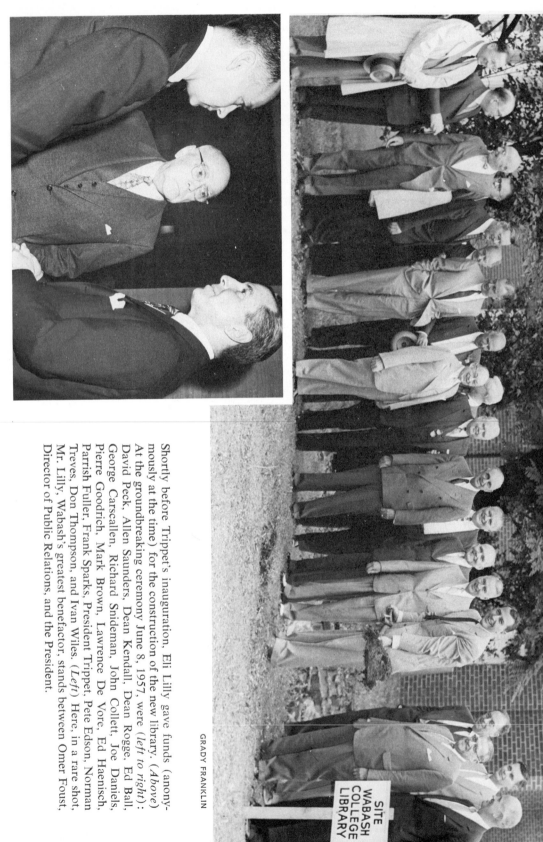

GRADY FRANKLIN

Shortly before Trippet's inauguration, Eli Lilly gave funds (anonymously at the time) for the construction of the new library. (*Above*) At the groundbreaking ceremony June 8, 1957, were (*left to right*): David Peck, Allen Saunders, Dean Kendall, Dean Rogge, Ed Ball, George Carscallen, Richard Snideman, John Collett, Joe Daniels, Pierre Goodrich, Mark Brown, Lawrence De Vore, Ed Haenisch, Parrish Fuller, Frank Sparks, President Trippet, Pete Edson, Norman Treves, Don Thompson, and Ivan Wiles. (*Left*) Here, in a rare shot, Mr. Lilly, Wabash's greatest benefactor, stands between Omer Foust, Director of Public Relations, and the President.

Senior Chapel. On the platform are Dean Rogge, President Trippet, Dean Kendall and Dr. Harry Cotton. Robert Mitchum, director of the Glee Club, stands next to the organ.

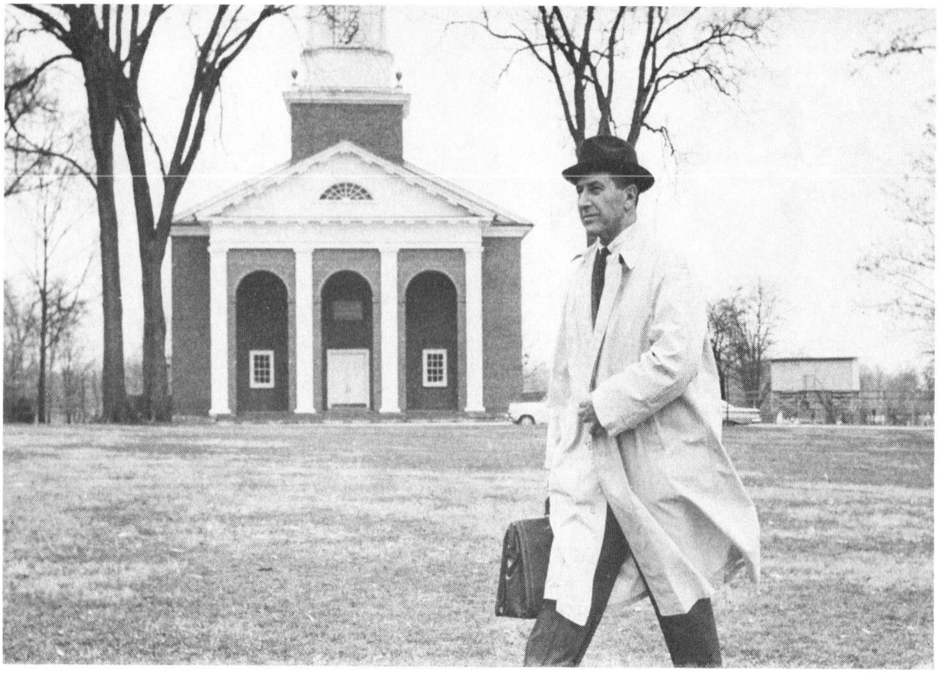

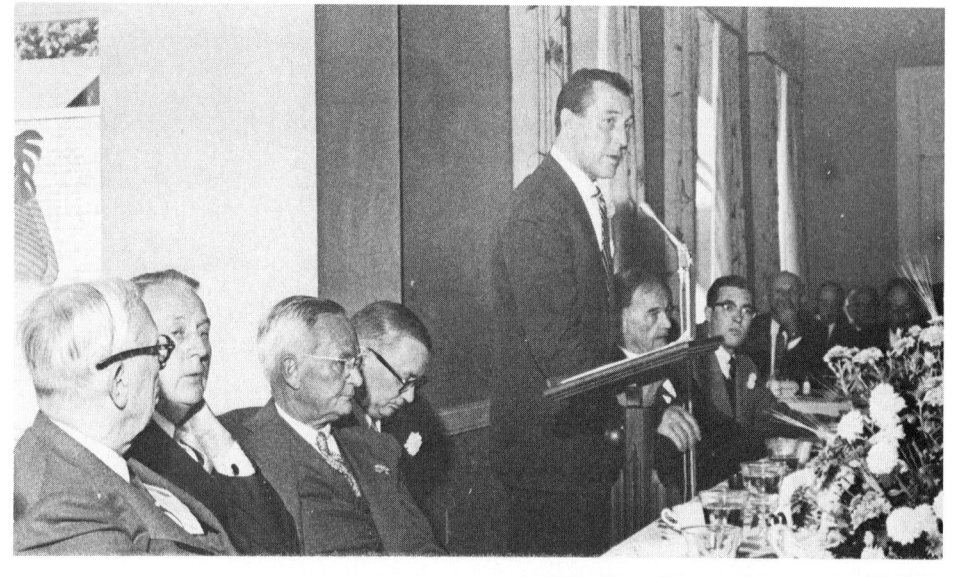

President Trippet on his way to Center Hall

CAPITOL PHOTOGRAPHERS

President Trippet welcomes guests at a luncheon on October 11, 1957, as a part of the college's 150th anniversary celebration. Seated (*left to right*) are Alfred P. Sloan, Jr. (honorary Chairman of the Board, General Motors Corporation), Dr. Frank Sparks, Frank W. Abrams (former Chairman of the Board, Standard Oil of New Jersey), and Charles D. LaFollette. Sloan, Abrams, and Irving S. Olds (former Chairman of the Board, United States Steel Corporation) were awarded honorary degrees during the celebration.

At commencement exercises on June 7, 1959, the college conferred an honorary degree on Dr. Ludwig Erhard, Vice-chancellor of West Germany and Minister of Finance. In the procession (*left to right*) are President Trippet, Dr. Erhard, and Eugene Beesley.

Pierre Goodrich, Florence Elston, Dr. Erhard, and Ike Elston at Elston Homestead after the commencement ceremony.

The winter, 1960, meeting of the Board of Trustees. *Clockwise from the upper left:* Richard Ristine, William Howard, John Collett, Allen Saunders, Lee McCanliss, Parrish Fuller, Eli Lilly, Pierre Goodrich, Ivan Wiles (chairman), President Trippet, Samuel Rea, David Peck, Norman Treves, E. B. Martindale, Eugene Beesley, Charles LaFollette, Pete Edson, and Joe Daniels. Board members not present: Ed Ball, Mark Brown, I. C. Elston, Jr., and Richard Snideman.

President Trippet chats with Fred Hadley and John Collett at a Wabash Glee Club party given by the Indianapolis Alumni Association, December 9, 1960, at the Columbia Club.

Vice-president Hadley, Chairman of the Board Wiles, President Trippet, and Treasurer Collett with a check for $450,000, the advance payment on the college's 1961 Ford Foundation Grant.

The annual banquet of Wabash alumni at Commencement, 1961.
From left to right: Vice-president Hadley, Robert S. Harvey, Robert Neal,
Ivan Wiles, Robert M. Smith, President Trippet, and Paul Husting.

President and Mrs. Trippet arrive at the 1961 Homecoming game with Butler
in a new (for him) 1930 Ford, the gift of Vice-president Hadley who
"wanted to make sure there was a Ford in Trippet's future."

President and Mrs. Trippet entertain British scholar Sir Steven Runciman
during one of his visits to campus. He was awarded an honorary degree in June, 1962.

President Trippet watches Coach Owen Huntsman train his runners.

At every commencement, the president renews
acquaintances and meets new friends of Wabash.

him detailed plans, his interest, while genuine, was perfunctory. It was clear to me, however, that he was quite taken with Eric Gugler's vision of how the building should look. Gradually I began to advance my ideas about the educational importance of associating great family names with a college like Wabash. Again, I would credit Ivan Wiles with persuading Mr. Lilly to let us put his name on the building. All of us were delighted when he finally agreed. But he maintained his shy, unassuming stance throughout the construction of the building, and even at the simple dedication ceremonies he seemed embarrassed. He deprecated his part in the whole project. When I expressed to him my personal thanks he said, "Well, don't forget, those shares of stock I gave you in the beginning only cost me about five cents a share." For all of his diffidence, I believe Mr. Lilly was quite proud of the library and pleased to have his name associated with the college. It amounted to a deepening of his commitment to the future of Wabash.

Some time later a totally unexpected conversation with Mr. Lilly reinforced the conviction I have just expressed. During an intermission at an Indianapolis Symphony concert he and I were chatting casually when he suddenly said to me, just as the lights were dimming for the resumption of the concert, "Byron, I have decided to give Wabash 10,000 shares of Lilly Company stock to endow the library. When you have time drop in to see me and we can talk about it." I was speechless with surprise and joy. During the balance of the concert I could think of nothing else. At the then market value of Lilly common stock that amounted, I calculated, to another million dollar gift to Wabash. It was a splendid thing for the future of the new library, and it was a major step toward a general push for a greatly increased Wabash endowment. The gift shortly thereafter was made, again with the request that it be treated as an anonymous gift.

Mr. Lilly's gifts for this project justify the importance I am giving to them in these recollections. But I would be remiss if I did not acknowledge my sense of indebtedness to the memory of numerous others who made smaller contributions to the same project. Pierre Goodrich's part in the creation of a distinctive feature of the library I have discussed in another part of these reflections. Controversial though his seminar room was, I was enthusiastic about his ideas for the room and I was proud of it once it was completed. Another detail in the building which pleased me was A. J. Daugherty's gift of butternut wood paneling for the archives room. Jack Daugherty and I had been fraternity brothers and good friends at Wabash during our undergraduate years. After graduation I had seen little of him but, mindful of his lifelong interest in woods and wood products, I appealed to him to make the archives-rare books room a handsome feature in the library. He responded with enthusiasm and that delightful, peaceful room is a consequence of his enthusiasm. For meditation and for writing, it became my favorite retreat in the college in my last years there.

Baxter Hall. I had thought that finding funds for a new social science building would be easy. It seemed to me nothing would be simpler than to appeal to wealthy businessmen friends and admirers of Frank Sparks to finance the construction of a building which would bear his name and which, in part at least, would be used to promote the economic principles which he had espoused. All that would be needed would be one major gift which would attract others. I tried out the idea on a few trustees. They liked it. So did two or three close Indiana friends of Dr. Sparks, for example, Glenn (Tommy) Thompson of Arvin Industries and Clarence Hamilton. H. E. (Eb) Hastings, executive director of Associated Colleges of Indiana, who had worked closely with Frank and who idolized him, thought it was a sure thing. He helped me to put together a list of prospective donors, and I began a quest for major gifts with the highest of hopes.

It was a quest which failed. I had felt sure that from among his wealthy associates on the board of the Council for Financial Aid to Education in New York I could win the challenge money necessary to appeal for the balance in gifts in Indiana. And I had what I considered an excellent opening for the New York search. In 1957 as a part of the celebration of the college's 125th anniversary, we had held an impressive convocation to honor Irving Olds (chairman of the board of U. S. Steel), Frank Abrams (chairman of the board of Standard Oil of New Jersey), and Alfred Sloan (retired chairman of the board of General Motors). In recognition of their leadership in promoting corporate aid to education, they were awarded honorary degrees. Irving Olds in particular seemed especially friendly toward Wabash and toward me as a consequence. These three, plus DeWitt Wallace , owner of the *Reader's Digest,* were my targets for financing a new Frank Hugh Sparks building on the Wabash campus. I remember saying to myself, "If I can't get at least a half million dollars for Wabash out of those four, I'd better quit."

I tried DeWitt Wallace first. When I called his office near New York for an appointment, his secretary was evasive. Mr. Wallace, she explained, would not be available for several days, she was uncertain about his schedule, et cetera. But she asked me where I was staying and said she would call back later in the day. I waited most of the day at the St. Regis Hotel. Her call never came. I was surprised, therefore, when the telephone rang about 7:30 the next morning. It was DeWitt Wallace himself. He explained he was downstairs in the lobby, and he suggested we have breakfast together. I took this as a good omen. During our breakfast I outlined to him my idea for a building to honor Dr. Sparks. He asked me what I thought the building would cost. I told him "something on the order of $1 million," half of which I was now seeking in New York. "So much?" he said. "And can't you find that money in Indiana?" he added. I assured him I could get that kind of money in Indiana but that I had other things in mind for which only Indiana money would be obtainable and, anyway, I thought Frank Sparks deserved national recognition. He smiled at that response and seemed to agree with me. Beyond saying he would think about it, however, he gave me no encouragement. As soon as I returned to Crawfordsville I wrote him a follow-up letter. I never received a reply.

On that same trip to New York I talked at length with Dr. W. Homer Turner,[3] executive director of the U. S. Steel Foundation. He was helpful and encouraging, but he pointed out that the kind of money I was seeking was beyond the reach of the U. S. Steel Foundation. It would have to come from individuals. With his help I also had a brief conversation with Irving Olds. He agreed to arrange a conference with Frank Abrams, Alfred Sloan and himself present at which I could present my story. Again my hopes soared.

The conference took place a few weeks later in New York. At the last minute Mr. Sloan had to cancel the appointment and I met only with Olds and Abrams. I took Steve Kurtz with me. It was Abrams who dashed my hopes. He listened courteously, but he made it clear he did not think well of the idea. He doubted that Mr. Sloan would be interested and without Sloan's participation nothing would happen. "Anyway" he added "I think it is premature to make this gesture to Frank Sparks." Irving Olds was gentler, but he too said "no." I was terribly discouraged.

I did not abandon my idea but I concluded this project would have to wait, maybe for years. Like so many other good things that happened at Wabash in the early 1960s, the realization of a new social science building was a consequence of the impetus given to our fund raising efforts by the Ford Foundation Challenge Grant. And the source of funds for the building, as far as I was concerned, was a complete surprise. One day following a meeting of the "rating committee" we had put together to identify prospects for major gifts, Norman Baxter, a member of the committee, asked several questions about the social science building project. One of his questions was something to the effect "Would the building bear the donor's name?" Sensing new possibilities I quickly answered "yes," and I did not mention my idea of a Frank H. Sparks building. Not long after that Norman told us that he, his brother, Emory, and his sister, plus the Baxter Foundation, would like to finance that particular project as a memorial to their father, Arthur. It was thrilling news.[4]

I never was able to determine who really triggered that very generous gift.

3. Bill Turner and I became friends in 1956–57 when he heard me speak at a conference of college presidents and businessmen. He liked the ideas I expressed and asked permission to print the speech for distribution to colleges and business corporations throughout the country as a courtesy gesture by the U. S. Steel Foundation. Repeatedly thereafter he was kind to me. He was one of the few people whom I consulted for advice and help when I left Wabash. During my years with ICFA in New York, this friendship deepened into a close companionship. BKT.

4. Two Baxter Foundation grants in 1962, totalling $600,000, made the construction possible.

Certainly not I. For a time I credited Fred Hadley with having stimulated the gift by virtue of his friendship with Emory. But once when I was relating that thought to Abbie Sparks, she scoffed at the idea. She was sure that Frank Sparks had won the gift for Wabash. Perhaps he did. However, from conversations I had had with Emory, I concluded that Arthur Baxter and Emory had "got off the Sparks bandwagon" some years earlier because of Frank's Christian Science views. Perhaps Al Campbell had something to do with the gift. Certainly he was helpful in retaining it somewhat later when Emory, a tough and touchy conservative, took angry offense at some remarks made publicly by a member of the faculty. My guess is that the moving spirit in this unexpected gift came from Norman Baxter. A quiet, thoughtful person, Norman's interest in the college had deepened when he became a trustee and, once the Ford Foundation Grant began to operate, he saw a chance to help the college in a major way and at the same time to honor the memory of his father, to whom he had been devoted.

In spite of my joy at the prospect of a new splendid home for the social sciences at Wabash, it was a strangely sad day for me when the dismantling of old South Hall began. Ugly and misused though that relic of the past was, its removal was like the death of an aged and beloved family member. I believe Eric Gugler, more than anyone else, shared my sense of regret and sadness. Eric had battled hard and in vain for a restoration of South Hall as it originally was. (Somewhere among the college papers there must be a set of Gugler's complete preliminary plans for a restored South Hall, including strip windows and a replica of the original tower.) He shook off his regret as he designed Baxter Hall. I regarded his plan as perhaps the happiest of all the buildings he designed at Wabash, with an excellent combination of grace and beauty and utility.

Improved Student Housing. As in the case of Baxter Hall, the Ford Foundation Challenge Grant provided the stimulus for the construction of Martindale Hall and for modernization and enlargement of fraternity housing.

While Dr. Sparks was still president of Wabash Lige Martindale had promised "at least" $50,000 toward the construction of another dormitory similar to Morris and Wolcott Halls. In the late 1950s I began to talk with him about moving ahead with this project with important differences — a larger dormitory with more functional internal arrangements and with multiple options for students as far as rooms were concerned. For such a building, Lige agreed, $50,000 would not be sufficient. He undertook to increase the amount of his gift. At meetings of the Board of Trustees and of the executive committee, of which he was a member, Lige rarely had much to say, but in his office or over cocktails I found him ready to talk freely. Our discussions included the possibility of his remembering Wabash generously in his will. His bequest to the college more than made up for the deficit between his gift and the actual

226

cost of the dormitory which bears his name. Gifts from others, including the holly paneling which came from Parish Fuller, plus money from the Ford grant made the building possible at the time it was built.

Beta Theta Pi took the lead in constructing a new house under a plan approved by the Board of Trustees at my recommendation. The college became the owner of the fraternity and thereafter functioned, at arm's length, as landlord for the physical property. Only in this way was it possible for donors to obtain tax credits for gifts to the college for fraternity house construction. Approval of the Internal Revenue Service was sought and obtained before the Beta House project was undertaken.

The response of numerous Beta alumni for funds under this plan was gratifying. The same thing proved to be true when Sigma Chi shortly afterward built its new house on the corner of Wabash Avenue and Crawford Street. The gifts that poured in for these projects illustrated, in several instances, that for some alumni allegiance to their fraternity is stronger than allegiance to the college. No better example of this, to me regrettable, fact can be found than the generous help Volney Brown gave in the construction of the new Beta House. Ever since his undergraduate years at Wabash, Beta Theta Pi had been one of the most important things in Volney's life. He took a continuing serious interest in the affairs of the undergraduate chapter. He rarely missed an annual meeting of the Board of Directors of Tau Association (owner of the old Beta house) of which for years he was a member. Often he attended the annual initiation ceremonies for pledges who qualified for membership. He could repeat with great sobriety and reverence key passages in the Beta ritual. And when it came to the singing of "Oh, pass the loving cup around . . ." he underwent something akin to a religious experience.

No doubt Volney Brown was fond of the college and proud of it too, but whatever he felt for Wabash was pale by comparison with his devotion to his fraternity. I was shocked to discover when I became president of Wabash that Volney had been giving only $25 a year to the college. Dr. Sparks had despaired of getting him to increase his gifts. Along with others he concluded that Volney was simply stingy with his money. And yet he was a moderately well-to-do, if not wealthy man. He inherited a substantial amount of money from his father. He was an important stockholder in the Indiana National Bank where he served as one of its vice presidents. His responsibilities in the bank were rather vague.

It occurred to me when I became president that here was one alumnus whose annual giving to the college I could substantially increase. I was not above exploiting our common fraternal bonds in the effort. Volney was one of the first alumni to whom I appealed for a large annual gift to the college. I had in mind something like $5,000 a year. My conversation with him in his office went quite well, I thought. When I had finished he squirmed uneasily in his

227

chair and in between puffs on his pipe he said, "Well, Byron, you are right. I should be giving more to the college and in the future I will." He was as good as his word. Thereafter, he gave $50 a year!

But when it came to the construction of a new Beta House his attitude was quite different. He immediately pledged $25,000 and indicated his willingness to give more if it were needed. He was enormously interested in the progress of the project and proud of the building when it was completed.

I felt good about Martindale Hall, the new Beta House, and the new Sigma Chi House. When alumni of Delta Tau Delta indicated their interest in following the same plan I was delighted, and I did what I could to help them initiate a drive for funds which, after I had left Wabash, was successfully completed. My interest in pushing the plan for college-owned fraternity housing was not only to provide better housing for fraternity students, but also, in view of the future uncertainty of fraternities, to put the college in an ownership position of their physical facilities.

The Improvement of Facilities for Intramural and Intercollegiate Sports. Only a beginning was made toward accumulating the funds required for expanding athletic facilities. But it was a good beginning. As I indicated earlier, the improvement of athletic facilities had a somewhat lower priority than other building projects. Moreover, there was among trustees less common agreement about what facilities were needed. Some favored tearing down the old gymnasium and building something new and modern. Others thought only an expansion of the existing gymnasium would be sufficient.

In the early stages of such discussions, I favored the former point of view. Someone had brought to my attention a young architect in Terre Haute, Ewing Miller, whose bold designs appealed to me. I liked the thought of having on the Wabash campus a gymnasium the architectural style of which would contrast sharply with the Georgian colonial style of Gugler's buildings. Parrish Fuller agreed with me and we asked Ewing to give us a sketch of what he would propose for a new gymnasium. He provided us with preliminary drawings for a radically different kind of building. It had the shape of a mushroom. He proposed locating the building at the southwest corner of Ingall's Field.

An artist's sketch of Miller's proposed gymnasium was reproduced in the promotional brochure we printed and distributed during the Ford Foundation Challenge Grant campaign. That sketch touched off decidely mixed comments. Lee McCanliss called the building "a monstrosity." He had the full backing of his close friend, Eric Gugler. Since Lee was one of the prospective donors for a new gymnasium, the Miller plans were quietly shelved.[5]

5. Parrish Fuller, a Sigma Chi, saw to it that Ewing Miller was the architect for the new Sigma Chi house. That accounts for the fact that while blending with the prevailing architectural style of the Wabash campus, the new fraternity house is distinctly different. BKT.

With the Miller plans discarded, we began conversations with Gugler and Ferd Eiseman about designing additions to the old gymnasium. And, once the financing of Baxter Hall was assured, I began a serious search for funds for athletic facilities. One night after a long discussion with Lee McCanliss in his room in the Gotham Hotel in New York, Lee agreed to give to Wabash $400,000 to apply on an expanded gymnasium, subject to a lifetime annuity of $25,000 a year. I had hoped for more, and I was troubled by Lee's remark that if he did this there would be nothing in his will for Wabash. Nevertheless, it was a beginning.

About the same time I began conversations with George Banta, Jr., in Menasha, Wisconsin, about the possibility of his helping with the program for improving athletic facilities. George Banta had attended Wabash only two years and his fraternity experience (Phi Delta Theta) at Wabash claimed more of his allegiance than the college itself. He had never been active in Wabash alumni circles and rarely returned to the campus. In Wisconsin he became heavily involved in Lawrence College where he served for years as a trustee and for a time as chairman of the board. He had given to Lawrence an excellent football stadium and supporting athletic facilities. My idea for approaching him came, not from within the Wabash family, but from my friend Doug Knight, then president of Lawrence and shortly afterward president of Duke University.

I took an immediate liking to George and our conversations were more productive than I had expected. He visited the Wabash campus, liked what he saw, enjoyed the opportunity I provided him to exchange thoughts with faculty members, and in my last months at the college, he agreed to finance the construction of the permanent bleachers on Ingall's Field as well as the rebuilding of the athletic track.

Meanwhile, John Collett, without any nudging from me, had decided to finance the construction of the excellent tennis courts, both indoor and outdoor, which Wabash now enjoys. As I have explained elsewhere, it was also John who suggested that I talk with Bert Reade in Indianapolis about a substantial gift to Wabash to help with the plan for a new gymnasium. This John and I did it together in my last month at the college, and soon thereafter the search for sufficient funds for the gymnasium received a very helpful boost.

I did not get to see these several athletic projects become the splendid realities they now are on the Wabash campus, but I left the college knowing they were assured. I felt good about what we had been able to do in a relatively short time concerning the Wabash building program. In saying this I have in mind not only the major projects which I have touched on but also numerous other improvements which were less conspicuous and less costly.

New boilers for the power plant, a new maintenance building, the conversion of Yandes to an art and language center, the construction of new entrances to the campus from Wabash Avenue and from Grant Avenue, the relocation of Forest Hall and Hovey Cottage, the Caperton carillon in the Chapel tower,[6] the expansion of office space in Center Hall, the conversion of the old chapel into office space for philosophy and religion, the gradual acquisition of more college-owned houses for faculty members, the program for planting new trees and new shrubbery — about all of such improvements I felt gratified. Especially gratifying was the realization of Eric Dean's dream of a miniature, exquisite chapel at the east end of the old chapel, a place symbolizing all religious faiths where individuals could meditate. Early on Commencement morning, June, 1965, from the hands of Eric Dean, I received my final communion in that chapel. The companionship of a handful of old friends, Reiley Adams and Lafe LaFollette among others, heightened the mixture of emotions that engulfed me.

The Wabash Mystique. It is easy to write as I have written about adding new buildings to the Wabash campus. It is quite a different matter to write about those intangible qualities that make up the day-to-day life of the college. When it comes to appraising the character and the quality of Wabash as a place of learning in the years 1956–1965, remembered pride and affection undoubtedly color my retrospective thoughts. I am uncertain whether my judgments about the parts played by faculty, students, trustees, and alumni in the life of the college in those years amount to an exaggeration or an understatement. I suspect it is the latter. It is a case of the heart speaking rather more than the mind. But that mixture of things felt and things known is a part of the Wabash Mystique. It leads me to believe that in those years there was a touch of greatness about Wabash for those who taught and studied there and for all those who were sensitive to and proud of the symbolism of the college.

The Wabash community was a robust, united, spirited, and, on the whole, happy collection of people. The morale of the faculty and student body was extraordinarily high. Their academic performance was solid and tough, marked by numerous flashes of brilliance. For several of these years the number of Wabash graduating seniors who won Woodrow Wilson Fellowships annually gave Wabash a remarkably high rank among the nation's liberal arts colleges. These and similar attainments were a tribute to the quality of the faculty as well as to the quality of the student body. They also reflected a high Wabash *esprit de corps.*

I must disclaim any personal credit for the Wabash academic achievements of which I am boasting. The character of the student body remained much as it had been in the immediate past. Except for raising the minimum standards for awarding scholarships to entering freshmen, there were no important changes in our admission requirements. The faculty was essentially

6. Given by Mrs. Woods A. Caperton in memory of her husband. Dedicated June 3, 1960.

the same faculty as that of the late Sparks years. I made few additions to the faculty. But there was something in the air about Wabash in those years, if I may put it that way, which gave a lift to the life-of-the-mind concept of the college.

It was a lift not limited to the classroom and the laboratory. The "something in the air" feeling about the place found happy expressions in the non-intellectual life of the college. Ken Keuffel's football teams were not the greatest in Wabash history. But they were smart and spirited, fun to watch and to cheer. The single wing formation which Ken brought to Wabash added an interesting touch to the boast that Wabash is different. The same sort of thing could be said of the continued spectacular success of Owen Huntsman's track teams and of Max Servies' wrestling teams. In the early part of the period Bob Brock's basketball teams were a source of college pride.

The ambitious productions of the Scarlet Masque under the direction of Charlie Scott were a part of the mystique. So was the Wabash Glee Club under Bob Mitchum's energetic direction. Once Yandes Hall had been refurbished for art, music, and languages, Harold McDonald in his quiet relaxed way brought about a fascinating spurt in studio art. It never failed to amuse and delight me to watch some of the college's heartiest athletes expressing on canvas their private inner abstractions.

The momentum of new energy and high expectations that were so apparent on campus spread among alumni, too. Especially after the coming of the Ford Foundation grant, alumni all over the country mobilized to help their alma mater. There were notable exceptions which mystified me. For the most part they were in the East. There I found a few alumni who preferred to play down their Indiana background and their affiliation with Wabash. Often they had received their education at Wabash by virtue of a scholarship, but on rising to success and prominence they contributed nothing in return. They sent their sons to Harvard or Yale, declined to attend alumni meetings, and ignored written appeals. But not withstanding these exceptions, the great majority of the Wabash alumni were enthusiastic and energetic for their alma mater. I could not begin to name the numerous alumni in all parts of the country whose good will and active support gave color and substance to the quest for a new level of excellence at Wabash.[7]

7. Alumni response during the Ford Foundation Grant campaign included a number of examples of the fierce loyalty to Wabash which is part of the Wabash Mystique. From Mexico I received from an alumnus who was listed "lost" in the alumni files a letter enclosing a one-hundred peso note. It was all he had, he said, but he wanted "to be a part" of what was taking place at the college. From an alumnus in Indianapolis for whom life had been hard, I remember receiving a pathetic little note with a check enclosed. The check was for an odd amount — something like $168.27. Later I discovered that during the Christmas post office rush, he had taken on a part-time job at night in order to supplement his modest income as a maintenance man in an Indianapolis hospital. He sent to Wabash the full amount of his Christmas post office earnings. BKT.

231

The mobilization of alumni forces was in no small measure the result of the stellar work of Myron Phillips as director of alumni affairs. His fervent devotion to Wabash was contagious among the many alumni of his own and later generations whom he knew. He made friends easily in older classes and he was good at getting them to work. He instituted the system of class agents and he encouraged a spirit of competition among classes for annual giving to the college. His annual award of "bacon" for the class agent whose classmates achieved the highest percentage of participation in the alumni fund became a comic high point at annual alumni banquets. (Homer Showalter and Doc Elliott year after year set records as class agents for others to emulate.) Alumni interest and alumni activities, particularly in the Midwest, quickened as a result.

Omer Foust, whom I persuaded to return to Wabash as director of public relations and who at Myron Phillips' death became director of alumni affairs was equally effective in the resurgence of Wabash alumni spirit in those years. There was new appeal in the college publications and colorful touches were added to collegiate public functions and ceremonies as a consequence of his lively imagination.

A third alumnus who was especially helpful in promoting the "something in the air" attribute of Wabash in those years, especially between 1960 and 1965, was Clarence Jackson. Omer Foust helped me to persuade Jack to become the chairman of the Wabash National Development Council, which was formed when the Ford Foundation announced its challenge grant to Wabash. Clarence Jackson took his assignment seriously, and he brought to bear on the drive for matching funds the remarkable talents for selling which had made him such a successful president and later chairman of the board of the American United Life Insurance Company. His bluff, hearty, Hoosier, no-nonsense way with people was extremely effective among alumni, and his sense of humor and his gift for story telling made our fund raising effort a happy adventure.

The Wabash Board of Trustees in the years 1956–1965 continued to be the basic source of strength it had been throughout the Sparks administration. Its membership was much the same but there were important changes nonetheless. In the Sparks years the board was dominated by Lee McCanliss. After his retirement the board functioned more nearly as an assembly of equals. Long-time trustees such as Allen Saunders, Lafe Lafollete, and Pete Edson had a more active part in the work of the board. David Peck, who became a trustee in 1955–56, became increasingly important in board decisions. The same thing was true of Norman Treves. No one person dominated the board's thinking. It was Ivan Wiles, Gene Beesley, and especially John Collett who became the moving spirits among trustees, and they provided a new impetus to the drive to make Wabash the kind of college which I have been describing.

Among new trustees there were two whose membership on the board was especially gratifying to me. One was Joe Daniels, who at my request agreed to rejoin the board for one term. The second was Frank Misch, vice president for finance of the Chrysler Corporation. Frank's storybook career with Chrysler was for me another thrilling example of the validity of the Wabash claims for the liberal arts. His joining the board added to its "blue chip" reputation.

As I recollect these impressions about Wabash trustees, alumni, faculty members, and students in the years 1956–1965, it occurs to me that perhaps we were witnessing a final expression of a collegiate way of life which was shortly to be swept away by the turbulent changes that overtook America in the late 1960s and early 1970s. There were rumblings of the issues which were to become pervasive a few years later — the Viet Nam war protests, the call for black power, the attack on the established order, Women's Lib, et cetera — but in the main tradition and traditional ways of thinking continued to shape the life of the college. It was still the era of the crewcut hair, of green rhynie pots, of the lusty singing of "Old Wabash," of required chapels (with unlimited cuts!), of formal Pan Hellenic dances. Until the last year or two of the period it was, as I said earlier, a spirited, unified, happy college. I felt good about the direction in which the college was moving.

My frequent references to the Ford Foundation Challenge Grant have already made clear the importance I attached to that event in the history of the college. By comparison with the major fund drive Wabash has recently launched, the amount of money involved in the campaign touched off by the Ford grant in the fall of 1961 was modest. But for that time and by comparison with previous money raising goals at Wabash, it was a very ambitious undertaking. It presented a dramatic opportunity for a decisive breakthrough in the rising fortunes of the college.

The conditions accompanying the Ford grant were precise and demanding. The foundation offered Wabash a grant of $2 million provided the college would obtain $4 million in other gifts within a three-year period. The foundation would make annual payments on its grant in proportion to the money raised by the college each year. No restrictions were placed on the uses to which the Ford contributions could be put. But the definitions of what kind of gifts would count for matching purposes were explicit. Pledges would not count. It was a case of "cash on the barrel head." Cash and negotiable securities were emphasized. Gifts of real estate and gifts in kind must have a clear and exact market value certified by the college's auditors. These were helpful conditions.

Half-way through the campaign, Lilly Endowment, to whom we had appealed for a major gift, added a further matching dimension to our efforts. Manning Pattillo, who was in his last months at the endowment, and I worked out the details together. The endowment offered an additional million dollars

233

to be matched by two million dollars in gifts from sources other than the Ford Foundation. The time limit corresponded to that set by the Ford Foundation. Under this arrangement every dollar received by the college from Lilly would entitle the college to fifty cents in matching money from Ford. Thus we were able to say to prospective donors in the later stages of the drive, "Every dollar given to Wabash will mean $1.50 in matching gifts from other sources." It was a superb selling device. The response of donors in those final months of the campaign enabled us to meet the conditions of the Ford grant ahead of schedule. With the resulting accumulation of funds we were able to proceed with confidence toward the high-priority objectives I had set for the college.

The Ford grant helped in another way also. Being chosen as one of the first six private colleges to receive Ford Foundation Challenge Grants brought to Wabash for the moment the kind of national recognition and publicity I had coveted for the college. The Ford Foundation's announcement of their program of challenge grants spoke of existing "pillars of strength" worthy of substantial support. I liked that category for Wabash and I was proud of the fact that Wabash was placed in the company of institutions like Wellesley, Swarthmore, Carleton, and Reed, who also were chosen for those first grants. Thereafter, at national educational meetings particularly, I sensed a new kind of respect for Wabash.

How did it happen? As far as I was concerned it was completely unexpected. The annual meeting of the Association of American Colleges was held in Denver in January, 1961. I was late in arriving for the meeting. But I had barely registered at the Denver Hilton, when I became aware of the excited gossip among presidents of private colleges about something "big" in the offing from the Ford Foundation. A staff team from the foundation had taken a suite of rooms at the Brown Palace Hotel and was already in the process of interviewing college presidents. Why the interviews? No one was sure, but everyone sniffed something important in the making. Two or three of my closer friends had already had their interviews. They were terribly excited and, as matters turned out, over-confident.

When I ran through the accumulated messages which were waiting for me when I registered, I found a crisp note on Ford Foundation stationery inviting me, if it proved convenient, to come to Suite such-and-such in the Brown Palace at two o'clock the following afternoon for a short conference. I found it quite "convenient" to keep the appointment. I was ushered into a spacious lounge which had been converted into something like an office. There were perhaps a half dozen Ford people casually seated about the room. The only person I recognized was Elizabeth Pascal. She greeted me warmly, but took no part in the discussion which followed.

James Armsey did most of the talking, and it was he who put questions to me. Although we later were to become good friends, I had never met Jim

Armsey before that Denver meeting. I had heard much about him, however. By reputation he was a sharp, tough kind of guy, outspoken and often caustic. At that time he was considered a major force in the Ford Foundation because of his closeness to Henry Heald, president of the foundation. His initial comments at that interview and his questions confirmed his no-nonsense reputation. But I immediately liked Jim Armsey. His eyes were friendly, and he had a nice grin. He reminded me of Vernon Hahn for some reason.

Armsey asked me what plans we had at Wabash for the decade of the 1960s. I outlined my objectives for Wabash. He pressed me a little about innovations. I answered something to the effect that, in view of the common propensity for innovations, sticking by tradition might prove to be a useful experiment. Armsey grinned. He then asked me what I thought the cost of the improvement program at Wabash would be. I really had not tried to estimate these costs, but I answered as if I had. "Between $6 and $10 million," I said. There was a note of skepticism when he asked, "Do you think you can get *that* kind of money for Wabash?" I admitted that I was not sure, but I insisted with perhaps more confidence than I actually felt that our prospects were good.

We talked a little about the Wabash position on federal aid to education. "Why should outsiders give you substantial help when you refuse to take government money which is available to you?" Armsey asked. "In our part of the country," I said, "we can attract support not in spite of our position on federal aid but because of it." He grinned again.

The whole interview was not more than twenty minutes. I came away with no idea how well or how poorly I had done on behalf of Wabash. Nor had I learned much about what the Ford Foundation had in mind. Armsey spoke vaguely about the possibility of a series of Ford grants to liberal arts colleges, but he gave no details and I asked no questions. He said it was possible he might be writing me for more information but his tone was that of polite dismissal.

Apparently there were that week approximately 100 such interviews. Later that same month elaborate questionnaires were sent by Armsey to approximately fifty of the college presidents interviewed. The questionnaires called for: (a) a list of assumptions about economic, political, and international conditions for the next ten years; (b) a list of assumptions about the future of American higher education generally and of private colleges in particular; (c) a ten-year projection, year by year, of operating costs and operating income for the college receiving the questionnaire; (d) a ten-year projection of gift money required for operating purposes; (e) similar projections for the cost of capital improvements; (f) a ten-year projection for enrollment and for faculty additions required; (g) a case statement for private colleges generally; and (h) a case statement for the particular college being questioned.

It was a searching, demanding set of questions and instructions. The exercise involved in responding to them forced college presidents to face up to the realities of financing private colleges in a way few, if any, had done before.

When in late January our packet of questions and instructions arrived, Ben Rogge, Bill Degitz, and I locked ourselves in a small room on the second floor of Center Hall and went to work. For hours at a time during the next three or four days, we hammered out our response to the questions. As an economist Ben's thoughts about the assumptions were especially helpful. And as an accountant Bill Degitz, responding to the projections Ben and I made about such matters as enrollment, teaching resources, number and specialties of faculty required, produced carefully projected operating budgets for the next ten years. Allowances were made for annual rates of inflation and for contingencies. Bill's first set of figures staggered Ben and me. We began all over again with a higher projection for both faculty-student ratios and for tuition fee charges. And so it went for days. With Ben's help I wrote the case for private colleges generally and for Wabash in particular.

When we had finished our work and put it in the mail, I began to feel that we were winners. I do not know why, but my confidence in our case for a major grant from Ford was unshakable. Confirmation of my feelings came after the passage of several weeks. Elizabeth Pascal wrote that she wished to visit the Wabash campus for a close look at the faculty. Her visit went off well. She didn't tell me, but I knew she had been favorably impressed. Thanks largely to John and Mary Collett her more cursory visit with a few trustees also went well. Somewhat later, at his request, I spent an hour with Jim Armsey in his office in New York. When I walked in his office I was pleased to see on his desk our report open at the pages where I had made the case for Wabash. He had underlined in red numerous passages. We talked about college finances, the prospects for fund raising at Wabash, my personal plans for the future, and especially we talked educational philosophy.[8] I came away from that visit convinced that Wabash would be one of the winning colleges.

Somewhat later Bill Degitz was asked to confer with Sidney Tickton about our financial projections. That summer Armsey flew out to Indianapolis to confer with trustees. I have related those conversations elsewhere in these reflections. When they were concluded, we knew we were in for the maximum grant — $2 million. No announcement was to be made, however, until September. It was a joyous prospect.

The development of strategy and the organization of our forces for the

---

8. In March of that year at the annual Conference on Higher Education in Chicago, Theodore Brameld of Boston University and I had given the principal speeches at the opening general session. Brameld took the position that liberal education should be directed toward a reconstruction of society. I took the traditional position that the business of liberal education is to educate people. Armsey had heard this debate and much of our conversation was about the thoughts I had expressed in Chicago. BKT.

campaign actually began before we were officially told the grant would be forthcoming. The executive committee of the Board of Trustees agreed that we should be ready for the drive for matching funds well in advance. We had everything to gain and nothing to lose. As Ivan Wiles said, we should be prepared to launch a major campaign for funds even if we should be unsuccessful in our bid for the Ford grant. John Collett, who shared my belief that we were sure winners, shrewdly proposed that major gifts from trustees which normally would have been made before June 30 be delayed in order that they would count as matching gifts in the fiscal year 1961–62. It is for that reason that the record for gifts in 1960–61 shows a decided decline over the preceding year.

By September of that year we were well along with our plans. For a short time we used the counsel of John Price Jones & Company. After Clarence Jackson took the chairmanship of the development board which we formed, it was generally agreed we did not need outside professional help. Such a decision was characteristic of the do-it-yourself attitude at Wabash. But although we early dispensed with professional fund raising counsel, the campaign included numerous professional touches. Omer Foust took the lead in designing and publishing a handsome promotional brochure which was widely distributed. About the same time Will H. Hays, Jr., became the moving spirit in the production of a film to promote our drive for funds. Calling on his Hollywood experience, Bill persuaded his friend, Ralph Edwards, to undertake the production of the movie as a personal contribution to Wabash. Bill did the scenario, wrote the script, and gave the movie its name, *Where is Wabash?* At the same time he increased his annual financial gifts to Wabash!

Such professional touches as the brochure and the movie were helpful instruments in the quest for funds we made in those three strenuous years. But the success of the venture depended, as is always the case in such matters, on the time and energy devoted to the campaign by numerous individuals who gladly sought and won gifts for Wabash. Among these Fred Hadley was an outstanding example. His hearty enthusiasm, his confidence, and the fun he had working for Wabash meant more to me than I can put in words.

It was John Collett who suggested to me in the winter of 1960–61 that Fred Hadley might make an excellent vice president for development at Wabash. It had been a troublesome post since I became president. Ed Gullion's brief term as vice president ended in a crisis. Bennett Kline, who succeeded Ed, made a promising beginning. His combined interest and experience in business and education made him an ideal person to promote and to administer the Wabash Institute for Personal Development. But Ben missed the business world, and his wife, Judie, I believe was far from happy about returning to her home town. I was not surprised when, after a couple of years, Ben decided to take an assignment with Corn Products, Inc., in New York. I was downcast by

Ben's leaving, and perhaps for that reason John Collett's recommendation of Fred Hadley appealed to me at once.

I had known Fred only casually up until that time. It would never have occurred to me that he might be persuaded to join forces with Wabash. For years he had been an important figure at Eli Lilly and Company. He was a wealthy man with numerous outside business and civic interests. He was a trustee of his alma mater, Amherst, and although I had always found him friendly toward Wabash, I assumed his collegiate allegiance would be Amherst. But circumstances combined to make Wabash and Fred Hadley right for each other at that moment in time.

Shortly after Gene Beesley became president and chief executive officer at Lilly's, Fred decided to give up his post as executive vice president and to take advantage of Lilly's early retirement plan. John Collett, as a close friend of Fred, knew this before it became public information. Apart from continuing his membership on several boards of directors, Fred had not yet made any business plans. Moreover, Fred's ardor for Amherst had cooled. Increasingly he disapproved of policies being followed there. The anti-fraternity policy offended him especially, and he transferred his Phi Psi membership to the struggling Phi Psi chapter at Wabash.

When John and I had what I had assumed would be the first of several exploratory conversations with Fred, I was astonished at the quickness and the enthusiasm with which he responded to the idea of becoming vice president of Wabash. He was excited and full of ideas which he pursued with me by telephone in the days that followed. A few days later I was in Minneapolis when he telephoned me shortly after midnight to say he was "ready to report for duty." It was an hilarious conversation.

Thus as we began the Ford grant campaign Fred Hadley was the new Wabash vice president. He and his wife, Jane, immersed themselves in the life of the college. They made friends quickly on campus and in Crawfordsville. No old time Wabash man could have been more "gung ho" for the college and all of its activities than Fred Hadley was. His work habits were unconventional. We established a development office in the Merchants Bank Building in Indianapolis. Fred divided his time between that office and his office in Center Hall. But he was essentially an outside man, not an office man. A superb golfer, he did much of his selling on the course. Extroverted and gregarious, he also sold Wabash at cocktail parties, banquets, business conventions, alumni meetings, and at an infinite variety of social occasions. His explosive laughter was contagious. People liked him and, warming to him, they warmed to Wabash at the same time.

The salary we paid to Fred Hadley, though respectable by college standards, was little more than expense money for him. But that was of no consequence to Fred. His frequent gifts to the college, often for special projects such

President Trippet applauds the efforts of the Little Giants.

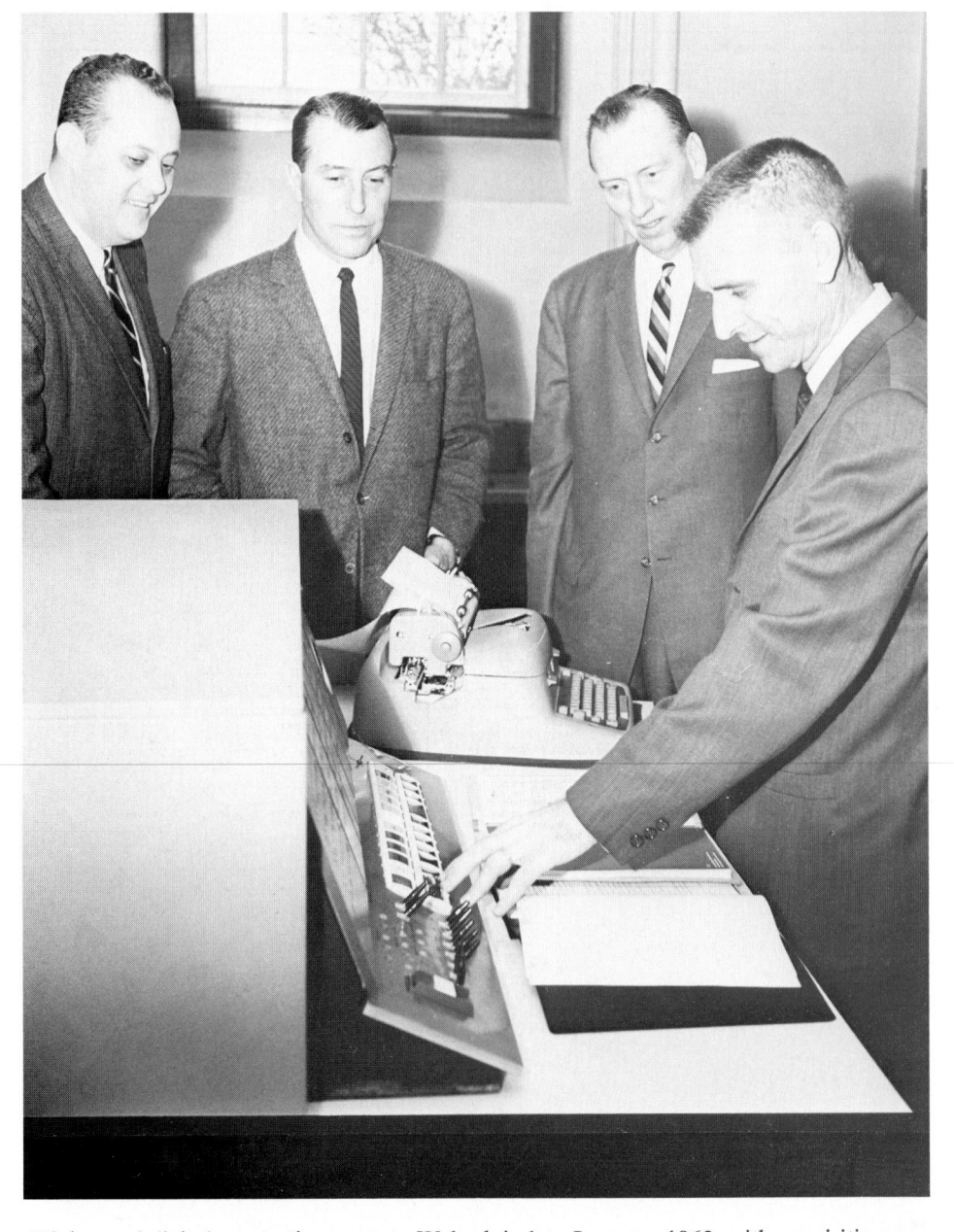

High speed digital computing came to Wabash in late January, 1962, with acquisition on a "temporary" rental basis of an IBM paper-tape 1620 computer. Grouped around the 1620 in the basement of Goodrich Hall are (*from left to right*): Robert B. Whittaker (1956), IBM sales representative; President Trippet; Ken Shutte, IBM sales manager; and Paul Mielke (1942), founder and first director of the computing laboratory. Math 15C, Computer Programming, offered by Mielke in the spring semester of that year, enrolled eighty-three students and eight faculty members. When Baxter Hall was completed a year and a half later, the laboratory was moved to new quarters in its basement.

At the groundbreaking ceremony for Baxter Hall, March 28, 1963, were (left to right): Paul Mielke, George Lovell, Dean Moore, R. Norman Baxter, Ben Rogge, Phil Wilder, President Trippet, Emory Baxter, Arthur R. Baxter, Will Hays, Jr., and Clarence Jackson. The faculty wing was completed in early spring, 1964, and the building dedicated after the Homecoming Chapel, October 16, 1964.

TEIICHI BETCHAKU

President Trippet with Mr. and Mrs. Waldo Stephens during their 1964 spring trip to campus to give an annual award in memory of their son, Dean, a member of the college coaching staff who was killed in an airplane accident in October, 1958. The 1964 winner, Don Schmidt, stands next to Mr. Stephens.

TEIICHI BETCHAKU

In January, 1965, a few months before he announced his resignation, President Trippet chats with colleagues in the Scarlet Inn. Facing Trippet is Robert S. Harvey, and to his left are Vice-president Hadley and Dean Kendall.

On the Campus Center steps, President Trippet checks his appointment book
for time to spend with a student.

The old Peter Kennedy place, the Trippets' home away from the campus

President Trippet in the library of the Caleb Mills House

(*Right*) The main staircase, Center Hall

FOUR WABASH PRESIDENTS

Above
President Trippet beneath the Samuel F. B. Morse portrait of Elihu Baldwin, the college's first president.

Right
During a break in a softball game, President Trippet talks to Lewis S. Salter, then a member of the physics department and now the twelfth president of Wabash College.

PAUL MIELKE

Above
During a return trip to campus, former President Trippet talks to his successor, President Paul Cook, at a football game.

PAUL MIELKE

as the Phi Psi building fund or a European trip for the glee club, more than offset his salary. They were spontaneous gifts to a place which he and his wife had come to love. And they were a prelude to the major capital gift he and Jane made to Wabash some years later.

The successful completion of the Ford Foundation challenge with all that it made possible for Wabash was, for me, the climax of the years 1956–65. I was glad when it was finished. But I was also filled with despair. I knew I must now prepare to leave Wabash, but I could see nothing worth living for beyond my departure. It was not all that bad, of course, but at the time I could only regard the future with acute melancholy.

In June, 1965, I resigned. A few weeks later I left Crawfordsville to begin a new life. Thanks to the generosity of the Board of Trustees, I could have relaxed for a year or two, but I felt impelled to lose myself in work. By October I was deeply involved in a new job.

My break with the college, at least to the naked eye, was complete. Since 1965, except for the brief service as trustee to which I referred earlier, I have had no official connection with Wabash. Only rarely have I returned to campus, and my visits there have been brief and perfunctory. The work opportunities that I elected to pursue took me far from Indiana — to Colorado, New York, and Mexico. Distance and the nature of my work limited contacts with Wabash friends and alumni and excluded involvement in Wabash affairs. I preferred it that way.

In spite of this elaborate effort to put the college and experience there out of mind, not a day has passed since 1965 that in one way or another Wabash and its people have not touched my thoughts and feelings. Obviously I have never broken the spell Wabash cast on me years ago. Nor do I now have the slightest desire to try further to break it. What a helpful realization that is. It enables me to look back on my Wabash years more calmly. If now and then my memory makes me wince, I nonetheless look back with abundant gratitude and abiding love.

EPILOGUE

WABASH ON MY MIND

Time and again, as I have been writing these reflections about the past at Wabash, I have found myself pausing to wonder about the future. Much of this wondering has been the kind of poetic musing to which I fear I am increasingly addicted. Even so, as far as the future of Wabash is concerned, it has led me to solid ground on the other side of mere wishful thinking.

Soon Wabash will celebrate its 150th anniversary. It will be an occasion for recollecting as I have recollected episodes out of the past. Alumni who gather for that celebration will recapture, perhaps in an illusory way, the happy associations of their youth and they will sing their praises of Wabash heroes, long since departed, who influenced their lives. Public rituals appropriate for such an anniversary will be repeated, paying tribute to the memory of those resolute men who founded Wabash and acknowledging the contributions, often sacrificial, of those who followed them over the years in service to the college. The principles for which Wabash has stood will be reaffirmed, and brave resolutions for keeping the Wabash faith will be recorded. It will be, as it should be, an exercise in love and gratitude and hope.

A hundred and fifty years hence, will men and women much like ourselves assemble on a similar mission? If they do, what will be the promises and the faiths by which they live? And how shall we of the twentieth century, resurrected for the occasion, appear to them? Will our recorded hopes and fears seem quaint and childish by the accepted standards of their time? Or will they too take renewed strength and resolution from our examples as we do from the examples of our predecessors? Impossible though it is to foretell, it is fascinating to contemplate.

As I have indulged in such musings, invariably I have been brought up short by the realization that my presuppositions about the future may be all wrong. It is a brave man who tries to predict what the conditions of life will be twenty-five years from now, to say nothing of what they will be after another

241

century and a half. The continued existence of a place like Wabash may prove to be impossible. So much depends on what happens to the society of which Wabash is only a small part. If it ceases to be even a relatively free society — economically as well as politically — then free private institutions like Wabash will disappear. Even if society continues to be relatively free, that will not insure the future of Wabash and places like it. There are ominous clouds on the horizon for such institutions. Who can predict what storms may break in the years ahead of us?

We have no oracles to consult about such questions. All we can do is to plan and work by such presuppositions as we have. With such light as our reason can provide, we must try to move ahead. Future generations will weigh our faith, and knowing that becomes a commandment for us, even though we shall never know their judgment.

Stray thoughts such as these prompt me to add this epilogue to what I have written about Wabash history. In a way I suppose it amounts to a personal testament of faith in the future of Wabash and of the species of American institution of which Wabash has been and continues to be a steadfast example.

What difference would it make if Wabash ceased to exist as a private liberal arts college? "None," a stranger might answer, "None whatsoever." Shocking though such a retort might be to loyal sons of Wabash, if we are honest we will have to acknowledge that it is a plausible answer.

The quantitative contribution which Wabash makes to the total enterprise of higher education in America is microscopic. The Wabash student body could be absorbed without being noticed by almost any state university. Whether or not its individual members were also absorbed by universities, the disappearance of the Wabash faculty would not affect the research and scholarly apparatus of American higher education. Wabash is not, and has never pretended to be, a center for the enlargement of the world's accumulated body of original knowledge. Nor would the closing of the Wabash library mean an appreciable loss to the nation's store of recorded knowledge. Good as it is as a working library for undergraduate learning, it is not a scholars' library. Apart from Wabashiana and a few manuscripts and documents of special interest to Indiana history, the Wabash library houses no treasured collections of interest to writers and research scholars elsewhere.

The splendid physical plant that Wabash enjoys would not necessarily be lost if Wabash went out of business. Under government sponsorship it could continue to be used for a variety of public purposes. It might become a satellite of one of the state's major universities. It might, with internal modifications, become a government-operated center for the aging, or possibly a rehabilitation complex for urban juvenile delinquents, or even a minimum security prison for a certain class of convicted law offenders. The continuous expansion of government services provides innumerable possibilities for use of the Wabash plant — at taxpayers expense, of course.

Liquidation of the Wabash financial endowment might present expensive legal complications for the Board of Trustees. But in time and in accordance with government regulations, both state and federal, these could be resolved. The balance of the investment portfolio could be put to other educational and charitable uses. Following all of this, the legal entity of Wabash College could be dissolved.

There would be those who would mourn the demise of Wabash, but they would be only a tiny handful in the total American society. In a short time Wabash would be forgotten. Viewed in this light it would appear that our stranger friend was correct when, in response to the question "What difference would it make?" he answered "None. None whatsoever." And it should be borne in mind that what I have been saying about Wabash in this context could also be said with equal validity of every other individual private liberal arts college in America without exception. It is a depressing thought.

This discussion of the question I have posed for Wabash leads logically to a larger and more important question. It is this: "What difference would it make if *all* private liberal arts colleges ceased to exist?" To this question answers come more haltingly, and there is nothing simple about them. Our stranger friend no longer would say "None. None whatsoever." More likely would be the answer "Well, if you insist on putting the question that way, yes it would make a difference — a very big difference." And so it would. If one faces up to the question squarely, the resulting difference, not only for the American system of higher education but also for American society as a whole, defies calculation.

The quantitative impact of such a loss on the nation's educational system would be severe. No longer are we talking of one individual private college. We are now contemplating the disappearance of an entire species of institution with hundreds and hundreds of variegated members. No longer are we talking about reallocating a few hundred students. Now we are talking about hundreds of thousands. Nor are we now trying to imagine the public uses to which a handful of buildings on one college campus could be put. We must think instead of thousands of such buildings, the majority of which have been constructed and equipped in the last twenty-five years. Shifting to tax-supported colleges and universities the total number of students now enrolled in private liberal arts colleges would be an extremely costly business requiring sharply increased annual government appropriations for operating expenses, to say nothing of financing additional plant expansion. No doubt many of the former private college plants could be merged into an enlarged system of public higher education. But an incalculable number of such campuses could not be efficiently incorporated.[1]

More serious consequences would affect the structure and quality of American society. In other countries on all continents, one can find great universities and technological institutes. But only in America does one find the private liberal arts college. It is so characteristic of the American scene that it is taken for granted. Here and there abroad one will find such an institution transplanted from American soil, such as Roberts College in the Near East or La Universidad de las Americas in Mexico. But such examples are rare. Moreover, these transplanted institutions encounter peculiar difficulties on foreign soil. Their educational aims often run counter to the prevailing political and social notions of what higher education is all about. Their instructional methodology, with emphasis on free expression of student thought, is often suspect. Without direction and support from within the United States, such institutions flounder badly.

It is only in America that private liberal arts colleges have flourished. For many years they were the only institutions of higher learning in the young republic. The earliest public universities were modeled after them. They spread westward in the late eighteenth and early nineteenth centuries as America expanded to the Pacific. Again and again the founding dates of western private colleges reveal a connection with the history of the American frontier. Hanover College, Wabash College, and Asbury College (DePauw University) were all chartered soon after Indiana became a state. The same thing can be said of the earliest colleges in Illinois, Missouri, Kansas, Colorado, California, Oregon — indeed in all of the western states.

Almost always such colleges reflected the missionary zeal of a particular church denomination. Wabash was an exception to the rule, as far as church connection was concerned, but the missionary zeal of individual Presbyterians was nonetheless the animating drive in the founding of Wabash. The common goal of these infant colleges was to bring to raw frontier country the civilizing impact of education within a Christian context. High among their objectives was the preparation of teachers and ministers who could accomplish this. The course offerings provided by these frontier colleges followed the example of older New England schools. It was "classical" education. Greek, Latin, mathe-

---

1. I do not have access to current statistical data as I write this. However, a study conducted by ICFA under my direction in the academic year, 1969–70, revealed the following facts about the then 515 member colleges of ICFA: total combined undergraduate enrollment, 650,000; combined annual operating costs, more than $1 billion; combined plant valuation, $4.3 billion; combined endowment funds, $2.8 billion. The member colleges of ICFA represent approximately two-thirds of the nation's private liberal arts colleges. Therefore, comparable figures for *all* private colleges would be substantially higher than those listed above. BKT.

matics, moral and natural philosophy, ancient and modern history — these were the heart of the curriculum. It was the same kind of education that influenced the thinking of those relatively young men who wrote the Constitution of the United States.

As the emphasis on the role of the Christian missionary gradually faded, the curricula of these liberal arts colleges underwent extensive modifications and expansion. But two legacies of their earliest history have continued to influence the role of modern liberal arts colleges, The first of these is a continuing commitment to a concept of education that gives highest priority to intellectual and emotional preparation for living, rather than to preparation for how to make a living. However much private colleges may differ from one another, they agree on the aims of liberal education. The *artes liberales* involved bodies of knowledge and intellectual disciplines considered appropriate for free men in the Hellenistic world. And the liberal arts in modern times are considered the appropriate arts for free men and women in a democratic society. Among other things, this includes an understanding and an appreciation of the past, an intellectual basis for interpreting the present, and some vision of the ends and the means for enjoying and improving the quality of human life. It is often called an impractical education. And that it is, unless in the long run an education which strives primarily to produce good human beings and good citizens is the most practical of all educations.

The second legacy is more difficult to identify. Perhaps it should be called simply idealism. Or perhaps it should be called the appeal to service for the common good. But whatever name we give it, there is something about the nature of a liberal arts college that stimulates habits of voluntary personal action in the public interest. This appeal to altruism is often especially pronounced at the most unsophisticated and obscure of private colleges. There is something naïve about it. And yet it frequently leads to impressive examples of individual lives devoted to the service of others. Repeatedly it is exemplified by the avocational interests of busy and successful college graduates who find time to give to one or several civic, religious, cultural, or charitable enterprises. It is as much emotional and psychological as it is intellectual. It reflects the subtle but important attitudes formed when students are energetic participants rather than auditors and spectators in the dialogue and the action of the collegiate experience. It is the sort of thing the Duke of Wellington had in mind when he said "The battle of Waterloo was won on the playing fields of Eton." It is fashionable now to sneer at the implications of such a quotation. Nevertheless, I believe there continue to be important values in the vestiges of missionary zeal and pioneer individual initiative that remain in private liberal arts colleges.

Of course, these same interests and concerns can be found in the college of arts and sciences in any large university. But there, other important priorities — specialized professional schools, research, semi-professional athletic spectacles, highly developed musical and dramatic entertainment, a variety of extension services to the general public, and so on — contribute to a different hierarchy of values for young people.

Despite common educational aims, American liberal arts colleges exhibit an astonishing range of differences. Some are tiny. Some are moderately large. Some continue to be closely identified with and influenced by a church. Others make a point of their non-sectarianism. Some are "godless." The great majority are coeducational. But many are exclusively for women. A handful remain which are exclusively for men. Some are feverishly innovative, free-wheeling, "far out," even freakish in their educational methodology and their life styles. Many more are conventional and traditional in such matters. A few — and Wabash is one of them — are so conservative that they are really highly experimental. In all of these and other ways, the diversification among private colleges is enormous.

This diversification has contributed to an experimentation in educational curricula that has been quite remarkable in the American system of higher education. Throughout the twentieth century, and especially since World War II, periodic extensive revisions of curricula, teaching methods, grading systems, academic calendars, and the like have been commonplace. Practically every liberal arts college in the country in one way or another has undergone such an experience. They study what others are doing. Whole faculties are caught up in the process, reviewing their own programs in the light of new developments, debating alternative approaches to liberal education, experimenting with new courses, new methods, and new requirements for entrance or for graduation. Often there develops considerable institutional pride in a "new plan" to which the name of the college is attached.

A good deal of this feverish activity probably has been much ado about nothing as far as significant new programs are concerned, but the process has served to refresh and revitalize individual colleges. Not infrequently this kind of activity has led to innovations that have influenced to some extent the whole of American higher education. The honors curriculum at Swarthmore. The work-study curriculum at Antioch. The Great Books curriculum at St. Johns. Those and numerous similar educational experiments have been widely adopted in whole or in part by other colleges, and they have influenced curricular changes in large universities. Some of the now standard practices for colleges and universities, such as the junior year abroad programs, resulted from early experimentation in private colleges.

The small size, the sense of community, and the propensity for experimentation that characterize liberal arts colleges make constant educational ferment a natural continuous activity for the private college. There is, of course, a corresponding self-criticism at work in the large university. But necessarily the nature of a complex university makes it exceedingly difficult to revolutionize its academic workings. Centrifugal influences work against change. The specialized department, within the specialized division, within the special purpose school, has a splintering effect on such sense of community as exists within the total university. Faculty leaders have divided loyalties and competing interests — the graduate school as well as the undergraduate college, the demands of research and publishing, the obligations of consulting assignments with government and industry. It could be argued that the bigger an institution, the more heavy-handed its bureaucratic organization and the more unwieldy its processes for making comprehensive changes.

There are differences, to be sure, between Indiana University and Northwestern University, but those differences are negligible compared to the differences between Wabash College and Indiana University or between Knox College and Northwestern University. Universities, whether public or private, are deeply involved in contractual services to government and industry and in varying degrees are dependent on government financial support for much of their most sophisticated research activities. Moreover, the general public has come to expect of universities a variety of public services that have nothing to do with undergraduate education and sometimes nothing to do with education. A small liberal arts college, however, privately organized, privately financed, and privately governed, is more independent and freer to pursue its role in American higher education than a multi-purpose university, public or private.

The liberal arts colleges, then, constitute the bulwark of privacy and independence in American education. Their disappearance from the American scene would almost certainly mean in time a nationalized system of higher education quite uniform in structure and organization and closely tied to service to the national goals, however those goals might from time to time be defined by the federal government.

What I have been saying bears directly on the pluralistic nature of American society. If one believes that the diversity and pluralism of American society in the past have been important parts of the genius of America among modern nations, then he should agree that it is in the national interest to preserve and to strengthen the pluralism of American society in the future. This means, among other things, seeing to it that private colleges not merely survive. It means seeing to it that they continue with renewed vitality and with enriched opportunities for improved service. This is not a task for government. It is a task for private individuals working with each other. If private colleges disappear from the American scene, the American faith in and practice of voluntary action would be severely weakened.

In the light of this reasoning, we might again ask the question "What difference would it make if Wabash should cease to exist?" "None. None whatsoever!" now seems a little too glib and relaxed. Quantitatively it might make no

247

difference. But in terms of the thoughts I have expressed about the importance of private colleges as a species of institution — yes, it would make a difference, perhaps quite an important difference. The demise of any private college is a loss to the system of private higher education. The stronger and the more famous the college has been, the greater is the loss. In Wabash, Indiana, the Midwest, and indeed the whole country have a proud and honored little college famed for its rugged independence and commitment to the liberal arts during almost a century and a half. Close that college permanently and something of intangible but very great value will be lost to Indiana, to the Midwest, and to the nation. Even to the strongest of remaining private colleges, it would be disheartening. To many others, accustomed to looking to the likes of Wabash for reassuring leadership, it would be an ominous catastrophe.

APPENDIX

THOUGHTS ON FINANCING
THE PRIVATE LIBERAL ARTS COLLEGE

Of the several arguments advanced that predict the doom of private colleges, the financial is the most compelling. For many presidents the task of meeting the annual budgeted deficit is a repetitive nightmare, one that explains why private colleges in recent years have increasingly banded together to seek financial assistance from state and federal governments. But if a private college is really "private," it must solve its financial problem by private, not governmental means. The only government aid which a private college must have is limited to protection of its tax-exempt status and policies that encourage rather than discourage private philanthropy. Lobbying for these essentials strikes me as a proper, indeed essential, activity on the part of private colleges. But to go beyond that amounts to contradictory and, in the long run, self-defeating efforts.

What are the "private means" by which a private college can improve its financial situation? The most common answer to that question is traditional — find more gift money from within the private sector. It continues to be a useful answer, as Wabash and many other colleges have demonstrated with successful multi-million dollar gift campaigns. As long as private, profit-making enterprise remains the basis of the American economy and as long as government policy encourages private giving in the public interest, the unrelenting search for gifts and grants for operating purposes is fundamental to the sound fiscal health of private colleges. And the potential for increased private giving to private colleges is far from exhausted. Gratifying though the growth of corporate giving to education has been in the past twenty years, it continues to lag far behind contributions from individuals and foundations. If, on the average, American business corporations annually would give for education one percent of net profits before taxes, the annual total would approach the magnitude of the federal government's current appropriations for education.

A better answer to the question, however, involves bold and ingenious changes within private colleges themselves, changes which go to the heart of the problem of per-student cost of operation. It means soul searching about such matters as productivity, instructional methodology, student-faculty ratios, plant utilization, multiplicity of course offerings, intercollegiate athletics, intramural programs, tuition fee pricing — everything that affects per-student costs. What I have in mind could be revolutionary. It would be both difficult and time-consuming. At points, especially for faculty members, it would be disagreeable, involving, as it must, the most sensitive and cherished of college shibboleths.

To be effective, such a new attack on the problem of operating costs would have to represent a consensus of solid conviction among faculty leaders, administrators and trustees. A preliminary step, lasting perhaps weeks, would be a continuing dialogue in the whole college community to clarify the issues and identify the problems. Among other things, this would mean a serious reexamination of what is meant by a private, independent college and how it differs from a university, private or public. (Such a dialogue might very well reveal that some faculty members in private colleges do not really believe there is any special value in "private" as distinguished from "public" institutions of higher education.)

The second step should be an in-depth analysis of the financial operation of the college. This should include an examination of traditional methods of meeting costs — repeated increases in tuition fees, more and more "student aid" for those unable to meet the higher charges, and ever-increasing requirements for gifts and grants for operating purposes. A projection of the consequences of continuing these methods for the balance of this century, coupled with a projection of the shrinking pool of young people who will enter college, will offer very sobering food for thought for any faculty and board of trustees.

The third step would be an examination of alternate approaches to academic programs and their funding. This is not simply a matter of asking "How and where can we make economies?" It means asking "What changes can we make in the interest of increasing productivity? What changes can we make that will decrease the per-student cost of operation?" Terms such as "increasing productivity" are distasteful to college professors, and there are those who argue — for example, Harold Bowen — that "productivity" on the part of college teachers can not be increased as one might increase productivity in a business.[1] Nevertheless, that is really what is at stake.

If it is clear to the faculty that the trustees are determined to achieve stated fiscal objectives and are inviting the faculty to decide how they can best

1. Former president of Grinnell College and of the University of Illinois, Bowen in recent years has written extensively about financing higher education. BKT.

be achieved, faculty leaders will respond constructively. There is always the chance, of course, that the procedure I am suggesting will result in a dichotomy between the faculty and the trustees, with the trustees insisting on the achievement of certain objectives and the faculty protesting that they cannot be achieved without sacrificing standards of quality. But my experience at Wabash as teacher, dean, and president encourages me to believe that, allowing plenty of time for full and free exchange of opinions and points of view, in the end solid and quite far-reaching changes could emerge which would revitalize the fiscal health of the college.

Applying this line of thought to Wabash College I find reassuring. Wabash has one of the largest endowment funds per student among all private American colleges. Thus it has a base from which it can experiment in ways that many colleges would find exceedingly difficult, if not imposible. I cannot resist the temptation, therefore, to suggest experiments or possibilities for exploration that might be considered at Wabash. I do not mean to say that the ideas which follow are the only ideas worth pursuing, but at least they are illustrative of the kind of "soul searching" I have been recommending as a prelude to achieving solvency for private college operations.

For several years now I have been convinced that Wabash should stop raising its tuition fees. Since 1946 Wabash has periodically raised tuition fees until now they are 500 percent higher than they were twenty-five years ago. If this practice is continued at about the same rate of increase, by the year 2000 the annual tuition fee charges will be on the order of $10,000 per year. Even allowing for further decline in the purchasing power of the dollar, this is absurd. Already families of moderately high income are finding the cost of sending two or three children to private colleges like Wabash a heavy burden. There comes a point when such families opt for a public university for their children, however much they might prefer a private college.

To offset this, Wabash, like all private colleges, has increased the amount of "student aid" every time it has increased tuition fees. But "student aid" of this kind is not fully funded. Thus, it becomes in reality an increased operating expenditure which somehow must be met on the revenue side of the annual budget. That usually means that larger sums in gifts and grants must be found each year to avoid an actual instead of only a budgeted deficit. Moreover, as the percentage of the student body receiving aid rises, an adverse psychological factor begins to operate among that portion of the student body which pays full tuition. When more than half of the student body is receiving some form of "student aid," it is natural for the new minority to ask themselves, "Why shouldn't we too receive some kind of discount?" I do not have access to current figures, so I am only guessing, but I would not be surprised if the total budgeted item for student aid (plus the staff and clerical costs for administer-

251

ing it) is now larger than the total operating budget of the college ten years ago.[2]

This trend will lead to a crisis demanding drastic action. What can be done to anticipate such a crisis? Well, why not reduce tuition fees steeply and at the same time eliminate all non-funded aid and the extra personnel required to administer that aid? In other words, if Wabash should announce that its tuition fees are being reduced to, let us say, $1,000 a year, but that henceforth, except for winners of endowed scholarships, all students will be required to pay full tuition as billed, what would happen? I am not sure what would happen, of course, but with adequate publicity it is conceivable that the number of applicants for admission would rise substantially. Instead of it being said, "Wabash is a good place to go if you can afford it," it might be said, "Wabash is a good place to go if you can qualify academically."

Sooner or later some well-endowed private college is going to take such a step as this — announcing a steep reduction in tuition fees and the elimination of "blue sky" student aid. When that happens, it will be headline news in educational circles, and others will begin to follow the example. Why should not Wabash take the lead?

One of the objections undoubtedly to be raised is that it would ruin the intercollegiate athletic program at Wabash. Such an objection would not come so much from faculty members as from trustees and alumni. I understand these feelings because I share the pride typical Wabash alumni have in the college's athletic tradition and the conviction that a vigorous athletic program is important to the character of the college. However, if the "soul searching" process is to be honestly pursued, the entire athletic program at Wabash would have to be thoroughly reexamined and, if necessary, revised.[3]

If the new tuition policy caused increased enrollments, another possible objection would be a substantially higher student-faculty ratio. The trustees might be enthusiastic, while the faculty would be greatly troubled. Nevertheless, the trustees should press for serious faculty consideration. Beardsly Ruml's old "Rule of Twenty" would be a good starting point for exploration. By that

2. In 1974–75 the total sum spent by Wabash College for financial aid and its administration was $1,097,550; the operating budget for the academic year 1964–65 was $1,773,000.

3. Fortunately, events of the past few years serve to effectively remove any basis in fact for this concern. In late 1975 the faculty and trustees concurred in the important decision to place all of the college's athletic programs under the scope of the new NCAA Division III rules: no more athletic scholarships would be awarded by Wabash College. Any athletes with financial need are eligible for need-based aid, but on precisely the same basis as any other student. The glowing success of Little Giant teams in intercollegiate contests over the past four or five years makes it clear that sound and successful varsity programs at Wabash are not dependent upon unfunded student aid in the form of athletic scholarships.

rule a student body of 1,000 (full-time equivalent students) would require a teaching faculty of not more than fifty (also full-time equivalents). To move to such a student-faculty ratio without impairing quality would require extensive changes in instructional methodology, which is always difficult for a faculty. But it could be done.

One such change involves the increased mechanization of those learning processes which are primarily repetitive. "Mechanization" is a dirty word for many professors, but as a supporting and supplementing method for the personal contact between teacher and student, it is worth trying. It is ironic that the sophisticated electronic hardware which has revolutionized large portions of American business and industry has by comparison made relatively little impact on collegiate teaching methodology. I say this notwithstanding the fact that practically every college boasts of its language laboratories, its computer center, and its depository for audio-visual aids.

Still another change would emphasize the concept of truly independent study. At Wabash and elsewhere what is called "independent study" is, in practice, "dependent study," requiring time-consuming faculty direction and supervision of student reading programs. The notion that unless something is learned in a class situation, with regular specific assignments and frequent written tests, it is not likely to be well-learned, is deeply engrained in both American college professors and American college students. My experience at Oxford convinces me that, for some disciplines at least (for example, history, literature, philosophy, and political science), frequent written examinations are not necessary for the serious-minded student. Nor are periodic grade reports necessary. In these areas lectures by gifted teachers, accompanied by required and recommended reading lists, can serve the serious-minded student probably better than daily assignments, quiz sections, and frequent examinations. Those who are insecure without the "spoon feed" method should not be in Wabash anyway.

The theoretical objective of the changes I have briefly explored would be to achieve an operating budget in which stable revenue (i.e., tuition fee income plus endowment income) would equal budgeted expenses. The chances are, however, that even after extensive changes, annual gifts and grants would be required to meet budget expenditures. But by comparison with the annual gifts and grants currently required for operating purposes, the amount required would be relatively modest. Even if the theoretical objective would be achieved, in the interest of maintaining high quality standards and offsetting administrative complacency, it would be desirable to include in each year's budget on the revenue side a manageable item for gifts and grants. What do I mean by "manageable"? I suggest something between five and ten percent of the total budgeted expenditures. For an operating budget of $3 million, then, only $150,000 need be raised in gifts and grants. Any enterprising president could agree that the fund-raising capacity of the college in any given year will greatly exceed such a figure. He would be right. The Board of Trustees might insist that the excess raised over $150,000 each year be added to a reserve account called "funds temporarily functioning as endowment" until that account is equal to one full year's operating expenses.[4] Such a reserve would enable the college if necessary to operate for a full year with no tuition and no endowment income. Such dire circumstances may be exceedingly remote possibilities. Nevertheless, the Achilles' heel for many private colleges in adverse times is that they have no reserves which can be converted into cash for emergency purposes.

Another innovative use of the excess unrestricted funds raised in any given year would be to give an annual bonus to all faculty and staff members, indeed to all employees of the college. While a common practice in business, so far as I know, no private college in America has experimented with annual bonuses. Such a practice should take into consideration progress made in the efficiency of operations each year as well as gift money raised, and precautions would have to be taken to insure that faculty and staff members do not begin to assume that an annual bonus is automatic. But with reasonably good fortune over a period of years, a bonus plan might contribute to highly beneficial results, including an income level for faculty members substantially above the faculty salary level at most colleges.

It might be objected, of course, that achieving this kind of fiscal health for Wabash could adversely affect alumni and corporate givings. I doubt it. In fact it might increase such giving. People with money to give like a winner, and the kind of achievement I am talking about enhances the Wabash reputation as a winner. Businessmen, I believe, would be especially responsive in their support, once they understood what Wabash was doing. They would like the example Wabash would be providing for private colleges generally. Howard Bowen once observed that the standard practice for financing colleges is simple. "They get as much money as they can from all sources every year and then spend it all." The refreshing example of a college no longer engaged in this standard practice would be appealing to all friends of private higher education.

The business of raising money for Wabash or for any private college is never-ending. Once the current major fund raising campaign is successfully completed, I assume that Wabash will not for some years to come engage in a multi-million dollar push for capital purposes. But the steady pursuit of annual gifts from alumni, friends and corporations will continue to be important. So also will be the quiet but persistent appeal for deferred gifts to augment endow-

4. Wabash has already had good experience with this kind of reserve account. Under the treasurership of John Collett, substantial gains were made by investing surplus cash in "funds temporarily functioning as endowment." BKT.

ment which, under Albert Campbell's direction, has been so effective in recent years.[5] Both of these continuing efforts could become richer in rewards as the college demonstrates its ability to operate with increased efficiency, while at the same time reducing its charges to students.

As I said earlier, what I have suggested as a new approach to the problem of financing Wabash may not be the best idea. Certainly it is not the only one worth examining. But I am convinced that some such ideas should be seriously considered sooner rather than later. Somehow, in some way the present trend of mounting costs, increasing tuition fees, larger budgeted deficits, and more and more annual gifts must be arrested. It is time that trustees, faculty members, and administrators join hands in a common quest for a goal that is admittedly difficult to reach, but which is of vital importance for Wabash and for the species of institution which it has represented with distinction for a century and a half. Just the possibilities of such an effort make me confident of a sturdy future for Wabash for as long as I care to look ahead.

1976

5. Albert Campbell, a graduate of DePauw and recipient of an honorary Wabash doctorate of laws (1972), joined the Wabash staff as its first director of deferred giving in 1962. Though he retired in 1976, he continues as a consultant to the Wabash development effort.

INDEX

When appropriate, the following information is given for individuals: class year (W); years as trustee (T), as member of administration or staff (S), of athletic staff (A), or of academic department; as well as honorary degrees. Administrative offices noted: president, dean, registrar, and librarian. Pages of major entries for an individual or topic are italicized. Only selected references are indexed for Byron K. Trippet.

Dean of the College, 19, 33, 39, 72, 84, 125–28, 137, 217–18.
See also Bodine, Cowles, Harvey, Kendall, Kurtz, McKinney, Powell, Rogge, Shearer, Thomas, and Trippet
Dean of the Faculty, 39, 128.
See also Kendall
Decision at Law, 192, 192n
Degitz, William B. (W 1942, S 1955–), 60, 85, 135, 138, 218, 236
DeLanney, Louis E. (Zoology 1949–66), 60, 121, 123
Delta Sigma Rho, 174n
Delta Tau Delta, 159, 228
DePauw University, 8, 46, 67, 119, 126, 160, 196, 213, 244
Detchon, I. Lee, 178, 198n
The Development of Constitutional Guarantees of Liberty, 186n
Devol, Benjamin F. (W 1927), 8, 147
De Vore, Lawrence E. (W 1911, T 1938–56), 22, 37, 159, *173–75,* 177
De Vore, Mabel (Mrs. L. E.), 177
De Vore, Margaret, 174
Diehl, Dolores (S 1953–76), 33
Dixon, James, 161
Doane, Frances. *See* Osborne, Frances
Domroese, Charlotte, 105
Domroese, Ewold, 105
Domroese, Frederick C. (German 1919–52, Registrar 1923–46), *103–7,* 116, 132
Dowd, Earl M., Jr. (W 1943), 145
Dunlap Construction Co., 181n
Dunlap, Jerald B. (W 1927), 181n
Duston, C. Owen (English 1954–70), 60, 128, 168–69, 218

Earlham College, 56, 74, 78n, 161
Eby, A. Dale (W 1917), v, 7, 8, 139
Edman, Irwin, 170
Edson, Peter (W 1920, T 1955–67, L.H.D. 1971), 158, 210, 232
Edwards, Ralph, 237
Ehrensberger, Ray (W 1929), 94, 98
Eiseman, Ferdinand, 62, 63, 64, 229
Elliott, Morris E. ("Doc") (W 1913), 210, 232

Elston, Florence (Mrs. I. C.), 176, 178, 186
Elston Homestead, 48, 174, 176, 177, 178, 178n, 186
Elston, Isaac C., Jr. (W 1894, T 1921–39/-1942–62), 23, 34, 48, 93, 157, 158, 174, *175–78,* 186, 189, 194, 196
Elston, Pearl (Mrs. I. C.), 176
Erhard, Ludwig (LL.D. 1959), 186–87
Essentials in Biology, 121, 121n
Evans, Edgar H. (W 1892, T 1918–52), 35–37, 55, 87–88, 128, 158, 159
Evansville Press, 161

Faculty, schism between scientists and humanists 5, 9, 16, 17, 19, high morale during early Hopkins years 27–8, 34, against Evans proposal 35–6, 39, initial doubts about Sparks 40–1, 47, 48, 50, 54, Sparks' post-war faculty 58–61, 67, 69, *81–90,* 91, 109, 113, 118, Johnson as the "conscience of the faculty" 122, Kendall as its best spokesman 128, 132, 139, Osborne as the faculty's "voice of conscience" 143, 150, faculty and trustee responsibilities and conflicts 151–5, 158, 187, 210, 230, 233, 242, 247, 250–1, 252, 254
Fahl, Robert E. (W 1950), 163
Farber, John C. (W 1915, French 1915–16), 12, 188–89, 192
Federal aid to education, 73–74, 249
Fertig, Walter L. (W 1938, English 1940–75), 82, 128, 141
Fields, Paul E. (Psychology 1947–49), 59, 59n, 99
Financial support, 9, 21, 22, 23, 31, 34, 35–7, Sparks' goal for financial support 54, 57–8, 65, 69–73, without federal aid 73–4, corporate aid 74–6, 79–80, Hutsinpillar Fund 117, influence of Beardsley Ruml 153–5, 164, Collett's help 165–8, Coss Fund 170n, Rubber Research, Inc. 172–3, De Vore professorship 175, 175n, 178, 181–2, 184, 185–6, 188–9, Treves funds 193, 195–6, Wabash Foundation 196–7, recent alumni apathy 207, 207n, Trippet's

261